Capital Market Instruments

FINANCIAL TIMES

Prentice Hall

In an increasingly competitive world, we believe it's quality of thinking that will give you the edge – an idea that opens new doors, a technique that solves a problem, or an insight that simply makes sense of it all. The more you know, the smarter and faster you can go.

That's why we work with the best minds in business and finance to bring cutting-edge thinking and best learning practice to a global market.

Under a range of leading imprints, including *Financial Times Prentice Hall*, we create world-class print publications and electronic products bringing our readers knowledge, skills and understanding which can be applied whether studying or at work.

To find out more about our business and publications, or tell us about the books you'd like to find, you can visit us at **www.business-minds.com**

For other Pearson Education publications, visit **www.pearsoned-ema.com**

Pearson
Education

Dedicated to the spirit of the Crazy Gang

Moorad Choudhry

For Chloë

Didier Joannas

Dedicated to my parents, Trajano and Idinha Pereira

Richard Pereira

To my wife Colette, who made life easy whenever work took control

Rod Pienaar

About the authors

Moorad Choudhry is a vice-president in structured finance services with JPMorgan in London. He started his City career in 1989 at the London Stock Exchange, before joining the sterling eurobond desk at Hoare Govett Securities Limited. He was later employed as a gilt-edged market-maker and treasury trader at ABN Amro Hoare Govett Sterling Bonds Limited. From there he moved to Hambros Bank Limited, where he set up and ran the Treasury division's sterling proprietary trading desk. He also worked as a strategy and risk management consultant to some of the world's leading investment banks, before joining JPMorgan in 2000. Moorad has an MA in econometrics from Reading University and an MBA from Henley Management College. He has lectured at London Guildhall University, and is a Senior Fellow at the Centre for Mathematical Trading and Finance, City University Business School.

Moorad lives in Surrey, England.

Author photo by Dawson Strange, Cobham, Surrey.

Didier Joannas is a regional director with SunGard Trading and Risk Systems in Hong Kong. He was previously employed as a quantitative analyst and arbitrage trader on the gilt-edged market-making desk at ABN Amro Hoare Govett Sterling Bonds Limited and ABN Amro Securities (UK) Limited. He obtained his doctorate in applied mathematics and aerodynamics at the University of St Étienne in France before joining Avions Marcel Dassault, the company behind such projects as the Ariane space rocket and the Rafale supersonic jet fighter. He then worked for Viel & Cie bond option brokers in Paris before joining ABN Amro Hoare Govett Sterling Bonds Limited in London in 1994.

Richard Pereira is a member of the credit derivatives and securitization team at Dresdner Kleinwort Wasserstein in London. He obtained a first-class degree in mathematics from Imperial College, University of London, before training as a Chartered Accountant. He then worked as a management consultant specializing in market and credit risk, and has been involved in advisory work at a number of investment banks. Richard joined Dresdner Kleinwort Wasserstein in 2001.

Rod Pienaar works as a business analyst with Deutsche Bank in London, as part of a project group providing systems analysis to the corporate and investment banking division. Rod obtained his undergraduate degree in business and commerce at the University of Witwatersrand in Johannesburg before training as a Chartered Accountant. He then moved to London where he worked as a management consultant specializing in market risk analysis, before joining Deutsche Bank in 2000.

Capital Market Instruments

Analysis and valuation

M O O R A D   C H O U D H R Y
D I D I E R   J O A N N A S
R I C H A R D   P E R E I R A
R O D   P I E N A A R

FINANCIAL TIMES
Prentice Hall

An imprint of **Pearson Education**

London ▪ New York ▪ San Francisco ▪ Toronto ▪ Sydney ▪ Tokyo ▪ Singapore
Hong Kong ▪ Cape Town ▪ Madrid ▪ Paris ▪ Milan ▪ Munich ▪ Amsterdam

Pearson Education limited

Head Office:
Edinburgh Gate
Harlow CM20 2JE
Tel: +44 (0)1279 623623
Fax: +44 (0)1279 431059

London Office:
128 Long Acre
London WC2E 9AN
Tel: +44 (0)20 7447 2000
Fax: +44 (0)20 7240 5771

Website: www.financialminds.com

First published in Great Britain in 2002

Note
To save endless repetition of 'he' or 'she', we have mainly used the male gender indiscriminately to denote both genders.

ISBN 0 273 65412 8

British Library Cataloguing in Publication Data
A CIP catalogue record for this book can be obtained from the British Library

10 9 8 7 6 5 4 3 2 1

Typeset by Pantek Arts Ltd, Maidstone, Kent
Printed and bound in Great Britain by Bookcraft, Midsomer Norton, Bath

The Publishers' policy is to use paper manufactured from sustainable forests.

Contents

PART FIVE

Equity instrument analysis

PART SIX

RATE applications software

Foreword

In the context of finance and capital markets, if one looks back just 30 years the world was a very different place. The movement of capital was subject to a range of restrictions, and currencies were locked into fixed exchange rates. For instance the concepts of securitization or even something as plain vanilla as an interest-rate swap were unheard of. The avenues available to companies for raising finance were severely limited. During the 1970s, as inflation took hold, there was no instrument available to investors in North America and Europe as straightforward as an index-linked bond that would enable them to protect their savings. However over the last 30 years the business of finance and banking has undergone a radical, not to say incredible, transformation. Corporate entities can obtain funding by issuing an endless variety of instruments, be it on an unsecured basis or backed by cash flow receipts from within their own sphere of business. Banks restructure their balance sheets on a regular basis, and investors have a range of products they can purchase to protect themselves against inflation risk.

Academics place the origin of this transformation at different points; some cite the presentation of the Black-Scholes option pricing model, along with Merton's work in 1973, while others point to the rapid development of computer processing power from the early 1980s onwards. In fact a combination of factors, ranging from these two very valid developments to economic necessity and borrower and investor requirements, have come together to give us the fascinating, dynamic and diverse capital markets industry we see today.

Participants in the capital markets are not limited to the vast range of products that are available for raising finance, moving assets off-balance sheet or hedging exposure to energy cycles or the weather (not to mention hedging more old-fashioned risks such as interest-rate or exchange rate volatility). They can ask an investment bank to design a product specifically to meet their individual requirements, and target it at specific groups of customers. For example it is arguable whether the growth of the so-called credit-card banks in the United States could have occurred so rapidly without the securitization mechanism that enabled them to raise lower-cost funding. Witness also the introduction of the synthetic collateralized debt obligation, allied with a credit derivative, following rapidly on the development of more conventional CDO structures. The increasing depth and complexity of the markets requires participants to be completely up to date on the latest analytical and valuation techniques if they are not to risk being left behind. It is clear that we operate in an environment in which there exists a long-term interest in the application of ever more sophisticated valuation and analytical techniques. The level of mathematical sophistication in use in financial markets today is phenomenal, not to mention very specialized.

Investment bankers stress the importance of constantly staying at the leading edge of research and market development to ensure that they continue to deliver quality and value to their clients. Furthermore much of the innovation and product development at financial institutions originates from ongoing discussion with their client base, as they seek to meet their requirements. This book is part of the continuing need to remain ahead of the curve. It contains insight into practical techniques and applications used in the market today, with a hint at what one might expect in the future. It also indicates the scope and significance of these techniques in the world of finance. Readers have a rich mix of topics to choose from. The equity instrument is covered in succinct fashion, which will be of interest to newcomers to equity research. For would-be fixed-income investors and issuers alike there is a review of asset-backed and mortgage-backed bonds, with a thought-provoking discussion on prepayment risk. The asset-backed theme continues with a review of the CDO product. Elsewhere there is a high-level look at fitting the yield curve, including the application of multiple regression in spline methods and the use of B-spline techniques in yield curve modelling. For the beginner there is an accessible introduction to the more commonly encountered yield curve models, such as Vasicek and Cox-Ingersoll-Ross. There is also (in Chapter 7) a succinct account of the use and applications of credit derivatives. The rapid growth of the credit derivative market illustrates perfectly the speed of development in the banking industry today.

Readers will notice the text become more involved by the time we reach the Heath-Jarrow-Morton interest-rate model, described and explained here in its single-factor form. One could say that the presentation by Heath, Jarrow and Morton in 1992 is as seminal a work as the Black-Scholes model, but in the field of interest-rate modelling rather than option pricing. Just as Black and Scholes presented for the first time a closed-form analytical solution to the problem of valuing options, based on the assumption of lognormal distribution of asset prices, so Heath, Jarrow and Morton, tackling the stochastic properties of the term structure of interest rates, showed how the drift element of the stochastic differential equation is a deterministic function of its volatility. This, in its own way, is perhaps as fundamental a result as the earlier work. Financial institutions are able to continue meeting their clients' ever more complex requirements by incorporating such pioneering work into their product development.

The following chapters present in an accessible and readable fashion some of the main techniques and applications used in the markets today. Future progress in finance and capital markets rests in the hands of the students and practitioners of today, who will need to build upon the solid foundations which currently exist, and so assist further developments over the next 30 years. Moorad Choudhry and his co-authors have made a noteworthy contribution to the literature on financial economics with this book, and I hope that this exciting and interesting new work spurs readers on to their own research and investigation.

Jane Douglas-Jones
Managing Editor, *FOW*
the risk management and derivatives magazine

Preface

This book is an introduction to some of the important issues in the capital markets today, with an emphasis on fixed-income instruments such as index-linked bonds, asset-backed securities, mortgage-backed securities, and related products such as credit derivatives. However, fundamental concepts in equity market analysis, foreign exchange and money markets, and certain other derivative instruments are also covered so as to complete the volume. The focus is on analysis and valuation techniques, presented for the purposes of practical application. Hence institutional and market-specific data is largely omitted for reasons of space and clarity, as this is abundant in existing literature.

Students and practitioners alike should be able to understand and apply the methods discussed here. The book has a practical approach to the main issues, with worked examples presented in the chapters. Some of the material in the book has previously been used by the authors as a reference and guide on consulting projects at a number of investment and commercial banks, including Citibank, CSFB, Standard Chartered, NatWest GFM (now RBS Financial Markets), Halifax plc and Co-operative Bank plc. The authors hope that readers find the book thought-provoking and that it enables them to become familiar with practical concepts of importance in the capital markets.

The book is aimed at those with just a basic understanding of the capital markets; however, it also investigates the instruments to sufficient depth to be of use to the more experienced practitioner. It is primarily aimed at front office, middle office and back office staff working in banks and other financial institutions and who are involved to some extent in the capital markets. Undergraduate and postgraduate students of finance and economics should also find the book useful. Other readers, including corporate and local authority treasurers, risk managers, capital market lawyers, auditors, financial journalists and professional students, may find the broad coverage to be of value. In particular, graduate trainees beginning their careers in financial services and investment banking should find the topic coverage ideal, as the authors have aimed to present the key concepts in both debt and equity capital markets.

Comments on the text are welcome and should be sent to the authors care of FT Prentice Hall.

Structure of the book

This book is organized into six parts. Part I sets the scene with a discussion on the financial markets, the time value of money and the determinants of the discount rate. Part II examines fixed-income instruments, and the analysis and valuation of bonds. This covers in overview fashion the main interest rate models, before looking in detail at some important areas of the markets, including:

- fitting the yield curve, and an introduction to spline techniques;
- the B-spline method of extracting the discount function;
- the option-adjusted spread;
- bond pricing in continuous time;
- inflation-indexed bonds.

Part III is an introduction to structured financial products, with a look at mortgage-backed bonds and collateralized debt obligations (CDOs).

In Part IV we introduce the main analytical techniques used for derivative instruments. This includes futures and swaps, as well as an introduction to options and the Black-Scholes model, still widely used today nearly 30 years after its introduction.

Part V considers the basic concepts in equity analysis, while the final part of the book describes the accompanying CD-ROM and RATE application software.

Study materials

Where possible, the main concepts and techniques have been illustrated with worked examples and case studies. The case studies are examples of actual real-world events at a number of investment banks.

Some of the content of this book was originally written as course notes, and used to form part of capital market courses taught at a number of professional bodies and teaching institutions, including the Securities Institute, International Faculty of Finance, London Guildhall University, City University Business School and FinTuition Limited. From these courses, a number of Microsoft Powerpoint slides have been made available for use as teaching aids, and these may be downloaded from Moorad Choudhry's website at www.YieldCurve.com. This site contains sample lecture notes and also lists details of training courses that are available on capital market topics, run by Moorad Choudhry and his associates.

RATE computer software

Included with this book is a specialist computer application, RATE software, which is designed to introduce readers to yield curve modelling. It also contains calculators for vanilla interest rate swaps and caps. This application was developed in C++ specially for this book. The full source code is also included on the CD-ROM, which may be of use to budding programmers.

Acknowledgements

Love, thanks and respect to Mum, Dad, Anuk and Sherif for ongoing help and support – it's something special. And my best to Molga, the Scottish wildcat, both elusive and exclusive ... or should I quote from another Orange Juice song, *A Place In My Heart...*?

A special very big thank you to Brian Eales at the Department of Economics, London Guildhall University – a true gentleman and great to work with – for his review comments on some of the chapters; his time and suggestions for improvement were much appreciated. Of course, any remaining errors in the text remain the responsibility of the authors. Thanks to Peter Matthews at ABN Amro Bank N.V., it's always a pleasure to meet up with former colleagues. Also thanks to Ruth Kentish, Clive Kentish, Chris Bessant, Vicky Dennis and Michele Cook at JPMorgan Chase; Professor Steven Satchell at Trinity College Cambridge for ongoing support; Professor Elias Dinenis at City University Business School; Daniel Shakhani at Goldman Sachs; and Aaron Nematnejad at Bloomberg – cheers chaps.

A warm thank you to Ian Abrams, now MD at Mizuho International in London, for sponsoring my MBA a while back. And I'd only gone into his office to ask for a reference! Thanks also to Dr Paul Darbyshire for the book endorsement, much appreciated.

Thanks to Barberman for being a top man (by the way, it was Del Amitri who recorded *Not Where Its At*, and I look forward to the next time we're at the Oval). I'd like to thank the author of the *Bristow* cartoon strip in the London *Evening Standard*, Mr Frank Dickens, for being spot on every day I've read it commuting home on the train from the City.

Hair styling by Jo Milbourn, and thanks for the therapy as well! ... and to Millie, Uncle Dig says "hello". Carl Scuderi in Oz, can you shift some copies of this book Down Under?

For inspiration, I'd like to thank Mr Frank Fabozzi, the Rockingbirds, the late William Hewlett, *An Introduction to Mathematical Finance* by Sheldon Ross, Mark Ramprakash (now with Surrey CCC), 'Hand In Glove' from the fabulous *Hatful of Hollow*, the fantastically brilliant Orange Juice, that August 1985 interview in *Melody Maker* with Johnny Marr, the first time I saw the enigmatic, inspirational and dynamic Nick King, Chris Dean and Martin Hewes of Redskins perform live, the Bodines, the sublime *Rattlesnakes* by Lloyd Cole and the Commotions, both books I've read on fixed income by Bruce Tuckman, Sir Brian Pitman, and the feeling on any record by Dexy's Midnight Runners, especially *Let's Make This Precious*. And from 1984, Lawrence, Maurice Deebank, Mick Lloyd and Gary Ainge of Felt.

What started out as something similar to what Martin Fry had in mind when he formed ABC has turned into something much more impressive! I was originally going to call the project *A Solid Bond In Your Heart*, following The Style Council, but decided on *Capital Market Instruments* instead. That's teamwork for you.

Moorad Choudhry
Surrey, England
February 2001

Thanks to Moorad 'Goldfinger' Choudhry for making me part of this adventure...

Didier Joannas
Hong Kong

Love to Viv, Des, Sylvia, Giselle, Gabrielle and Bethany. Thanks to Jeremy Vice, Punit Khare, Andrey Chiritin and Yun Kang Liu. And a special thank you to Moorad for getting me involved in this project.

Richard Pereira
London

I'd like to thank Michael Lewis for reviewing the RATE source code with a practised and critical eye...

Rod Pienaar
London

'One 109 at ten o'clock, Bill. Going down. All clear?'
'All clear [sir]. I'm covering you.'
This was perfect teamwork.

Wing Leader
Air Vice-Marshall J.E. 'Johnnie' Johnson CB CBE DSO DFC
(1915–2001)

Part I

Introduction

Part I is a very brief introduction to capital market instruments, designed to set the scene and introduce the concept of time value of money. There are a large number of textbooks that deal with the subjects of macroeconomics and corporate finance, and so these issues are not considered here. Instead we concentrate on the financial arithmetic that is the basic building block of capital market instruments analysis. We also consider briefly the determinants of interest rates or discount rates, which are key ingredients used in the valuation of capital market instruments.

Introduction to financial market instruments

This book is concerned with the valuation and analysis of capital market securities, and also associated derivative instruments, which are not *securities* as such but are often labelled thus. The range of instruments is large and diverse, and it would be possible to stock a library full of books on various aspects of this subject. Space dictates that the discussion be restricted to basic, fundamental concepts as applied in practice across commercial and investment banks and financial institutions around the world.

The importance of adequate, practical and accessible methods of analysis cannot be understated, as this assists greatly in maintaining an efficient and orderly financial system. By employing sound analytics, market participants are able to determine the fair pricing of securities, and thereby ascertain whether opportunities for profit or excess return exist. In this chapter we define cash market securities and place them in the context of corporate financing and capital structure; we then define *derivative* instruments, specifically financial derivatives.

Capital market financing

In this section we briefly introduce the structure of the capital market, from the point of view of corporate financing. An entity can raise finance in a number of ways, and the flow of funds within an economy – and the factors that influence this flow – plays an important part in the economic environment in which a firm operates. As in any market, pricing factors are driven by the laws of supply and demand, and price itself manifests itself in the *cost of capital* to a firm and the *return* expected by investors who supply that capital. Although we speak in terms of a corporate firm, many different entities raise finance in the capital markets. These include sovereign governments, supranational bodies such as the World Bank, local authorities and state governments, and public sector bodies or *parastatals*. However, equity capital funding tends to be the preserve of the corporate firm.

Financing instruments

The key distinction in financing arrangements is between *equity* and *debt*. Equity finance represents ownership rights in the firm issuing equity, and may be raised either by means of a share offer or as previous year profits invested as retained earnings. Equity finance is essentially permanent in nature, as it is rare for firms to repay equity; indeed in most countries there are legal restrictions on doing so.

Debt finance represents a loan of funds to the firm by a *creditor*. A useful way to categorize debt is in terms of its maturity. Hence very short-term debt is best represented by a bank overdraft or short-term loan; for longer-term debt a firm can take out a bank loan or raise funds by issuing a bond. Bonds may be secured on the firm's assets or unsecured, or they may be issued against incoming cash flows or other assets, which is known as *securitization*. The simplest type of bond is known as a *plain vanilla* or *conventional* bond, or in the US markets a *bullet* bond. Such a bond features a fixed *coupon* and fixed *term to maturity*, so for example a US Treasury security such as the 6% 2009 pays interest on its nominal or face value of 6% each year until 15 August 2009, when it is redeemed and the principal is paid back to bondholders.

A firm's financing arrangements are specified in a number of ways, which include:

- The *term* or maturity: financing that is required for less than one year is regarded as short term, and money market securities are short term in this way. Borrowing between one year and ten years is considered medium term, while longer-dated requirements are regarded as long term. There is also permanent financing, for example preference shares.
- The size of funding: the amount of capital required.
- The *risk* borne by suppliers of finance and the *return* demanded by them as the cost of bearing such risk. The risk of all financial instruments issued by one issuer is governed by the state of the firm and the economic environment in which it operates, but specific instruments bear specific risks. Secured creditors are at less risk of loss compared with unsecured creditors, while the owners of equity (shareholders) are last in line for repayment of capital in the event of the winding-up of a company. The return achieved by the different forms of finance reflects the risk exposure each form represents.

A common observation[1] is that although shares and share valuation are viewed as very important in finance and finance textbooks, in actual cash terms they represent a minor source of corporate finance. Statistics[2] indicate that the major sources of funding are retained earnings and debt.

1. For example, see Higson (1995) p. 181.
2. Ibid., see the table on p. 180.

Market mechanism for determining financing price

In a free market economy, which apart from a handful of exceptions is now the norm for all countries around the world, the capital market exhibits the laws of supply and demand. This means that the market price of finance is brought into *equilibrium* by the price mechanism. A simple illustration of this is given in Figure 1.1, which shows that the cost of finance will be the return level at which saving and investment are in equilibrium.

In Figure 1.1 the supply curve sloping upwards represents the investors' willingness to give up an element of present consumption when higher returns are available. The demand curve sloping downwards illustrates an increasing pipeline of projects that become more worthwhile as the cost of capital decreases. In the pioneering work of Fisher (1930) it was suggested that the cost of capital, in fact the rate of return required by the market, was made up of two components: the real return ri and the expected rate of inflation i. Extensive research since then has indicated that this is not the complete picture; for instance Fama (1975) showed that in the USA during the 1950s and 1960s the change in the nominal level of interest rates was actually a reasonably accurate indicator of inflation, but that the real rate of interest remained fairly stable. Generally speaking, the market's view on expected inflation is a major factor in driving nominal interest rates. On the other hand, the real interest rate is generally believed[3] to be driven by factors that influence the total supply of savings and the demand for capital, which include overall levels of income and saving and government policies on issues such as personal and corporate taxation.

We look briefly at firm capital structure in Part V on equities.

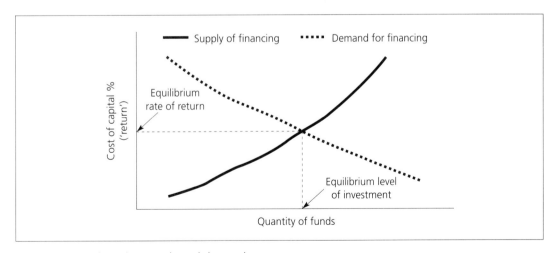

FIGURE 1.1 ■ Financing supply and demand curves

3. For example, *see* Higson (1995), Chapter 11.

Securities

The financial markets can be said to be an integration of market participants, the trading and regulatory environment (which includes stock and futures exchanges) and market instruments. These instruments can be further divided into cash securities and derivatives. Securities are known as cash market instruments (or simply *cash*) because they represent actual cash by value. A security product is issued by the party requiring finance, and as such represents a liability to the issuer. Conversely, a security is an asset of the buyer or holder. Contrary to what might be thought given the publicity and emphasis on derivatives, financial markets are first and foremost cash securities, with the markets themselves being (in essence) a derivative of the wider economy.

In the first instance, securities may be categorized as debt or equity. Such classification determines their ownership and participation rights with regard to the issuing entity. Generally speaking, a holding of equity or *common stock* confers both ownership and voting rights. Debt securities do not confer such rights but rank ahead of equities in the event of a winding-up of the company.

Following this classification, securities are defined primarily in terms of their issuer, term to maturity (if not an equity) and currency. They may also be categorized in terms of:

- the rights they confer on the holder, such as voting and ownership rights;
- whether they are unsecured or secured against fixed or floating assets;
- the cash flows they represent;
- how liquid they are, that is the ease with which they can be bought and sold in the secondary market;
- whether or not they offer a guaranteed return and/or redemption value;
- the tax liability they represent;
- their structure, for example if they are hybrid or composite securities, or whether their return or payoff profile is linked to another security.

The characteristics of any particular security influence the way it is valued and analyzed. Debt securities originally were issued with an annual fixed interest or *coupon* liability, stated as a percentage of *par* value, so that their cash flows were known with certainty during their lifetime. This is the origin behind the term *fixed income* (or in sterling markets, *fixed interest*) security, although there are many different types of debt security issued that do not pay a fixed coupon. Equity does not pay a fixed coupon as the dividend payable is set each year, depending on the level of corporate after-tax profit for each year,[4] and even a dividend in time of profit is no longer obligatory – witness the number of corporations that have never paid a dividend, such as Microsoft Corporation.[5]

4. The exception is *preference shares* (in the USA, preferred stock), which combine certain characteristics of equity with others of debt.
5. Given the performance of the company's share price since it was first listed, this fact is not likely to concern the owners of the shares too much...

Derivative instruments

In this book we consider the principal financial derivatives, which are forwards, futures, swaps and options. We also briefly discuss the importance of these instruments in the financial markets, and the contribution they have made to market efficiency and liquidity. Compared with a cash market security, a derivative is an instrument whose value is linked to that of an underlying asset. An example would be a crude oil future, the value of which will track the value of crude oil. Hence the value of the future derives from that of the underlying crude oil. Financial derivatives are contracts written on financial securities or instruments, for example equities, bonds or other financial derivatives. In the following chapters we consider the main types of financial derivatives, namely forward contracts, futures, swaps and options. We ignore derivatives of other markets, such as energy or weather, which are esoteric enough to warrant separate, specialist treatment.

Forward contracts

A forward contract is a tailor-made instrument, traded *over the counter* (OTC) directly between the counterparties; that is, agreed today for expiry at a point in the future. In the context of the financial markets, a forward involves an exchange of an asset in return for cash or another asset. The price for the exchange is agreed at the time the contract is written and is made good on delivery, irrespective of the value of the underlying asset at the time of contract expiry. Both parties to a forward are obliged to carry out the terms of the contract when it matures, which makes it different to an *option* contract.

Forward contracts have their origin in the agricultural commodity markets, and it is easy to see why.[6] A farmer expecting to harvest his wheat crop in four months' time is concerned that the price of wheat in four months may have fallen below the level it is at today. He can enter into a forward contract today for delivery when the crop is harvested; however, the price the farmer receives will have been agreed today, so removing the uncertainty over what he will receive. The best known examples of forward contracts are forwards in foreign exchange (FX), which are in fact interest rate instruments. A forward FX deal confirms the price today for a quantity of foreign currency that is delivered at some point in the future. The market in currency forwards is very large and liquid.

---

6. See the footnote on p. 10 of Kolb (2000), who also cites further references on the historical origin of financial derivatives.

Futures contracts

Futures contracts, or simply futures, are exchange-traded instruments that are standardized contracts; this is the primary difference between futures and forwards. The first organized futures exchange was the Chicago Board of Trade, which opened for futures trading in 1861. The basic model of futures trading established in Chicago has been adopted around the world.

Futures contracts are standardized, which means each contract represents the same quantity and type of underlying asset. The terms under which delivery is made into an expired contract are also specified by the exchange. Traditionally, futures were traded on an exchange's floor (in the 'pit'), but this has been increasingly supplanted by electronic screen trading – so much so that by January 2001 the only trading floor still in use in London was that of the International Petroleum Exchange. The financial futures exchange, LIFFE, now trades exclusively on screen. Needless to say, the two exchanges in Chicago, the Chicago Board of Trade and the Chicago Board Options Exchange, retain pit trading.

The differences between forwards and futures relate mainly to the mechanism by which the two instruments are traded. We have noted that futures are standardized contracts, rather than tailor-made ones. This means that they expire on set days of the year, and none other. Second, futures trade on an exchange, rather than OTC. Third, the counterparty to every futures trade on the exchange is the exchange *clearing house*, which guarantees the other side to every transaction. This eliminates counterparty risk, and the clearing house is able to provide guarantees because it charges all participants a *margin* to cover their trade exposure. Margin is an initial deposit of cash or risk-free securities by a trading participant, plus a subsequent deposit to account for any trading losses, made at the close of each business day. This enables the clearing house to run a default fund. Although there are institutional differences between futures and forwards, the valuation of both instruments follows similar principles.

Swap contracts

Swap contracts are derivatives that exchange one set of cash flows for another. The most common swaps are interest-rate swaps, which exchange (for a period of time) fixed-rate payments for floating-rate payments, or floating-rate payments of one basis for floating payments of another basis.

Swaps are OTC contracts and so can be tailor-made to suit specific requirements. These requirements can be for the nominal amount, maturity or level of interest rate. The first swaps were traded in 1981 and the market is now well developed and liquid. Interest rate swaps are now so common as to be considered 'plain vanilla' products, similar to the way fixed coupon bonds are viewed.

Option contracts

The fourth type of derivative instrument is fundamentally different from the other three products we have just introduced. This is because its payoff profile is unlike those of the other instruments, due to the optionality element inherent in the instrument. The history of options also goes back a long way, although practical use of financial options is generally thought of as dating from after the introduction of the acclaimed Black-Scholes pricing model for options, which was first presented by its authors in 1973.

The basic definition of option contracts is well known. A *call option* entitles its holder to buy the underlying asset at a price and time specified in the contract terms, the price specified being known as the *strike* or *exercise* price; while a *put option* entitles its holder to sell the underlying asset. A European option can only be exercised on maturity, while an American option may be exercised by its holder at any time from the time it is purchased to its expiry. The party that has sold the option is known as the writer, and its only income is the price or *premium* that it charges for the option. This premium should in theory compensate the writer for the risk exposure he is taking on when he sells the option. The buyer of the option has a risk exposure limited to the premium he paid. If a call option strike price is below that of the underlying asset price on expiry it is said to be *in-the-money*, otherwise it is *out-of-the-money*. When they are first written or struck, option strike prices are often set at the current underlying price, which is known as *at-the-money*.

For an excellent and accessible introduction to options we recommend Galitz (1995).

Securities and derivatives

Securities are commonly described as *cash* instruments because they represent actual cash, so that a 5% ten-year £100 million corporate bond pays 5% on the nominal value each year, and on maturity the actual nominal value of £100 million is paid out to bond holders. The risk to holders is potentially the entire nominal value or *principal,* if the corporate entity defaults on the loan. Generally, the physical flow of cash is essential to the transaction, as for when an entity wishes to raise finance. For other purposes, such as hedging or speculation, physical cash flow is not necessarily essential and the objectives can be achieved with non-cash or off-balance sheet instruments. The amount at risk in a derivative transaction is usually, but not always, considerably less than its nominal value. The use of derivatives can provide users with near-identical exposures as those in the cash market, such as changes in foreign exchange rates, interest rates or equity indices, but with reduced or no exposure to the principal or nominal value.

For instance, a position in a ten-year £100 million sterling interest-rate swap has similar exposure to a position in the ten-year bond mentioned above, in terms of profit or loss arising from changes in sterling interest rates. However, if the bond issuer is declared bankrupt, potentially the full value of the bond may be lost, whereas (if the same corporate is the swap counterparty) the loss for the swap holder would be considerably less than £100 million. As the risk with derivatives is lower than that for cash instruments (with the exception of writers of options), the amount of capital allocation required to be set aside by banks trading derivatives is considerably less than that for cash. This is a key reason behind the popularity of derivatives, together with their flexibility and liquidity.

The issue of banking capital is a particularly topical one, since the rules governing this are in the process of being reformed. We will therefore not discuss it in this book, however interested readers should consult Choudhry (2001).

In the next chapter we consider the basic building blocks of finance, the determination of interest rates and the time value of money.

SELECTED BIBLIOGRAPHY AND REFERENCES

Choudhry, M., *The Repo Handbook*, Butterworth Heinemann, 2001.

Fama, E., 'Short-term interest rates as predictors of inflation', *American Economic Review*, 1975, pp. 269–82.

Fisher, I., *The Theory of Interest*, Macmillan 1930.

Galitz, L., *Financial Engineering*, revised edition, FT Pitman 1995, Chapters 10–11.

Higson, C., *Business Finance*, 2nd edition, Butterworths 1995.

Kolb, R., *Futures, Options and Swaps*, 3rd edition, Blackwell 2000.

Van Horne, J., *Financial Management and Policy*, 10th edition, Prentice Hall 1995.

CHAPTER 2

Market-determined interest rates, and the time value of money

For any application, the discount rate used is the market-determined rate. This rate is used to value capital market instruments. The rate of discount reflects the fact that cash has a current value and any decision to forgo consumption of cash today must be compensated at some point in the future. So when a cash-rich individual or entity decides to invest in another entity, whether by purchasing the latter's equity or debt, he (or it) is forgoing the benefits of consuming a known value of cash today for an unknown value at some point in the future. That is, he is sacrificing consumption today for the (hopefully) greater benefits of consumption later. The investor will require compensation for two things; first, for the period of time that his cash is invested and therefore unusable, and second for the risk that his cash may fall in value or be lost entirely during this time. The beneficiary of the investment, who has issued shares or bonds, must therefore compensate the investor for bearing these two risks. This makes sense, because if compensation was not forthcoming the investor would not be prepared to part with his cash.

The compensation payable to the investor is available in two ways. First, through the receipt of cash income, in the form of interest income if the investment is a loan or a bond, dividends from equity, rent from property and so on, and second through an increase in the value of the original capital over time. The first is interest return or gain and the second is capital gain. The sum of these two is the overall rate of return on the investment.

The market-determined interest rate

The rate of interest

The interest rate demanded in return for an investment of cash can be considered the required rate of return. In an economist's world of no inflation and no default or other risk, the real interest rate demanded by an investor would be the equilibrium rate at which the supply of funds available from investors meets the demand for funds from entrepreneurs. The time preference of individuals determines whether they will be borrowers or lenders, that is whether they wish to consume now or invest for consumption later. As this is not an economics text book, we will not present even an overview analysis; however, the rate of interest at which both borrowing and lending takes place will reflect the time preference of individuals.

Assume that the interest rate is 4%. If this is too low, there will be a surplus of people who wish to borrow funds over those who are willing to lend. If the rate was 6% and this was considered too high, the opposite would happen, as there would be an excess of lenders over borrowers. The *equilibrium rate of interest* is that rate at which there is a balance between the supply of funds and the demand for funds.[1] The interest rate is the return received from holding cash or money, or the cost of *credit* – the price payable for borrowing funds. Sometimes the term *yield* is used to describe this return.

The rate of inflation

The equilibrium rate of interest would be the rate observed in the market in an environment of no inflation and no risk. In an inflationary environment, the compensation paid to investors must reflect the expected level of inflation. Otherwise, borrowers would be repaying a sum whose real value was being steadily eroded. We illustrate this in simple fashion.

Assume that the markets expect that the general level of prices will rise by 3% in one year. An investor forgoing consumption of £1 today will require a minimum of £1.03 at the end of the year, which is the same value (in terms of purchasing power) that he had at the start. His total rate of return required will clearly be higher than this, to compensate for the period of time when the cash was invested. Assume further that the equilibrium *real* rate of interest is 2.50%. The total rate of return required on an investment of £1 for one year is calculated as:

$$\text{Repayment of principal} = £1 \times (1 + \text{real interest rate}) \times \frac{\text{Price level at year-end}}{\text{Price level at start of year}}$$

$$= £1 \times (1.025) \times \frac{£1.03}{£1}$$

$$= £1(1.025)(1.03)$$

$$= £1.05575$$

1. There is of course not one interest rate but many different interest rates. This reflects the different status of individual borrowers and lenders in a capital market.

or 5.575%. This is known as the *nominal* rate of interest. The nominal interest rate is determined using the Fisher equation after Fisher (1930) and is shown as (2.1),

$$1 + r = (1 + p)(1 + i)$$
$$= 1 + p + i + pi$$

(2.1)

where

    r is the nominal rate of interest

    p is the real rate of interest

    i is the expected rate of inflation and is given by:

$$i = \frac{\text{Price level at end of period}}{\text{Price level at start of period}} - 1.$$

A market-determined interest rate must also account for what is known as the *liquidity premium,* which is the price paid for the conflict of interest between borrowers who wish to borrow (at preferably fixed rates) for as long a period as possible, and lenders who wish to lend for as short a period as possible. A short-dated instrument is generally easier to transact in the secondary market than a long-dated instrument; that is, it is more *liquid.* The trade-off is that in order to entice lenders to invest for longer time periods, a higher interest rate must be offered. Combined with investors' expectations of inflation, this means that rates of return (or yields) are generally higher for longer-dated investments. This manifests itself most clearly in an upward sloping *yield curve.* Yield curves are considered in a later chapter; in Figure 2.1 we show a hypothetical upward-sloping yield curve with the determinants of the nominal interest rate indicated.

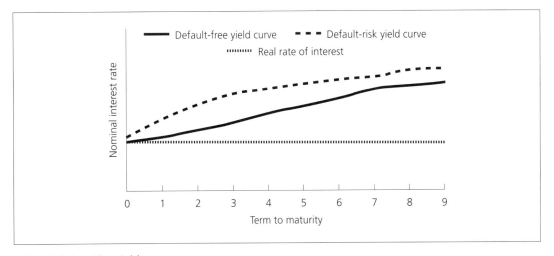

FIGURE 2.1 ▪ The yield curve

Figure 2.1 shows two curves. The lower one incorporates the three elements we have discussed: the real rate, expected inflation and liquidity. However, it would only apply to investments that bore no *default* risk, the risk that the borrower would default on the loan and not repay it.[2] Investments that are default-free are typified by government bonds issued by developed economy countries, for example US Treasury securities or UK gilts. Investments that expose the investor to default risk, for example a corporate bond, must offer a return that incorporates a risk premium, over and above the risk-free interest rate. If this were not the case, investors would be reluctant to enter into such investments. The risk premium factor is indicated by the higher yield curve in Figure 2.1.

The time value of money

Present value and discounting

We now review a key concept in cash flow analysis, that of discounting and *present value*. It is essential to have a firm understanding of the main principles summarized here before moving on to other areas. When reviewing the concept of the time value of money, we assume that the interest rates used are the market-determined rates of interest.

Financial arithmetic has long been used to illustrate that £1 received today is not the same as £1 received at some point in the future. Faced with a choice between receiving £1 today or £1 in one year's time we would not be indifferent given a rate of interest of, say, 10% that was equal to our required nominal rate of interest. Our choice would be between £1 today or £1 plus 10p – the interest on £1 for one year at 10% per annum. The notion that money has a time value is a basic concept in the analysis of financial instruments. Money has a time value because of the opportunity to invest it at a rate of interest.

A loan that has one interest payment on maturity is accruing *simple interest*. On short-term instruments there is usually only the one interest payment on maturity, hence simple interest is received when the instrument expires. The terminal value of an investment with simple interest is given by:

$$F = P (1 + r) \qquad (2.2)$$

where

F is the terminal value or *future value*
P is the initial investment or present *value*
r is the interest rate.

---

2. The borrower may be unable to repay it, say because of bankruptcy or liquidation, or unwilling to repay it, for example because of war or revolution or another reason.

The market convention is to quote interest rates as *annualized* interest rates, which is the interest that is earned if the investment term is one year. Consider a three-month deposit of £100 in a bank, placed at a rate of interest of 6%. In such an example the bank deposit will earn 6% interest for a period of 90 days. As the annual interest gain would be £6, the investor will expect to receive a proportion of this, which is:

$$£600 \times \frac{90}{365}.$$

The investor will receive £1.479 interest at the end of the term. The total proceeds after the three months are therefore £100 plus £1.479. If we wish to calculate the terminal value of a short-term investment that is accruing simple interest we use the following expression:

$$F = P\left(1 + r \times \frac{\text{days}}{\text{year}}\right). \tag{2.3}$$

The fraction $\frac{\text{days}}{\text{year}}$ refers to the numerator, which is the number of days the investment runs, divided by the denominator, which is the number of days in the year. In the sterling markets the number of days in the year is taken to be 365; however, most other markets (including the dollar and euro markets) have a 360-day year convention. For this reason we simply quote the expression as 'days' divided by 'year' to allow for either convention.

Let us now consider an investment of £100 made for three years, again at a rate of 6%, but this time fixed for three years. At the end of the first year the investor will be credited with interest of £6. Therefore for the second year the interest rate of 6% will be accruing on a principal sum of £106, which means that at the end of year 2 the interest credited will be £6.36. This illustrates how *compounding* works, which is the principle of earning interest on interest. The outcome of the process of compounding is the *future value* of the initial amount. The expression is given in (2.4):

$$FV = PV(1 + r)^n \tag{2.4}$$

where

 FV is the future value
 PV is initial outlay or *present value*
 r   is the periodic rate of interest (expressed as a decimal)
 n   is the number of periods for which the sum is invested.

When we compound interest we have to assume that the reinvestment of interest payments during the investment term is at the same rate as the first year's interest. That is why we stated that the 6% rate in our example was *fixed* for three years. We can see, then, that compounding increases our returns, compared with investments that accrue only on a simple interest basis.

Now let us consider a deposit of £100 for one year, at a rate of 6% but with quarterly interest payments. Such a deposit would accrue interest of £6 in the normal way, but £1.50 would be credited to the account every quarter, and this would then benefit from compounding. Again assuming that we can reinvest at the same rate of 6%, the total return at the end of the year will be:

$$100 \times [(1 + 0.015) \times (1 + 0.015) \times (1 + 0.015) \times (1 + 0.015)] = 100 \times [(1 + 0.015)^4]$$

which gives us 100×1.06136, a terminal value of £106.136. This is some 13 pence more than the terminal value using annual compounded interest.

In general, if compounding takes place m times per year, then at the end of n years mn interest payments will have been made; the future value of the principal is given by (2.5) below:

$$FV = PV \left(1 + \frac{r}{m}\right)^{mn}.$$

(2.5)

As we showed in our example, the effect of more frequent compounding is to increase the value of the total return when compared with annual compounding. The effect of more frequent compounding is shown below, where we consider the annualized interest rate factors, for an annualized rate of 6%.

$$\text{Interest rate factor} = \left(1 + \frac{r}{m}\right)^m$$

Compounding frequency	Interest rate factor	
Annual	$(1 + r)$	= 1.060000
Semi-annual	$\left(1 + \frac{r}{2}\right)^2$	= 1.060900
Quarterly	$\left(1 + \frac{r}{4}\right)^4$	= 1.061364
Monthly	$\left(1 + \frac{r}{12}\right)^{12}$	= 1.061678
Daily	$\left(1 + \frac{r}{365}\right)^{365}$	= 1.061831

This shows us that the more frequent the compounding, the higher the interest rate factor. The last case also illustrates how a limit occurs when interest is compounded continuously. Equation (2.5) can be rewritten as follows:

$$FV = PV\left[\left(1 + \frac{r}{m}\right)^{m/r}\right]^{rn}$$

$$= PV\left[\left(1 + \frac{1}{m/r}\right)^{m/r}\right]^{rn} \qquad (2.6)$$

$$= PV\left[\left(1 + \frac{1}{n}\right)^{n}\right]^{rn}$$

where $n = m/r$. As compounding becomes continuous and m and hence n approach infinity, the expression in the square brackets in (2.6) approaches a value known as e, which is shown below as:

$$e = \lim_{n\to\infty}\left(1 + \frac{1}{n}\right)^{n} = 2.718281\ldots$$

If we substitute this into (2.6) above, this gives us:

$$FV = PVe^{rn} \qquad (2.7)$$

where we have continuous compounding. In (2.7) e^{rn} is known as the *exponential function* of rn and it tells us the continuously compounded interest rate factor. If $r = 6\%$ and $n = 1$ year, then:

$$e^{r} = (2.718281)^{0.05} = 1.061837$$

This is the limit reached with continuous compounding.

The convention in both wholesale and personal (retail) markets is to quote an annual interest rate. A lender who wishes to earn the interest at the rate quoted has to place his funds on deposit for one year. Annual rates are quoted irrespective of the maturity of a deposit, from overnight to ten years or longer. For example, if one opens a bank account that pays interest at a rate of 3.5% but then closes it after six months, the actual interest earned will be equal to 1.75% of the sum deposited. The actual return on a three-year building society bond (fixed deposit) that pays 6.75% fixed for three years is 21.65% after three years. The quoted rate is the annual one-year equivalent. An overnight deposit in the wholesale or *interbank* market is still quoted as an annual rate, even though interest is earned for only one day.

The convention of quoting annualized rates is to allow deposits and loans of different maturities and different instruments to be compared on the basis of the interest rate applicable. We must be careful when comparing interest rates for products that have different payment frequencies. As we have seen, the actual interest earned will be greater for a deposit earning 6% on a semi-annual basis compared with 6% on an annual basis. The convention in the money markets is to quote the equivalent interest rate applicable when taking into account an instrument's payment frequency.

We saw how a *future value* could be calculated given a known *present value* and rate of interest. For example, £100 invested today for one year at an interest rate of 6% will generate $100 \times (1 + 0.06) = £106$ at the end of the year. The future value of £100 in this case is £106. We can also say that £100 is the *present value* of £106 in this case.

In equation (2.4) we established the following future value relationship:

$$FV = PV(1 + r)^n$$

By reversing this expression, we arrive at the present value calculation given in (2.8):

$$PV = \frac{FV}{(1 + r)^n} \tag{2.8}$$

where the symbols represent the same terms as before. Equation (2.8) applies in the case of annual interest payments and enables us to calculate the present value of a known future sum.

To calculate the present value for a short-term investment of less than one year we will need to adjust what would have been the interest earned for a whole year by the proportion of days of the investment period. Rearranging the basic equation, we can say that the present value of a known future value is:

$$PV = \frac{FV}{\left(1 + r \times \frac{\text{days}}{\text{year}}\right)} \tag{2.9}$$

Given a present value and a future value at the end of an investment period, what then is the interest rate earned? We can rearrange the basic equation again, to solve for the *yield*.

When interest is compounded more than once a year, the formula for calculating present value is modified, as shown in (2.10):

$$PV = \frac{FV}{\left(1 + \frac{r}{m}\right)^{mn}} \tag{2.10}$$

where, as before, FV is the cash flow at the end of year n, m is the number of times a year interest is compounded, and r is the rate of interest or discount rate. Illustrating this, the present value of £100 that is received at the end of five years at a rate of interest of 5%, with quarterly compounding, is:

$$PV = \frac{100}{\left(1 + \frac{00.5}{4}\right)^{(4)(5)}}$$

$$= £78.00.$$

Interest rates in the money markets are always quoted for standard maturities; for example, overnight, 'tom next' (the overnight interest rate starting tomorrow, or 'tomorrow to the next'), spot next (the overnight rate starting two days forward), one week, one month, two months and so on up to one year. If a bank or corporate customer wishes to deal for non-standard periods, an interbank desk will calculate the rate chargeable for such an 'odd date' by *interpolating* between two standard-period interest rates. If we assume that the rate for all dates in between two periods increases at the same steady state, we can calculate the required rate using the formula for *straight-line* interpolation, shown in (2.11):

$$r = r_1 + (r_2 - r_1) \times \frac{n - n_1}{n_2 - n_1} \qquad (2.11)$$

where

    r is the required odd-date rate for n days
    r_1 is the quoted rate for n_1 days
    r_2 is the quoted rate for n_2 days.

Let us imagine that the one-month (30-day) offered interest rate is 5.25% and that the two-month (60-day) offered rate is 5.75%.[3] If a customer wishes to borrow money for a 40-day period, what rate should the bank charge? We can calculate the required 40-day rate using straight-line interpolation. The increase in interest rates from 30 to 40 days is assumed to be 10/30 of the total increase in rates from 30 to 60 days. The 40-day offered rate would therefore be:

    5.25% + (5.75% − 5.25%) × 10/30 = 5.4167%.

What about the case of an interest rate for a period that lies just before or just after two known rates and not roughly in between them? When this happens we *extrapolate* between the two known rates, again assuming a straight-line relationship between the two rates and for a period after (or before) the two rates. So if the one-month offered rate is 5.25% while the two-month rate is 5.75%, the 64-day rate is:

    5.25 + (5.75 − 5.25) × 34/30 = 5.8167%.

Discount factors

An n-period discount factor is the present value of one unit of currency (£1 or $1) that is payable at the end of period n. Essentially, it is the present-value relationship expressed

---

3. This is the convention in the sterling market, that is 'one month' is 30 days.

in terms of £1. If $d(n)$ is the n-year discount factor, then the five-year discount factor at a discount rate of 6% is given by:

$$d(5) = \frac{1}{(1 + 0.06)^5} = 0.747258.$$

The set of discount factors for every time period from one day to 30 years or longer is termed the *discount function*. Discount factors may be used to price any financial instrument that is made up of a future cash flow. For example, what would be the value of £103.50 receivable at the end of six months if the six-month discount factor is 0.98756? The answer is given by:

0.98756 × 103.50 = 102.212.

In addition, discount factors may be used to calculate the future value of any present investment. From the example above, £0.98756 would be worth £1 in six months' time, so by the same principle a present sum of £1 would be worth:

$1/d(0.5) = 1 / 0.98756 = 1.0126$

at the end of six months.

It is possible to obtain discount factors from current bond prices. Assume a hypothetical set of bonds and bond prices as given in Table 2.1, and assume further that the first bond in the table matures in precisely six months' time (these are semi-annual coupon bonds).

TABLE 2.1 ▪ Hypothetical set of bonds and bond prices

Coupon	Maturity date	Price
7%	7 June 2001	101.65
8%	7 December 2001	101.89
6%	7 June 2002	100.75
6.5%	7 December 2002	100.37

Taking the first bond, this matures in precisely six months' time, and its final cash flow will be 103.50, comprised of the £3.50 final coupon payment and the £100 redemption payment. The price or present value of this bond is 101.65, which allows us to calculate the six-month discount factor as:

$d(0.5) \times 103.50 = 101.65$

which gives $d(0.5)$ equal to 0.98213.

From this first step we can calculate the discount factors for the following six-month periods. The second bond in Table 2.1, the 8% 2001, has the following cash flows:

■ £4 in six months' time

■ £104 in one year's time.

The price of this bond is 101.89, which again is the bond's present value, and this consists of the sum of the present values of the bond's total cash flows. So we are able to set the following:

101.89 = 4 × d(0.5) + 104 × d(1).

However, we already know d(0.5) to be 0.98213, which leaves only one unknown in the above expression. Therefore we may solve for d(1) and this is shown to be 0.94194.

If we carry on with this procedure for the remaining two bonds, using successive discount factors, we obtain the complete set of discount factors as shown in Table 2.2. The continuous function for the two-year period from today is shown as the discount function, in Figure 2.2.

TABLE 2.2 ■ Discount factors calculated using bootstrapping technique

Coupon	Maturity date	Term (years)	Price	d (n)
7%	7 June 2001	0.5	101.65	0.98213
8%	7 December 2001	1	101.89	0.94194
6%	7 June 2002	1.5	100.75	0.92211
6.5%	7 December 2002	2	100.37	0.88252

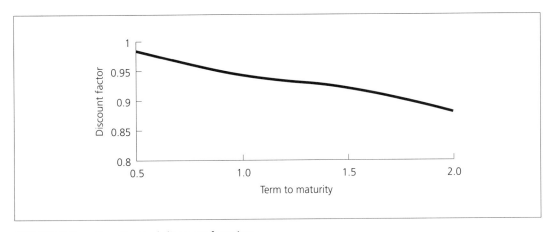

FIGURE 2.2 ■ Hypothetical discount function

This technique, which is known as bootstrapping, is conceptually neat, although problems arise when we do not have a set of bonds that mature at precise six-month intervals. In addition, liquidity issues connected with specific individual bonds can cause complications. However, it is still worth being familiar with this approach.

Note from Figure 2.2 how discount factors decrease with increasing maturity: this is intuitively obvious, since the present value of something to be received in the future diminishes the further into the future we go.

SELECTED BIBLIOGRAPHY AND REFERENCES

Blake, D., *Financial Market Analysis*, McGraw-Hill 1990.

Fisher, I., *Theory of Interest*, Macmillan 1930.

Lee, T., *Economics for Professional Investors*, 2nd edition, Prentice Hall 1998.

Part II

Debt capital market cash instruments

Part II of this book concentrates on vanilla debt market instruments. We begin with money market instruments. The first products in any capital market are money market instruments such as Treasury bills and bankers acceptances. These, together with other cash money market products, are considered in Chapter 3. The next three chapters are devoted to fixed-income instruments or bonds. The analysis generally restricts itself to default-free bonds. Chapter 4 is a large one, which begins by describing bonds in the 'traditional' manner, and then follows with the current style of describing the analysis of bonds. There is also a description of the bootstrapping technique of calculating spot and forward rates. In Chapter 7 we summarize some of the most important interest-rate models used in the market today. This is a well-researched topic and the bibliography for this chapter is consequently quite sizeable. The crux of the analysis presented is the valuation of future cash flows. We consider the pricing of cash flows whose future value is known, in intermediate-level terms. The reader requires an elementary understanding of statistics, probability and calculus to make the most of these chapters. There are a large number of texts that deal with the mathematics involved; an overview of these is given in Choudhry (2001).

We look first at default-free zero-coupon bonds. The process begins with the fair valuation of a set of cash flows. If we are analyzing a financial instrument comprised of a cash flow stream of nominal amount C_i, paid at times $i = 1, 2, ..., N$ then the value of this instrument is given by:

$$PV = \sum_{i=1}^{N} C_i P(0, t_i)$$

where $P(0, t_i)$ is the price today of a zero-coupon bond of nominal value 1 maturing at each point i, or in other words the i-period discount factor. This expression can be written as:

$$PV = \sum_{i=1}^{N} C_i \exp[-(t_i)r(0, t_i)]$$

which indicates that in a no-arbitrage environment the present value of the cash flow stream is obtained by discounting the set of cash flows and summing them. Therefore in theory it is straightforward to calculate the present value of any cash flow stream (and by implication virtually any financial instrument) using the yields observed on a set of risk-free and default-free zero-coupon bonds.

In a market where such default-free zero-coupon bonds existed for all maturities, it would be relatively straightforward to extract the discount function to the longest-dated maturity, and we could use this discount function to value other cash flows and instruments. However, this is a theoretical construct because in practice there is no market with such a preponderance of risk-free zero-coupon bonds; indeed zero-coupon bonds are a relative rarity in government markets around the world. In practice then, the set of such zero-coupon bonds is limited and is influenced by liquidity and other market considerations. We require therefore an efficient and tractable method for extracting the zero-coupon yield curve from coupon-paying bonds of varying maturity. This vital issue is introduced in Chapter 8, and is followed in Chapter 9 by an advanced-level treatment of the B-spline method of extracting the discount function. This is a most efficient technique.

The final chapter in Part II considers the analysis of inflation-indexed bonds, an important asset class in a number of capital markets around the world.

REFERENCE

Choudhry, M., *Bond Market Securities*, FT Prentice Hall 2001.

Money market instruments and foreign exchange

Money market securities are debt securities with maturities of up to 12 months. Market issuers include sovereign governments, which issue Treasury bills; corporates issuing commercial paper; and banks issuing bills and certificates of deposit. Investors are attracted to the market because the instruments are highly liquid and carry relatively low credit risk. Investors in the money market include banks, local authorities, corporations, money market investment funds and individuals. However, the money market essentially is a wholesale market and the denominations of individual instruments are relatively large.

In this chapter we review the cash instruments traded in the money market, as well as the two main money market derivatives: interest rate futures and forward rate agreements.

Overview

The cash instruments traded in the money market include:

- Treasury bills
- time deposits
- certificates of deposit
- commercial paper
- bankers acceptances
- bills of exchange.

We can also add the market in repurchase agreements or *repos*, which are essentially secured cash loans, to this list.

A Treasury bill is used by sovereign governments to raise short-term funds, while certificates of deposit (CDs) are used by banks to raise finance. The other instruments are used by corporates and occasionally banks. Each instrument represents an obligation on the borrower to repay the amount borrowed on the maturity date, together with interest if this applies. The instruments above fall into one of two main classes of money market securities: those quoted on a *yield* basis and those quoted on a *discount* basis. These two terms are discussed below.

The calculation of interest in the money markets often differs from the calculation of accrued interest in the corresponding bond market. Generally, the day-count convention in the money market is the exact number of days that the instrument is held, divided by the number of days in the year. In the sterling market the year base is 365 days, so the interest calculation for sterling money market instruments is given by (3.1):

$$i = \frac{n}{365} \, . \tag{3.1}$$

The majority of currencies, including the US dollar and the euro, calculate interest based on a 360-day base.

Settlement of money market instruments can be for value today (generally only when traded in before midday), tomorrow, or two days forward (known as *spot*).

Securities quoted on a yield basis

Two of the instruments in the list above are yield-based instruments.

Money market deposits

These are fixed-interest-term deposits of up to one year with banks and securities houses. They are also known as *time deposits* or *clean deposits*. They are not negotiable, so cannot be liquidated before maturity. The interest rate on the deposit is fixed for the term and related to the London Interbank Offered Rate (Libor) of the same term. Interest and capital are paid on maturity.

The effective rate on a money market deposit is the annual equivalent interest rate for an instrument with a maturity of less than one year.

Certificates of deposit

Certificates of deposit are receipts from banks for deposits that have been placed with them. They were introduced in the sterling market in 1958. The deposits themselves carry a fixed rate of interest related to Libor and have a fixed term to maturity, so cannot be withdrawn before maturity. However, the certificates themselves can be traded in a secondary market, that is, they are negotiable.[1] CDs are therefore very similar to negotiable money market deposits, although the yields are about 0.15% below the equivalent deposit

---

1. A small number of CDs are non-negotiable.

Libor

The term LIBOR or 'Libor' comes from London Interbank Offered Rate and is the interest rate at which one London bank offers funds to another London bank of acceptable credit quality, in the form of a cash deposit. The rate is 'fixed' by the British Bankers Association at 1100 hours every business day morning (in practice, the fix is usually about 20 minutes later) by taking the average of the rates supplied by member banks. The term Libid is the bank's 'bid' rate – the rate at which it pays for funds in the London market. The quote spread for a selected maturity is therefore the difference between Libor and Libid. The convention in London is to quote the two rates as Libor–Libid, thus matching the yield convention for other instruments. In some other markets the quote convention is reversed. Euribor is the interbank rate offered for euros as reported by the European Central Bank. Other money centres also have their rates fixed, so for example Stibor is the Stockholm banking rate, while pre-euro the Portuguese escudo rate fixing out of Lisbon was Lisbor.

rates because of the added benefit of liquidity. Most CDs issued are of between one and three months' maturity, although they do trade in maturities of one to five years. Interest is paid on maturity, except for CDs lasting longer than one year, where interest is paid annually or, occasionally, semi-annually.

Banks, merchant banks and building societies issue CDs to raise funds to finance their business activities. A CD will have a stated interest rate and fixed maturity date and can be issued in any denomination. On issue, a CD is sold for face value, so the settlement proceeds of a CD on issue always equal its nominal value. The interest is paid, together with the face amount, on maturity. The interest rate is sometimes called the *coupon*, but unless the CD is held to maturity this will not equal the yield, which is of course the current rate available in the market and varies over time. In the USA CDs are available in smaller denomination amounts to retail investors.[2] The largest group of CD investors, however, are banks themselves, money market funds, corporates and local authority treasurers.

Unlike coupons on bonds, which are paid in rounded amounts, CD coupons are calculated to the exact day.

2. This was first introduced by Merrill Lynch in 1982.

CD yields

The coupon quoted on a CD is a function of the credit quality of the issuing bank, its expected liquidity level in the market, and of course the maturity of the CD (because this will be considered relative to the money market yield curve). As CDs are issued by banks as part of their short-term funding and liquidity requirement, issue volumes are driven by the demand for bank loans and the availability of alternative sources of funds for bank customers. The credit quality of the issuing bank is the primary consideration, however. In the sterling market the lowest yield is paid by 'clearer' CDs, which are CDs issued by the clearing banks such as RBS NatWest, HSBC and Barclays plc. In the US market 'prime' CDs, issued by highly rated domestic banks, trade at a lower yield than non-prime CDs. In both markets CDs issued by foreign banks, such as French or Japanese banks, will trade at higher yields.

Euro-CDs, which are CDs issued in a different currency to the home currency, also trade at higher yields; in the USA this is because of reserve and deposit insurance restrictions.

If the current market price of the CD including accrued interest is P and the current quoted yield is r, the yield can be calculated given the price, using (3.2):

$$r = \left[\frac{M}{P} \times \left[1 + C \left(\frac{N_{im}}{B} \right) \right] - 1 \right] \times \left(\frac{B}{N_{sm}} \right). \tag{3.2}$$

The price can be calculated given the yield, using (3.3):

$$P = M \times \left[1 + C \left(\frac{N_{im}}{B} \right) \right] / \left[1 + r \left(\frac{N_{sm}}{B} \right) \right]$$

$$= F / \left[1 + r \left(\frac{N_{sm}}{B} \right) \right] \tag{3.3}$$

where

C is the quoted coupon on the CD
M is the face value of the CD
B is the year base (365 or 360)
F is the maturity value of the CD
N_{im} is the number of days between issue and maturity
N_{sm} is the number of days between settlement and maturity
N_{is} is the number of days between issue and settlement.

After issue a CD can be traded in the secondary market. The secondary market in CDs in the UK is very liquid and CDs will trade at the rate prevalent at the time, which will invariably be different from the coupon rate on the CD at issue. When a CD is traded in the secondary market, the settlement proceeds will need to take into account interest that has accrued on the paper and the different rate at which the CD has now been dealt. The formula for calculating the settlement figure is given at (3.4), which applies to the sterling market and its 365-day count basis.

$$\text{Proceeds} = \frac{M \times \text{Tenor} \times C \times 100 + 36500}{\text{Days remaining} \times r \times 100 + 36500}. \tag{3.4}$$

The *tenor* of a CD is the life of the CD in days, while *days remaining* is the number of days left to maturity from the time of trade.

The return on holding a CD is given by (3.5):

$$\text{Return} = \left[\frac{\left(1 + \text{purchase yield} \times \frac{\text{days from purchase to maturity}}{B}\right)}{1 + \text{sale yield} \times \frac{\text{days from sale to maturity}}{B}} - 1 \right] \times \frac{B}{\text{days held}}. \tag{3.5}$$

Securities quoted on a discount basis

The remaining money market instruments are all quoted on a *discount* basis, and so are known as 'discount' instruments. This means that they are issued on a discount to face value, and are redeemed on maturity at face value. Hence Treasury bills, bills of exchange, bankers acceptances and commercial paper are examples of money market securities that are quoted on a discount basis, that is, they are sold on the basis of a discount to par. The difference between the price paid at the time of purchase and the redemption value (par) is the interest earned by the holder of the paper. Explicit interest is not paid on discount instruments, rather interest is reflected implicitly in the difference between the discounted issue price and the par value received at maturity. Note that in some markets commercial paper is quoted on a yield basis, but not in the UK or in the USA where it is a discount instrument.

Treasury bills

Treasury bills (or T-bills) are short-term government 'IOUs', often with a three-month maturity. For example, if a bill is issued on 10 January it will mature on 10 April. Bills of one-month and six-month maturity are also issued, but only rarely in the UK market. On maturity, the holder of a T-bill receives the par value of the bill by presenting it to the central bank. In the UK most such bills are denominated in sterling, but issues are also made in euros. In a capital market, T-bill yields are regarded as the *risk-free* yield, because they represent the yield from short-term government debt. In emerging markets they are often the most liquid instruments available for investors.

A sterling T-bill with a £10 million face value issued for 91 days will be redeemed on maturity at £10 million. If the three-month yield at the time of issue is 5.25%, the price of the bill at issue is:

$$P = \frac{10m}{\left(1 + 0.0525 \times \frac{91}{365}\right)} = £9,870,800.69$$

In the UK and US markets the interest rate on discount instruments is quoted as a *discount rate* rather than a yield. This is the amount of discount expressed as an annualized percentage of the face value, and not as a percentage of the original amount paid. By definition, the discount rate is always lower than the corresponding yield. If the discount rate on a bill is d, then the amount of discount is given by:

$$d_{Value} = M \times d \times \frac{n}{B}. \tag{3.6}$$

The price P paid for the bill is the face value minus the discount amount, given by:

$$P = 100 \times \left[1 - \frac{d.\left(\frac{N_{sm}}{365}\right)}{100}\right]. \tag{3.7}$$

If we know the yield on the bill, then we can calculate its price at issue by using the simple present-value formula, as shown at (3.8):

$$P = M / \left[1 + r\left(\frac{N_{sm}}{365}\right)\right]. \tag{3.8}$$

The discount rate d for T-bills is calculated using (3.9):

$$d = (1 - P) \times \frac{B}{n}. \tag{3.9}$$

The relationship between discount rate and true yield is given by:

$$d = \frac{r}{(1 + r \times \frac{n}{B})}$$

$$r = \frac{d}{1 - d \times \frac{n}{B}}. \tag{3.10}$$

If a T-bill is traded in the secondary market, the settlement proceeds from the trade are calculated using (3.11):

$$Proceeds = M - \left(\frac{M \times \text{days remaining} \times d}{B \times 100}\right). \tag{3.11}$$

Bankers acceptances

A *bankers acceptance* is a written promise issued by a borrower to a bank to repay borrowed funds. The lending bank lends funds and in return accepts the bankers acceptance. The acceptance is negotiable and can be sold in the secondary market. The investor who buys the acceptance can collect the loan on the day that repayment is due. If the borrower defaults, the investor has legal recourse to the bank that made the first acceptance. Bankers acceptances are also known as *bills of exchange, bank bills, trade bills* or *commercial bills*.

Essentially, bankers acceptances are instruments created to facilitate commercial trade transactions. The instrument is called a 'bankers acceptance' because a bank accepts the ultimate responsibility to repay the loan to its holder. The use of bankers acceptances to finance commercial transactions is known as *acceptance financing*. The transactions for which acceptances are created include import and export of goods, the storage and shipping of goods between two overseas countries (where neither the importer nor the exporter is based in the home country)[3] and the storage and shipping of goods between two entities based at home. Acceptances are discount instruments and are purchased by banks, local authorities and money market investment funds. The rate that a bank charges a customer for issuing a bankers acceptance is a function of the rate at which the bank thinks it will be able to sell it in the secondary market. A commission is added to this rate. For ineligible bankers acceptances (see below), the issuing bank will add an amount to offset the cost of the additional reserve requirements.

Eligible bankers acceptance

An accepting bank that chooses to retain a bankers acceptance in its portfolio may be able to use it as collateral for a loan obtained from the central bank during open market operations, for example the Bank of England in the UK and the Federal Reserve in the USA. Not all acceptances are eligible to be used as collateral in this way, since they must meet certain criteria set by the central bank. The main requirements for eligibility are that the acceptance must be within a certain maturity band (a maximum of six months in the USA and three months in the UK), and that it must have been created to finance a self-liquidating commercial transaction. In the USA eligibility is also important because the Federal Reserve imposes a reserve requirement on funds raised via bankers acceptances that are ineligible. Bankers acceptances sold by an accepting bank are potential liabilities of the bank, but the Fed imposes a limit on the amount of eligible bankers acceptances that a bank may issue. Bills eligible for deposit at a central bank enjoy a finer rate than ineligible bills, and also act as a benchmark for prices in the secondary market.

3. A bankers acceptance created to finance such a transaction is known as a *third-party acceptance*.

US Treasury bills

The Treasury bill market in the USA is one of the most liquid and transparent debt markets in the world. Consequently, the bid–offer spread on them is very narrow. The Treasury issues bills at a weekly auction each Monday, made up of 91-day and 182-day bills. Every fourth week the Treasury also issues 52-week bills. As a result, there are large numbers of Treasury bills outstanding at any one time. The interest earned on Treasury bills is not liable to state and local income taxes.

Federal funds

Commercial banks in the USA are required to keep reserves on deposit at the Federal Reserve. Banks with reserves in excess of required reserves can lend these funds to other banks, and these interbank loans are called *federal funds* or *fed funds* and are usually overnight loans. Through the fed funds market, commercial banks with excess funds are able to lend to banks that are short of reserves, thus facilitating liquidity. The transactions are very large denominations and are lent at the *fed funds rate*, which is a volatile interest rate because it fluctuates with market shortages.

Prime rate

The *prime interest rate* in the USA is often said to represent the rate at which commercial banks lend to their most creditworthy customers. In practice, many loans are made at rates below the prime rate, so the prime rate is not the best rate at which highly rated firms may borrow. Nevertheless, the prime rate is a benchmark indicator of the level of US money market rates, and is often used as a reference rate for floating-rate instruments. As the market for bank loans is highly competitive, all commercial banks quote a single prime rate, and the rate for all banks changes simultaneously.

Commercial paper

Commercial paper (CP) is a short-term money market funding instrument issued by corporates. In the UK and USA it is a discount instrument, with sterling paper being dealt on a 365-day basis. CP trades essentially as T-bills but with higher yields because it is an unsecured corporate obligation. CP is an important part of the US money market, and began as a US instrument before being introduced in other money centres around the world. The instrument ranges in maturity from 30 to 270 days (although typical maturities are 30 to 90 days) and is usually issued in response to investor demand or for short-term working capital considerations. As the paper is unsecured, investor sentiment usually requires that any issue be rated by a rating agency such as Moody's Investors Services or Standard & Poor's, although high-yield CP also exists.

Another significant market exists in Euro-commercial paper (ECP), which is similar in concept to CP but is not restricted to the 270-day maturity.[4] The market in ECP exists in money centres globally. Standard settlement of ECP is for spot value (which is two business days forward), whereas standard settlement of US and UK settlement is on a same-day basis. ECP can be issued as both a discount instrument or a yield-bearing instrument, although the latter is rarer.

For yield-bearing ECP, the calculation of settlement proceeds in the secondary market is given by (3.12):

$$\text{Proceeds} = M \times \left[\frac{1 + \frac{C \times T}{36000}}{1 + \frac{r \times N}{36000}} \right] \qquad (3.12)$$

where

M is the face amount
C is the coupon
r is the yield
T is the paper's original maturity or *tenor*
N is the time from settlement to maturity.

For paper issued on a discount basis the proceeds are given by:

$$\text{Proceeds} = \left[\frac{M}{1 + \frac{r \times N}{36000}} \right]. \qquad (3.13)$$

The majority of ECP is issued in US dollars, although euro, sterling and Japanese yen are also popular currencies.

Foreign exchange

The price quotation for currencies generally follows a convention used by the SWIFT and Reuters dealing systems, and is a three-letter code used to identify a currency, such as USD for US dollar and GBP for sterling. The rate convention is to quote everything in terms of one unit of the US dollar, so that the dollar and Swiss franc rate is quoted as USD/CHF, and is the number of Swiss francs to one US dollar. The exception is for sterling, which is

---

4. In the US market this is a Securities and Exchange Commission requirement.

Asset-backed commercial paper

The rise in securitisation has led to the growth of short-term instruments backed by the cash flows from other assets, known as *asset-backed commercial paper* (ABCP). Securitisation is looked at in greater detail in Chapter 11; here we discuss briefly the basic concept of ABCP.

Generally, securitisation is used as a funding instrument by companies for three main reasons: it offers lower-cost funding compared with traditional bank-loan or bond financing; it is a mechanism by which assets such as corporate loans or mortgages can be removed from the balance sheet, thus improving the lender's return on assets or return on equity ratios; and it increases a borrower's funding options. When entering into securitisation, an entity may issue term securities against assets into the public or private market, or it may issue commercial paper via a special vehicle known as a *conduit*. These conduits are usually sponsored by commercial banks.

Entities usually access the commercial paper market in order to secure permanent financing, rolling over individual issues as part of a longer-term *programme* and using interest-rate swaps to arrange a fixed rate if required. Conventional CP issues are typically supported by a line of credit from a commercial bank, and so this form of financing is in effect a form of bank funding.

---

quoted as GBP/USD and is the number of US dollars to the pound. The rate for euros has been quoted both ways round, for example EUR/USD, although some banks, for example RBS Financial Markets in the UK, quote euros to the pound, that is GBP/EUR.

Spot exchange rates

A *spot* foreign exchange trade is an outright purchase or sale of one currency against another currency, with delivery two working days after the trade date. Non-working days do not count, so a trade on a Friday is settled on the following Tuesday. There are some exceptions to this, for example trades of US dollar against Canadian dollar are settled the next working day; note that in some currencies, generally in the Middle East, markets are closed on Friday but open on Saturday. A settlement date that falls on a public holiday in the country of one of the two currencies is delayed for settlement by that day. An FX transaction is possible between any two currencies; however, to reduce the number of quotes that need to be made the market generally quotes only against the US dollar or occasionally sterling or euro, so that the exchange rate between two non-dollar currencies is calculated from the rate for each currency against the dollar. The resulting exchange rate is known as a *cross-rate*. Cross-rates themselves are also traded between banks, in addition to dollar-based rates. This is usually because the relationship between two rates is closer than that of either against the dollar; for example, the Swiss franc moves more closely in line with the euro than against the dollar, so in practice one observes that the dollar/Swiss franc rate is more a function of the euro/Swiss franc rate.

The spot FX quote is a two-way bid-offer price, just as in the bond and money markets, and indicates the rate at which a bank is prepared to buy the base currency against the variable currency; this is the 'bid' for the variable currency, so is the lower rate. The other side of the quote is the rate at which the bank is prepared to sell the base currency against the variable currency. For example, a quote of 1.6245–1.6255 for GBP/USD means that the bank is prepared to buy sterling for $1.6245, and to sell sterling for $1.6255. The convention in the FX market is uniform across countries, unlike the money markets. Although the money market convention for bid-offer quotes is, for example, $5\frac{1}{2}\%$–$5\frac{1}{4}\%$, meaning that the 'bid' for paper – the rate at which the bank will lend funds, say in the certificate of deposit market – is the higher rate and always on the left, this convention is reversed in certain countries. In the FX markets the convention is always the same one just described.

The difference between the two sides in a quote is the bank's dealing spread. Rates are quoted to 1/100th of a cent, known as a *pip*. In the quote above, the spread is 10 pips; however, this amount is a function of the size of the quote number, so that the rate for USD/JPY at, say, 110.10–110.20 indicates a spread of 0.10 yen. Generally only the pips in the two rates are quoted, so that the quote above would be simply '45–55'. The 'big figure' is not quoted.

EXAMPLE   *3.1 Exchange cross-rates*

Consider the following two spot rates:

EUR/USD	1.0566–1.0571
AUD/USD	0.7034–0.7039

The EUR/USD dealer buys euros and sells dollars at 1.0566 (the left side), while the AUD/USD dealer sells Australian dollars and buys US dollars at 0.7039 (the right side). To calculate the rate at which the bank buys euros and sells Australian dollars, we need:

1.0566/0.7039 = 1.4997

which is the rate at which the bank buys euros and sells Australian dollars. In the same way the rate at which the bank sells euros and buys Australian dollars is given by:

1.0571/0.7034 or 1.5028

Therefore the spot EUR/AUD rate is 1.4997–1.5028.

The derivation of cross-rates can be depicted in the following way. If we assume two exchange rates XXX/YYY and XXX/ZZZ, the cross-rates are:

YYY/ZZZ = XXX/ZZZ ÷ XXX/YYY
ZZZ/YYY = XXX/YYY ÷ XXX/ZZZ

Given two exchange rates YYY/XXX and XXX/ZZZ, the cross-rates are:

YYY/ZZZ = YYY/XXX × XXX/ZZZ
ZZZ/YYY = 1 ÷ (YYY/XXX × XXX/ZZZ)

Forward exchange rates

Forward outright

The spot exchange rate is the rate for immediate delivery (notwithstanding that actual delivery is two days forward). A *forward contract* or simply *forward* is an outright purchase or sale of one currency in exchange for another currency for settlement on a specified date at some point in the future. The exchange rate is quoted in the same way as the spot rate, with the bank buying the base currency on the bid side and selling it on the offered side. In some emerging markets no liquid forward market exists, so forwards are settled in cash against the spot rate on the maturity date. These *non-deliverable forwards* are considered in Choudhry (2001), Chapter 32.

Although some commentators have stated that the forward rate may be seen as the market's view of where the spot rate will be on the maturity date of the forward transaction, this is incorrect. A forward rate is calculated on the current interest rates of the two currencies involved, and the principle of no-arbitrage pricing ensures that there is no profit to be gained from simultaneous (and opposite) dealing in spot and forward. Consider the following strategy:

- borrow US dollars for six months starting from the spot value date;
- sell dollars and buy sterling for value spot;
- deposit the long sterling position for six months from the spot value date;
- sell forward today the sterling principal and interest that mature in six months' time into dollars.

The market will adjust the forward price so that the two initial transactions, if carried out simultaneously, will generate a zero profit/loss. The forward rates quoted in the trade will be calculated on the six months deposit rates for dollars and sterling; in general the calculation of a forward rate is given as:

$$Fwd = spot \times \frac{\left(1 + \text{variable currency deposit rate} \times \frac{\text{days}}{B}\right)}{\left(1 + \text{base currency deposit rate} \times \frac{\text{days}}{B}\right)}. \tag{3.14}$$

The year day-count base B will be either 365 or 360, depending on the convention for the currency in question.

EXAMPLE   *3.2 Forward rate*

90-day GBP deposit rate	5.75%
90-day USD deposit rate	6.15%
Spot GBP/USD rate	1.6315 (mid-rate)

The forward rate is given by:

$$1.6315 \times \frac{\left(1 + 0.0575 \times \frac{90}{365}\right)}{\left(1 + 0.0615 \times \frac{90}{365}\right)} = 1.6296$$

Therefore to deal forward the GBP/USD mid-rate is 1.6296, so in effect £1 buys $1.6296 in three months' time as opposed to $1.6315 today. Under different circumstances sterling may be worth more in the future than at the spot date.

Forward swaps

Expression (3.14) illustrates how a forward rate is calculated and quoted in theory. In practice, since spot rates change rapidly, often many times even in one minute, it would be tedious to keep recalculating the forward rate so often. Therefore banks quote a forward spread over the spot rate, which can then be added or subtracted to the spot rate as it changes. This spread is known as the *swap points*. An approximate value for the number of swap points is given by:

$$\text{Forward swap} \approx \text{spot x deposit rate differential} \times \frac{\text{days}}{B}. \tag{3.15}$$

The approximation is not accurate enough for forwards maturing more than 30 days from now, in which case another equation must be used. This is given as (3.16). It is also possible to calculate an approximate deposit rate differential from the swap points by rearranging (3.15).

$$\text{Forward swap} = \text{spot} \times \frac{\left(\text{variable currency depo rate} \times \frac{\text{days}}{B} - \text{base currency depo rate} \times \frac{\text{days}}{B}\right)}{\left(1 + \text{base currency depo rate} \times \frac{\text{days}}{B}\right)} \tag{3.16}$$

EXAMPLE *3.3 Forward swap points*

Spot EUR/USD   1.0566–1.0571
Forward swap   0.0125–0.0130
Forward outright   1.0691–1.0701

The forward outright is the spot price + the swap points, so in this case:

1.0691 = 1.0566 + 0.0125
1.0701 = 1.0571 + 0.0130.

Spot EUR/USD rate   0.9501
31-day EUR rate   3.15%
31-day USD rate   5.95%

$$\text{Forward swap} = 0.9501 \times \frac{0.0595 \times \frac{31}{360} - 0.0315 \times \frac{31}{360}}{1 + 0.0315 \times \frac{31}{360}}$$

or +24 points.

The swap points are quoted as two-way prices in the same way as spot rates. In practice, a middle spot price is used and then the forward swap spread around the spot quote. The difference between the interest rates of the two currencies will determine the magnitude of the swap points and whether they are added or subtracted from the spot rate. When the swap points are positive and the forwards trader applies a bid–offer spread to quote a two-way price, the left-hand side of the quote is smaller than the right-hand side as usual. When the swap points are negative, the trader must quote a 'more negative' number on the left-hand side and a 'more positive' number on the right-hand side. The 'minus' sign is not shown however, so that the left-hand side may appear to be the larger number. Basically, when the swap price appears larger on the right, it means that it is negative and must be subtracted from the spot rate and not added.

Forwards traders can be considered to be interest rate traders rather than foreign exchange traders; although they will be left positions that arise from customer orders, in general they will manage their book based on their view of short-term deposit rates in the currencies they are trading. In general a forward trader expecting the interest rate differential to move in favour of the base currency – for example, a rise in base currency rates or a fall in the variable currency rate – will 'buy and sell' the base currency. This is equivalent to borrowing the base currency and depositing in the variable currency. The relationship between interest rates and forward swaps means that banks can take advantage of different opportunities in different markets. Assume that a bank requires funding in one currency but is able to borrow in another currency at a relatively cheaper rate. It may wish to borrow in the second currency and use a forward contract to convert the borrowing to the first currency. It will do this if the all-in cost of borrowing is less than the cost of borrowing directly in the first currency.

Forward cross-rates

A forward cross-rate is calculated in the same way as spot cross-rates. The formulae given for spot cross-rates can be adapted to forward rates.

Forward-forwards

A forward-forward swap is a deal between two forward dates rather than from the spot date to a forward date; this is the same terminology and meaning as in the bond markets, where a forward or a forward-forward rate is the zero-coupon interest rate between two points both beginning in the future. In the foreign exchange market, an example would be a contract to sell sterling three months forward and buy it back in six months' time. Here, the swap is for the three-month period between the three-month date and the six-month date. The reason a bank or corporate might do this is to hedge a forward exposure or because of a particular view it has on forward rates, in effect deposit rates.

EXAMPLE *3.4 Forward-forward contract*

GBP/USD spot rate	1.6315–20
Three-month swap	45–41
Six-month swap	135–125

If a bank wished to sell GBP three months forward and buy them back six months forward, this is identical to undertaking one swap to buy GBP spot and sell GBP three months forward, and another to sell GBP spot and buy it six months forward. Swaps are always quoted as the quoting bank buying the base currency forward on the bid side, and selling the base currency forward on the offered side; the counterparty bank can 'buy and sell' GBP 'spot against three months' at a swap price of –45, with settlement rates of spot and (spot – 0.0045). It can 'sell and buy' GBP 'spot against six months' at the swap price of –125 with settlement rates of spot and (spot – 0.0125). It can therefore do both simultaneously, which implies a difference between the two forward prices of (–125) – (–45) = –90 points. Conversely the bank can 'buy and sell' GBP 'three months against six months' at a swap price of (–135) – (–41) or –94 points. The two-way price is therefore 94–90 (we ignore the negative signs).

SELECTED BIBLIOGRAPHY AND REFERENCES

Choudhry, M., *The Bond and Money Markets*, Butterworth-Heinemann 2001.

Roth, P., *Mastering Foreign Exchange and Money Markets*, FT Prentice Hall 1996.

Stigum, M., Robinson, F., *Money Market and Bond Calculations*, Irwin 1996.

Walmsley, J., *The Foreign Exchange and Money Markets Guide*, 2nd edition, Wiley 2000.

CHAPTER 4

Fixed-income securities I

Bonds are debt capital market instruments that represent a cash flow payable during a specified time period heading into the future. This cash flow represents the interest payable on the loan and the loan redemption. So a bond essentially is a loan, albeit one that is tradeable in a secondary market. This differentiates bond market securities from commercial bank loans.

For some considerable time the analysis of bonds was frequently presented in what might be called 'traditional' terms, with a description limited to gross redemption yield or *yield to maturity*. However, these days basic bond analysis is presented in slightly different terms, as described in a range of books and articles such as those by Ingersoll (1987), Shiller (1990), Neftci (2000), Jarrow (1996), Van Deventer (1997) and Sundaresan (1997), among others. For this reason we review the basic elements in this chapter, but then consider the academic approach and description of bond pricing, and review the term structure of interest rates. Interested readers may wish to consult the texts in the bibliography at the end of the chapter for further information.

In the analysis that follows bonds are assumed to be *default-free*, which means that there is no possibility that the interest payments and principal repayment will not be made. Such an assumption is accurate when one is referring to government bonds such as US Treasuries, UK gilts and so on. However, it is unreasonable when applied to bonds issued by corporates or lower-rated sovereign borrowers. Nevertheless it is still relevant to understand the valuation and analysis of bonds that are default-free, because the pricing of bonds that carry default risk is based on the price of risk-free government securities. Essentially, the price investors charge borrowers that are not of risk-free credit standing is the price of government securities plus some *credit risk* premium.

Bond pricing and yield: the traditional approach

Bond pricing

The interest rate that is used to discount a bond's cash flows (therefore called the *discount* rate) is the rate required by the bondholder. It is therefore known as the bond's yield. The yield on the bond will be determined by the market and reflects the price demanded by investors for buying it, which is why it is sometimes called the bond's *return*. The required yield for any bond will depend on a number of political and economic factors, including what yield is being earned by other bonds of the same class. Yield is always quoted as an annualized interest rate, so that for a semi-annually coupon-paying bond exactly half of the annual rate is used to discount the cash flows.

The *fair price* of a bond is the present value of all its cash flows. Therefore when pricing a bond we need to calculate the present value of all the coupon interest payments and the present value of the redemption payment, and sum these. The price of a conventional bond that pays annual coupons can therefore be given by:

$$P = \frac{C}{(1+r)} + \frac{C}{(1+r)^2} + \frac{C}{(1+r)^3} + \ldots \frac{C}{(1+r)^N} + \frac{M}{(1+r)^N}$$

$$= \sum_{n=1}^{N} \frac{C}{(1+r)^n} + \frac{M}{(1+r)^N}$$

(4.1)

where

P is the price
C is the annual coupon payment (for semi-annual coupons it will be $C/2$)
r is the discount rate (therefore, the required yield)
N is the number of years to maturity (therefore, the number of interest periods in an annually paying bond; for a semi-annual bond the number of interest periods is $N \times 2$)
M is the maturity payment or par value (usually 100% of currency).

For longhand calculation purposes the first half of (4.1) is usually simplified and is sometimes encountered in one of the two ways shown in (4.2):

$$P = C \left[\frac{1 - \left[\frac{1}{(1+r)^N} \right]}{r} \right]$$

or

(4.2)

$$P = \frac{C}{r} \left[1 - \frac{1}{(1+r)^N} \right].$$

The price of a bond that pays semi-annual coupons is given by the expression at (4.3), which is our earlier expression modified to allow for the twice-yearly discounting:

$$P = \frac{C/2}{\left(1 + \frac{1}{2}\,r\right)} + \frac{C/2}{\left(1 + \frac{1}{2}\,r\right)^2} + \frac{C/2}{\left(1 + \frac{1}{2}\,r\right)^3} + \ldots + \frac{C/2}{\left(1 + \frac{1}{2}\,r\right)^{2N}} + \frac{M}{\left(1 + \frac{1}{2}\,r\right)^{2N}}$$

$$= \sum_{t=1}^{2T} \frac{C/2}{\left(1 + \frac{1}{2}\,r\right)^n} + \frac{M}{\left(1 + \frac{1}{2}\,r\right)^{2N}} \tag{4.3}$$

$$= \frac{C}{r}\left[1 - \frac{1}{\left(1 + \frac{1}{2}\,r\right)^{2N}}\right] + \frac{M}{\left(1 + \frac{1}{2}\,r\right)^{2N}}.$$

Note how we set $2N$ as the power to which to raise the discount factor, as there are two interest payments every year for a bond that pays semi-annually. Therefore a more convenient function to use might be the number of interest periods in the life of the bond, as opposed to the number of years to maturity, which we could set as n, allowing us to alter the equation for a semi-annually paying bond as:

$$P = \frac{C}{r}\left[1 - \frac{1}{\left(1 + \frac{1}{2}\,r\right)^n}\right] + \frac{M}{\left(1 + \frac{1}{2}\,r\right)^n}. \tag{4.4}$$

The formula at (4.4) calculates the fair price on a coupon payment date, so that there is no *accrued interest* incorporated into the price. It also assumes that there is an even number of coupon payment dates remaining before maturity. The concept of accrued interest is an accounting convention, and treats coupon interest as accruing every day that the bond is held; this amount is added to the discounted present value of the bond (the *clean price*) to obtain the market value of the bond, known as the *dirty price.*

The date used as the point for calculation is the *settlement date* for the bond – the date on which a bond will change hands after it is traded. For a new issue of bonds the settlement date is the day when the stock is delivered to investors and payment is received by the bond issuer. The settlement date for a bond traded in the *secondary market* is the day that the buyer transfers payment to the seller of the bond and when the seller transfers the bond to the buyer. Different markets will have different settlement conventions; for example, UK gilts normally settle one business day after the trade date (the notation used in bond markets is 'T + 1') whereas eurobonds settle on T + 3. The term *value date* is sometimes used in place of settlement date. The two terms are, however, not strictly synonymous. A settlement date can only fall on a business day, so that a gilt traded on a Friday will settle on a Monday. A value date can, however, sometimes fall on a non-business day, for example, when accrued interest is being calculated.

If there is an odd number of coupon payment dates before maturity the formula at (4.4) is modified as shown in (4.5).

$$P = \frac{C}{r} \left[1 - \frac{1}{\left(1 + \frac{1}{2} r\right)^{2N+1}} \right] + \frac{M}{\left(1 + \frac{1}{2} r\right)^{2N+1}}. \tag{4.5}$$

The standard formula also assumes that the bond is traded for settlement on a day that is precisely one interest period before the next coupon payment. The price formula is adjusted if dealing takes place in between coupon dates. If we take the *value date* for any transaction, we then need to calculate the number of calendar days from this day to the next coupon date. We then use the following ratio i when adjusting the exponent for the discount factor:

$$i = \frac{\text{Days from value date to next coupon date}}{\text{Days in the interest payment}}.$$

The number of days in the interest period is the number of calendar days between the last coupon date and the next one, and it will depend on the day count basis used for that specific bond. The price formula is then modified as shown at (4.6):

$$P = \frac{C}{(1 + r)^i} + \frac{C}{(1 + r)^{1+i}} + \frac{C}{(1 + r)^{2+i}} + \ldots + \frac{C}{(1 + r)^{n-1+i}} + \frac{M}{(1 + r)^{n-1+i}} \tag{4.6}$$

where the variables C, M, n and r are as before. Note that (4.6) assumes r for an annually paying bond and is adjusted to $r/2$ for a semi-annual coupon-paying bond.

There also exist *perpetual* or *irredeemable* bonds which have no redemption date, so that interest on them is paid indefinitely. They are also known as *undated* bonds. An example of an undated bond is the $3\frac{1}{2}\%$ War Loan, a UK gilt originally issued in 1916 to help pay for the 1914–18 war effort. Most undated bonds date from a long time in the past and it is unusual to see them issued today. In structure, the cash flow from an undated bond can be viewed as a continuous annuity. The fair price of such a bond is given from (4.1) by setting $N = \infty$, such that:

$$P = \frac{C}{r}. \tag{4.7}$$

In most markets bond prices are quoted in decimals, in minimum increments of 1/100ths. This is the case with Eurobonds, euro-denominated bonds and gilts. Certain markets, including the US Treasury market, South African and Indian government bonds, quote prices in *ticks*, where the minimum increment is 1/32nd. One tick is therefore equal to 0.03125. A US Treasury might be priced at '98–05', which means '98 and 5 ticks'. This is equal to 98 and 5/32nds, which is 98.15625.

Bonds that do not pay a coupon during their life are known as *zero-coupon* bonds or *strips*, and the price for these bonds is determined by modifying (4.1) to allow for the fact that $C = 0$. We know that the only cash flow is the maturity payment, so we may set the price as:

$$P = \frac{M}{(1 + r)^N} \qquad (4.8)$$

where M and r are as before and N is the number of years to maturity. The important factor is to allow for the same number of interest periods as coupon bonds of the same currency. That is, even though there are no actual coupons, we calculate prices and yields on the basis of a *quasi-coupon* period. For a US dollar or a sterling zero-coupon bond, a five-year zero-coupon bond would be assumed to cover ten quasi-coupon periods, which would set the price equation as:

$$P = \frac{M}{\left(1 + \frac{1}{2}r\right)^{2n}} \cdot \qquad (4.9)$$

We have to note carefully the quasi-coupon periods in order to maintain consistency with conventional bond pricing.

An examination of the bond price formula tells us that the yield and price for a bond are closely related. A key aspect of this relationship is that the price changes in the opposite direction to the yield. This is because the price of the bond is the net present value of its cash flows; if the discount rate used in the present value calculation increases, the present values of the cash flows will decrease. This occurs whenever the yield level required by bondholders increases. In the same way, if the required yield decreases, the price of the bond will rise.

Bond yield

We have observed how to calculate the price of a bond using an appropriate discount rate known as the bond's *yield*. We can reverse this procedure to find the yield of a bond where the price is known, which would be equivalent to calculating the bond's *internal rate of return* (IRR). The IRR calculation is taken to be a bond's *yield to maturity* or *redemption yield* and is one of various yield measures used in the markets to estimate the return generated from holding a bond. In most markets bonds are generally traded on the basis of their prices, but because of the complicated patterns of cash flows that different bonds can have, they are generally compared in terms of their yields. This means that a market-maker will usually quote a two-way price at which he will buy or sell a particular bond, but it is the *yield* at which the bond is trading that is important to the market-maker's customer. This is because a bond's price does not actually tell us anything useful about what we are getting. Remember that in any market there will be a number of bonds with different issuers, coupons and terms to maturity. Even in a homogeneous market such as the gilt market, different gilts will trade according to their own specific character-istics. To compare bonds in the market, therefore, we need the yield on any bond, and it is yields that we compare, not prices.

The yield on any investment is the interest rate that will make the present value of the cash flows from the investment equal to the initial cost (price) of the investment. Mathematically, the yield on any investment, represented by r, is the interest rate that satisfies equation (4.10) below, which is simply the bond price equation we've already reviewed:

$$P = \sum_{n=1}^{N} \frac{C}{(1 + r)^n} .$$
(4.10)

But, as we have noted, there are other types of yield measure used in the market for dif-ferent purposes. The simplest measure of the yield on a bond is the *current yield*, also known as the *flat yield, interest yield* or *running yield*. The running yield is given by:

$$rc = \frac{C}{P} \times 100$$
(4.11)

where rc is the current yield.

In (4.11) C is not expressed as a decimal. Current yield ignores any capital gain or loss that might arise from holding and trading a bond and does not consider the time value of money. It essentially calculates the bond coupon income as a proportion of the price paid for the bond, and to be accurate would have to assume that the bond was more like an annuity rather than a fixed-term instrument.

The current yield is useful as a 'rough and ready' interest rate calculation; it is often used to estimate the cost of or profit from a short-term holding of a bond. For example, if other short-term interest rates, such as the one-week or three-month rates, are higher than the current yield, holding the bond is said to involve a *running cost*. This is also known as *negative carry* or *negative funding*. The terms are used by bond traders, market makers and *leveraged* investors. The *carry* on a bond is a useful measure for all market practitioners because it illustrates the cost of holding or *funding* a bond. The funding rate is the bondholder's short-term cost of funds. A private investor could also apply this to a short-term holding of bonds.

The *yield to maturity* or *gross redemption yield* is the most frequently used measure of return from holding a bond.[1] Yield to maturity (YTM) takes into account the pattern of

---

1. In this book the terms *yield to maturity* and *gross redemption yield* are used synonymously. The latter term is encountered in sterling markets.

coupon payments, the bond's term to maturity and the capital gain (or loss) arising over the remaining life of the bond. We saw from our bond price formula in the previous section that these elements were all related and were important components determining a bond's price. If we set the IRR for a set of cash flows to be the rate that applies from a start date to an end date, we can assume the IRR to be the YTM for those cash flows. The YTM therefore is equivalent to the *internal rate of return* on the bond – the rate that equates the value of the discounted cash flows on the bond to its current price. The calculation assumes that the bond is held until maturity, and therefore it is the cash flows to maturity that are discounted in the calculation. The calculation also employs the concept of the time value of money.

As we would expect, the formula for YTM is essentially that for calculating the price of a bond. For a bond paying annual coupons, the YTM is calculated by solving equation (4.1). Note that the expression at (4.1) has two variable parameters: the price P and yield r. It cannot be rearranged to solve for yield r explicitly, and in fact the only way to solve for the yield is to use the process of numerical iteration. The process involves estimating a value for r and calculating the price associated with the estimated yield. If the calculated price is higher than the price of the bond at the time, the yield estimate is lower than the actual yield, and so it must be adjusted until it converges to the level that corresponds with the bond price.[2] For the YTM of a semi-annual coupon bond, we have to adjust the formula to allow for the semi-annual payments, shown at (4.3).

To differentiate redemption yield from other yield and interest rate measures described in this book, we henceforth refer to it as *rm*.

EXAMPLE *4.1 Yield to maturity for semi-annual coupon bond*

A semi-annual paying bond has a price of £98.50, an annual coupon of 6%, and there is exactly one year before maturity. The bond therefore has three remaining cash flows, comprising two coupon payments of £3 each and a redemption payment of £100. Equation (4.10) can be used with the following inputs:

$$9850 = \frac{3.00}{\left(1 + \frac{1}{2} rm\right)} + \frac{103.00}{\left(1 + \frac{1}{2} rm\right)^2}$$

Note that we use half of the YTM value *rm* because this is a semi-annual paying bond. The expression above is a quadratic equation, which is solved using the standard solution for quadratic equations, which is noted below:

---

2. Bloomberg (the electronic analytics and trading system) also uses the term *yield to workout* where 'workout' refers to the maturity date for the bond.

$$ax^2 + bx + c = 0$$

$$x = \frac{-b \pm \sqrt{b^2 - 4ac}}{2a}.$$

In our expression if we let $x = (1 + rm/2)$, we can rearrange the expression as follows:

$$98.50x^2 - 3.0x - 103.00 = 0.$$

We then solve for a standard quadratic equation, and as such there will be two solutions, only one of which gives a positive redemption yield. The positive solution is $rm/2 = 0.037929$ so that $rm = 7.5859\%$.

As an example of the iterative solution method, suppose that we start with a trial value for rm of $r_1 = 7\%$ and plug this into the right-hand side of equation (4.10). This gives a value for the right-hand side of:

$$RHS_1 = 99.050$$

which is higher than the left-hand side (LHS = 98.50); the trial value for rm was therefore too low. Suppose then that we try next $r_2 = 8\%$ and use this as the right-hand side of the equation. This gives:

$$RHS_2 = 98.114$$

which is lower than the LHS. Because RHS1 and RHS2 lie on either side of the LHS value, we know that the correct value for rm lies between 7% and 8%. Using the formula for linear interpolation:

$$rm = r_1 + (r_2 - r_1) \frac{RHS_1 - LHS}{RHS_1 - RHS_2}$$

our linear approximation for the redemption yield is $rm = 7.587\%$, which is near to the exact solution.

Note that the redemption yield as calculated in this section is the *gross redemption yield* – the anticipated yield that results from payment of coupons without deduction of any withholding tax. The *net redemption yield* is obtained by multiplying the coupon rate C by (1 – marginal tax rate). The net yield is what is expected to be received if the bond is traded in a market where bonds pay coupon *net*, which means net of a withholding tax. The net redemption yield is always lower than the gross redemption yield.

The key assumption behind the YTM calculation is that the rate rm remains stable for the entire period of the life of the bond. By assuming the same yield we can say that all coupons are reinvested at the same yield *rm*. For the bond in example 4.1 this means that if all the cash flows are discounted at 7.59% they will have a total net present value of 98.50. This is patently unrealistic since we can predict with virtual certainty that interest rates for instruments of similar maturity to the bond at each coupon date will not remain at this rate for the life of the bond. In practice however, investors require a rate of return that is equivalent to the price that they are paying for a bond and the redemption yield is, to put it simply, as good a measurement as any.

A more accurate measurement might be to calculate present values of future cash flows using the discount rate that is equal to the market's view on where interest rates will be at that point, known as the *forward* interest rate. However, forward rates are *implied* interest rates, and a YTM measurement calculated using forward rates can be as speculative as one calculated using the conventional formula. This is because the *actual* market interest rate at any time is invariably different from the rate implied earlier in the forward markets. So a YTM calculation made using forward rates would not be realized in practice either.[3] We shall see later how the *zero-coupon* interest rate is the true interest rate for any term to maturity. The YTM is, despite the limitations presented by its assumptions, the main measure of return used in the markets. It is of course an expected return.

We have noted the difference between calculating redemption yield on the basis of both annual and semi-annual coupon bonds. Analysis of bonds that pay semi-annual coupons incorporates semi-annual discounting of semi-annual coupon payments. This is appropriate for most UK and US bonds. However, government bonds in most of continental Europe and most Eurobonds pay annual coupon payments, and the appropriate method of calculating the redemption yield is to use annual discounting. The two yields measures are not therefore directly comparable. We could make a Eurobond directly comparable with a UK gilt by using semi-annual discounting of the Eurobond's annual coupon payments. Alternatively, we could make the gilt comparable with the Eurobond by using annual discounting of its semi-annual coupon payments. The price/yield formulae for different discounting possibilities we encounter in the markets are listed below (as usual we assume that the calculation takes place on a coupon payment date so that accrued interest is zero).

Semi-annual discounting of annual payments:

$$P_d = \frac{C}{\left(1 + \frac{1}{2}rm\right)^2} + \frac{C}{\left(1 + \frac{1}{2}rm\right)^4} + \frac{C}{\left(1 + \frac{1}{2}rm\right)^6} + \ldots + \frac{C}{\left(1 + \frac{1}{2}rm\right)^{2N}} + \frac{M}{\left(1 + \frac{1}{2}rm\right)^{2N}}. \quad (4.12)$$

Annual discounting of semi-annual payments:

---

3. Such an approach is used to price interest rate swaps, however.

$$P_d = \frac{C/2}{(1 + rm)^{\frac{1}{2}}} + \frac{C/2}{(1 + rm)} + \frac{C/2}{(1 + rm)^{\frac{3}{2}}} + \ldots + \frac{C/2}{(1 + rm)^N} + \frac{M}{(1 + rm)^N}. \tag{4.13}$$

Consider a bond with a dirty price of 97.89, a coupon of 6% and five years to maturity. This bond would have the following gross redemption yields under the different yield calculation conventions:

Discounting	Payments	Yield to maturity (%)
Semi-annual	Semi-annual	6.500
Annual	Annual	6.508
Semi-annual	Annual	6.428
Annual	Semi-annual	6.605

This proves what we have already observed, namely that the coupon and discounting frequency will impact the redemption yield calculation for a bond. We can see that increasing the frequency of discounting will lower the yield, while increasing the frequency of payments will raise the yield. When comparing yields for bonds that trade in markets with different conventions, it is important to convert all the yields to the same calculation basis.

Intuitively we might think that doubling a semi-annual yield figure will give us the annualized equivalent; in fact this will result in an inaccurate figure due to the multiplicative effects of discounting, and one that is an underestimate of the true annualized yield. The correct procedure for producing an annualized yield from semi-annual and quarterly yields is given by the expressions below.

The general conversion expression is given by:

$$rm_a = (1 + \text{interest rate})^m - 1 \tag{4.14}$$

where m is the number of coupon payments per year.

Specifically, we can convert between yields using the expressions given at (4.15) and (4.16):

$$rm_a = \left[\left(1 + \tfrac{1}{2}rm_s\right)^2 - 1\right]$$
$$rm_s = \left[\left(1 + rm_a\right)^{\frac{1}{2}} - 1\right] \times 2 \tag{4.15}$$

$$rm_a = \left[\left(1 + \tfrac{1}{4}rm_q\right)^4 - 1\right]$$
$$rm_q = \left[\left(1 + rm_a\right)^{\frac{1}{4}} - 1\right] \times 4 \tag{4.16}$$

where rm_q, rm_s and rm_a are respectively the quarterly, semi-annually and annually compounded yields to maturity.

4.2 Comparing bond yield

A UK gilt paying semi-annual coupons and a maturity of ten years has a quoted yield of 4.89%. A European government bond of similar maturity is quoted at a yield of 4.96%. Which bond has the higher effective yield?

The effective annual yield of the gilt is:

$$rm = \left(1 + \tfrac{1}{2} \cdot 0.0489\right)^2 - 1 = 4.9498\%.$$

Therefore the gilt does indeed have the lower yield.

The market convention is sometimes simply to double the semi-annual yield to obtain the annualized yields, despite the fact that this produces an inaccurate result. It is only acceptable to do this for rough calculations. An annualized yield obtained by multiplying the semi-annual yield by two is known as a *bond equivalent yield*.

The major disadvantage of the YTM measure has already been alluded to. Another disadvantage of the yield to maturity measure of return is where investors do not hold bonds to maturity. The redemption yield will not be of great value where the bond is not being held to redemption. Investors might then be interested in other measures of return, which we can look at later.

To reiterate then, the redemption yield measure assumes that:

■ the bond is held to maturity;

■ all coupons during the bond's life are reinvested at the same (redemption yield) rate.

Therefore the YTM can be viewed as an *expected* or *anticipated* yield and is closest to reality perhaps where an investor buys a bond on first issue and holds it to maturity. Even then, the actual realized yield on maturity would be different from the YTM figure because of the inapplicability of the second condition above.

In addition, as coupons are discounted at the yield specific for each bond, it actually becomes inaccurate to compare bonds using this yield measure. For instance, the coupon cash flows that occur in two years' time from both a two-year and five-year bond will be discounted at different rates (assuming we do not have a flat yield curve). This would occur because the YTM for a five-year bond is invariably different to the YTM for a two-year bond. However, it would clearly not be correct to discount a two-year cash flow at different rates, because we can see that the present value calculated today of a cash flow in two years' time should be the same whether it is sourced from a short- or long-dated bond. Even if the first condition noted above for the YTM calculation is satisfied, it is clearly unlikely for any but the shortest maturity bond that all coupons will be reinvested at the same rate. Market interest rates are in a state of constant flux and hence this would affect money reinvestment rates. Therefore, although yield to maturity is the main market measure of bond levels, it is not a true interest rate. This is an important result and we shall explore the concept of a true interest rate later in this chapter.

Accrued interest, clean and dirty bond prices

The consideration of bond pricing up to now has ignored coupon interest. All bonds (except zero-coupon bonds) accrue interest on a daily basis, and this is then paid out on the coupon date. The calculation of bond prices using present value analysis does not account for coupon interest or *accrued interest*. In all major bond markets the convention is to quote the price as a *clean price*. This is the price of the bond as given by the net present value of its cash flows, but excluding coupon interest that has accrued on the bond since the last dividend payment. As all bonds accrue interest on a daily basis, even if a bond is held for only one day, interest will have been earned by the bondholder. However, we have referred already to a bond's *all-in* price, which is the price that is actually paid for the bond in the market. This is also known as the *dirty price* (or *gross price*), which is the clean price of a bond plus accrued interest. In other words, the accrued interest must be added to the quoted price to get the total consideration for the bond.

Accruing interest compensates the seller of the bond for giving up all of the next coupon payment, even though he will have held the bond for part of the period since the last coupon payment. The clean price for a bond will move with changes in market interest rates; assuming that these are constant in a coupon period, the clean price will be constant for this period. However, the dirty price for the same bond will increase steadily from one interest payment date until the next one. On the coupon date, the clean and dirty prices are the same and the accrued interest is zero. Between the coupon payment date and the next *ex dividend* date the bond is traded *cum dividend*, so that the buyer gets the next coupon payment. The seller is compensated for not receiving the next coupon payment by receiving accrued interest instead. This is positive and increases up to the next ex dividend date, at which point the dirty price falls by the present value of the amount of the coupon payment. The dirty price at this point is below the clean price, reflecting the fact that accrued interest is now negative. This is because after the ex dividend date the bond is traded 'ex dividend'; the seller not the buyer receives the next coupon and the buyer has to be compensated for not receiving the next coupon by means of a lower price for holding the bond.

The net interest accrued since the last ex dividend date is determined using (4.17),

$$AI = C \times \left[\frac{N_{xt} - N_{xc}}{\text{day base}} \right] \tag{4.17}$$

where

AI	is the next accrued interest
C	is the bond coupon
N_{xc}	is the number of days between the *ex dividend* date and the coupon payment date (seven business days for UK gilts)
N_{xt}	is the number of days between the *ex dividend* date and the date for the calculation
day base	is the day-count base (365 or 360).

Interest accrues on a bond from and including the last coupon date up to and excluding what is called the *value date*. The value date is almost always the *settlement* date for the bond, or the date when a bond is passed to the buyer and the seller receives payment. Interest does not accrue on bonds whose issuer has subsequently gone into default. Bonds that trade without accrued interest are said to be trading *flat* or *clean*. By definition therefore:

Clean price of a bond = dirty price – accrued interest.

For bonds that are trading ex-dividend, the accrued coupon is negative and would be subtracted from the clean price. The calculation is given by:

$$AI = -C \times \frac{\text{days to } next \text{ coupon}}{\text{day base}}. \qquad (4.18)$$

Certain classes of bonds, for example US Treasuries and Eurobonds, do not have an *ex dividend* period and therefore trade *cum dividend* right up to the coupon date.

The accrued interest calculation for a bond is dependent on the day-count basis specified for the bond in question. When bonds are traded in the market the actual consideration that changes hands is made up of the clean price of the bond together with the accrued interest that has accumulated on the bond since the last coupon payment; these two components make up the dirty price of the bond. When calculating the accrued interest, the market will use the appropriate day-count convention for that bond. A particular market will apply one of five different methods to calculate accrued interest:

▪ *Actual/365*: Accrued = coupon × days/365.

▪ *Actual/360*: Accrued = coupon × days/360.

▪ *Actual/actual*: Accrued = coupon × days/actual number of days in the interest period.

▪ *30/360*: See below.

▪ *30E/360*: See below.

When determining the number of days in between two dates, include the first date but not the second; thus, under the actual/365 convention, there are 37 days between 4 August and 10 September. The last two conventions assume 30 days in each month, so for example there are '30 days' between 10 February and 10 March. Under the 30/360 convention, if the first date falls on the 31st, it is changed to the 30th of the month, and if the second date falls on the 31st *and* the first date is on the 30th or 31st, the second date is changed to the 30th. The difference under the 30E/360 method is that if the second date falls on the 31st of the month it is automatically changed to the 30th.

EXAMPLE *4.3 Accrued interest*

Accrual calculation for 7% Treasury 2002

This gilt has coupon dates of 7 June and 7 December each year. £100 nominal of the bond is traded for value 27 August 1998. What is accrued interest on the value date?

On the value date 81 days have passed since the last coupon date. Under the old system for gilts, actual/365, the calculation was:

$$7 \times \frac{81}{365} = 1.55342.$$

Under the current system of actual/actual, which came into effect for gilts in November 1998, the accrued calculation uses the actual number of days between the two coupon dates, giving us:

$$7 \times \frac{81}{183} \times 0.5 = 1.54918.$$

EXAMPLE *4.4*

Mansur buys £25,000 nominal of the 8% 2015 gilt for value on 27 August 1998, at a price of 102.4375. How much does he actually pay for the bond?

The clean price of the bond is 102.4375. The dirty price of the bond is:

102.4375 + 1.55342 = 103.99092.

The total consideration is therefore 1.0399092 × 25,000 = £25,997.73.

EXAMPLE *4.5*

A Norwegian government bond with a coupon of 8% is purchased for settlement on 30 July 1999 at a price of 99.50. Assume that this is seven days before the coupon date and therefore the bond trades ex-dividend. What is the all-in price?

The accrued interest $= -8 \times \dfrac{7}{365} = -0.153424$.

The all-in price is therefore $99.50 - 0.1534 = 99.3466$.

EXAMPLE *4.6 Day-count bases*

A bond has coupon payments on 1 June and 1 December each year. What is the day-base count if the bond is traded for value date on 30 October, 31 October and 1 November 1999 respectively? There are 183 days in the interest period.

	30 October	31 October	1 November
Actual/365	151	152	153
Actual/360	151	152	153
Actual/actual	151	152	153
30/360	149	150	151
30E/360	149	150	150

Bond pricing and yield: the current approach

We are familiar with two types of fixed-income security, *zero-coupon bonds*, also known as *discount bonds* or *strips*, and *coupon bonds*. A zero-coupon bond makes a single payment on its maturity date, while a coupon bond makes regular interest payments at regular dates up to and including its maturity date. A coupon bond may be regarded as a set of strips, with each coupon payment and the redemption payment on maturity being equivalent to a zero-coupon bond maturing on that date. The literature we review in this section is set in a market of default-free bonds, whether they are zero-coupon bonds or coupon bonds. The market is assumed to be liquid so that bonds may be freely bought and sold. Prices of bonds are determined by the economy-wide supply and demand for the bonds at any time, so they are *macroeconomic* and not set by individual bond issuers or traders.

Zero-coupon bonds

A zero-coupon bond is the simplest fixed-income security. It is an issue of debt – the issuer promises to pay the face value of the debt to the bondholder on the date the bond matures. There are no coupon payments during the life of the bond, so it is a discount instrument, issued at a price that is below the face or *principal* amount. We denote as $P(t, T)$ the price of a discount bond at time t that matures at time T, with $T \geq t$. The term to maturity of the bond is denoted with n, where $n = T - t$. The price increases over time until the maturity date, when it reaches the maturity or *par value*. If the par value of the bond is £1, then the *yield to maturity* of the bond at time t is denoted by $r(t,T)$, where r is actually 'one plus the percentage yield' that is earned by holding the bond from t to T. So we have:

$$P(t, T) = \frac{1}{[r(t, T)]^n}.$$

(4.19)

The yield may be obtained from the bond price and is given by:

$$r(t, T) = \left[\frac{1}{P(t, T)} \right]^{1/n}$$

(4.20)

which is sometimes written as:

$$r(t, T) = P(t, T)^{-(1/n)}.$$

(4.21)

Analysts and researchers frequently work in terms of logarithms of yields and prices, or continuously compounded rates. One advantage of this is that it converts the non-linear relationship in (4.20) into a linear relationship.[4]

The bond price at time t_2 where $t \leq t_2 \leq T$ is given by:

$$P(t_2, T) = P(t, T)e^{(t_2 - t)r(t, T)}$$

(4.22)

which is natural, given that the bond price equation in continuous time is:

---

4. A linear relationship in X would be a function $Y = f(X)$ in which the X values change via a power or index of 1 only and are not multiplied or divided by another variable or variables. So, for example, terms such as X^2, $\sqrt{X}$ and other similar functions are not linear in X, nor are terms such as XZ or X/Z where Z is another variable. In econometric analysis, if the value of Y is solely dependent on the value of X, then its rate of change with respect to X, or the derivative of Y with respect to X, denoted dY/dX, is independent of X. Therefore if $Y = 5X$, then $dY/dX = 5$, which is independent of the value of X. However if $Y = 5X^2$, then $dY/dX = 10X$, which is not independent of the value of X. Hence this function is not linear in X. The classic regression function $e(Y \mid Xi) = \alpha + \beta X_i$ is a linear function with slope β and intercept α and the regression 'curve' is represented geometrically by a straight line.

$$P(t,T) = e^{-r(t,T)(t,T)} \tag{4.23}$$

so that the yield is given by:

$$r(t, T) = -\log\left(\frac{P(t, T)}{n}\right) \tag{4.24}$$

which is sometimes written as:

$$\log r(t, T) = -\left(\frac{1}{n}\right)\log P(t, T). \tag{4.25}$$

The expression in (4.22) includes the exponential function, hence the use of the term continuously compounded.

The *term structure of interest rates* is the set of zero-coupon yields at time t for all bonds ranging in maturity from $(t, t + 1)$ to $(t, t + m)$ where the bonds have maturities of $\{0,1,2, \dots, m\}$. A good definition of the term structure of interest rates is given by Sundaresan, who states that it 'refers to the relationship between the yield to maturity of default-free zero-coupon securities and their maturities' (Sundaresan 1997, p. 176).

The *yield curve* is a plot of the set of yields for $r(t, t + 1)$ to $r(t, t + m)$ against m at time t. For example, Figures 4.1–4.3 show the log zero-coupon yield curve for US Treasury strips, UK gilt strips and French OAT strips on 27 September 2000. Each of the curves exhibit peculiarities in their shape, although the most common type of curve is gently upward sloping, as is the French curve. The UK curve is *inverted*. We explore further the shape of the yield curve later in this chapter.

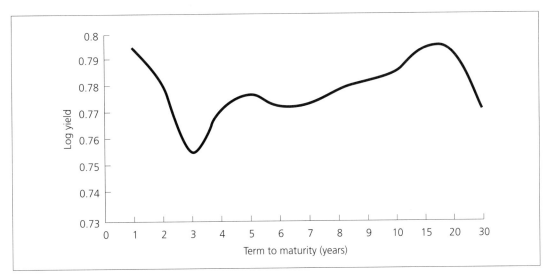

FIGURE 4.1 ■ US Treasury zero-coupon yield curve, September 2000

Source: Bloomberg L.P.

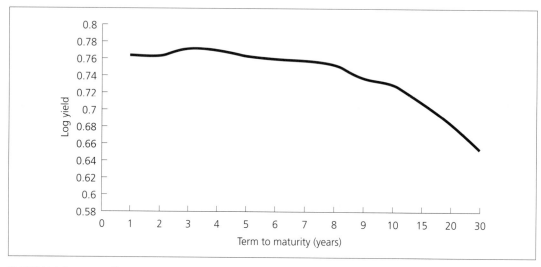

FIGURE 4.2 ▪ UK gilt zero-coupon yield curve, September 2000
Source: Bloomberg L.P.

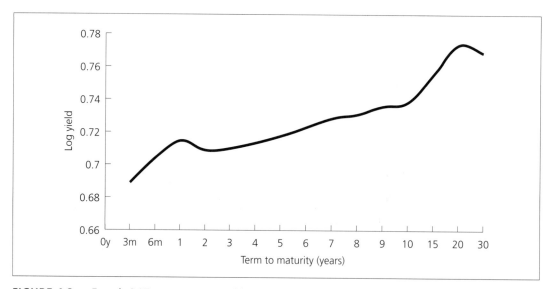

FIGURE 4.3 ▪ French OAT zero-coupon yield curve, September 2000
Source: Bloomberg L.P.

Coupon bonds

The majority of bonds in the market make periodic interest or *coupon* payments during their life, and are known as coupon bonds. We have already noted that such bonds may be viewed as a package of individual zero-coupon bonds. The coupons have a nominal value that is a percentage of the nominal value of the bond itself, with steadily longer maturity dates; while the final redemption payment has the nominal value of the bond itself and is redeemed on the maturity date. We denote a bond issued at time i and maturing at time T as having a w-element vector of payment dates $(t_1, t_2,...,t_{w-1}, T)$ and matching date payments $(C_1, C_2,..., C_{w-1}, C_w)$. In the academic literature these coupon payments are assumed to be made in continuous time, so that the stream of coupon payments is given by a positive function of time $C(t), i < t \leq T$. An investor who purchases a bond at time t that matures at time T pays $P(t, T)$ and will receive the coupon payments as long as he continues to hold the bond.[5]

The yield to maturity at time t of a bond that matures at T is the interest rate that relates the price of the bond to the future returns on the bond, that is, the rate that *discounts* the bond's cash flow stream C_w to its price $P(t, T)$. This is given by:

$$P(t, T) = \sum_{t_i > t} C_i e^{-(t_i - t)r(t, T)} \qquad (4.26)$$

which says that the bond price is given by the present value of the cash flow stream of the bond, discounted at the rate $r(t, T)$. For a zero-coupon bond (4.26) reduces to (4.24). In the academic literature, where coupon payments are assumed to be made in continuous time, the $\sum$ summation in (4.26) is replaced by the $\int$ integral. We will look at this in a moment.

In some texts the plot of the yield to maturity at time t for the term of the bonds m is described as the term structure of interest rates, but it is generally accepted that the term structure is the plot of zero-coupon rates only. Plotting yields to maturity is generally described as graphically depicting the yield curve, rather than the term structure. Of course, given the law of one price, there is a relationship between the yield-to-maturity yield curve and the zero-coupon term structure, and given the first one can derive the second.

The expression at (4.26) obtains the continuously compounded yield to maturity $r(t, T)$. It is the use of the exponential function that enables us to describe the yield as continuously compounded.

The market frequently uses the measure known as *current yield,* which is:

$$rc = \frac{C}{P_d} \times 100 \qquad (4.27)$$

where P_d is the dirty price of the bond. The measure is also known as the *running yield* or *flat yield.* Current yield is not used to indicate the interest rate or discount rate and therefore should not be mistaken for the yield to maturity.

---

5. In theoretical treatment this is the discounted clean price of the bond. For coupon bonds in practice, unless the bond is purchased for value on a coupon date, it will be traded with interest accrued. The interest that has accrued on a pro-rata basis from the last coupon date is added to the clean price of the bond, to give the market 'dirty' price that is actually paid by the purchaser. This was covered in the previous section.

Bond pricing in continuous time[6]

Fundamental concepts

In this section we present an introduction to the bond price equation in continuous time. The necessary background on price processes is given in Choudhry (2001).

Consider a trading environment where bond prices evolve in a w-dimensional process:

$$X(t) = [X_1(t), X_2(t), X_3(t), ..., X_w(t)], \; t > 0 \tag{4.28}$$

where the random variables are termed *state variables* that reflect the state of the economy at any point in time. The markets assume that the state variables evolve through a process described as geometric Brownian motion or a Weiner process. It is therefore possible to model the evolution of these variables, in the form of a stochastic differential equation.

The market assumes that the cash flow stream of assets, such as bonds and (for equities) dividends, is a function of the state variables. A bond is characterized by its coupon process:

$$C(t) = \tilde{C} \, [X_1(t), X_2(t), X_3(t), ..., X_w(t), t]. \tag{4.29}$$

The coupon process represents the cash flow that the investor receives during the time that he holds the bond. Over a small incremental increase in time of dt from the time t the investor can purchase $1 + C(t)dt$ units of the bond at the end of the period $t + dt$. Assume that there is a very short-term discount security such as a Treasury bill that matures at $t + dt$, and during this period the investor receives a return of $r(t)$. This rate is the annualized short-term interest rate or *short rate*, which in the mathematical analysis is defined as the rate of interest charged on a loan that is taken out at time t and which matures almost immediately. For this reason the rate is also known as the *instantaneous rate*. The short rate is given by:[7]

$$r(t) = r(t, t) \tag{4.30}$$

and

---

6. This section follows the approach adopted in such texts as Avellaneda (2000), Baxter and Rennie (1996), Neftci (2000), Campbell *et al.* (1997), Ross (1999) and Shiller (1990). These are all excellent texts and strongly recommended. For an accessible and highly readable introduction, Ross's book is worth buying for Chapter 4 alone, as is Avellaneda's for his Chapter 12. For a general introduction to the main pricing concepts see Campbell *et al.*, Chapter 10. Chapter 3 in Jarrow (1996) is an accessible introduction to discrete-time bond pricing. Sundaresan (1997) is an excellent overview text on the fixed-income market as a whole, and is highly recommended. Further recommended references are given in the bibliography.

$$r(t) = -\frac{\partial}{\partial T}\log P(t, t). \qquad (4.31)$$

If we continuously reinvest the short-term security such as the T-bill at this short rate, we obtain a cumulative amount that is the original investment multiplied by (4.32).[8]

$$M(t) = \exp\left[\int_0^t r(s)ds\right] \qquad (4.32)$$

where M is a money market account that offers a return of the short rate $r(t)$.

If we say that the short rate is constant, making $r(t) = r$, then the price of a risk-free bond that pays £1 on maturity at time T is given by:

$$P(t, T) = e^{-r(T-t)}. \qquad (4.33)$$

What (4.33) states is that the bond price is simply a function of the continuously compounded interest rate, with the right-hand side of (4.33) being the discount factor at time t. At $t = T$ the discount factor will be 1, which is the redemption value of the bond and hence the price of the bond at this time.

Consider the following scenario; a market participant may undertake the following:

■ he can invest $e^{-r(T-t)}$ units cash in a money market account today, which will have grown to a sum of £1 at time T;

■ he can purchase the risk-free zero-coupon bond today, which has a maturity value of £1 at time T.

The market participant can invest in either instrument, both of which we know beforehand to be risk-free, and both of which have identical payouts at time T and have no cash flow between now and time T. As interest rates are constant, a bond that paid out £1 at T must have the same value as the initial investment in the money market account, which is

7. Generally, the expression $r(t, T)$ is used to denote the zero-coupon interest rate, starting at time t and maturing at time T, with $T>t$. Generally t is taken to be now, so that $t = 0$. The rate is the return on a risk-free zero-coupon bond of price P at time t and maturity T, so we may define it as $P(t, T) = 1/[1 + r(t, T)]^T$. The term $r(t)$ is generally used to express the spot interest rate at the limit of $r(t, T)$ as T approaches t. Thus $r(t)$ may be regarded as the continuously compounded rate of return on a risk-free zero-coupon bond of infinitesimal maturity. The spot rate is therefore a theoretical construct, as it is unlikely to be observed directly on a market instrument. The zero-coupon rate on an instrument of infinitesimal maturity is sometimes expressed as $r(t, t)$ or as we do here, $r(t)$. So at time $t = 0$ we have $r(t) = \lim_{T \to 0} r(t, T)$.

8. This expression uses the integral operator. The integral is the tool used in mathematics to calculate sums of an infinite number of objects, that is where the objects are uncountable. This is different to the Σ operator which is used for a countable number of objects. For a readable and accessible review of the integral and its use in quantitative finance, see Neftci (2000), pp. 59–66, a summary of which is given in Appendix 3.1 of Choudhry (2001).

$e_t^{-r(T-t)}$. Therefore equation (4.33) must apply. This is a restriction placed on the zero-coupon bond price by the requirement for markets to be arbitrage-free.

If the bond was not priced at this level, arbitrage opportunities would present themselves. Consider if the bond was priced higher than $e_t^{-r(T-t)}$. In this case, an investor could sell short the bond and invest the sale proceeds in the money market account. On maturity at time T, the short position will have a value of −£1 (negative, because the investor is short the bond) while the money market will have accumulated £1, which the investor can use to pay the proceeds on the zero-coupon bond. However, the investor will have surplus funds because at time t:

$$P(t,T) - e^{-r(T-t)} > 0$$

and so he will have profited from the transaction at no risk to himself.

The same applies if the bond is priced below $e_t^{-r(T-t)}$. In this case the investor borrows $e_t^{-r(T-t)}$ and buys the bond at its price $P(t, T)$. On maturity the bond pays £1, which is used to repay the loan amount; however, the investor will gain because:

$$e^{-r(T-t)} - P(t,T) > 0.$$

Therefore the only price at which no arbitrage profit can be made is if:

$$P(t,T) = e^{-r(T-t)}.$$

In the academic literature the price of a zero-coupon bond is given in terms of the evolution of the short-term interest rate, in what is termed the *risk-neutral measure*.[9] The short rate $r(t)$ is the interest rate earned on a money market account or short-dated risk-free security such as the T-bill suggested above, and it is assumed to be continuously compounded. This makes the mathematical treatment simpler. With a zero-coupon bond we assume a payment on maturity of 1 (say \$1 or £1), a one-off cash flow payable on maturity at time T. The value of the zero-coupon bond at time t is therefore given by:

$$P(t,T) = \exp\left(-\int^T r(s)ds\right) \qquad (4.34)$$

which is the redemption value of 1 divided by the value of the money market account, given by (4.32).

The bond price for a coupon bond is given in terms of its yield as:

$$P(t,T) = \exp(-(T-t)r(T-t)). \qquad (4.35)$$

Expression (4.34) is very commonly encountered in the academic literature. Its derivation does not occur so frequently however; readers will find it in Ross (1999), pp. 54–6. Readers are also recommended to refer to Neftci (2000), Chapter 18.

9. This is part of the *arbitrage pricing theory*. For details on this see Cox *et al.* (1985). Duffie (1992) is a fuller treatment for those with a strong grounding in mathematics.

4 ■ Fixed-income securities I

The expression (4.34) represents the zero-coupon bond pricing formula when the spot rate is continuous or *stochastic*, rather than constant. The rate $r(s)$ is the risk-free return earned during the very short or *infinitesimal* time interval $(t, t + dt)$. The rate is used in the expressions for the value of a money market account (4.32) and the price of a risk-free zero-coupon bond (4.35).

Stochastic rates in continuous time

In the academic literature the bond price given by (4.35) evolves as a *martingale* process under the risk-neutral probability measure $\tilde{P}$. This is an advanced branch of fixed-income mathematics, and is outside the scope of this book; however, it will be described in introductory fashion in Chapter 7.[10] Under this analysis the bond price is given as:

$$P(t, T) = E_t^{\tilde{P}}\left[e^{-\int_t^T r(s)ds}\right] \tag{4.36}$$

where the right-hand side of (4.36) is viewed as the randomly evolved *discount factor* used to obtain the present value of the £1 maturity amount. Expression (4.36) also states that bond prices are dependent on the entire spectrum of short-term interest rates $r(s)$ in the future during the period $t < s < T$. This also implies that the term structure at time t contains all the information available on short rates in the future.[11]

From (4.36) we say that the function $T \rightarrow P_t^T$, $t < T$ is the discount curve (or *discount function*) at time t. Avellaneda (2000) notes that the markets usually replace the term $(T - t)$ with a term meaning *time to maturity*, so the function becomes:

$$\tau \rightarrow P_t^{t+\tau}, t > 0$$

where $\tau = (T - t)$.

Under a constant spot rate, the zero-coupon bond price is given by:

$$P(t, T) = e^{-r(t, T)(T - t)}. \tag{4.37}$$

From (4.36) and (4.37) we can derive a relationship between the yield $r(t, T)$ of the zero-coupon bond and the short rate $r(t)$, if we equate the two right-hand sides, namely:

$$e^{-r(T, t)(T - t)} = E_t^{\tilde{P}}\left[e^{-\int_t^T r(s)ds}\right]. \tag{4.38}$$

Taking the logarithm of both sides we obtain:

---

10. Interested readers should consult Nefcti (2000), Chapters 2, 17–18; another accessible text is Baxter and Rennie (1996), while Duffie (1992) is a leading reference for those with a strong background in financial mathematics.

11. This is related to the view of the short rate evolving as a martingale process. For a derivation of (4.36) see Nefcti (2000), p. 417.

$$r(t, T) = \frac{-\log E_t^{\tilde{P}}\left[e^{-\int_t^T r(s)ds}\right]}{T-t}.$$

(4.39)

This describes the yield on a bond as the average of the spot rates that apply during the life of the bond, and under a constant spot rate the yield is equal to the spot rate.

With a zero-coupon bond and assuming that interest rates are positive, $P(t, T)$ is less than or equal to 1. The yield of the bond is, as we have noted, the continuously compounded interest rate that equates the bond price to the discounted present value of the bond at time t. This is given by:

$$r(t, T) = -\frac{\log(P(t, T))}{T-t}$$

(4.40)

so we obtain:

$$P(t, T) = e^{-(T-t)r(T-t)}.$$

(4.41)

In practice, this means that an investor will earn $r(t, T)$ if he purchases the bond at t and holds it to maturity.

Coupon bonds

Using the same principles as in the previous section, we can derive an expression for the price of a coupon bond in the same terms of a risk-neutral probability measure of the evolution of interest rates. Under this analysis, the bond price is given by:

$$P_c = 100.E_t^{\tilde{P}}\left(e^{-\int_t^{t_N} r(s)ds}\right) + \sum_{n:t_n>t}^{N} \frac{C}{w} E_t^{\tilde{P}}\left(e^{-\int_t^{t_n} r(s)ds}\right)$$

(4.42)

where

P_c is the price of a coupon bond
C is the bond coupon
t_n is the coupon date, with $n \leq N$, and $t = 0$ at the time of valuation
w is the coupon frequency[12]

and where 100 is used as the convention for *principal* or bond nominal value (that is, prices are quoted per cent, or per 100 nominal).

Expression (4.42) is written in some texts as:

---

12. Conventional or *plain vanilla* bonds pay coupon on an annual or semi-annual basis. Other bonds, notably certain floating-rate notes and mortgage and other asset-backed securities, also pay coupon on a monthly basis, depending on the structuring of the transaction.

$$P_c = 100e^{-rN} + \int_n^N Ce^{-rn}dt. \tag{4.43}$$

We can simplify (4.42) by substituting Df to denote the discount factor part of the expression and assuming an annual coupon, which gives us:

$$P = 100.Df_N + \sum_{n:t_n \geq t}^{N} C.Df_n \tag{4.44}$$

which states that the market value of a risk-free bond on any date is determined by the discount function on that date.

We know from Chapter 2 that the actual price paid in the market for a bond includes accrued interest from the last coupon date, so that the price given by (4.44) is known as the *clean price*, while the traded price, which includes accrued interest, is known as the *dirty price*.

Forward rates

An investor can combine positions in bonds of differing maturities to guarantee a rate of return that begins at a point in the future. That is, the trade ticket would be written at time t but would cover the period T to $T + 1$, where $t < T$ (sometimes written as beginning at T_1 and ending at T_2, with $t < T_1 < T_2$). The interest rate earned during this period is known as the *forward rate*.[13] The mechanism by which this forward rate can be guaranteed is described in Example 4.7, following the approach of Jarrow (1996) and Campbell *et al.* (1997) among others.

EXAMPLE *4.7 The forward rate*

An investor buys at time t_1 unit of a zero-coupon bond maturing at time T, priced at $P(t, T)$ and simultaneously sells $P(t, T)/P(t, T + 1)$ bonds that mature at $T + 1$. From Table 4.1 we see that the net result of these transactions is a zero cash flow. At time T there is a cash inflow of 1, and then at time $T + 1$ there is a cash outflow of $P(t, T)/P(t, T + 1)$. These cash flows are identical to a loan of funds made during the period T to $T + 1$, contracted at time t. The interest rate on this loan is given by $P(t, T)/P(t, T + 1)$, which is therefore the forward rate. That is:

$$f(t, T) = \frac{P(t, T)}{P(t, T + 1)}. \tag{4.45}$$

---

13. See the footnote on p. 639 of Shiller (1990) for a fascinating insight into the origin of the term 'forward rate', which is ascribed to John Hicks (1946).

Together with our earlier relationships on bond price and yield, from (4.45) we can define the forward rate in terms of yield, with the return earned during the period $(T, T + 1)$, being:

$$f(t, T, T + 1) = \frac{1}{(P(t, T + 1)/P(t, T))} = \frac{(r(t, T + 1))^{(T + 1)}}{r(t, T)^T}. \tag{4.46}$$

TABLE 4.1

Transactions	Time $\longrightarrow$		
	t	T	T + 1
Buy 1 unit of T-period bond	$-P(t,T)$	+1	
Sell $P(t,T)/P(t, T+1)$ $T+1$ period bonds	$+[(P(t,T)/P(t, T+1)]P(t, T+1)$		$-P(t,T)/P(t, T+1)$
Net cash flows	0	+1	$-P(t,T)/P(t, T+1)$

From (4.45) we can obtain a bond price equation in terms of the forward rates that hold from t to T:

$$P(t, T) = \frac{1}{\prod_{k=t}^{T-1} f(t, k)}. \tag{4.47}$$

A derivation of this expression can be found in Jarrow (1996), Chapter 3. Expression (4.47) states that the price of a zero-coupon bond is equal to the nominal value, here assumed to be 1, receivable at time T after it has been discounted at the set of forward rates that apply from t to T.[14]

When calculating a forward rate, remember that it is as if we are writing an interest rate contract *today* that comes into effect at a start date some time in the *future*. In other words, we are trading a forward contract. The law of one price, or no-arbitrage, is used to calculate the rate. For a loan that begins at T and matures at $T + 1$, similarly in the way we described in Example 4.7, consider a purchase of a $T + 1$ period bond and a sale of p amount of the T-period bond. The net cash position at t must be zero, so p is given by:

$$p = \frac{P(t, T + 1)}{P(t, T)}$$

---

14. The symbol $\prod$ means 'take the product of', and is defined as $\prod_{i=1}^{n} x_i = x_1 \cdot x_2 \cdot \ldots \cdot x_n$, so that $\prod_{k=t}^{T-1} f(t,k) = f(t,t) \cdot f(t,t + 1) \cdot \ldots f(t, T - 1)n$ which is the result of multiplying the rates that obtain when the index k runs from t to $T - 1$.

and to avoid arbitrage the value of p must be the price of the $T + 1$-period bond at time T. Therefore the forward yield is given by:

$$f(t, T + 1) = -\frac{\log P(t, T + 1) - \log P(t, T)}{(T + 1) - T}.$$ (4.48)

If the period between T and the maturity of the later-dated bond is reduced, so we now have bonds that mature at T and T_2 and $T_2 = T + \Delta t$; then as the incremental change in time Δt becomes progressively smaller, we obtain an instantaneous forward rate, which is given by:

$$f(t, T) = -\frac{\partial}{\partial T} \log P(t, T).$$ (4.49)

This rate is defined as the forward rate and is the price today of forward borrowing at time T. The forward rate for borrowing today, where $T = t$, is equal to the instantaneous short rate $r(t)$. At time t the spot and forward rates for the period (t, t) will be identical; at other maturity terms they will differ.

For all points other than at (t, t) the forward rate yield curve will lie above the spot rate curve if the spot curve is positively sloping. The opposite applies if the spot rate curve is downward sloping. Campbell *et al.* (1997, p. 400–1) observe that this property is a standard one for marginal and average cost curves. That is, when the cost of a marginal unit (say, of production) is above that of an average unit, then the average cost will increase with the addition of a marginal unit. This results in the average cost rising when the marginal cost is above the average cost. Equally, the average cost per unit will decrease when the marginal cost lies below the average cost.

The term structure of interest rates

We have already referred to the yield curve or *term structure of interest rates*. Strictly speaking, only a spot rate yield curve is a term structure, but one sometimes encounters the two expressions being used synonymously. At any time t there will be a set of coupon and/or zero-coupon bonds with different terms to maturity and cash flow streams. There will be certain fixed maturities that are not represented by actual bonds in the market, as there will be more than one bond maturing at or around the same redemption date. The debt capital markets and the pricing of debt instruments revolve around the term structure, and for this reason this area has been extensively researched in the academic literature.

There are a number of ways to estimate and interpret the term structure, and in this section we review the research highlights. The bootstrapping method described below follows the approach described in Windas (1993), which is a very accessible account of this basic technique.

The bootstrapping approach using bond prices

In this section we describe how to obtain zero-coupon and forward interest rates from the yields available from coupon bonds, using a method known as *bootstrapping*. In a government bond market such as that for US Treasuries or UK gilts, the bonds are considered to be *default-free*. The rates from a government bond yield curve describe the risk-free rates of return available in the market *today*; however they also *imply* (risk-free) rates of return for *future time periods*. These implied future rates, known as *implied forward rates*, or simply *forward rates*, can be derived from a given spot yield curve using bootstrapping. This term reflects the fact that each calculated spot rate is used to determine the next period spot rate, in successive steps.

Table 4.2 shows a hypothetical benchmark gilt yield curve for value as at 7 December 2000. The observed yields of the benchmark bonds that compose the curve are displayed in the last column. All rates are annualized and assume semi-annual compounding. The bonds all pay on the same coupon dates of 7 June and 7 December, and since the value date is a coupon date, there is no accrued interest on any of the bonds.[15] The *clean* and *dirty* prices for each bond are identical.

TABLE 4.2 ■ Hypothetical UK government bond yields, 7 December 2000

Bond	Term to maturity (years)	Coupon	Maturity date	Price	Gross redemption yield
4% Treasury 2001	0.5	4%	7 June 2001	100	4%
5% Treasury 2001	1	5%	7 December 2001	100	5%
6% Treasury 2002	1.5	6%	7 June 2002	100	6%
7% Treasury 2002	2	7%	7 December 2002	100	7%
8% Treasury 2003	2.5	8%	7 June 2003	100	8%
9% Treasury 2003	3	9%	7 December 2003	100	9%

The gross redemption yield or *yield to maturity* of a coupon bond describes the single rate that present-values each of its future cash flows to a given price. This yield measure suffers from a fundamental weakness in that each cash flow is present-valued at the same rate – an unrealistic assumption in anything other than a flat yield curve environment. The bonds in Table 4.2 pay semi-annual coupons on 7 June and 7 December and have the same time period – six months – between 7 December 2000, their valuation date, and 7 June 2001, their next coupon date. However, since each issue carries a different yield,

15. Benchmark gilts pay coupon on a semi-annual basis on 7 June and 7 December each year.

the next six-month coupon payment for each bond is present-valued at a different rate. In other words, the six-month bond present-values its six-month coupon payment at its 4% yield to maturity, the one-year at 5%, and so on. Because each of these issues uses a different rate to present-value a cash flow occurring at the same future point in time, it is unclear which of the rates should be regarded as the true interest rate or benchmark rate for the six-month period from 7 December 2000 to 7 June 2001. This problem is repeated for all other maturities.

For the purposes of valuation and analysis however, we require a set of true interest rates, and so these must be derived from the redemption yields that we can observe from the benchmark bonds trading in the market. These rates we designate as rs_i, where rs_i is the *implied spot rate* or *zero-coupon rate* for the term beginning on 7 December 2000 and ending at the end of period i.

We begin calculating implied spot rates by noting that the six-month bond contains only one future cash flow: the final coupon payment and the redemption payment on maturity. This means that it is in effect trading as a zero-coupon bond, because there is only one cash flow left for this bond – its final payment. Since this cash flow's present value, future value and maturity term are known, the unique interest rate that relates these quantities can be solved using the compound interest equation below:

$$FV = PV \times \left(1 + \frac{rs_i}{m}\right)^{(nm)}$$

(4.50)

$$rs_i = m \times \left(\sqrt[(nm)]{\frac{FV}{P}} - 1\right)$$

where

    FV is the future value
    PV is the present value
    rs_i is the implied i-period spot rate
    m is the number of interest periods per year
    n is the number of years in the term.

The first rate to be solved is referred to as the implied six-month spot rate and is the true interest rate for the six-month term beginning on 2 January and ending on 2 July 2000.

Equation (4.50) relates a cash flow's present value and future value in terms of an associated interest rate, compounding convention and time period. Of course if we rearrange it, we may use it to solve for an implied spot rate. For the six-month bond the final cash flow on maturity is £102, comprised of the £2 coupon payment and the £100 (*par*) redemption amount. So we have for the first term: $i = 1$, FV = £102, PV = £100, $n = 0.5$ years and $m = 2$. This allows us to calculate the spot rate as follows:

$$rs_i = m \times \left({}^{(nm)}\sqrt{FV/PV} - 1 \right)$$
$$rs_1 = 2 \times \left({}^{(0.5 \times 2)}\sqrt{£102/£100} - 1 \right) \qquad (4.51)$$
$$rs_1 = 0.04000$$
$$rs_1 = 4.000\%.$$

Thus the implied six-month spot rate or zero-coupon rate is equal to 4%.[16] We now need to determine the implied one-year spot rate for the term from 7 December 2000 to 7 June 2001. We note that the one-year issue has a 5% coupon and contains two future cash flows: a £2.50 six-month coupon payment on 7 June 2001 and a £102.50 one-year coupon and principal payment on 7 December 2001. Since the first cash flow occurs on 7 June – six months from now – it must be present-valued at the 4% six-month spot rate established above. Once this present value is determined, it may be subtracted from the £100 total present value (its current price) of the one-year issue to obtain the present value of the one-year coupon and cash flow. Again, we then have a single cash flow with a known present value, future value and term. The rate that equates these quantities is the implied one-year spot rate. From equation (4.50) the present value of the six-month £2.50 coupon payment of the one-year benchmark bond, discounted at the implied six-month spot rate, is:

$$PV_{\text{6-mo cash flow, 1-yr bond}} = £2.50/(1 + 0.04/2)(0.5 \times 2)$$
$$= £2.45098.$$

The present value of the one-year £102.50 coupon and principal payment is found by subtracting the present value of the six-month cash flow, determined above, from the total present value (current price) of the issue:

$$PV_{\text{1-yr cash flow, 1-yr bond}} = £100 - £2.45098$$
$$= £97.54902.$$

The implied one-year spot rate is then determined by using the £97.54902 present value of the one-year cash flow determined above:

$$rs_2 = 2 \times \left({}^{(1 \times 2)}\sqrt{£102.50/£97.54902} - 1 \right)$$
$$= 0.0501256$$
$$= 5.01256\%.$$

The implied 1.5-year spot rate is solved in the same way:

$$PV_{\text{6-mo cash flow, 1.5-yr bond}} = £3.00 / (1 + 0.04 / 2)^{(0.5 \times 2)}$$
$$= £2.94118$$

---

16. Of course intuitively we could have concluded that the six-month spot rate was 4%, without the need to apply the arithmetic, since we had already assumed that the six-month bond was a quasi-zero-coupon bond.

$$PV_{\text{1-yr cash flow, 1.5-yr bond}} = £3.00 / (1 + 0.0501256/2)^{(1\times2)}$$
$$= £2.85509$$

$$PV_{\text{1.5-yr cash flow, 1.5-yr bond}} = £100 - £2.94118 - £2.85509$$
$$= £94.20373$$

$$rs_3 = 2 \times \left({}^{(1.5\times2)}\sqrt{£103/£94.20373} - 1 \right)$$
$$= 0.0604071$$
$$= 6.04071\%.$$

Extending the same process for the two-year bond, we calculate the implied two-year spot rate rs_4 to be 7.0906%. The implied 2.5-year and three-year spot rates rs_5 and rs_6 are 8.1709% and 9.2879% respectively.

The interest rates rs_1, rs_2, rs_3, rs_4, rs_5 and rs_6 describe the true zero-coupon interest rates for the six-month, one-year, 1.5-year, two-year, 2.5-year and three-year terms that begin on 7 December 2000 and end on 7 June 2001, 7 December 2001, 7 June 2002, 7 December 2002, 7 June 2003 and 7 December 2003 respectively. They are also called *implied spot rates* because they have been calculated from redemption yields observed in the market from the benchmark government bonds that were listed in Table 4.2.

Note that the one-year, 1.5-year, two-year, 2.5-year and three-year implied spot rates are progressively greater than the corresponding redemption yields for these terms. This is an important result, and occurs whenever the yield curve is positively sloped. The reason for this is that the present values of a bond's shorter-dated cash flows are discounted at rates that are lower than the bond's redemption yield; this generates higher present values that, when subtracted from the current price of the bond, produce a lower present value for the final cash flow. This lower present value implies a spot rate that is greater than the issue's yield. In an inverted yield curve environment we observe the opposite result: that is, implied rates that lie below the corresponding redemption yields. If the redemption yield curve is flat, the implied spot rates will be equal to the corresponding redemption yields.

Once we have calculated the spot or zero-coupon rates for the six-month, one-year, 1.5-year, two-year, 2.5-year and three-year terms, we can determine the rate of return that is implied by the yield curve for the sequence of six-month periods beginning on 7 December 2000, 7 June 2001, 7 December 2001, 7 June 2002 and 7 December 2002. These period rates are referred to as *implied forward rates* or *forward-forward rates* and we denote these as rf_i, where rf_i is the implied six-month forward interest rate today for the ith period.

Since the implied six-month zero-coupon rate (spot rate) describes the return for a term that coincides precisely with the first of the series of six-month periods, this rate describes the risk-free rate of return for the first six-month period. It is therefore equal to the first period spot rate. Thus we have $rf_1 = rs_1 = 4\%$, where rf_1 is the risk-free forward rate for the first six-month period beginning at period 1. We show now how the risk-free rates for the second, third, fourth, fifth and sixth six-month periods, designated rf_2, rf_3, rf_4, rf_5 and rf_6 respectively, may be solved from the implied spot rates.

The benchmark rate for the second semi-annual period rf_2 is referred to as the one-period forward six-month rate, because it goes into effect one six-month period from now ('one-period forward') and remains in effect for six months ('six-month rate'). It is therefore the six-month rate in six months' time, and is also referred to as the six-month forward-forward rate. This rate, in conjunction with the rate from the first period rf_1, must provide returns that match those generated by the implied one-year spot rate for the entire one-year term. In other words, £1 invested for six months from 7 December 2000 to 7 June 2001 at the first period's benchmark rate of 4% and then reinvested for another six months from 7 June 2001 to 7 December 2001 at the second period's (as yet unknown) implied *forward* rate must enjoy the same returns as £1 invested for one year from 7 December 2000 to 7 December 2001 at the implied one-year *spot* rate of 5.0125%. This reflects the law of no-arbitrage.

A moment's thought will convince us that this must be so. If this were not the case, we might observe an interest rate environment in which the return received by an investor over any given term would depend on whether an investment is made at the start of the period for the entire maturity term or over a succession of periods within the whole term and reinvested. If there were any discrepancies between the returns received from each approach, there would exist an unrealistic arbitrage opportunity, in which investments for a given term carrying a lower return might be sold short against the simultaneous purchase of investments for the same period carrying a higher return, thereby locking in a risk-free, cost-free profit. Therefore forward interest rates must be calculated so that they are *arbitrage-free*. Forward rates are not therefore a prediction of what spot interest rates are likely to be in the future, rather a mathematically derived set of interest rates that reflect the current spot term structure and the rules of no-arbitrage. Excellent mathematical explanations of the no-arbitrage property of interest rate markets are contained in Ingersoll (1987), Jarrow (1996) and Shiller (1990), among others.

The existence of a no-arbitrage market makes it straightforward to calculate forward rates; we know that the return from an investment made over a period must equal the return made from investing in a shorter period and successively reinvesting to a matching term. If we know the return over the shorter period, we are left with only one unknown, the full-period forward rate, which is then easily calculated. In our example, having established the rate for the first six-month period, the rate for the second six-month period – the one-period forward six-month rate – is determined as below.

The future value of £1 invested at rf_1, the period 1 forward rate, at the end of the first six-month period, is calculated as follows:

$$FV_1 = \pounds 1 \times \left(1 + \frac{rf_1}{2}\right)^{(0.5 \times 2)}$$

$$= \pounds 1 \times \left(1 + \frac{0.04}{2}\right)^1$$

$$= \pounds 1.02000.$$

The future value of £1 at the end of the one-year term, invested at the implied benchmark one-year spot rate, is determined as follows:

$$FV_2 = \pounds 1 \times \left(1 + \frac{rf_2}{2}\right)^{(1 \times 2)}$$

$$= \pounds 1 \times \left(1 + \frac{0.0501256}{2}\right)^1$$

$$= \pounds 1.050754.$$

The implied benchmark one-period forward rate rf_2 is the rate that equates the value of FV_1 (£1.02) on 7 June 2001 to FV_2 (£1.050754) on 7 December 2001. From equation (4.50) we have:

$$rf_2 = 2 \times \left(^{(0.5 \times 2)}\sqrt{\frac{FV_2}{FV_1}} - 1\right)$$

$$= 2 \times \left(\frac{\pounds 1.050754}{\pounds 1.02} - 1\right)$$

$$= 0.060302$$

$$= 6.0302\%.$$

In other words, £1 invested from 7 December to 7 June at 4% (the implied forward rate for the first period) and then reinvested from 7 June to 7 December 2001 at 6.0302% (the implied forward rate for the second period) would accumulate the same returns as £1 invested from 7 December 2000 to 7 December 2001 at 5.01256% (the implied one-year spot rate).

The rate for the third six-month period – the two-period forward six-month interest rate – may be calculated in the same way:

$$FV_2 = \pounds 1.050754$$

$$FV_3 = \pounds 1 \times (1 + rs_3/2)^{(1.5 \times 2)}$$

$$= \pounds 1 \times (1 + 0.0604071/2)^3$$

$$= \pounds 1.093375$$

$$rf_3 = 2 \times \left({}^{(0.5 \times 2)}\sqrt{\frac{FV_3}{FV_4}} - 1 \right)$$

$$= 2 \times \left(\sqrt[1]{\pounds 1.093375 \Big/ \pounds 1.050754} - 1 \right)$$

$$= 0.081125$$

$$= 8.1125\%.$$

In the same way, the three-period forward six-month rate rf_4 is calculated to be 10.27247%. The rest of the results are shown in Table 4.3. We say *one-period* forward rate because it is the forward rate that applies to the six-month period. The results of the implied spot (zero-coupon) and forward rate calculations along with the given redemption yield curve are illustrated graphically in Figure 4.4.

The simple bootstrapping methodology can be applied using a spreadsheet for actual market redemption yields. However in practice we will not have a set of bonds with exact and/or equal periods to maturity and coupons falling on the same date. Nor will they all be priced conveniently at par. In designing a spreadsheet spot-rate calculator therefore, the coupon rate and maturity date is entered as standing data and usually interpolation is used when calculating the spot rates for bonds with uneven maturity dates. A spot curve model that uses this approach in conjunction with the bootstrapping method is available for downloading at www.YieldCurve.com. Market practitioners usually use discount factors to extract spot and forward rates from market prices.

TABLE 4.3 ▪ Implied spot and forward rates

Term to maturity	Yield to maturity	Implied spot rate	Implied one-period forward rate
0.5	4.0000%	4.00000%	4.00000%
1	5.0000%	5.01256%	6.03023%
1.5	6.0000%	6.04071%	8.11251%
2	7.0000%	7.09062%	10.27247%
2.5	8.0000%	8.17090%	12.24833%
3	9.0000%	9.28792%	14.55654%

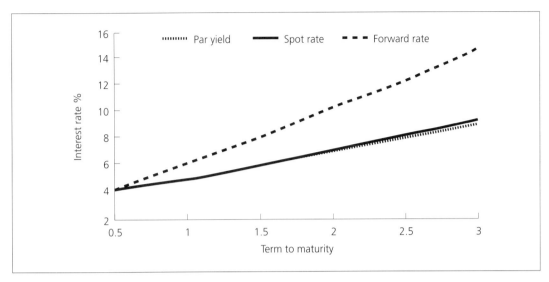

FIGURE 4.4 ■ Par, spot and forward yield curves

The theoretical approach described above is neat and appealing, but in practice there are a number of issues that will complicate the attempt to extract zero-coupon rates from bond yields. The main problem is that it is highly unlikely that we will have a set of bonds that are both precisely six months (or one interest period) apart in maturity and priced precisely at par. We also require our procedure to fit as smooth a curve as possible. Setting our coupon bonds at a price of par simplified the analysis in our illustration of bootstrapping, so in reality we need to apply more advanced techniques. A basic approach for extracting zero-coupon bond prices is described in the next section.

Calculating spot rates in practice

Researchers have applied econometric techniques to the problem of extracting a zero-coupon term structure from coupon bond prices. The most well-known approaches are described in McCulloch (1971, 1975), Schaefer (1981), Nelson and Siegel (1987), Deacon and Derry (1994), Adams and Van Deventer (1994) and Waggoner (1997), to name but a few. The most accessible article is probably the one by Deacon and Derry.[17] In addition, a good overview of all the main approaches is contained in James and Webber (2000), and Chapters 15–18 of their book provide an excellent summary of the research highlights to date.

17. This is in the author's personal opinion. Those with a good grounding in econometrics will find all these references both readable and accessible. Further recommended references are given in the bibliography.

We have noted that a coupon bond may be regarded as a portfolio of zero-coupon bonds. By treating a set of coupon bonds as a larger set of zero-coupon bonds, we can extract an (implied) zero-coupon interest rate structure from the yields on the coupon bonds.

If the actual term structure is observable, so that we know the prices of zero-coupon bonds of £1 nominal value P_1, P_2, ..., P_N then the price P_C of a coupon bond of nominal value £1 and coupon C is given by:

$$P_C = P_1 C + P_2 C + \ldots + P_N (1 + C).$$ (4.52)

Conversely, if we can observe the coupon bond yield curve, so that we know the prices P_{C1}, P_{C2},..., P_{CN}, then we may use (4.52) to extract the implied zero-coupon term structure. We begin with the one-period coupon bond, for which the price is:

$$P_{C1} = P_1 (1 + C)$$

so that

$$P_1 = \frac{PC_1}{(1 + C)}.$$ (4.53)

This process is repeated. Once we have the set of zero-coupon bond prices P_1, P_2,....,P_{N-1} we obtain P_N using:

$$P_N = \frac{P_{CN} - P_{N-1}C - \ldots - P_1 C}{1 + C}.$$ (4.54)

At this point we apply a regression technique known as *ordinary least squares* (OLS) to fit the term structure. The next chapter discusses this area in greater detail; we have segregated this so that readers who do not require extensive familiarity with this subject may skip the next chapter. Interested readers should also consult the references at the end of this chapter.

Expression (4.52) restricts the prices of coupon bonds to be precise functions of the other coupon bond prices. In fact, this is unlikely in practice because specific bonds will be treated differently according to liquidity, tax effects and so on. For this reason we add an *error term* to (4.52) and estimate the value using cross-sectional regression against all the other bonds in the market. If we say that these bonds are numbered $i = 1, 2, \ldots, I$ then the regression is given by:

$$P_{C_i N_i} = P_1 C_i + P_2 C_i + \ldots + P_{Ni} (1 + C_i) + u_i$$ (4.55)

for $i = 1, 2, \ldots, I$ and where C_i is the coupon on the ith bond and N_i is the maturity of the ith bond. In (4.55) the regressor parameters are the coupon payments at each interest period date, and the coefficients are the prices of the zero-coupon bonds P_1 to P_N where $j = 1, 2, \ldots, N$. The values are obtained using OLS, as long as we have a complete term structure, and that $I \geq N$.

In practice, we will not have a complete term structure of coupon bonds and so we are not able to identify the coefficients in (4.55). McCulloch (1971, 1975) described a *spline estimation* method, which assumes that zero-coupon bond prices vary smoothly with term to maturity. In this approach we define P_N, a function of maturity $P(N)$, as a *discount function* given by:

$$P(N) = 1 + \sum_{j=1}^{J} a_j f_j(N). \qquad (4.56)$$

The function $f_j(N)$ is a known function of maturity N, and the coefficients a_j must be estimated. We arrive at a regression equation by substituting (4.56) into (4.55) to give us (4.57), which can be estimated using OLS.

$$\prod_i = \sum_{j=1}^{J} a_j X_{ij} + u_i, \qquad i = 1, 2, \ldots, I \qquad (4.57)$$

where

$$\prod_i \equiv P_{C_i N_i} - 1 - C_i N_i$$
$$X_{ij} \equiv f_j(N_i) + C_i \sum_{l=1}^{Ni} f_j(l).$$

The function $f_j(N)$ is usually specified by setting the discount function as a polynomial. In certain texts, including McCulloch, this is carried out by applying what is known as a *spline* function. Considerable academic research has gone into the use of spline functions as a yield curve fitting technique; however, we are not able to go into the required level of detail here, which is left to the next chapter. For a specific discussion on using regression techniques for spline curve fitting methods, see Suits *et al.* (1978), a highly accessible account, which is also summarized (with permission) in Choudhry (2001).

Term structure hypotheses

As befits a subject that has been the target of extensive research, a number of hypotheses have been put forward that seek to explain the term structure of interest rates. These hypotheses describe why yield curves assume certain shapes, and relate maturity terms with spot and forward rates. In this section we briefly review these hypotheses.

The expectations hypothesis

Simply put, the *expectations hypothesis* states that the slope of the yield curve reflects the market's expectations about future interest rates. There are in fact four main versions of the hypothesis, each distinct from the other and each incompatible with the others. The expectations hypothesis has a long history, first being described in 1896 by Fisher and later developed by Hicks (1946) among others.[18] As Shiller (1990) describes, the thinking behind it probably stems from the way market participants discuss their views on future interest rates when assessing whether to purchase long-dated or short-dated bonds. For instance, if interest rates are expected to fall, investors will purchase long-dated bonds in order to 'lock in' the current high long-dated yield. If all investors act in the same way, the yield on long-dated bonds will of course decline as prices rise in response to demand; this yield will remain low as long as short-dated rates are expected to fall, and will revert to a higher level only once the demand for long-term rates is reduced. Therefore, down-ward-sloping yield curves are an indication that interest rates are expected to fall, while an upward-sloping curve reflects market expectations of a rise in short-term interest rates.

Let us briefly consider the main elements of the discussion. The *unbiased expectations hypothesis* states that current forward rates are unbiased predictors of future spot rates. Let $f_t(T,T+1)$ be the forward rate at time t for the period from T to $T+1$. If the one-period spot rate at time T is r_T, then according to the unbiased expectations hypothesis:

$$f_t(T, T+1) = E_t[r_T] \tag{4.58}$$

which states that the forward rate $f_t(T,T+1)$ is the expected value of the future one-period spot rate given by r_T at time T.

The *return-to-maturity expectations hypothesis* states that the return generated from an investment of term t to T by holding a $(T-t)$-period bond will be equal to the expected return generated by holding a series of one-period bonds and continually rolling them over on maturity. More formally, we write:

$$\frac{1}{P(t, T)} = E_t[(1 + r_t)(1 + r_{t+1})......(1 + r_{T-1})]. \tag{4.59}$$

The left-hand side of (4.59) represents the return received by an investor holding a zero-coupon bond of price P to maturity, which is equal to the expected return associated with rolling over £1 from time t to time T by continually reinvesting one-period maturity bonds, each of which has a yield of the future spot rate r_t. A good argument for this hypothesis is contained in Jarrow (1996, p. 52), which states that essentially in an environment of *economic equilibrium* the returns on zero-coupon bonds of similar maturity cannot be significantly different, otherwise investors would not hold bonds with the lower return. A similar argument can be put forward with relation to coupon bonds of differing maturities. Any difference in yield would not therefore disappear as equilibrium was re-established. However, there are a number of reasons why investors will hold shorter-dated bonds, irre-spective of the yield available on them, so it is possible for the return-to-maturity version

18. See the footnote on p. 644 of Shiller (1990) for a fascinating historical note on the origins of the expectations hypothesis. An excellent overview of the hypothesis itself is contained in Ingersoll (1987, p. 389–92).

of the hypothesis not to apply. In essence this version represents an equilibrium condition in which expected *holding period returns* are equal, although it does not state that this return is the same from different bond-holding strategies.

From (4.58) and (4.59) we can determine that the unbiased expectations hypothesis and the return-to-maturity hypothesis are not compatible with each other, unless there is no correlation between future interest rates. As Ingersoll (1987) notes, although it would be both possible and interesting to model such an economic environment, it is not related to reality, as interest rates are highly correlated. Given positive correlation between rates over a period of time, bonds with maturity terms longer than two periods will have a higher price under the unbiased expectations hypothesis than under the return-to-maturity version. Bonds of exactly two-period maturity will have the same price.

The *yield-to-maturity expectations hypothesis* is described in terms of yields. It is given by:

$$\left[\frac{1}{P(t, T)}\right]^{\frac{1}{T-t}} = E_t\left[\{(1 + r_t)(1 + r_{t+1})...(1 + r_{T-1})\}^{\frac{1}{T-t}}\right] \tag{4.60}$$

where the left-hand side specifies the yield to maturity of the zero-coupon bond at time t. In this version the expected holding period *yield* on continually rolling over a series of one-period bonds will be equal to the yield that is guaranteed by holding a long-dated bond until maturity.

The *local expectations* hypothesis states that all bonds will generate the same expected rate of return if held over a small term. It is given by:

$$\frac{E_t[P(t + 1, T)]}{P(t, T)} = 1 + r_t. \tag{4.61}$$

This version of the hypothesis is the only one that is consistent with no-arbitrage, because the expected rates of return on all bonds are equal to the risk-free interest rate. For this reason the local expectations hypothesis is sometimes referred to as the *risk-neutral expectations hypothesis*.

Liquidity premium hypothesis

The *liquidity premium hypothesis* arises from the natural desire for borrowers to borrow long while lenders prefer to lend short. It states that current forward rates differ from future spot rates by an amount that is known as the *liquidity premium*. It is expressed as:

$$f_t(T, T + 1) = E_t[r_T] + \pi_t(T, T + 1). \tag{4.62}$$

Expression (4.62) states that the forward rate $f_t(T,T + 1)$ is the expected value of the future one-period spot rate given by r_T at time T plus the liquidity premium, which is a function of the maturity of the bond (or term of loan). This premium reflects the conflicting requirements of borrowers and lenders, while traders and speculators will borrow short and lend long, in an effort to earn the premium. The liquidity premium hypothesis has been described in Hicks (1946).

Segmented markets hypothesis

The *segmented markets hypothesis* seeks to explain the shape of the yield curve by stating that different types of market participants invest in different sectors of the term structure, according to their requirements. So, for instance, the banking sector has a requirement for short-dated bonds, while pension funds will invest in the long end of the market. This was first described in Culbertson (1957). There may also be regulatory reasons why different investors have preferences for particular maturity investments. A *preferred habitat* theory was described in Modigliani and Sutch (1966), which states not only that investors have a preferred maturity but also that they may move outside this sector if they receive a premium for so doing. This would explain 'humped' shapes in yield curves. The preferred habitat theory may be viewed as a version of the liquidity preference hypothesis, where the preferred habitat is the short end of the yield curve, so that longer-dated bonds must offer a premium in order to entice investors to hold them. This is described in Cox, Ingersoll and Ross (1985).

SELECTED BIBLIOGRAPHY AND REFERENCES

Adams, K., Van Deventer, D., 'Fitting yield curves and forward rate curves with maximum smoothness', *Journal of Fixed Income* 4, 1994, pp. 52–62.

Avellaneda, M., Laurence, P., *Quantitative Modelling of Derivative Securities*, Chapman & Hall/CRC 2000, Chapters 10–12.

Baxter, M., Rennie, A., *Financial Calculus*, Cambridge University Press 1996, Chapter 5.

Campbell, J., Lo, A., MacKinlay, A., *The Econometrics of Financial Markets*, Princeton University Press 1997, Chapters 10–11.

Choudhry, M., *Bond Market Securities*, FT Prentice Hall 2001, Chapters 4, 5.

Cox, J., Ingersoll, J., Ross, S., 'An inter-temporal general equilibrium model of asset prices', *Econometrica* 53, 1985.

Culbertson, J., 'The term structure of interest rates', *Quarterly Journal of Economics* 71, 1957, pp. 485–517.

Deacon, M., Derry, A., 'Estimating the term structure of interest rates', *Bank of England working paper* 24, July 1994.

Duffie, D., *Dynamic Asset Pricing Theory*, Princeton University Press 1992.

Fabozzi, F., *Bond Markets, Analysis and Strategies*, 2nd edition, Prentice Hall 1993, Chapter 5.

Fabozzi, F., *Fixed Income Mathematics*, McGraw-Hill 1997.

Fabozzi, F. (ed.), *The Handbook of Fixed Income Securities*, 5th edition, McGraw-Hill 1997.

Fabozzi, F., *Valuation of Fixed Income Securities and Derivatives*, 3rd edition, FJF Associates 1998.

Fabozzi, F., *Treasury Securities and Derivatives*, FJF Associates 1998.

Guajarati, D., *Basic Econometrics*, 3rd edition, McGraw-Hill 1995.

Hicks, J., *Value and Capital*, 2nd edition, Oxford University Press 1946.

Ingersoll, J., *Theory of Financial Decision Making*, Rowman & Littlefied 1987, Chapter 18.

James, J., Webber, N., *Interest Rate Modelling*, Wiley 2000.

Jarrow, R., *Modelling Fixed Income Securities and Interest Rate Options*, McGraw-Hill 1996, Chapter 3.

Kitter, G., *Investment Mathematics for Finance and Treasury Professionals*, Wiley 1999, Chapters 3, 5.

McCulloch, J., 'Measuring the term structure of interest rates', *Journal of Business* 44, 1971, pp. 19–31.

McCulloch, J., 'The tax-adjusted yield curve', *Journal of Finance* 30, 1975, pp. 811–30.

Modigliani, F., Sutch, R., 'Innovations in interest rate policy', *American Economic Review* 56, 1966, pp. 178–197.

Neftci, S., *An Introduction to the Mathematics of Financial Derivatives*, 2nd edition, Academic Press 2000, Chapter 18.

Nelson, C., Siegel, A., 'Parsimonious modelling of yield curves', *Journal of Business* 60: 4, 1987, pp. 473–89

Questa, G., *Fixed Income Analysis for the Global Financial Market*, Wiley 1999.

Ross, S. M., *An Introduction to Mathematical Finance*, Cambridge University Press 1999.

Schaefer, S., 'Measuring a tax-specific term structure of interest rates in the market for British government securities', *Economic Journal* 91, 1981, pp. 415–38.

Shiller, R., 'The term structure of interest rates', in Friedman, B., Hanh, F. (eds), *Handbook of Monetary Economics*, North Holland 1990, Chapter 13.

Suits, D., Mason, A., Chan, L., 'Spline functions fitted by standard regression methods', *Review of Economics and Statistics* 60, 1978, pp. 132–9.

Sundaresan, S., *Fixed Income Markets and Their Derivatives*, South-Western Publishing 1997.

Tuckman, B., *Fixed Income Securities*, Wiley 1996.

Van Deventer, D., Imai, K., *Financial Risk Analytics*, Irwin 1997, pp. 9–11.

Waggoner, D., 'Spline methods for extracting interest rate curves from coupon bond prices', *Federal Reserve Bank of Atlanta, Working Paper*, 97-10, 1997.

Windas, T., *An Introduction to Option-Adjusted Spread Analysis*, Bloomberg 1993, Chapter 5.

In addition, interested readers may wish to consult the following recommended references on term structure analysis.

Constantinides, G., 'A theory of the nominal term structure of interest rates', *The Review of Financial Studies* 5: 4, 1992, pp. 531–52.

Cox, J., Ingersoll, J., Ross, S., 'A re-examination of traditional hypotheses about the term structure of interest rates', *Journal of Finance* 36, 1981, pp. 769–9.

Cox, J., Ingersoll, J., Ross, S., 'A theory of the term structure of interest rates', *Econometrica* 53, 1985, pp. 385–407.

Culbertson, J., 'The term structure of interest rates', *Quarterly Journal of Economics* LXXI, 1957, pp. 489–504.

McCulloch, J.H., 'A reexamination of traditional hypotheses about the term structure: a comment', *Journal of Finance* 63: 2, 1993, pp. 779–89.

Shiller, R., Campbell, J., Schoenholtz, K., 'Forward rates and future policy: interpreting the term structure of interest rates', *Brookings Papers on Economic Activity* 1, 1983, pp. 173–223.

Stambaugh, R., 'The information in forward rates: implications for models of the term structure', *Journal of Financial Economics* 21, 1988, pp. 41–70.

CHAPTER 5

Fixed-income securities II: interest rate risk

In this chapter we discuss the sensitivity of bond prices to changes in market interest rates, and the key concepts of duration and convexity.

Introduction

Bonds pay a part of their total return during their lifetime, in the form of coupon interest, so that the term to maturity does not reflect the true period over which the bond's total return is earned. Additionally, to gain an idea of the trading characteristics of a bond, and compare this to other bonds (for example, bonds of similar maturity), term to maturity is insufficient and so we need a more accurate measure. A plain vanilla coupon bond pays out a proportion of its return during the course of its life, in the form of coupon interest. If we were to analyze the properties of a bond, we should conclude quite quickly that its maturity gives us little indication of how much of its return is paid out during its life, nor any idea of the timing or size of its cash flows, and hence its sensitivity to moves in market interest rates. For example, if comparing two bonds with the same maturity date but different coupons, the higher coupon bond provides a larger proportion of its return in the form of coupon income than does the lower coupon bond. The higher coupon bond provides its return at a faster rate; its value is theoretically therefore less subject to subsequent fluctuations in interest rates.

We may wish to calculate an average of the time to receipt of a bond's cash flows, and use this measure as a more realistic indication of maturity. However, cash flows during the life of a bond are not all equal in value, so a more accurate measure would be to take the average time to receipt of a bond's cash flows, but weighted in the form of the cash flows' present value. This is, in effect, *duration*. We can measure the speed of payment of a bond, and hence its price risk relative to other bonds of the same maturity, by measuring the average maturity of the bond's cash flow stream. Bond analysts use duration to measure this property (it is sometimes known as *Macaulay's duration*, after its inventor, who introduced it in 1938).[1] Duration is the weighted average time until the receipt of cash flows from a bond, where the weights are the present values of the cash flows, measured in years. At the time that he introduced the concept, Macaulay used the duration measure as an alternative for the length of time that a bond investment had remaining to maturity.

Duration

To recall, the price/yield formula for a plain vanilla bond is given at (5.1) below, assuming complete years to maturity paying annual coupons, and with no accrued interest at the calculation date. Note that the symbol for yield to maturity reverts to r in this section.

$$P = \frac{C}{(1 + r)} + \frac{C}{(1 + r)^2} + \frac{C}{(1 + r)^3} + \dots + \frac{C}{(1 + r)^n} + \frac{M}{(1 + r)^n} \qquad (5.1)$$

If we take the first derivative of this expression we obtain (5.2):

$$\frac{dP}{dr} = \frac{(-1)C}{(1 + r)^2} + \frac{(-2)C}{(1 + r)^3} + \dots + \frac{(-n)C}{(1 + r)^{n+1}} + \frac{(-n)M}{(1 + r)^{n+1}}. \qquad (5.2)$$

If we rearrange (5.2) we will obtain the expression at (5.3), which is our equation to calculate the approximate change in price for a small change in yield:

$$\frac{dP}{dr} = -\frac{1}{(1 + r)}\left[\frac{1C}{(1 + r)} + \frac{2C}{(1 + r)^2} + \dots + \frac{nC}{(1 + r)^n} + \frac{nM}{(1 + r)^n}\right]. \qquad (5.3)$$

Readers may feel a sense of familiarity regarding the expression in brackets in equation (5.3), because this is the weighted average time to maturity of the cash flows from a bond, where the weights are, as in our example above, the present values of each cash flow. The expression at (5.3) gives us the approximate measure of the change in price for a small change in yield. If we divide both sides of (5.3) by P we obtain the expression for the approximate percentage price change, given at (5.4):

$$\frac{dP}{dr}\frac{1}{P} = -\frac{1}{(1+r)}\left[\frac{1C}{(1+r)} + \frac{2C}{(1+r)^2} + \dots + \frac{nC}{(1+r)^n} + \frac{nM}{(1+r)^n}\right]\frac{1}{P}. \qquad (5.4)$$

1. Macaulay, F., *Some Theoretical Problems Suggested by the Movements of Interest Rates, Bond Yields and Stock Prices in the United States since 1865*, National Bureau of Economic Research, NY 1938. This work is available from Risk Classics Library, under the title *Interest Rates, Bond Yields and Stock Prices in the United States since 1856*.

If we divide the bracketed expression in (5.4) by the current price of the bond P we obtain the definition of Macaulay duration, given at (5.5):

$$D = \frac{\frac{1C}{(1+r)} + \frac{2C}{(1+r)^2} + \dots + \frac{nC}{(1+r)^n} + \frac{nM}{(1+r)^n}}{P} \,. \tag{5.5}$$

Equation (5.5) is simplified using Σ, as shown by (5.6):

$$D = \frac{\sum_{n=1}^{N} \frac{nC_n}{(1+r)^n}}{P} \tag{5.6}$$

where C represents the bond cash flow at time n.

The Macaulay duration value given by (5.6) is measured in years. However, as a measure of interest rate sensitivity, and for use in hedge calculations, duration can be transformed into *modified duration*. This was the primary measure of interest rate risk used in the markets, and is still widely used, despite the advent of the *value-at-risk* measure for market risk.

If we substitute the expression for Macaulay duration (5.5) into equation (5.4) for the approximate percentage change in price, we obtain (5.7) below:

$$\frac{dP}{dr}\frac{1}{P} = -\frac{1}{(1+r)} D. \tag{5.7}$$

This is the definition of modified duration, given as (5.8):

$$MD = \frac{D}{(1+r)}. \tag{5.8}$$

Modified duration is clearly related to duration then, and we can use it to indicate that, for small changes in yield, a given change in yield results in an inverse change in bond price. We can illustrate this by substituting (5.8) into (5.7), giving us (5.9):

$$\frac{dP}{dr}\frac{1}{P} = -MD. \tag{5.9}$$

If we are determining duration longhand, there is another arrangement we can use to shorten the procedure. Instead of equation (5.1) we use (5.10) as the bond price formula, which calculates price based on a bond being comprised of an annuity stream and a redemption payment, and summing the present values of these two elements. Again we assume an annual coupon bond priced on a date that leaves a complete number of years to maturity and with no interest accrued.

$$P = C \left[\dfrac{1 - \dfrac{1}{(1 + r)^n}}{r} \right] + \dfrac{M}{(1 + r)^n} \cdot \tag{5.10}$$

This expression calculates the price of a bond as the present value of the stream of coupon payments and the present value of the redemption payment. If we take the first derivative of (5.10) and then divide this by the current price of the bond P, the result is another expression for the modified duration formula, given at (5.11):

$$MD = \dfrac{\dfrac{C}{r^2} \left[1 - \dfrac{1}{(1 + r)^n} \right] + \dfrac{n \left(M - \frac{C}{r} \right)}{(1 + r)^{n+1}}}{P} \cdot \tag{5.11}$$

For an irredeemable bond, duration is given by:

$$D = \dfrac{1}{rc} \tag{5.12}$$

where $rc = (C/P_d)$ is the *running yield* (or *current yield*) of the bond. This follows from equation (5.6) as $N \rightarrow \infty$, recognizing that for an irredeemable bond $r = rc$ (rc is the bond's current or flat yield). Equation (5.12) provides the limiting value to duration. For bonds trading at or above par, duration increases with maturity and approaches this limit from below. For bonds trading at a discount to par, duration increases to a maximum at around 20 years and then declines towards the limit given by (5.12). So, in general, duration increases with maturity, with an upper bound given by (5.12).

Properties of Macaulay duration

A bond's duration is always less than its maturity. This is because some weight is given to the cash flows in the early years of the bond's life, which brings forward the average time at which cash flows are received. In the case of a zero-coupon bond, there is no present value weighting of the cash flows, for the simple reason that there are no cash flows, and so duration for a zero-coupon bond is equal to its term to maturity. Duration varies with coupon, yield and maturity. The following three factors imply higher duration for a bond:

■ the lower the coupon;

■ the lower the yield;

■ broadly, the longer the maturity.

Duration increases as coupon and yield decrease. As the coupon falls, more of the relative weight of the cash flows is transferred to the maturity date and this causes duration to rise. Because the coupon on index-linked bonds is generally much lower than on vanilla bonds, the duration of index-linked bonds will be much higher than for vanilla bonds of the same maturity. As yield increases, the present values of all future cash flows fall, but the present values of the more distant cash flows fall relatively more than those of the nearer cash flows. This has the effect of increasing the relative weight given to nearer cash flows, and hence of reducing duration.

Modified duration

Although it is common for newcomers to the market to think intuitively of duration much as Macaulay originally did – as a proxy measure for the time to maturity of a bond – such an interpretation is to miss the main point of duration, which is as a measure of price volatility or interest rate risk.

Using the first term of a Taylor's expansion of the bond price function,[2] we can show the following relationship between price volatility and the duration measure, which is expressed as (5.13) below:

$$\Delta P = -\left[\frac{1}{(1 + r)}\right] \times \text{Macaulay duration} \times \text{change in yield} \tag{5.13}$$

where r is the yield to maturity for an annual-paying bond (for a semi-annual coupon bond, we use $\frac{r}{2}$). If we combine the first two components of the right-hand side, we obtain the definition of modified duration. Equation (5.13) expresses the approximate percentage change in price as being equal to the modified duration multiplied by the change in yield. We saw in the previous section how the formula for Macaulay duration could be modified to obtain the *modified duration* for a bond. There is a clear relationship between the two measures. From the Macaulay duration of a bond can be derived its modified duration, which gives a measure of the sensitivity of a bond's price to small changes in yield. As we have seen, the relationship between modified duration and duration is given by:

$$MD = \frac{D}{1 + r} \tag{5.14}$$

where MD is the modified duration in years. However, it also measures the approximate change in bond price for a 1% change in bond yield. For a bond that pays semi-annual coupons, the equation becomes:

2. For an accessible explanation of the Taylor expansion, see Butler, C., *Mastering Value-at-Risk*, FT Prentice Hall, 1998, pp. 112–14.

$$MD = \frac{D}{(1 + \frac{1}{2}r)} \cdot \qquad (5.15)$$

This means that the following relationship holds between modified duration and bond prices:

$$\Delta P = MD \times \Delta r \times P. \qquad (5.16)$$

In the UK markets the term *volatility* is sometimes used to refer to modified duration, but this is becoming increasingly uncommon in order to avoid confusion with option markets' use of the same term, which often refers to *implied volatility* and is something quite different.

EXAMPLE *5.1 Using modified duration*

An 8% annual coupon bond is trading at par with a duration of 2.85 years. If yields rise from 8% to 8.5%, then the price of the bond will fall by:

$$\Delta P = -D \times \frac{\Delta(r)}{1 + r} \times P$$

$$= -(2.85) \times \left(\frac{0.005}{1.080}\right) \times 100$$

$$= -£1.3194.$$

That is, the price of the bond will now be £98.6806.

The modified duration of a bond with a duration of 2.85 years and yield of 8% is obviously:

$$MD = \frac{2.85}{1.08}$$

which gives us *MD* equal to 2.639 years.

Consider a five-year 8% annual bond priced at par with a duration of 4.31 years: the modified duration can be calculated to be 3.99. This tells us that for a 1% move in the yield to maturity, the price of the bond will move (in the opposite direction) by 3.99%.

We can use modified duration to approximate bond prices for a given yield change. This is illustrated using (5.16) above:

$$\Delta P = -MD \times (\Delta r) \times P. \qquad (5.17)$$

For a bond with a modified duration of 3.99, priced at par, an increase in yield of one basis point (100 basis points = 1%) leads to a fall in the bond's price of:

$\Delta P = (-3.24/100) \times (+ 0.01) \times 100.00$

$\Delta P = £0.0399$, or 3.99 pence.

In this case 3.99 pence is the *basis point value* (BPV) of the bond, which is the change in the bond price given a one basis point change in the bond's yield. The basis point value of a bond can be calculated using (5.18):

$$BPV = \frac{MD}{100} \cdot \frac{P}{100} \qquad\qquad (5.18)$$

Basis point values are used in hedging bond positions. To hedge a bond position requires an opposite position to be taken in the hedging instrument. So, if we are long a ten-year bond, we may wish to sell short a similar ten-year bond as a hedge against it. A short position in a bond will be hedged through a purchase of an equivalent amount of the hedging instrument. In fact there are a variety of hedging instruments available, both on- and off-balance sheet. Once the hedge is put on, any loss in the primary position should, in theory, be offset by a gain in the hedge position, and vice versa. The objective of a hedge is to ensure that the price change in the primary instrument is equal to the price change in the hedging instrument. If we are hedging a position with another bond, we use the BPVs of each bond to calculate the amount of the hedging instrument required. This is important because each bond will have different BPVs, so that to hedge a long position in, say, £1 million nominal of a 30-year bond does not mean we simply sell £1 million of another 30-year bond. This is because the BPVs of the two bonds will almost certainly be different. Also there may not be another 30-year bond in that particular bond.

What if we have to hedge with a ten-year bond? How much nominal of this bond would be required? We need to know the ratio given at (5.19) to calculate the nominal hedge position:

$$\frac{BPV_p}{BPV_b} \qquad\qquad (5.19)$$

where

BPV_p is the basis point value of the primary bond (the position to be hedged);
BPV_b is the basis point value of the hedging instrument.

The *hedge ratio* is used to calculate the size of the hedge position and is given at (5.20).

$$\frac{BPV_p}{BPV_b} \times \frac{\text{change in yield for primary bond position}}{\text{change in yield for hedge instrument}}. \qquad\qquad (5.20)$$

The second ratio in (5.20) is known as the *yield beta*.

EXAMPLE *5.2 The nature of the modified duration approximation*

Table 5.1 ■ The nature of the modified duration approximation

Bond	Maturity (years)	Modified duration	Price duration of basis point	Yield									
				6.00%	6.50%	7.00%	7.50%	7.99%	**8.00%**	8.01%	8.50%	9.00%	10.00%
8% 2009	10	6.76695	0.06936	114.72017	110.78325	107.02358	103.43204	100.067	**100.00000**	99.932929	96.71933	93.58234	87.71087

Yield change	Price change	Estimate using price duration
Down 1 bp	0.06713	0.06936
Up 1 bp	0.06707	0.06936
Down 200 bps	14.72017	13.872
Up 200 bps	12.28913	13.872

Table 5.1 shows the change in price for a hypothetical bond, the 8% 2009, for a selection of yields. We see that for a one basis point (bp) change in yield, the change in price given by the dollar duration figure, while not completely accurate, is a reasonable estimation of the actual change in price. For a large move however, say 200 bps, the approximation is significantly in error and analysts would not use it. Notice also for our hypothetical bond how the dollar duration value, calculated from the modified duration measurement, underestimates the change in price resulting from a fall in yields, but overestimates the price change for a rise in yields. This is a reflection of the price/yield relationship for this bond. Some bonds will have a more pronounced convex relationship between price and yield and the modified duration calculation will underestimate the price change resulting from both a fall or a rise in yields.

Convexity

Duration can be regarded as a first-order measure of interest rate risk: it measures the *slope* of the present value/yield profile. It is, however, only an approximation of the actual change in bond price, given a small change in yield to maturity. This is also true of modified duration, which describes the price sensitivity of a bond to small changes in yield.

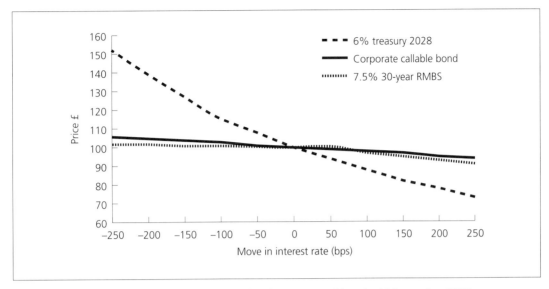

FIGURE 5.1 ■ Illustration of price sensitivity for three types of bonds, 15 December 2000

However, as Figure 5.1 illustrates, the approximation is an underestimate of the actual price at the new yield because the price/yield relationship is not linear for even plain vanilla instruments. This is the weakness of the duration measure. We see that the long-dated gilt has a reasonably convex profile, but that the callable bond and the mortgage-backed bond have slightly concave profiles, a feature known as negative convexity. The modified duration measure is a reasonable approximation for bonds with fixed coupon payments and maturity date, but inadequate for bonds that exhibit uncertainties in cash flow and maturity. For any bond, modified duration becomes increasingly inaccurate for increasing magnitude of interest rate change. For this reason, an adjustment to the estimation of price change is made using the *convexity* measure.

Convexity is a second-order measure of interest rate risk; it measures the curvature of the present value/yield profile. Convexity can be regarded as an indication of the error we make when using duration and modified duration, because it measures the degree to which the curvature of a bond's price/yield relationship diverges from the straight-line estimation. The convexity of a bond is positively related to the dispersion of its cash flows; thus, other things being equal, if one bond's cash flows are more spread out in time than another's, then it will have a higher *dispersion* and hence a higher convexity. Convexity is also positively related to duration.

The second-order differential of the bond price equation with respect to the redemption yield r is:

$$\frac{\Delta P}{P} = \frac{1}{P}\frac{\Delta P}{\Delta r}(\Delta r) + \frac{1}{2P}\frac{\Delta^2 P}{\Delta r^2}(\Delta r)^2 \qquad (5.21)$$

$$= -MD(\Delta r) = \frac{CV}{2}(\Delta r)^2$$

where CV is the convexity.

From equation (5.21), convexity is the rate at which price variation to yield changes with respect to yield. That is, it describes a bond's modified duration changes with respect to changes in yield. It can be approximated by expression (5.22):

$$CV = 10^8 \left(\frac{\Delta P'}{P} + \frac{\Delta P''}{P}\right) \qquad (5.22)$$

where

$\Delta P'$ is the change in bond price if yield increases by one basis point (0.01);
$\Delta P''$ is the change in bond price if yield decreases by one basis point (0.01).

Appendix 5.1 provides the mathematical derivation of the formula.

EXAMPLE   *5.3 Convexity*

A 5% annual coupon bond is trading at par with three years to maturity. If the yield increases from 5.00 to 5.01%, the price of the bond will fall (using the bond price equation) to:

$$P'_d = \frac{5}{(0.0501)}\left[1 - \frac{1}{(1.0501)^3}\right] + \frac{100}{(1.0501)^3}$$

$$= 99.97277262$$

or by $\Delta P_d = -0.02722738$. If the yield falls to 4.99%, the price of the bond will rise to:

$$P''_d = \frac{5}{(0.0499)}\left[1 - \frac{1}{(1.0499)^3}\right] + \frac{100}{(1.0499)^3}$$

$$= 100.027237$$

or by $\Delta P''_d = 0.02723695$. Therefore:

$$CV = 10^8 \left(\frac{-0.02722738}{100} + \frac{0.02723695}{100}\right)$$

$$= 9.57$$

that is, a convexity value of approximately 9.57.

The unit of measurement for convexity using (5.22) is the number of interest periods. For annual coupon bonds this is equal to the number of years; for bonds paying coupon on a different frequency we use (5.23) to convert the convexity measure to years:

$$CV_{years} = \frac{CV}{C^2} \qquad (5.23)$$

The convexity measure for a zero-coupon bond is given by:

$$CV = \frac{n(n + 1)}{(1 + r)^2}. \qquad (5.24)$$

Convexity is a second-order approximation of the change in price resulting from a change in yield. This is given by:

$$\Delta P = \tfrac{1}{2} \times CV \times (\Delta r)^2 . \qquad (5.25)$$

The reason we multiply the convexity by $\tfrac{1}{2}$ to obtain the convexity adjustment is because the second term in the Taylor expansion contains the coefficient $\tfrac{1}{2}$. The convexity approximation is obtained from the Taylor expansion of the bond price formula. An illustration of the Taylor expansion of the bond price/yield equation is given in Appendix 5.2.

The formula is the same for a semi-annual coupon bond. Note that the value for convexity given by the expressions above will always be positive; that is, the approximate price change due to convexity is positive for both yield increases and decreases.

EXAMPLE *5.4 Second-order interest rate risk*

A 5% annual coupon bond is trading at par with a modified duration of 2.639 and convexity of 9.57. If we assume a significant market correction and yields rise from 5% to 7%, the price of the bond will fall by:

$$\Delta P_d = -MD \times (\Delta r) \times P_d + \frac{CV}{2} \times (\Delta r)^2 \times P_d$$

$$= -(2.639) \times (0.02) \times 100 + \frac{9.57}{2} \times (0.02)^2 \times 100$$

$$= -5.278 + 0.1914$$

$$= -£5.0866$$

to £94.9134. The first-order approximation, using the modified duration value of 2.639, is −£5.278, which is an overestimation of the fall in price by £0.1914.

EXAMPLE *5.5 Convexity effect*

The 5% 2009 bond is trading at a price of £96.23119 (a yield of 5.5%) and has precisely ten years to maturity. If the yield rises to 7.5%, a change of 200 basis points, the percentage price change due to the convexity effect is given by:

$$(0.5) \times 96.23119 \times (0.02)^2 \times 100 = 1.92462\%$$

If we use an HP calculator to find the price of the bond at the new yield of 7.5% we see that it is £82.83980, a change in price of 13.92%. The convexity measure of 1.92462% is an approximation of the error we would make when using the modified duration value to estimate the price of the bond following the 200 basis point rise in yield.

If the yield of the bond were to fall by 200 basis points, the convexity effect would be the same, as given by the expression at (5.25).

Convexity is an attractive property for a bond to have. What level of premium will be attached to a bond's higher convexity? This is a function of the current yield levels in the market, as well as market volatility. Remember that modified duration and convexity are functions of yield level, and that the effect of both is magnified at lower yield levels. As well as the relative level, investors will value convexity more if the current market conditions are volatile. The cash effect of convexity is noticeable only for large moves in yield. If an investor expects market yields to move only by relatively small amounts, he will attach a lower value to convexity; and vice versa for large movements in yield. Therefore the yield premium attached to a bond with higher convexity will vary according to market expectations of the future size of interest rate changes.

The convexity measure increases with the square of maturity, and it decreases with both coupon and yield. As the measure is a function of modified duration, index-linked bonds have greater convexity than conventional bonds. We discussed how the price/yield profile will be more convex for a bond of higher convexity, and that such a bond will outperform a bond of lower convexity, whatever happens to market interest rates. High convexity is therefore a desirable property for bonds to have. In principle, a more convex bond should fall in price less than a less convex one when yields rise, and rise in price more when yields fall. That is, convexity can be equated with the potential to outperform. Thus, other things being equal, the higher the convexity of a bond, the more desirable it should be in principle to investors. In some cases investors may be prepared to accept a bond with a lower yield in order to gain convexity. We noted also that convexity is, in principle, of more value if uncertainty, and hence expected market volatility, is high, because the convexity effect of a bond is amplified for large changes in yield. The value of convexity is therefore greater in volatile market conditions.

For a conventional vanilla bond convexity is almost always positive. Negative convexity resulting from a bond with a concave price/yield profile would not be an attractive property for a bondholder; the most common occurrence of negative convexity in the cash markets is with callable bonds and certain types of mortgage-backed securities.

We illustrated that for most bonds, and certainly when the convexity measure is high, the modified duration measurement for interest rate risk becomes more inaccurate for large changes in yield. In such situations it becomes necessary to use the approximation, given by our convexity equation, to measure the error we have made in estimating the price change based on modified duration only. The expression was given earlier in this chapter.

The following points highlight the main convexity properties for conventional vanilla bonds.

A fall in yields leads to an increase in convexity. A decrease in bond yield leads to an increase in the bond's convexity; this is a property of positive convexity. Equally, a rise in yields leads to a fall in convexity.

For a given term to maturity, a higher coupon results in lower convexity. For any given redemption yield and term to maturity, the higher a bond's coupon, the lower its convexity. Therefore among bonds of the same maturity, zero-coupon bonds have the highest convexity.

For a given modified duration, a higher coupon results in higher convexity. For any given redemption yield and modified duration, a higher coupon results in a higher convexity. Contrast this with the earlier property; in this case, for bonds of the same modified duration, zero-coupon bonds have the lowest convexity.

The basic redemption yield, modified duration and convexity measures are unsuitable for bond instruments that exhibit uncertain cash flow and maturity characteristics, and other techniques must be used in the analysis of such products. One such technique is the *option-adjusted spread* model, which is considered in the next chapter.

Appendix 5.1 Measuring convexity

The modified duration of a plain vanilla bond is:

$$MD = \frac{D}{(1 + r)} . \tag{5.26}$$

We also know that:

$$\frac{dP}{dr} \frac{1}{P} = - MD. \tag{5.27}$$

This shows that for a percentage change in the yield we have an inverse change in the price by the amount of the modified duration value.

If we multiply both sides of (5.27) by any particular change in the bond yield, given by dr, we obtain expression (5.28):

$$\frac{dP}{P} = -MD \times dr. \tag{5.28}$$

Using the first two terms of a Taylor expansion, we obtain an approximation of the bond price change, given by (5.29):

$$dP = \frac{dP}{dr}\, dr + \frac{1}{2}\frac{d^2P}{dr^2}\,(dr)^2 + \text{approximation error}. \tag{5.29}$$

If we divide both sides of (5.29) by P to obtain the percentage price change, the result is the expression at (5.30):

$$\frac{dP}{P} = \frac{dP}{dr}\frac{1}{P}\,dr + \frac{1}{2}\frac{d^2P}{dr^2}\frac{1}{P}\,(dr)^2 + \frac{\text{approximation error}}{P}. \tag{5.30}$$

The first component of the right-hand side of (5.29) is the expression at (5.28), which is the cash price change given by the duration value. Therefore equation (5.29) is the approximation of the price change. Equation (5.30) is the approximation of the price change as given by the modified duration value. The second component in both expressions is the second derivative of the bond price equation. This second derivative captures the convexity value of the price/yield relationship and is the cash value given by convexity. As such, it is referred to as *dollar convexity* in the US markets. The dollar convexity is stated as:

$$CV_{dollar} = \frac{d^2P}{dr^2}. \tag{5.31}$$

If we multiply the dollar convexity value by the square of a bond's yield change we obtain the approximate cash value change in price resulting from the convexity effect. This is shown by (5.32):

$$dP = \left(CV_{dollar}\right)(dr)^2. \tag{5.32}$$

If we then divide the second derivative of the price equation by the bond price, we obtain a measure of the percentage change in bond price as a result of the convexity effect. This is the measure known as *convexity* and is the convention used in virtually all bond markets. This is given by the expression at (5.33):

$$CV = \frac{d^2P}{dr^2}\frac{1}{P}. \tag{5.33}$$

To measure the amount of the percentage change in bond price as a result of the convex nature of the price/yield relationship we can use (5.34):

$$\frac{dP}{P} = \frac{1}{2} CV (dr)^2. \tag{5.34}$$

For longhand calculations, note that the second derivative of the bond price equation is (5.35), which can be simplified to (5.36). The usual assumptions apply to the expressions: that the bond pays annual coupons and has a precise number of interest periods to maturity. If the bond is a semi-annual paying one, the yield value r is replaced by $r/2$:

$$\frac{d^2P}{dr^2} = \sum_{n=1}^{N} \frac{n(n+1)C}{(1+r)^{n+2}} + \frac{n(n+1)M}{(1+r)^{n+2}}. \tag{5.35}$$

Alternatively, we differentiate to the second order the bond price equation as given by (5.36), giving us the alternative expression (5.37):

$$P = \frac{C}{r} = \left[1 - \frac{1}{(1+r)^n}\right] + \frac{100}{(1+r)^n} \tag{5.36}$$

$$\frac{d^2P}{dr^2} = \frac{2C}{r^3}\left[1 - \frac{1}{(1+r)^n}\right] - \frac{2C}{r^2(1+r)^{n+1}} + \frac{n(n+1)(100 - \frac{C}{r})}{(1+r)^{n+2}} \tag{5.37}$$

Appendix 5.2 Taylor expansion of the price/yield function

Let us summarize the bond price formula as (5.38), where C represents all the cash flows from the bond, including the redemption payment:

$$P = \sum_{n=1}^{N} \frac{C_n}{(1+r)^n}. \tag{5.38}$$

We therefore derive the following:

$$\frac{dP}{dr} = -\sum_{n=1}^{N} \frac{C_n \cdot n}{(1+r)^{n+1}} \tag{5.39}$$

$$\frac{d^2P}{dr^2} = \sum_{n=1}^{N} \frac{C_n \cdot n(n+1)}{(1+r)^{n+2}} \tag{5.40}$$

This then gives us:

$$\Delta P = \left[\frac{dP}{dr}\Delta r\right] + \left[\frac{1}{2!}\frac{d^2P}{dr^2}(\Delta r)^2\right] + \left[\frac{1}{3!}\frac{d^3P}{dr^3}(\Delta r)^3\right] + \dots \tag{5.41}$$

The first expression in (5.41) is the modified duration measure, while the second expression measures convexity. The more powerful the changes in yield, the more expansion is required to approximate the change to greater accuracy. Expression (5.41) therefore gives us the equations for modified duration and convexity, shown by (5.42) and (5.43) respectively.

$$MD = -\frac{dP/dr}{P} \qquad (5.42)$$

$$CV = -\frac{d^2P/dr^2}{P} \qquad (5.43)$$

We can therefore state the following:

$$\frac{\Delta P}{P} = [-(MD)\Delta r] + \left[\tfrac{1}{2}(CV)(\Delta r)^2\right] + \text{residual error} \qquad (5.44)$$

$$\Delta P = -[P(MD)\Delta r] + \left[\frac{P}{2}(CV)(\Delta r)^2\right] + \text{residual error} \qquad (5.45)$$

SELECTED BIBLIOGRAPHY AND REFERENCES

Bierwag, G.O., 'Immunization, duration and the term structure of interest rates', *Journal of Financial and Quantitative Analysis*, December 1977, pp. 725–41.

Bierwag, G.O., 'Measures of duration', *Economic Inquiry* 16, October 1978, pp. 497–507.

Blake, D., Orszag, M., 'A closed-form formula for calculating bond convexity', *Journal of Fixed Income* 6, 1996, pp. 88–91.

Burghardt, G., *The Treasury Bond Basis*, McGraw-Hill 1994, Chapter 2.

Butler, C., *Mastering Value-at-Risk*, FT Prentice Hall 1998.

Dattatreya, R., *Fixed Income Analytics: State-of-the-Art Debt Analysis and Valuation Modeling*, McGraw-Hill 1991.

Garbade, K., *Fixed Income Analytics*, MIT Press 1996, Chapters 3, 4, 12.

Golub, B., Tilman, L., *Risk Management: Approaches in Fixed Income Markets*, Wiley 2000, Chapter 2.

Macaulay, F., *The Movements of Interest Rates, Bond Yields and Stock Prices in the United States since 1856*, Risk Classics Library 1999.

Windas, T., *An Introduction to Option-Adjusted Spread Analysis*, Bloomberg Publications 1993.

CHAPTER 6

Fixed-income securities III: option-adjusted spread analysis

The modified duration and convexity methods we have described are only suitable for use in the analysis of conventional fixed income instruments with known fixed cash flows and maturity date. They are not satisfactory for use with bonds that contain *embedded options,* such as callable bonds, or instruments with unknown final redemption dates, such as mortgage-backed bonds.[1] For these and other bonds that exhibit uncertainties in their cash flow pattern and redemption date, so-called *option-adjusted* measures are used. The most common of these is option-adjusted spread (OAS) and option-adjusted duration (OAD). The techniques were developed to allow for the uncertain cash flow structure of non-vanilla fixed income instruments, and to model the effect of the option element of such bonds.

A complete description of option-adjusted spread is outside the scope of this book; here we present an overview of the basic concepts. Accessible accounts of this technique are given in Wilson and Fabozzi (1990); another excellent introduction is Windas (1993).

Introduction

Option-adjusted spread analysis uses simulated interest rate paths as part of its calculation of bond yield and convexity. Therefore an OAS model is a *stochastic* model. The OAS refers to the yield spread between a callable or mortgage-backed bond and a government benchmark bond. The government bond chosen ideally will have similar coupon and duration values. Thus the OAS is an indication of the value of the option element of the bond, as well as the premium required by investors in return for accepting the default risk

---

1. The term 'embedded' is used because the option element of the bond cannot be stripped out and traded separately, for example the call option inherent in a callable bond.

of the corporate bond. When OAS is measured as a spread between two bonds of similar default risk, the yield difference between the bonds reflects the value of the option element only. This is rare, and the market convention is to measure OAS over the equivalent benchmark government bond. OAS is used in the analysis of corporate bonds that incorporate call or put provisions, as well as mortgage-backed securities with prepayment risk. For both applications the spread is calculated as the number of basis points over the yield of the government bond that would equate the price of both bonds.

The essential components of the OAS technique are as follows:

■ a simulation method such as Monte Carlo is used to generate sample interest rate paths, and a cash flow pattern generated for each interest rate path;

■ the value of the bond for each of the future possible rate paths is found, by discounting in the normal manner each of the bond's cash flows at the relevant interest rate (plus a spread) along the points of each path. This produces a range of values for the bond, and for a given price the OAS is the spread at which the average of the range of values equates the given price.

Thus OAS is a general stochastic model, with discount rates derived from the standard benchmark term structure of interest rates. This is an advantage over more traditional methods in which a single discount rate is used. The calculated spread is a spread over risk-free forward rates, accounting for both interest rate uncertainty and the price of default risk. As with any methodology, OAS has both strengths and weaknesses; however it provides more realistic analysis than the traditional yield-to-maturity approach. It has been widely adopted by investors since its introduction in the late 1980s.

A theoretical framework

All bond instruments are characterized by the promise to pay a stream of future cash flows. The term structure of interest rates and associated discount function is crucial to the valuation of any debt security, and underpins any valuation framework.[2] Armed with the term structure we can value any bond, assuming it is liquid and default-free, by breaking it down into a set of cash flows and valuing each cash flow with the appropriate discount factor. Further characteristics of any bond, such as an element of default risk or embedded option, are valued incrementally over its discounted cash flow valuation.

---

2. The term structure of interest rates is the spot rate yield curve; spot rates are viewed as identical to zero-coupon bond interest rates where there is a market of liquid zero-coupon bonds along regular maturity points. As such a market does not exist anywhere, the spot rate yield curve is considered a theoretical construct, which is most closely equated by the zero-coupon term structure derived from the prices of default-free liquid government bonds (*see* Chapter 4).

Valuation under known interest rate environments

We showed in Chapter 4 how forward rates can be calculated using the no-arbitrage argument. We use this basic premise to introduce the concept of OAS. Consider the spot interest rates for two interest periods:

Term (interest periods)	Spot rate
1	5%
2	6%

The reader familiar with Chapter 4 will easily determine that the one-period interest rate starting one period from now is 7.009%. This is the implied one-period forward rate.

We may use the spot rate term structure to value a default-free zero-coupon bond, so for example a two-period bond would be priced at £89.[3] Using the forward rate we obtain the same valuation, which is exactly what we expect.[4]

This framework can be used to value other types of bonds. Let us say we wish to calculate the price of a two-period bond that has the following cash flow stream:

Period 1	£5
Period 2	£105

Using the spot rate structure in Table 6.1 on page 108, the price of this bond is calculated to be £98.21.[5] This would be the bond's fair value if it were liquid and default-free. Assume, however, that the bond is a corporate bond and carries an element of default risk, and is priced at £97. What spread over the risk-free price does this indicate? We require the spread over the implied forward rate that would result in a discounted price of £97. Using iteration, this is found to be 67.6 basis points.[6] The calculation is:

$$P = \frac{5}{1 + (0.05 + 0.00676)} + \frac{105}{[1 + (0.05 + 0.00676)] \times [1 + (0.07009 + 0.00676)]}$$

$$= 97.00$$

The spread of 67.6 basis points is implied by the observed market price of the bond, and is the spread over the expected path of interest rates. Another way of considering this is that it is the spread premium earned by holding the corporate bond instead of a risk-free bond with identical cash flows.

---

3. £100/(1.06)^2 = £88.9996.

4. £100/(1.05) × (1.07009) = £89.

5. [£5/1.05 + £105/(1.05) × (1.07009)] = £98.21.

6. For students, problems requiring the use of iteration can be found using the 'Goal Seek' function in Microsoft Excel, under the 'Tools' menu.

This framework can be used to evaluate relative value. For example, if the average sector spread of bonds with similar credit risk is observed to be 73 basis points, a fairer value for the example bond might be:

$$P = \frac{5}{1 + (0.05 + 0.0073)} + \frac{105}{[1 + (0.05 + 0.0073)] \times [1 + (0.07009 + 0.0073)]}$$

$$= 96.905$$

which would indicate that our bond is overvalued.

The approach just described is the OAS methodology in essence. However, it applies only in an environment in which the future path of interest rates is known with certainty. The spread calculated is the OAS spread under conditions of no uncertainty. We begin to appreciate though that this approach is preferable to the traditional one of comparing redemption yields; whereas the latter uses a single discount rate, the OAS approach uses the correct spot rate for each period's cash flow.

However, our interest lies with conditions of interest rate uncertainty. In practice, the future path of interest rates is not known with certainty. The range of possible values of future interest rates is a large one, although the probability of higher or lower rates that are very far away from current rates is low. For this reason the OAS calculation is based on the most likely future interest rate path among the universe of possible rate paths. This is less relevant for vanilla bonds, but for securities whose future cash flow is contingent on the level of future interest rates, such as mortgage-backed bonds, it is very important. The first step, then, is to describe the interest rate process in terms that capture the character of its dynamics.[7]

Ideally the analytical framework under conditions of uncertainty would retain the arbitrage-free character of our earlier discussion. But by definition the evolution of interest rates will not match the calculated forward rate, thus creating arbitrage conditions. This is not surprising. For instance, if the calculated one-period forward rate shown above actually *turns out to be* 7.50%, the maturity value of the bond at the end of period 2 would be £100.459 rather than £100. This means that there was an arbitrage opportunity at the original price of £89. For the bond price to have been arbitrage-free at the start of period 1, it would have been priced at £88.59.[8]

---

7. This is interest rate modelling, an extensive and complex, not to mention heavily researched, subject. We present it here in accessible, intuitive terms. The next chapter introduces it in more formal fashion.

8. The price of the bond at the start of period is £89, shown earlier. This is worth (89 × 1.05) or £93.45 at the end of period 1, and hence £100 at the end of period 2 (93.45 × 1.07009). However if an investor at the time of rolling over the one-period bond can actually invest at 7.50%, this amount will mature to (83.45 × 1.075) or £100.459. In this situation, *in hindsight* the arbitrage-free price of the bond at the start of period 1 would be 100/(1.05 × 1.075) or £88.59.

This is a meaningless argument, short of advocating the employment of a clairvoyant. However, it illustrates how different eventual interest rate paths correspond to different initial fair values. As interest rates can follow a large number of different paths, of varying possibility, so bond prices can assume a number of fair values. The ultimate arbitrage-free price is as unknown as future interest rate levels! Let us look then at how the OAS methodology uses the most likely interest rate path when calculating fair values.

Valuation under uncertain interest rate environments

We begin by assuming that the current spot rate term structure is consistent with bond prices of zero option-adjusted spread, so that their price is the average expected for all possible evolutions of the future interest rate. By assuming this we may state that the most likely future interest rate path, which lies in the centre of the range of all possible interest rate paths, will be a function of interest rate volatility. Here we use volatility to mean the average annual percentage deviation of interest rates around their mean value. So an environment of 0% volatility would be one of interest rate certainty and would generate only one possible arbitrage-free bond price. This is a worthwhile scenario, since it enables us to generalize the example in the previous section as the arbitrage-free model in times of uncertainty, but when volatility is 0%.

A rise in volatility generates a range of possible future paths around the expected path. The actual expected path that corresponds to a zero-coupon bond price incorporating zero OAS is a function of the dispersion of the range of alternative paths around it. This dispersion is the result of the dynamics of the interest rate process, so this process must be specified for the current term structure. We can illustrate this with a simple binomial model example. Consider again the spot rate structure shown early on. Assume that there are only two possible future interest rate scenarios, outcome 1 and outcome 2, both of equal probability. The dynamics of the short-term interest rate are described by a constant drift rate a, together with a volatility rate σ. These two parameters describe the evolution of the short-term interest rate. If outcome 1 occurs, the one-period interest rate one period from now will be:

$$5\% \times \exp(a + \sigma)$$

while if outcome 2 occurs, the period one rate will become:

$$5\% \times \exp(a - \sigma)$$

In Figure 6.1 we present the possible interest rate paths under conditions of 0% and 25% volatility levels, and maintain our assumption that the current spot rate structure price for a risk-free zero-coupon bond is identical to the price generated using the structure to obtain a zero option-adjusted spread. To maintain the no-arbitrage condition, we know

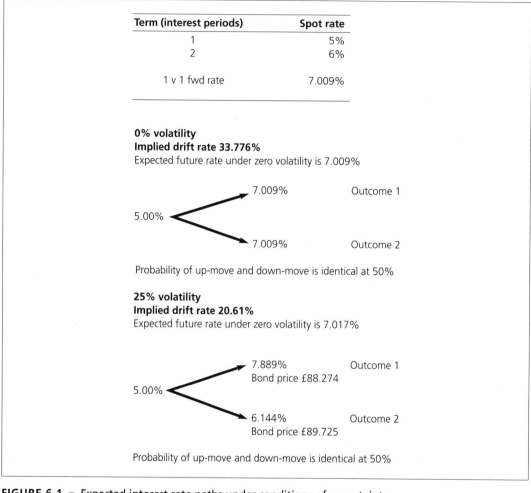

FIGURE 6.1 ▨ Expected interest rate paths under conditions of uncertainty

that the price of the bond at the start of period 1 must be £89, so we calculate the implied drift rate by an iterative process. This is shown in Figure 6.1.

At 0% volatility the prices generated by the up and down moves are equal, because the future interest rates are equal. Hence the forward rate is the same as before: 7.009%. When there is a multiple interest rate path scenario, the fair value of the bond is determined as the average of the discounted values for each rate path. Under conditions of certainty (0% volatility), the price of the bond is, not surprisingly, unchanged at both paths. The average of these is obviously £89. Under 25% volatility the up-move interest rate is 7.889% and the down-move rate is 6.144%. The average of these rates is 7.017%. We can check the values by calculating the value of the bond at each outcome (or 'node') and then obtaining the average of these values; this is shown to be £89. Beginners can view the simple spreadsheet used to calculate the rates in Appendix 6.1, with the iterative process undertaken using the Microsoft Excel 'Goal Seek' function.

We now consider the corporate bond with £5 and £105 cash flows at the end of periods 1 and 2 respectively. In an environment of certainty, the bond price of £97 implied an OAS of 67.6 basis points (bps). In the uncertain environment we can use the same process as above to determine the spread implied by the same price. The process involves discounting the cash flows across each path with the spread added, to determine the price at each node. The price of the bond is the average of all the resulting prices; this is then compared to the observed market price (or required price). If the calculated price is lower than the market price, then a higher spread is required, and if the calculated price is higher than the market price, then the spread is too high and must be lowered.

Applying this approach to the model in Figure 6.1, under the 0% volatility the spread implied by the price of £97 is, unsurprisingly, 67.6 bps. In the 25% volatility environment however, this spread results in a price of £97.296, which is higher than the observed price. This suggests the spread is too low. By iteration we find that the spread that generates a price of £97 is 89.76 bps, which is the bond's option-adjusted spread. This is shown below.

Outcome 1:

$$P = \frac{5}{[1 + (0.05 + 0.00897)]} + \frac{105}{[1 + (0.05 + 0.00897)] \times [1 + (0.07887 + 0.00897)]}$$

$$= £95.865$$

Outcome 2:

$$P = \frac{5}{[1 + (0.05 + 0.00897)]} + \frac{105}{[1 + (0.05 + 0.00897)] \times [1 + (0.06144 + 0.00897)]}$$

$$= £98.135$$

The calculated price is the average of these two values and is [(95.87 + 98.13)/2] or £97 as required. The OAS of 89.76 bps in the binomial model is a measure of the value attached to the option element of the bond at 25% volatility.

The final part of this discussion introduces the value of the embedded option in a bond. Our example bond from earlier is now semi-annually paying and carries a coupon value of 7%. It has a redemption value of £101.75. Assume that the bond is callable at the end of period 1, and that it is advantageous for the issuer to call the bond at this point if interest rates fall below 7%. We assume further that the bond is trading at the fair value implied by the discounting calculation earlier. With a principal nominal amount of £101.75, this suggests a market price of (101.75/97.00) or £104.89. We require the OAS implied by this price now that there is an embedded option element in the bond. Under conditions of 0% volatility the value of the call is zero, as the option is out-of-the-money when interest rates are above 7%. In these circumstances the bond behaves exactly as before, and the OAS remains 67.6 bps. However, in the 25% volatility environment it becomes advantageous to the issuer to call the bond in the down-state environment, as rates are below 7%. In fact we can calculate that the spread over the interest rate paths that would produce an average price of 104.89 is 4 bps, which means that the option carries a cost to the bondholder of (67.6 – 4) or 63.6 bps. We illustrate this property in general terms in Figure 6.2. A conventional bond has a convex price/yield profile, but the introduction of a call feature limits the upside price performance of a bond, since there is a greater chance of it being called as market yields fall.

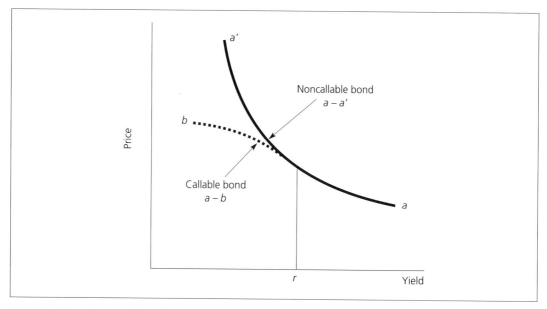

FIGURE 6.2 ▪ Impact of a call option on the price/yield profile of a corporate bond

The methodology in practice

In practice, the forward rate term structure is extracted using regression methods from the price of default-free government coupon bonds. Generally, OAS models used in the market are constructed so that they generate government prices that are identical to the prices observed in the market, because they assume that government bonds are fair value. This results in an implied forward rate yield curve that is the 'expected' path of future interest rates around which other rate possibilities are dispersed. Under this assumption then, an OAS value is a measure of the return over the government yield that an investor can expect to achieve by holding the option-embedded bond that is being analyzed. Banks generally employ a simulation model such as Monte Carlo to generate the 'tree' of possible interest rate scenarios. This is a series of computer-generated random numbers that are used to derive interest rate paths. To generate the paths, the simulation model runs using the two parameters introduced earlier: the deterministic drift term and the volatility term. Interest rates are assumed to be lognormally distributed.

When conducting relative value analysis, we strip a security down into the constituent cash flows relevant to each interest rate path. This is straightforward for vanilla bonds; however, for bonds such as mortgage-backed securities the cash flows are determined after assuming a level of prepayment. The results generated from the prepayment model are themselves based on interest rate scenarios. The OAS is then calculated by discounting the cash flows corresponding to each node on the interest rate tree, and is the spread that equates the calculated average price to the observed market price. In practice the model is run the other way: assuming a fair value spread over government bonds, the fair value price of a bond is the average price that is obtained by discounting all the cash flows at each relevant interest rate, together with the fair value spread.

EXAMPLE *6.1 Callable corporate bond and Treasury bond*

We conclude this chapter with an illustration of the OAS technique. Consider a five-year semi-annual corporate bond with a coupon of 8%. The bond incorporates a call feature that allows the issuer to call it after two years, and is currently priced at $104.25. This is equivalent to a yield to maturity of 6.979%. We wish to measure the value of the call feature to the issuer, and we can do this using the OAS technique. Assume that a five-year Treasury security also exists with a coupon of 8%, and is priced at $109.11, a yield of 5.797%. The higher yield of the corporate bond reflects the market-required premium, due to the corporate bond's default risk and call feature.

The valuation of both securities is shown in Table 6.1.

Our starting point is the redemption yield curve, from which we calculate the current spot rate term structure. This was done using RATE software and is shown in column 4. Using the spot rate structure, we calculate the present value of the Treasury security's cash flows, which is shown in column 7. We wish to calculate the OAS that equates the price of the Treasury to that of the corporate bond. By iteration, this is found to be 110.81 bps. This is the semi-annual OAS spread. The annualized OAS spread is double this. With the OAS spread added to the spot rates for each period, the price of the Treasury matches that of the corporate bond, as shown in column 9. The adjusted spot rates are shown in column 8. Figure 6.3 illustrates the yield curve for the Treasury security and the corporate bond.

TABLE 6.1 ■ OAS analysis for corporate callable bond and Treasury bond

Bond	Price	Yield
Corporate bond	104.25	6.98%
Treasury 8% 2006	109.11	5.80%

OAS spread 110.81 bps

Period	YTM	Date	Spot rate	Discount factor	Cash flow	Present value	OAS adjusted spot rate	PV of OAS-adjusted cash flows
0	5.000	25 February 2001	5.000	1				
1	5.000	27 August 2001	5.069	0.97521333	4	3.901125962	6.177	3.88016
2	5.150	25 February 2002	5.225	0.95034125	4	3.798913929	6.333	3.75822
3	5.200	26 August 2002	5.277	0.92582337	4	3.699381343	6.385	3.64011
4	5.250	25 February 2003	5.329	0.90137403	4	3.600632571	6.437	3.52394
5	5.374	25 August 2003	5.463	0.87567855	4	3.495761898	6.571	3.40300
6	5.500	25 February 2004	5.597	0.84928019	4	3.389528778	6.705	3.28196
7	5.624	25 August 2004	5.734	0.82277146	4	3.281916075	6.842	3.16080
8	5.750	25 February 2005	5.870	0.79585734	4	3.173623771	6.978	3.04022
9	5.775	25 August 2005	5.895	0.77285090	4	3.079766213	7.003	2.93453
10	5.800	27 February 2006	5.920	0.74972455	104	77.6869373	7.028	73.62754
						109.1075878		104.25049

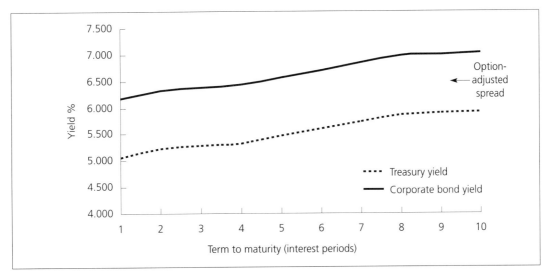

FIGURE 6.3 ■ Yield curves illustrating OAS yield

Appendix 6.1 Calculating interest rate paths

TABLE 6.2 ■ Calculating interest rate paths

Price	89				
Period 1 rate	1.05				
Volatility	0.25				
Drift	0.206054017				

Up state	0.078891779	1.078892	Bond price	88.2740022	Average	88.9996
Down state	0.061440979	1.061441		89.72528584		
					Fwd rate %	0.070166379

	F	G	H	I	J	K	L
17							
18	Price		89				
19	Period 1 rate		1.05				
20	Volatility		0.25				
21	Drift		0.206054017				
22							
23							
24	Up state	=0.05*EXP(G21+G20)	=1+G24	Bond price	=100/(G19*H24)	Average	=(J24+J25)/2
25	Down state	=0.05*EXP(G21−H19)	=1+G25		=100/(G19*H25)		
26							
27						Fwd rate %	=(G24+G25)/2

SELECTED BIBLIOGRAPHY AND REFERENCES

Si Chen, 'Understanding option-adjusted spreads: the implied prepayment hypothesis', *Journal of Portfolio Management*, summer 1996, pp. 104–13.

Wilson, R., Fabozzi, F., *The New Corporate Bond Market*, Probus Publishing 1990, Chapter 11.

Windas, T., *An Introduction to Option-Adjusted Spread Analysis*, Bloomberg Publications 1993.

CHAPTER 7

Interest rate modelling

Chapter 4 introduced the concept of the yield curve. The analysis and valuation of debt market instruments revolves around the yield curve. Yield curve or *term structure* modelling has been extensively researched in the financial economics literature; it is possibly the most heavily covered subject in that field. It is not possible to deliver a comprehensive summary in just one chapter, but our aim here is to cover the basic concepts. As ever, interested readers are directed to the bibliography listing, which contains the more accessible titles in this area.

In this chapter we review a number of interest rate models, generally the more well-known ones. In the next two chapters we discuss some of the techniques used to fit a smooth yield curve to market-observed bond yields, and present an advanced treatment of the B-spline curve fitting methodology.

Introduction

Term structure modelling is based on theory that describes the behaviour of interest rates. A model would seek to identify the elements or *factors* that are believed to explain the dynamics of interest rates. These factors are random or *stochastic* in nature, so that we cannot predict with certainty the future level of any factor. An interest rate model must therefore specify a statistical process that describes the stochastic property of these factors, in order to arrive at a reasonably accurate representation of the behaviour of interest rates.

The first term structure models described in the academic literature described the interest rate process as one where the *short rate*[1] follows a statistical process and where all other interest rates are a function of the short rate. So the dynamics of the short rate drive all other term interest rates. These models are known as *one-factor models*.

---

1. The short rate is a theoretical construct that refers to the interest rate that would be charged on a loan of funds that is repaid almost instantaneously.

A one-factor model assumes that all term rates follow on from when the short rate is specified; that is, they are not randomly determined. Two-factor interest rate models have also been described. For instance, the model described by Brennan and Schwartz (1979) specified the factors as the short rate and a long-term rate, while a model described by Fong and Vasicek (1991) specified the factors as the short rate and short-rate volatility.

Basic concepts

The original class of interest rate models describe the dynamics of the short rate; the later class of models, known as 'HJM' models, describe the dynamics of the forward rate, and we will introduce these later. The foundation of interest rate modelling is grounded in probability theory, so readers may wish to familiarize themselves with this subject. An excellent introduction to this area is given in Ross (1999), while a fuller treatment is given in the same author's better known book, *Probability Models* (2000).

In a one-factor model of interest rates, the short rate is assumed to be a random or stochastic variable, with the dynamics of its behaviour being uncertain and acting in an unpredictable manner. A random variable such as the short rate is defined as a variable whose future outcome can assume more than one possible value. Random variables are either *discrete* or *continuous*. A discrete variable moves in identifiable breaks or jumps. So, for example, while time is continuous, the trading hours of an exchange-traded future are not continuous, because the exchange will be shut outside business hours. Interest rates are treated in academic literature as being continuous, whereas in fact rates such as central bank base rates move in discrete steps. A continuous variable moves in a manner that has no breaks or jumps. So if an interest rate can move in a range from 5% to 10%, if it is continuous it can assume any value between this range, for instance a value of 5.671291%. Although this does not reflect market reality, assuming that interest rates and the processes they follow are continuous allows us to use calculus to derive useful results in our analysis.

The short rate is said to follow a stochastic process, so although the rate itself cannot be predicted with certainty, since it can assume a range of possible values in the future, the process by which it changes from value to value can be assumed, and hence modelled. The dynamics of the short rate therefore are a stochastic process or *probability distribution*. A one-factor model of the interest rate actually specifies the stochastic process that describes the movement of the short rate.

The analysis of stochastic processes employs mathematical techniques originally used in physics. An instantaneous change in value of a random variable x is written as dx. The changes in the random variable are assumed to be normally distributed. The shock to this random variable that generates it to change value, also referred to as *noise*, follows a randomly generated process known as a Weiner process or geometric Brownian motion.

An introduction to this is given in Choudhry (2001). A variable following a Weiner process is a random variable, termed x or z, whose value alters instantaneously, but whose patterns of change follow a normal distribution with mean 0 and standard deviation 1. If we assume that the yield r of a zero-coupon bond follows a continuous Weiner process with mean 0 and standard deviation 1, this would be written as:

$dr = dz$.

Changes or 'jumps' in the yield that follow a Weiner process are scaled by the volatility of the stochastic process that drives interest rates, which is given by σ. So the stochastic process for the change in yields is given by:

$dr = \sigma dz$.

The value of this volatility parameter is user-specified; that is, it is set at a value that the user feels most accurately describes the current interest rate environment. Users often use the volatility implied by the market price of interest rate derivatives such as caps and floors.

So far we've said that the zero-coupon bond yield is a stochastic process following a geometric Brownian motion that drifts with no discernible trend; however, in this scenario, over time the yield would continuously rise to a level of infinity or fall to infinity, which is not an accurate representation of reality. We need to add to the model a term that describes the observed trend of interest rates moving up and down in a cycle. This expected direction of the change in the short rate is the second parameter in an interest rate model, which in some texts is referred to by a letter such as a or b and in other texts is referred to as μ.

The short-rate process can therefore be described in the functional form given by (7.1):

$$dr = a\,dt + \sigma dz \qquad (7.1)$$

where

dr is the change in the short rate
a is the expected direction of change of the short rate or *drift*
dt is the incremental change in time
σ is the standard deviation of changes in the short rate
dz is the random process.

Equation (7.1) is sometimes seen with dW or dx in place of dz. It assumes that on average the instantaneous change in interest rates is given by the function adt, with random shocks specified by σdz. It is similar to a number of models, such as those first described by Vasicek (1977), Ho and Lee (1986), Hull and White (1990) and others.

To reiterate then, (7.1) states that the change in the short rate r over an infinitesimal period of time dt, termed dr, is a function of:

- the drift rate or expected direction of change in the short rate a;
- a random process dz.

The two significant properties of the geometric Brownian motion are:

- the drift rate is equal to the expected value of the change in the short rate. Under a zero drift rate, the expected value of the change is also zero and the expected value of the short rate is given by its current value;
- the variance of the change in the short rate over a period of time T is equal to T, while its standard deviation is given by $\sqrt{T}$.

The model given by (7.1) describes a stochastic short-rate process, modified with a drift rate to influence the direction of change. However, a more realistic specification would also build in a term that describes the long-run behaviour of interest rates to drift back to a long-run level. This process is known as *mean reversion*, and is perhaps best known from the Hull-White model. A general specification of mean reversion would be a modification given by:

$$dr = a(b - r)dt + \sigma dz \tag{7.2}$$

where b is the long-run mean level of interest rates and where a now describes the speed of mean reversion. Equation (7.2) is known as an Ornstein-Uhlenbeck process. When r is greater than b, it will be pulled back towards b, although random shocks generated by dz will delay this process. When r is below b, the short rate will be pulled up towards b.

Itô's lemma

Having specified a term structure model, for market practitioners it becomes necessary to determine how security prices related to interest rates fluctuate. The main instance of this is where we wish to determine how the price P of a bond moves over time and as the short rate r varies. The formula used for this is known as Itô's lemma. For the background on the application of Itô's lemma see Hull (1997) or Baxter and Rennie (1996). Itô's lemma transforms the dynamics of the bond price P in terms of the interest rate r, into a stochastic process in the following form:

$$dP = P_r dr + \tfrac{1}{2} P_{rr}(dr)^2 + P_t. \tag{7.3}$$

The subscripts indicate partial derivatives.[2] The terms dr and $(dr)^2$ are dependent on the stochastic process that is selected for the short rate r. If this process is the Ornstein-Uhlenbeck process that was described in (7.2), then the dynamics of P can be specified as (7.4).

$$
\begin{aligned}
dP &= P_r\,[a(b-r)dt + \sigma\,dz] + \tfrac{1}{2}\,P_{rr}\,\sigma^2\,dt + P_t dt \\
&= \left[P_r\,a(b-r) + \tfrac{1}{2}\,P_{rr}\,\sigma^2 + P_t\right]dt + P_r\sigma\,dz \qquad\qquad (7.4) \\
&= a(r,\,t)dt + \sigma(r,\,t)\,dz.
\end{aligned}
$$

What we have done is to transform the dynamics of the bond price in terms of the drift and volatility of the short rate. Equation (7.4) states that the bond price depends on the drift of the short rate, and the volatility.

Itô's lemma is used as part of the process of building a term structure model. The generic process this follows involves:

▪ specifying the random or stochastic process followed by the short rate, for which we must make certain assumptions about the short rate itself;

▪ using Itô's lemma to transform the dynamics of the zero-coupon bond price in terms of the short rate;

▪ imposing no-arbitrage conditions, based on the principle of hedging a position in one bond with one in another bond of a different maturity (for a one-factor model), in order to derive the partial differential equation of the zero-coupon bond price (for a two-factor model we would require two bonds as hedging instrument);

▪ solving the partial differential equation for the bond price, which is subject to the condition that the price of a zero-coupon bond on maturity is 1.

In the next section we review some of the models that are used in this process.

One-factor term structure models

In this section we discuss briefly a number of popular term structure models and summarize the advantages and disadvantages of each, which renders them useful or otherwise under certain conditions and user requirements.

The Vasicek model

The Vasicek model (1977) was the first term structure model described in the academic literature and is a yield-based one-factor equilibrium model. It assumes that the short-rate

2. This is the great value of Itô's lemma – a mechanism by which we can transform a partial differential equation.

process follows a normal distribution. The model incorporates mean reversion and is popular with certain practitioners as well as academics because it is analytically tractable.[3] Although it has a constant volatility element, the mean reversion feature means that the model removes the certainty of a negative interest rate over the long term. However, other practitioners do not favour the model because it is not necessarily arbitrage-free with respect to the prices of actual bonds in the market.

So the instantaneous short rate described in the Vasicek model is:

$$dr = a(b - r)dt + \sigma dz \tag{7.5}$$

where a is the speed of the mean reversion and b is the mean reversion level or the long-run value of r.

z is the standard Weiner process, or Brownian motion, with a 0 mean and 1 standard deviation. In Vasicek's model the price at time t of a zero-coupon bond that matures at time T is given by:

$$P(t, T) = A(t,T)e^{-B(t, T)r(t)} \tag{7.6}$$

where $r(t)$ is the short rate at time t and

$$B(t, T) = \frac{1 - e^{-a(T - t)}}{a}$$

and

$$A(t, T) = \exp\left[\frac{(B(t, T) - T + t)(a^2b - \sigma^2/2)}{a^2} - \frac{\sigma^2 B(t, T)^2}{4a}\right].$$

The derivation of (7.6) is given in a number of texts (not least the original article!); we recommend section 5.3 in Van Deventer and Imai (1997) for its accessibility.

Note that in certain texts the model is written as:

$$dr = \kappa(\theta - r)dt + \sigma dz$$

or

$$dr = a(\mu - r)dt + \sigma dZ$$

but it just depends on which symbol the particular text is using. We use the form shown at (7.5) because it is consistent with discussion elsewhere in this book.

In Vasicek's model the short rate r is normally distributed, so therefore it can be negative with positive probability. The occurrence of negative rates is dependent on the initial

---

3. *Tractability* is much prized in a yield curve model, and refers to the ease with which a model can be implemented, that is, with which yield curves can be computed.

interest rate level and the parameters chosen for the model, and is an extreme possibility. For instance, a very low initial rate, such as that observed in the Japanese economy for some time now, and volatility levels set with the market, have led to negative rates when using the Vasicek model. This possibility, which also applies to a number of other interest rate models, is inconsistent with a no-arbitrage market because investors will hold cash rather than opt to invest at a negative interest rate.[4] However, for most applications the model is robust and its tractability makes it popular with practitioners.

The Ho-Lee model

The Ho-Lee model (1986) was an early arbitrage-free yield-based model. It is often called the extended Merton model because it is an extension of an earlier model described by Merton (1970).[5] It is called an arbitrage model because it is used to fit a given initial yield curve. The model assumes a normally distributed short rate, and the drift of the short rate is dependent on time, which makes the model arbitrage-free with respect to observed prices in the market, as these are the inputs to the model.

The model is given at (7.7):

$$dr = a(t)dt + \sigma dz. \tag{7.7}$$

The bond price equation is given as:

$$P(t, T) = A(t, T)e^{-r(t)(T-t)} \tag{7.8}$$

where $r(t)$ is the rate at time t and

$$\ln A(t, T) = \ln \left(\frac{P(0, T)}{P(0, t)} \right) - (T - t) \frac{\delta \ln P(0, t)}{\delta t} - \frac{1}{2} \sigma^2 (T - t)^2.$$

There is no mean reversion feature incorporated, so that interest rates can fall to negative levels, which is a cause for concern for market practitioners.

The Hull-White model

The model described by Hull and White (1990) is another well-known model that fits the theoretical yield curve that one would obtain using Vasicek's model extracted from the actual observed market yield curve. As such, it is sometimes referred to as the extended Vasicek model, with time-dependent drift.[6] The model is popular with practitioners precisely because it enables them to calculate a theoretical yield curve that is identical to

---

4. This is stated in Black (1995).
5. The reference in the bibliography is a later publication of a collection of Merton's earlier papers.

yields observed in the market, which can then be used to price bonds and bond derivatives and also to calculate hedges.

The model is given at (7.9):

$$dr = a\left(\frac{b(t)}{a} - r\right)dt + \sigma dz \tag{7.9}$$

where a is the rate of mean reversion and $\frac{b(t)}{a}$ is a time-dependent mean reversion.

The price at time t of a zero-coupon bond with maturity T is:

$$P(t, T) = A(t, T)e^{-B(t, T)r(t)}$$

where $r(t)$ is the short rate at time t and

$$B(t, T) = \frac{1-e^{-a(T-t)}}{a}$$

$$\ln A(t, T) = \ln\left[\frac{P(0, T)}{P(0, t)}\right] - B(T, t)\frac{\delta P(0, t)}{\delta t} - \frac{v(t, T)^2}{2}$$

and

$$v(t, T)^2 = \frac{1}{2a^3}\sigma^2 (e^{-aT} - e^{-at})^2(e^{2at} - 1).$$

Further one-factor term structure models

The academic literature and market application have thrown up a number of term structure models as alternatives to the Vasicek model, and models based on it, such as the Hull-White model. As with these two models, each possesses a number of advantages and disadvantages. As we noted in the previous section, the main advantage of Vasicek-type models is their analytic tractability, with the assumption of the dynamics of the interest rate allowing the analytical solution of bonds and interest-rate instruments. The main weakness of these models is that they permit the possibility of negative interest rates. While negative interest rates are not a market impossibility,[7] the thinking would appear to be that they are a function of more than one factor, therefore modelling them using Vasicek-type models is not tenable. This aspect of the models does not necessarily preclude their use in practice, and will depend on the state of the economy at the time.

To consider an example, during 1997–8 Japanese money market interest rates were frequently below $\frac{1}{2}$ of 1%, and at this level even low levels of volatility below 5% will imply negative interest rates with high probability if using Vasicek's model. In this envi-

6. Haug (1998) also states that the Hull-White model is essentially the Ho-Lee model with mean reversion.

7. Negative interest rates manifest themselves most obviously in the market for specific bonds in repo which have gone excessively special. However, academic researchers often prefer to work with interest rate environments that do not consider negative rates a possibility (for example, see Black (1995)).

ronment, practitioners may wish to use models that do not admit the possibility of nega-tive interest rates, perhaps those that model more than the short rate alone – the so-called two-factor and multi-factor models. We look briefly at these in the next section. First we consider, again briefly, a number of other one-factor models. As usual, readers are encouraged to review the bibliography articles for the necessary background and further detail on application.

The Cox-Ingersoll-Ross model

Although published officially in 1985, the Cox-Ingersoll-Ross (CIR) model was apparently described in academic circles in 1977 or perhaps earlier, which would make it the first interest rate model. Like the Vasicek model, it is a one-factor model that defines interest rate movements in terms of the dynamics of the short rate; however, it incorporates an additional feature whereby the variance of the short rate is related to the level of interest rates, and this feature has the effect of not allowing negative interest rates. It also reflects a higher interest rate volatility in periods of relatively high interest rates, and correspon-ding lower volatility when interest rates are lower.

The model is given at (7.10):

$$dr = k(b - r)dt + \sigma \sqrt{r} dz. \tag{7.10}$$

The derivation of the zero-coupon bond price equation given at (7.11) is contained in Ingersoll (1987), Chapter 18. The symbol τ represents the term to maturity of the bond or $(T - t)$.

$$P(r, \tau) = A(\tau)e^{-B(\tau)r} \tag{7.11}$$

where

$$A(\tau) = \left[\frac{2\gamma e^{(\gamma + \lambda + k)\frac{\tau}{2}}}{g(\tau)} \right]^{\frac{2kb}{\sigma^2}}$$

$$B(\tau) = \frac{-2(1 - e^{-\gamma\tau})}{g(\tau)}$$

$$g(\tau) = 2\gamma + (k + \lambda + \gamma)(e^{\gamma\tau} - 1)$$

$$\gamma = \sqrt{(k + \lambda)^2 + 2\sigma^2}.$$

Some researchers[8] have stated that the difficulties in determining parameters for the CIR model have limited its use among market practitioners.

---

8. For instance see Van Deventer and Imai (1997) citing Fleseker (1993) on p. 336, although the authors go on to state that the CIR model is deserving of further empirical analysis and remains worthwhile for practical application.

The Black-Derman-Toy model

The Black-Derman-Toy (BDT) model (1990) also removes the possibility of negative interest rates and is commonly encountered in the markets. The parameters specified in the model are time-dependent, and the dynamics of the short-rate process incorporate changes in the level of the rate. The model is given at (7.12):

$$d[\ln(r)] = [\vartheta(t) - \phi(t)\ln(r)]dt + \sigma(t)dz \qquad (7.12)$$

The model is popular among market practitioners because:

■ it fits the market-observed yield curve, similar to the Hull-White model;

■ there is no allowance for negative interest rates;

■ it models the volatility levels of interest rates in the market.

Against this, the model is not considered particularly tractable or able to be programmed for rapid calculation. Nevertheless it is important in the market, particularly for interest rate derivative market-makers. An excellent and accessible description of the BDT model is contained in Sundaresan (1997) on pp. 240–4; Tuckman (1996) pp. 102–6 is also recommended.

The Heath-Jarrow-Morton model

We have devoted a separate section to the approach described by Heath, Jarrow and Morton (1992) because it is a radical departure from the earlier family of interest rate models. As usual, a fuller exposition can be found in the references listed in the bibliography.

The Heath-Jarrow-Morton (HJM) approach to the specification of stochastic state variables is different to that used in earlier models. The previous models describe interest rate dynamics in terms of the short rate as the single or (in two- and multi-factor models) key state variable. With multi-factor models, the specification of the state variables is the fundamental issue in the practical application of the models themselves. In the HJM model, the entire term structure and not just the short rate is taken to be the state variable. It has been seen previously how the term structure can be defined in terms of default-free zero-coupon bond prices, yields, spot rates or forward rates. The HJM approach uses forward rates. So in the single-factor HJM model the change in forward rates at current time t, with a maturity at time u, is captured by:

■ a volatility function;

■ a drift function;

■ a geometric Brownian or Weiner process that describes the shocks or *noise* experienced by the term structure.

The importance of the Heath-Jarrow-Morton presentation is that in a market that permits no arbitrage, where interest rates including forward rates are assumed to follow a Weiner process, the drift term and the volatility term in the model's stochastic differential equation are not independent from each other, and in fact the drift term is a deterministic function of the volatility term. This has significant practical implications for the pricing and hedging of interest rate options.

The single-factor HJM model

The general form of the HJM model is very complex, principally because it is a multi-factor model. We will begin by describing the single-factor HJM model. This section is based on Chapter 5 of Baxter and Rennie (1996) and follows the approach in that text (with permission). This is an accessible and excellent text and is strongly recommended. Another recommended reading is James and Webber (2000).

In previous analysis we have defined the *forward rate* as the interest rate applicable to a loan made at a future point in time and repayable instantaneously. We assume that the dynamics of the forward rate follow a Weiner process. The *spot rate* is the rate for borrowing undertaken now and maturing at T, and we know from previous analysis that it is the geometric average of the forward rates from 0 to T, that is:

$$r(0, T) = T^{-1} \int_t^T f(0, t)d. \tag{7.13}$$

We also specify a money market account that accumulates interest at the continuously compounded spot rate r.

A default-free zero-coupon bond can be defined in terms of its current value under an *initial probability measure*, which is the Weiner process that describes the forward rate dynamics, and its price or present value under this probability measure. This leads us to the HJM model, in that we are required to determine what is termed a 'change in probability measure', such that the dynamics of the zero-coupon bond price are transformed into a *martingale*. This is carried out using Itô's lemma and a transformation of the differential equation of the bond price process. It can then be shown that in order to prevent arbitrage there would have to be a relationship between the drift rate of the forward rate and its volatility coefficient.

First we look at the forward rate process. We know (from the previous chapter) that for a term $[0, T]$ at time t the stochastic evolution of the forward rate $f(t, T)$ can be described as:

$$df(t, T) = a(t, T)dt + \sigma(t, T)dz_t \tag{7.14}$$

or alternatively in integral form as:

$$f(t, T) = f(0, T) + \int_0^t a(s, T)ds + \int_0^t \sigma(s, T)dz_s \tag{7.15}$$

where a is the drift parameter, σ the volatility coefficient and z_t is the Weiner process or Brownian motion. The terms dZ or dW are sometimes used to denote the Weiner process.

In (7.14) the drift and volatility coefficients are functions of time t and T. For all forward rates $f(t, T)$ in the period $[0, T]$ the only source of uncertainty is the Brownian motion. In practice this would mean that all forward rates would be perfectly positively correlated, irrespective of their terms to maturity. However, if we introduce the feature that there is more than one source of uncertainty in the evolution of interest rates, it would result in less than perfect correlation of interest rates, which is what is described by the HJM model.

Before we come to that, however, we wish to describe the spot rate and the money market account processes. In (7.15), under the particular condition of the maturity point T as it tends towards t (that is $T \to t$), the forward rate tends to approach the value of the short rate (spot rate), so we have:

$$\lim_{T \to t} f(t, T) = f(t, t) = r(t)$$

so that it can be shown that:

$$r(t) = f(0, t) + \int_0^t a(s, t)ds + \int_0^t \sigma(s, t)dz_s. \tag{7.16}$$

The money market account is also described by a Weiner process. We denote by $M(t, t) \equiv M(t)$ the value of the money market account at time t, which has an initial value of 1 at time 0 so that $M(0, 0) = 1$. This account earns interest at the spot rate $r(t)$ which means that at time t the value of the account is given by:

$$M(t) = e^{\int_0^t r(s)ds} \tag{7.17}$$

which is the interest accumulated at the continuously compounded spot rate $r(t)$. It can be shown by substituting (7.16) into (7.17) that:

$$M(t) = \exp[\int_0^t f(0, s)ds + \int_0^t \int_0^s a(u, s)du\, ds + \int_0^t \int_0^s \sigma(u, s)dz_u ds]. \tag{7.18}$$

To simplify the description we write the double integrals in (7.18) (!) in the form given below:

$$\int_0^t \int_s^t a(s, u)du\, ds + \int_0^t \int_s^t o(s, u)du\, dz_s.$$

The description of the process by which this simplification is achieved can be found on the author's website at www.YieldCurve.com.

Using the simplification above, it can be shown that the value of the money market account, which is growing by an amount generated by the continuously compounded spot rate $r(t)$, is given by:

$$M(t) = \exp[\int_0^t f(0, u)du + \int_0^t \int_s^t a(s, u)du\, ds + \int_0^t \int_s^t \sigma(s, u)du\, dz_s]. \tag{7.19}$$

The expression for the value of the money market account can be used to determine the expression for the zero-coupon bond price, which we denote $B(t, T)$. The money market account earns interest at the spot rate $r(t)$, while the bond price is the present value of 1 discounted at this rate. Therefore the inverse of (7.19) is required, which is:

$$M^{-1}(t) = e^{-\int_0^t r(u)du}. \qquad (7.20)$$

Hence the present value at time 0 of the bond $B(t, T)$ is:

$$B(t, T) = e^{-\int_0^t r(u)du} B(t, T).$$

and it can be shown that as a Weiner process the present value is given by:

$$B(t, T) = \exp[-\int_0^t f(0, u)du - \int_0^t \int_s^T o(s, u)du \, dz_s - \int_0^t \int_s^T a(s, u)du \, ds]. \qquad (7.21)$$

It can be shown that the forward rate expressed as an integral is:

$$f(t, T) = f(0, T) + \int_0^t a(s, T)ds + \sigma dz \qquad (7.22)$$

which assumes that the forward rate is normally distributed. Crucially, the different forward rates of maturity $f(0,1)$, $f(0,2)\ldots f(0, T)$ are assumed to be perfectly correlated. The random element is the Brownian motion dz, and the impact of this process is felt over time, rather than over different maturities.

The forward rate for any maturity period T will develop as described by the drift and volatility parameters $a(t, T)$ and $\sigma(t, T)$. In the single-factor HJM model the random character of the forward-rate process is captured by the Brownian motion dz.[9] Under HJM the primary assumption is that for each T the drift and volatility processes are dependent only on the history of the Brownian motion process up to the current time t, and on the forward rates themselves up to time t.

The multi-factor HJM model

Under the single-factor HJM model the movement in forward rates of all maturities is perfectly correlated. This can be too much of a restriction for market application, for example when pricing an interest rate instrument that is dependent on the yield spread between two points on the yield curve. In the multi-factor model, each of the state variables is described by its own Brownian motion process.[10] So, for example, in an m-factor model there would be m Brownian motions in the model, dz_1, dz_2, ..., dz_m. This allows each T-maturity forward rate to be described by its own volatility level $\sigma_i(t, T)$ and Brownian motion process dz_i. Under this approach, the different forward rates given by the different

---

9. Note that certain texts use α for the drift term and W_t for the random term.
10. For a good introduction, see Chapter 6 in Baxter and Rennie (1996).

maturity bonds that describe the current term structure evolve under more appropriate random processes, and different correlations between forward rates of differing maturities can be accommodated.

The multi-factor HJM model is given at (7.23):

$$f(t, T) = f(0, T) + \int_0^t a(s, T)ds + \sum_{i=1}^m \int_0^t \sigma_i(s, T)dz_i(s).$$ (7.23)

Equation (7.23) states that the dynamics of the forward rate process, beginning with the initial rate $f(0, T)$, are specified by the set of Brownian motion processes and the drift parameter.

For practical application the evolution of the forward-rate term structure is usually carried out as a binomial-type path-dependent process. However, path-independent processes have also been used. The HJM approach has become popular in the market, both for yield curve modelling and for pricing derivative instruments, due to the realistic effect of matching yield curve maturities to different volatility levels, and it is reasonably tractable when applied using the binomial-tree approach. Simulation modelling based on Monte Carlo techniques are also used. For further detail on the former approach see Jarrow (1996).

Choosing a term structure model

Selection of an appropriate term structure model is more of an art than a science. The different types of model available, and the different applications and user requirements, mean that it is not necessarily clear-cut which approach should be selected. For example, a practitioner's requirements will determine whether a single-factor model or a two- or multi-factor model is more appropriate. The Ho-Lee and BDT models, for example, are *arbitrage* models, which means that they are designed to match the current term structure. With arbitrage (or arbitrage-free) models, assuming that the specification of the evolution of the short rate is correct, the law of no arbitrage can be used to determine the price of interest rate derivatives.

There is also a class of interest rate models known as *equilibrium* models, which make an assumption of the dynamics of the short rate in the same way as arbitrage models do, but are not designed to match the current term structure. With equilibrium models, therefore, the price of zero-coupon bonds given by the model-derived term structure is not required to (and does not) match prices seen in the market. This means that the prices of bonds and interest rate derivatives are not given purely by the short rate process. Overall then, arbitrage models take the current yield curve as described by the market prices of default-free bonds as given, whereas equilibrium models do not.

What considerations must be taken into account when deciding which term structure model to use? Some of the key factors include:

- *Ease of application*: The key input to arbitrage models is the current spot rate term structure, which is straightforward to determine using the market price of bonds currently trading in the market. This is an advantage over equilibrium models, whose inputs are more difficult to obtain.

- *Capturing market imperfections*: The term structure generated by an arbitrage model will reflect the current market term structure, which may include pricing irregularities due to liquidity, tax and other considerations. If this is not desired, it is a weakness of the arbitrage approach. Equilibrium models would not reflect pricing imperfections.

- *Pricing bonds and interest rate derivatives*: Traditional seat-of-the-pants market making often employs a combination of the trader's nous, the range of prices observed in the market (often from inter-dealer broker screens) and gut feeling to price bonds. For a more scientific approach, or for relative value trading,[11] a yield curve model may well be desirable. In this case an equilibrium model is clearly the preferred model, as the trader will want to compare the theoretical price given by the model compared to the actual price observed in the market. An arbitrage model would not be appropriate because it would take the observed yield curve, and hence the market bond price, as given, and so would assume that the market bond prices were correct. Put another way, using an arbitrage model for relative value trading would suggest to the trader that there was no gain to be made from entering into, say, a yield curve spread trade. Pricing derivative instruments, such as interest rate options or swaptions, requires a different emphasis. This is because the primary consideration of the derivative market-maker is the technique and price of hedging the derivative. That is, upon writing a derivative contract the market-maker will simultaneously hedge the exposure using either the underlying asset, or a combination of this and other derivatives such as exchange-traded futures. The derivative market-maker generates profit through extracting premium and from the difference in price over time between the price of the derivative and the underlying hedge position. For this reason only an arbitrage model is appropriate, as it would price the derivative relative to the market, which is important for a market-maker; an equilibrium model would price the derivative relative to the theoretical market, which would not be appropriate since it is a market instrument that is being used as the hedge.

---

11. For example, yield curve trades – where bonds of different maturities are spread against each other, with the trader betting on the change in spread as opposed to the direction of interest rates – are a form of relative value trade.

■ *Use of models over time*: Initially, the parameters used in an interest rate model, most notably the drift, volatility and (if applicable) mean reversion rate, reflect the state of the economy up to that point. This state is not constant, and so consequently over time any model must be continually *recalibrated* to reflect the current market state. That is, the drift rate used today when calculating the term structure may well be a different value tomorrow. This puts arbitrage models at a disadvantage, because their parameters will be changed continuously in this way. Put another way, use of arbitrage models is not consistent over time. Equilibrium model parameters are calculated from historic data or from intuitive logic, and so may not be changed as frequently. However, their accuracy over time may suffer. It is up to users to decide whether they prefer the continual tweaking of the arbitrage model over the more consistent use of the equilibrium model.

This is just the beginning; there is a range of issues that must be considered by users when selecting an interest rate model. For example, in practice it has been observed that models incorporating mean reversion work more accurately than those that do not feature this. Another factor is the computer-processing power available to the user, and it is often the case that single-factor models are preferred precisely because processing is more straightforward. A good account of the different factors to be considered when assessing which model to use is given in Chapter 15 of James and Webber (2000), and Tuckman (1996), Chapter 9.

SELECTED BIBLIOGRAPHY AND REFERENCES

Baxter, M., Rennie, A., *Financial Calculus*, Cambridge University Press 1996, pp. 57–62.

Black, F., 'Interest rates as options', *Journal of Finance*, December 1995, pp. 1371–6.

Black, F., Derman, E., Toy, W., 'A one-factor model of interest rates and its application to Treasury bond options', *Financial Analysts Journal*, spring 1990, pp. 33–9.

Brennan, M., Schwartz, E., 'A continuous-time approach to the pricing of bonds', *Journal of Banking and Finance 3*, 1979, pp. 133–55.

Campbell, J., 'A defence of traditional hypotheses about the term structure of interest rates', *Journal of Finance 41*, 1986, pp. 183–93.

Chen, R-R., Scott, L., 'Pricing interest rate options in a two-factor Cox-Ingersoll-Ross model of the term structure', *Review of Financial Studies*, winter 1992, pp. 613–36.

Choudhry, M., *Bond Market Securities*, FT Prentice Hall 2001.

Cox, J., Ingersoll, J., Ross, S., 'A theory of the term structure of interest rates', *Econometrica 53*, March 1985, pp. 385–407.

Fleseker, B., 'Testing the Heath-Jarrow-Morton/Ho-Lee Model of Interest Contingent Claims Pricing', *Journal of Financial and Quantitive Analysis*, 1993 pp. 483–96.

Fong, H.G., Vasicek, O., 'Fixed income volatility management', *Journal of Portfolio Management*, summer 1991, pp. 41–6.

Haug, E., *The Complete Guide to Option Pricing Formulas*, McGraw-Hill 1998, Chapter 4.

Heath, D., Jarrow, R., Morton, A., 'Bond pricing and the term structure of interest rates: a new methodology for contingent claims valuation', *Econometrica* 60, January 1992, pp. 77–105.

Ho, T., Lee, S-B., 'Term structure movements and pricing interest rate contingent claims', *Journal of Finance*, December 1986, pp. 1011–29.

Hull, J., *Options, Futures and other Derivatives*, 3rd edition, Prentice Hall 1997, pp. 220–2.

Hull, J., White, A., 'Pricing interest rate derivative securities', *Review of Financial Studies*, 1990, pp. 573–92.

Ingersoll, J., *Theory of Financial Decision Making*, Rowman & Littlefield 1987.

James, J., Webber, N., *Interest Rate Modelling*, Wiley 2000, Chapters 5–15.

Jarrow, R., *Modeling Fixed Income Securities and Interest Rate Options*, McGraw-Hill 1996.

Merton, R., *Continuous Time Finance*, Blackwell 1993, Chapter 11.

Rebonato, R., *Interest Rate Option Models*, Wiley 1996.

Rebonato, R., Cooper, I., 'The limitations of simple two-factor interest rate models', *Journal of Financial Engineering*, March 1996.

Ross, S.M., *An Introduction to Mathematical Finance*, Cambridge University Press 1999.

Ross, S.M., *Probability Models*, Academic Press 2000.

Sundaresan, S., *Fixed Income Markets and their Derivatives*, South Western Publishing 1997.

Tuckman, B., *Fixed Income Securities*, Wiley 1996.

Van Deventer, D., Imai, K., *Financial Risk Analytics*, Irwin 1997, Chapter 5.

Vasicek, O., 'An equilibrium characterization of the term structure', *Journal of Financial Economics* 5, 1977, pp. 177–88.

CHAPTER 8

Fitting the yield curve

In this chapter we consider some of the techniques used to actually fit the term structure. In theory we could use the bootstrapping approach described earlier. For a number of reasons, this does not produce accurate results, and so other methods are used instead. The term structure models described in the previous chapter defined the interest rate process under various assumptions about the nature of the stochastic process that drives these rates. However, the zero-coupon curve derived by models such as those described by Vasicek (1977), Brennan and Schwartz (1979) and Cox, Ingersoll and Ross (1985) does not fit the observed market rates or spot rates implied by market yields, and generally market yield curves are found to contain more variable shapes than those derived using term structure models. Hence the interest rate models described in Chapter 7 are required to be *calibrated* to the market, and in practice they are calibrated to the market yield curve. This is carried out in two ways: the model is either calibrated to market instruments such as money market products and interest rate swaps, which are used to construct the yield curve, or the yield curve is constructed from market instrument rates and the model is calibrated to this constructed curve. If the latter approach is preferred, there are a number of *non-parametric* methods that may be used. We will consider these later.

In this chapter we present an overview of some of the methods used to fit the yield curve.

Yield curve smoothing[1]

Introduction

An approach that has been used to estimate the term structure was described by Carleton and Cooper (1976). It assumes that default-free bond cash flows are payable on specified discrete dates, with a set of unrelated discount factors that apply to each cash flow. These

1. Large parts of this section previously appeared in Choudhry (2001).

discount factors are then estimated as regression coefficients, with each bond cash flow acting as the independent variables, and the bond price for that date acting as the dependent variable.[2] Using simple linear regression in this way produces a discrete discount function, not a continuous one, and forward rates that are estimated from this function are very jagged. An approach more readily accepted by the market was described by McCulloch (1971), who fitted the discount function using polynomial splines. This method produces a continuous function, and one that is linear so that the *ordinary least squares* regression technique can be employed. In a later study, Langetieg and Smoot (1981)[3] use an extended McCulloch method, fitting *cubic splines* to zero-coupon rates instead of the discount function, and using non-linear methods of estimation.

That is the historical summary of early efforts. But let's get back to the beginning. We know that the term structure can be described as the complete set of discount factors, the discount function, which can be extracted from the price of default-free bonds trading in the market. The bootstrapping technique described in Chapter 4 may be used to extract the relevant discount factors. However, there are a number of reasons why this approach is problematic in practice. First, it is unlikely that the complete set of bonds in the market will pay cash flows at precise six-month intervals every six months from today to 30 years or longer. An adjustment needs to be made for cash flows received at irregular intervals, and for the lack of cash flows available at longer maturities. Another issue is the fact that the technique presented earlier allows practitioners to calculate the discount factor for six-month maturities, whereas it may be necessary in practice to determine the discount factor for non-standard periods, such as four-month or 14.2-year maturities. This is often the case when pricing derivative instruments.

A third issue concerns the market price of bonds. This often reflects specific investor considerations, which include:

■ the liquidity or lack thereof of certain bonds, caused by issue sizes, market-maker support, investor demand, non-standard maturity, and a host of other factors;

■ the fact that bonds do not trade continuously, so that some bond prices will be 'newer' than others;

■ the tax treatment of bond cash flows, and the effect that this has on bond prices;

■ the effect of the bid–offer spread on the market prices used.

The statistical term used for bond prices subject to these considerations is *error*. It is also common to come across the statement that these effects introduce *noise* into market prices.

2. The basics of regression are summarized in Appendix 5.1 of Choudhry (2001). Readers who wish to get a firm grasp of econometric techniques used in financial market analysis should consult Gujarati (1995).
3. Reference in Vasicek and Fong (1982).

Smoothing techniques

A common technique that may be used, but which is not accurate enough and so not recommended for market use, is *linear interpolation*. In this approach the set of bond prices is used to graph a redemption yield curve (as in the previous section), and where bonds are not available for the required maturity term, the yield is interpolated from actual yields. Using UK gilt yields for 9 November 2000, we plot this as shown in Figure 8.1. The interpolated yields are marked on the x-axis with an asterisk. Figure 8.1 looks reasonable for any practitioner's purpose. However, spot and forward yields that are obtained from this curve using the linear interpolation technique are apt to behave in unrealistic fashion, as shown in Figure 8.2.[4] The forward curve is very bumpy, and each bump will correspond to a bond used in the original set. The spot rate has a kink at three years and again at nine years, and so the forward curve jumps significantly at these points. This curve would appear to be particularly unrealistic.

For this reason, market analysts do not usually consider linear interpolation and instead use exponential interpolation, multiple regression or spline-based methods. One approach might be to assume a functional form for the discount function and estimate parameters of this form from the prices of bonds in the market. We consider these approaches next.

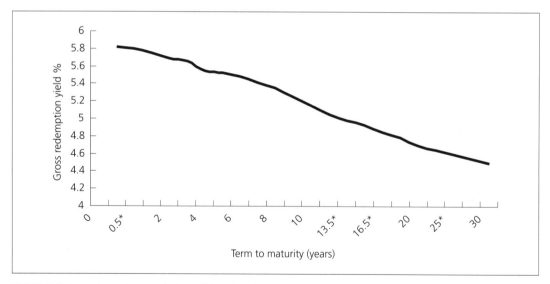

FIGURE 8.1 ■ Linear interpolation of bond yields, 9 November 2000
Source: Bloomberg L.P.

4. The spot and forward yield curves were calculated using the RATE application software.

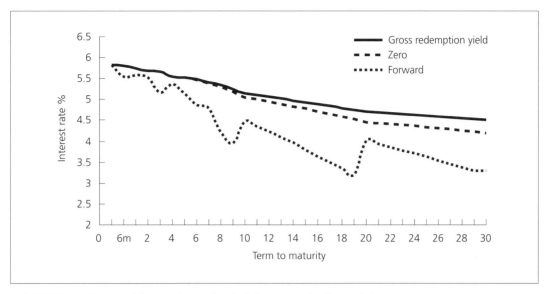

FIGURE 8.2 ■ Spot and forward rates implied from rates in Figure 8.1

Using a cubic polynomial

A simple functional form for the discount function is a *cubic polynomial*. This approach consists of approximating the set of discount factors using a cubic function of time. If we say that *d(t)* is the discount factor for maturity *t*, we approximate the set of discount factors using the following cubic function:

$$\hat{d}(t) = a_0 + a_1(t) + a_2(t)^2 + a_3(t)^3. \tag{8.1}$$

In some texts the coefficients sometimes are written as *a*, *b*, and *c* rather than a_1 and so on.

The discount factor for *t* = 0, that is at time now, is 1. Therefore a_0 = 1, and (8.1) can then be rewritten as:

$$\hat{d}(t) - 1 = a_1(t) + a_2(t)^2 + a_3(t)^3. \tag{8.2}$$

The market price of a traded coupon bond can be expressed in terms of discount factors. So at (8.3) we show the expression for the price of an *N*-maturity bond paying identical coupons *C* at regular intervals and redeemed at maturity at *M*:

$$P = d(t_1)C + d(t_2)C + \ldots + d(t_N)(C + M). \tag{8.3}$$

Using the cubic polynomial equation (8.2), expression (8.3) is transformed into:

$$P = C\left[1 + a_1(t_1) + a_2(t_1)^2 + a_3(t_1)^3\right] + \ldots + (C + M)\left[1 + a_1(t_N) + a_2(t_N)^2 + a_3(t_N)^3\right]. \tag{8.4}$$

We require the coefficients of the cubic function in order to start describing the yield curve, so we rearrange (8.4) in order to express it in terms of these coefficients. This is shown at (8.5):

$$P = M + \sum C + a_1[C(t_1) + ... + (C + M)(t_N)] + a_2[C(t_1)^2 + ...$$
$$+ (C + M)(t_N)^2] + a_3[C(t_1)^3 + ... + (C + M)(t_N)^3]. \qquad (8.5)$$

In the same way, we can express the pricing equation for each bond in our data set in terms of the unknown parameters of the cubic function. From (8.5) we may write:

$$P - (M + \sum C) = a_1 X_1 + a_2 X_2 + a_3 X_3 \qquad (8.6)$$

where X_i is the appropriate expression in square brackets in (8.5); this is the form in which the expression is encountered commonly in textbooks.

In practice, the cubic polynomial approach is too limited a technique, requiring one equation per bond, and does not have the required flexibility to fit market data satisfactorily. The resulting curve is not really a curve but rather a set of independent discount factors that have been fit with a line of best fit. In addition, the impact of small changes in the data can be significant at the non-local level, so for example a change in a single data point at the early maturities can result in badly behaved longer maturities. An alternative approach is for a *piecewise cubic polynomial* to be used, whereby $d(t)$ is assumed to be a different cubic polynomial over each maturity range. This means that the parameters a_1, a_2, and a_3 will be different over each maturity range. We will look at a special case of this use, the cubic spline, a little later.

Non-parametric methods

Besides the cubic polynomial approach described in the previous section there are two main approaches to fitting the term structure. These are usually grouped into *parametric* and *non-parametric* curves. Parametric curves are based on term structure models such as the Vasicek model or Longstaff and Schwartz model. Non-parametric curves are not derived from an interest rate model and are general approaches, described using a set of parameters. They include spline-based methods.

Spline-based methods

A spline is a statistical technique and a form of interpolation. There is more than one way of applying them, and the most straightforward method to understand the process is the spline function fitted using regression techniques. For the purposes of yield curve construction, this method can cause curves to jump wildly and make them over-sensitive to changes in parameters.[5] However, we feel it is the most accessible method to understand; an introduction to the basic technique, as described in Suits *et al.* (1978), is given in Appendix 5.2 of Choudhry (2001).[6]

An *n*-th order spline is a piecewise polynomial approximation with *n*-degree polynomials that are differentiable *n*-1 times. Piecewise means that the different polynomials are connected at arbitrarily selected points known as *knot points* (see Appendix 5.2 of Choudhry (2001)). A cubic spline is a three-order spline, and is a piecewise cubic polynomial that is differentiable twice along all its points.

The *x*-axis in the regression is divided into segments at arbitrary points – the knot points. At each knot point the slopes of adjoining curves are required to match, as must the curvature. Figure 8.3 is a cubic spline. The knot points are selected at 0, 2, 5, 10 and 25 years. At each of these points the curve is a cubic polynomial, and with this function we could accommodate a high and low in each space bounded by the knot points.

Cubic spline interpolation assumes that there is a cubic polynomial that can estimate the yield curve at each maturity gap. A spline can be thought of as a number of separate polynomials of $y = f(X)$ where X is the complete range, divided into user-specified segments,

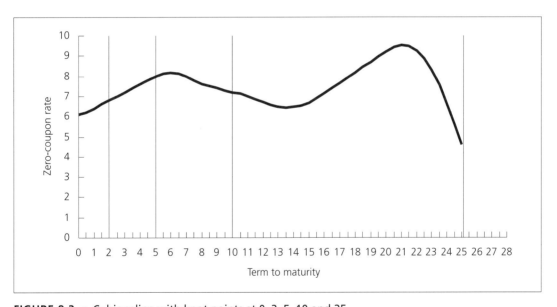

FIGURE 8.3 ▪ Cubic spline with knot points at 0, 2, 5, 10 and 25

which are joined smoothly at the knot points. If we have a set of bond yields r_0, r_1, r_2, ... r_n at maturity points t_0, t_1, t_2, ... t_n, we can estimate the cubic spline function in the following way:

■ the yield on bond i at time t is expressed as a cubic polynomial of the form $r_i(t) = a_i + b_i t + c_i t^2 + d_i t^3$ for the interval over t_i and t_{i-1};

■ the coefficients of the cubic polynomial are calculated for all n intervals between the $n + 1$ data points, which results in $4n$ unknown coefficients that must be computed;

■ these equations can be solved because they are made to fit the observed data. They are twice differentiable at the knot points, and these derivatives are equal at these points;

■ the constraints specified are that the curve is instantaneously straight at the start of the curve (the shortest maturity) and instantaneously straight at the end of the curve, the longest maturity, that is $r''(0) = 0$.

An accessible and readable account of this technique can be found in Van Deventer and Imai (1997).

The general formula for a cubic spline is:

$$s(\tau) = \sum_{i=0}^{3} a_i \tau^i + \frac{1}{3!} \sum_{p=1}^{n-1} b_p (\tau - X_p)^3 \qquad (8.7)$$

where τ is the time of receipt of cash flows and where X_p refers to the points where adjacent polynomials are joined (these are the knot points), with

$$\{X_0, ..., X_n\}, X_p < X_{p+1}, P = 0, ..., n-1$$

In addition

$$(\tau - X_p) = \max (\tau - X_p, 0).$$

The cubic spline is twice differentiable at the knot points. In practice, the spline is written down as a set of basis functions, with the general spline being made up of a combination of these. One way to do this is by using what are known as *B-splines*. For a specified number of knot points $\{X_0, ..., X_n\}$ this is given by (8.8):

$$B_p(\tau) = \sum_{j=p}^{p+4} \left(\prod_{i=p, i \neq 1}^{p+4} \frac{1}{X_i - X_j} \right) (\tau - X_p)^3 \qquad (8.8)$$

where $B_p(\tau)$ are cubic splines which are approximated on $\{X_0, ..., X_n\}$ with the following function:

$$\delta(\tau) = \delta(\tau | \lambda_{-3}, ..., \lambda_{n-1}) = \sum_{p=-3}^{n-1} \lambda_p B_p(\tau) \qquad (8.9)$$

with $\lambda = (\lambda_{-3}, ..., \lambda_{n-1})$ the required coefficients.

The maturity periods $\tau_1,\ldots,\tau_n$ specify the B-splines so that:

$$B = \{B_p\,(\tau_j)\}_{p=-3,\ldots,n-1,\ j=1,\ldots,m}$$

and

$$\hat{\delta} = (\delta(\tau_1),\ldots,\delta(\tau_m))$$

This allows us to set:

$$\hat{\delta} = B'\lambda \tag{8.10}$$

and therefore the regression equation:

$$\lambda^* = \arg\min_{\lambda}\{\varepsilon'\varepsilon \,|\, \varepsilon = P - D\lambda\} \tag{8.11}$$

with $D=CB'$.

$\varepsilon'\varepsilon$ are the minimum errors. The regression at (8.11) is computed using ordinary least squares regression.

An advanced illustration of the use of B-splines is given in the next chapter. Appendix 5.2 of Choudhry (2001) provides background on splines fitted using regression methods.

Nelson and Siegel curves

The curve-fitting technique first described by Nelson and Siegel (1985) has since been applied and modified by other authors, which is why the techniques are sometimes described as a 'family' of curves. These curves provide a satisfactory rough fit of the complete term structure, with some loss of accuracy at the very short and very long ends. In the original curve the authors specify four parameters. The approach is not a bootstrapping technique, rather a method for estimating the zero-coupon rate function from the yields observed on T-bills, under an assumed function for forward rates.

The Nelson and Siegel curve states that the implied forward rate yield curve may be modelled along the entire term structure using the following function:

$$rf(m,\,\beta) = \beta_0 + \beta_1 \exp\left(\frac{-m}{t_1}\right) + \beta_2\left(\frac{m}{t_1}\right)\exp\left(\frac{-m}{t_1}\right) \tag{8.12}$$

where

$\beta = (\beta_0,\beta_1,\beta_2,t_1)$ is the vector of parameters describing the yield curve, and m is the maturity at which the forward rate is calculated. There are three components: the constant term, a decay term and term reflecting the 'humped' nature of the curve. The shape of the curve will gradually lead into an asymptote at the long end, the value of which is given by β_0, with a value of $\beta_0 + \beta_1$ at the short end.

A version of the Nelson and Siegel curve is the Svensson model (1995), with an adjustment to allow for the humped characteristic of the yield curve. This is fitted by adding an extension, as shown by (8.13):

$$rf(m, \beta) = \beta_0 + \beta_1 \exp\left(\frac{-m}{t_1}\right) + \beta_2 \left(\frac{m}{t_1}\right) \exp\left(\frac{-m}{t_1}\right) + \beta_3 \left(\frac{m}{t_2}\right) \exp\left(\frac{-m}{t_2}\right) \tag{8.13}$$

The Svensson curve is modelled therefore using six parameters, with additional input of β_3 and t_2.

Nelson and Siegel curves are popular in the market because they are straightforward to calculate. Jordan and Mansi (2000) state that one of the advantages of these curves is that they force the long-date forward curve into a horizontal asymptote, while another is that the user is not required to specify knot points, the choice of which determines the effectiveness or otherwise of cubic spline curves. The disadvantage they note is that these curves are less flexible than spline-based curves and there is therefore a chance that they do not fit the observed data as accurately as spline models.[7] James and Webber (2000, p. 444–5) also suggest that Nelson and Siegel curves are slightly inflexible due to the limited number of parameters – they are accurate for yield curves that have only one hump, but are unsatisfactory for curves that possess both a hump and a trough. As they are only reasonable for approximations, Nelson and Siegel curves would not be appropriate for no-arbitrage applications.

Comparing curves

Whichever curve is chosen will depend on the user's requirements and the purpose for which the model is required. The choice of modelling methodology is usually a trade-off between simplicity and ease of computation and accuracy. Essentially, the curve chosen must fulfil the qualities of:

- *Accuracy*: Is the curve a reasonable fit of the market curve? Is it flexible enough to accommodate a variety of yield curve shapes?
- *Model consistency*: Is the curve-fitting method consistent with a theoretical yield curve model such as Vasicek or Cox-Ingersoll-Ross?
- *Simplicity*: Is the curve reasonably straightforward to compute, that is, is it *tractable*?

7. This is an excellent article, strongly recommended. A good overview to curve fitting is given in the introduction, and the main body of the article gives a good insight into the type of research that is currently being undertaken in yield curve analysis.

The different methodologies all fit these requirements to a greater or lesser extent. A good summary of the advantages and disadvantages of some popular modelling methods can be found in James and Webber (2000, Chapter 15).

SELECTED BIBLIOGRAPHY AND REFERENCES

Anderson, N., Breedon, F., Deacon, M., Derry, A., Murphy, M., *Estimating and Interpreting the Yield Curve*, Wiley 1996.

Brennan, M., Schwartz, E., 'A continuous time approach to the pricing of bonds', *Journal of Banking and Finance*, July 1979, pp. 133–55.

Carleton, W., Cooper, I., 'Estimation and uses of the term structure of interest rates', *Journal of Finance*, September 1976, pp. 1067–83.

Choudhry, M., *Bond Market Securities*, FT Prentice Hall 2001.

Cox, J., Ingersoll, J., Ross, S., 'A theory of term structure of interest rates', *Econometrica* 53, March 1985, pp. 385–407.

Deacon, M., Derry, A., 'Estimating the term structure of interest rates', *Bank of England Working Paper* 24, July 1994.

Gujarati, D., *Basic Econometrics*, 3rd edition, McGraw-Hill 1995.

James, J., Webber, N., *Interest Rate Modelling*, Wiley 2000.

Jordan, J., Mansi, S., 'How well do constant-maturity Treasuries approximate the on-the-run term structure?', *Journal of Fixed Income* 10:2, September 2000, pp. 35–45.

McCulloch, J.H., 'Measuring the term structure of interest rates', *Journal of Business*, January 1971, pp. 19–31.

Nelson, C., Siegel, A., 'Parsimonious modelling of yield curves', *Journal of Business, Volume 6*, 1987, pp. 473–83.

Questa, G., *Fixed Income Analysis for the Global Financial Market*, Wiley 1999.

Steeley, J.M., 'Estimating the gilt-edged term structure: basis splines and confidence intervals', *Journal of Business Finance and Accounting* 18, 1991, pp. 513–30.

Suits, D., Mason, A., Chan, L., 'Spline functions fitted by standard regression methods', *Review of Economics and Statistics* 60, 1978, pp. 132–9.

Svensson, L., 'Estimating forward interest rates with the extended Nelson & Siegel method', *Sveriges Riksbank Quarterly Review*, 1995: 3, pp. 13–25.

Tuckman, B., *Fixed Income Securities*, Wiley 1996.

Van Deventer, D., Imai, K., *Financial Risk Analytics*, Irwin 1997.

Vasicek, O., 'An equilibrium characterization of the term structure', *Journal of Financial Economics* 5, 1977, pp. 177–88.

Vasicek, O., Fong, H.G., 'Term structure modelling using exponential splines', *Journal of Finance* 37(2), May 1982, pp. 339–48.

CHAPTER 9

Spline methodology and fitting the yield curve

Introduction

For market practitioners, zero-coupon rate curves are the basic tools used to value interest rate-based instruments. Curves are built using market data such as money market rates, swap rates, interest rate futures or bond prices as inputs. Despite the name, it is not in fact the 'zero-coupon' rates that are the most important output from a curve-fitting methodology, but rather the discount factors. It is these that are crucial for the pricing of interest rate-based instruments.

In this chapter, we provide an advanced methodology to extract discount factors from a set of bond prices. The objective is to be as explicit as possible so that non-mathematicians may be able to incorporate the methodology into their daily activity. We begin with basic definitions; more experienced readers can skip this and go directly to p. 140.

Basic concepts

A zero-coupon rate is the interest rate that is generated by an investment in cash over a certain period of time. The name comes from the fact that no intermediate payment is made to the investor – there is only the one cash flow on maturity. Zero-coupon rates are usually expressed on an annual basis. A zero-coupon rate is fully described by its *value* (such as 8% or 10%), its period (for example, two years), its day-count convention (for example 30/360 or actual/365) and its compounding frequency (such as annual, semi-annual and so on). Day-count conventions were considered in Chapter 4. We consider here two simple examples to illustrate the basic concept.

EXAMPLE *9.1*

Consider a two-year zero-coupon rate, on 30/360, annual basis, that is 10% for value on 1 January 2001. If an investor were to invest $100 on 1 January 2001 until 31 December 2002 he would get £121 at the end of the two-year period, given by:

121 = 100[*investment*] × (1 + 10%)[*year*1] × (1 +10%)[*year*2]

In this case the day-count convention is irrelevant because the period of the zero coupon is an exact number of years.

EXAMPLE *9.2*

In this example we see how the day-count convention is relevant. Assume this same investor were to invest £100 on 1 January 2001 until 14 June 2002 and that the corresponding zero-coupon rate for the period is again 10% (30/360, annual). The investor would receive $114.88 at the end of the period, given by:

114.88 = 100 × (1 + 10%) × (1 + 10%)$^{(150 + 14)/360}$

This reflects the fact that in 2002 there will be five full months (i.e. 5 × 30 or 150 days) plus 14 days in June, for a total of 164 days.

Present value and discount factor

The present value of a future cash flow is its value today. For instance, using the data in Example 9.1, the present value of a two-year cash flow of 121 is 100. A discount factor is defined by a *date* and an *amount*. It is the coefficient by which we need to multiply a future cash flow to obtain its present value.

A discount factor is always less or equal to 1 and tends to zero when its date tends to infinity. In Example 9.1 the amount of the two-year discount factor is 100/121 or 0.8264463.

Bootstrapping

We have already described in Chapter 4 the bootstrapping methodology to extract a zero-coupon curve from a set of bonds. This methodology offers some comfort and peace of mind, because when recalculating the price of the bonds used in the application algorithm, we back out their original market value. That is, the technique allows us to construct zero rates that fit the original bond market prices. This reflects the bootstrapping methodology. This 'perfect match' allows for easy testing and benchmarking of the implementation of the method. Nevertheless, it is far from being satisfactory; because of some major distortions in the resulting zero curve computed, it often leads to negative forward rates and to unrealistic figures as far as the zero-coupon rates themselves are concerned.

For this reason, market practitioners require other more advanced techniques to get around the unsuitable results obtained from this traditional technique. This more advanced analytic is used by traders to price interest rate instruments, as well as by risk managers to measure the risk exposure entered into and the risk-adjusted profit performance of the front book.

An advanced methodology: the cubic B-spline

The methodology we describe now is based on a cubic B-spline representation of the discount curve. The reasoning behind this approach is that B-splines provide very smooth curves that are easy to manipulate if necessary; for instance, it is relatively straightforward to make a B-spline curve go through specific points. (B-splines are described later in this chapter.)

The methodology uses a least-squares method to try to minimize the gap between a set of bonds' theoretical prices – that is, the prices that would be obtained using the advanced methodology – and their observed market prices. This is illustrated with an example built using UK government bonds. Of course, it is perfectly permissible to use, say, AAA-rated corporate bonds from various institutions to obtain a discount curve for AAA-rated companies.

In their 1982 paper, Vasicek *et al.* offered an alternative method using 'third order exponential splines'. This essentially assumes that discount curves are a linear combination of exponential functions within given time buckets. Alternatively, it can be seen as a more complex method than the one described in this book: instead of using splines to describe the discount curve itself, it operates a change of variable in the discount factor function from t (the time) to the new variable x, using the logarithm function:

$$t = \frac{1}{\alpha} \log(1 - x).$$

The corresponding new discount function is then approximated using splines. Finally, they then solve a minimization problem where α (called 'the limiting value of the forward rates') is the unknown and where the function to minimize is itself a minimization problem.

However, this approach is not fully described here; rather it can be seen as a comparison to or an 'upgrade' from our proposed methodology. Once the basic concepts of splines and optimization (least-square methods) are well understood and have been implemented, it is possible to switch methodology with a limited amount of effort.

Notation

We describe our methodology using the following notation:

N	is the number of bonds used to compute the discount curve
Q	is the S-dimensional control vector whose components $(Q_i)_{i=0..S-1}$ are the unknowns of the optimization problem
P_i^{tb}	is the theoretical value of bond number i computed using the advanced methodology
P_i^{ma}	is the market value (dirty price) of bond number i
n_i	is the number of cash flows for bond number i
C_j^i	is the cash flow number j of bond number i
x_j^i	is the date at which C_j^i is expected to be paid
$Df(x)$	is the discount factor computed using the advanced methodology for a given date x
$B_{k,3}$	is the cubic B-spline number k
$(t_i)_{i=0..S+3}$	is a set of dates used to define the B-splines.

By definition, for the discount factor we have:

$$Df(x) = \sum_{k=0}^{S-1} Q_k B_{k,3}(x) \qquad (9.1)$$

Using the above notation we can express the theoretical value of a bond, that is its theoretical dirty price, as:

$$P_i^{tb} = \sum_{j=1}^{n_i} C_j^i \, Df\left(x_j^i\right) = \sum_{j=1}^{n_i} C_j^i \sum_{k=0}^{S-i} Q_k B_{k,3}\left(x_j^i\right). \qquad (9.2)$$

Our objective is to minimize the expression:

$$F(Q) = \sum_{i=1}^{N} \left(P_i^{tb} - P_i^{ma}\right)^2. \qquad (9.3)$$

So we have:

$$\Leftrightarrow \underset{Q \in \Re^S}{Min} \sum_{i=1}^{N} \left(P_i^{tb} - P_i^{ma}\right)^2$$

$$\underset{Q \in \Re^S}{Min\, F\,(Q)} \qquad \Leftrightarrow \underset{Q \in \Re^S}{Min} \sum_{i=1}^{N} \left(\sum_{j=1}^{ni} C_j^i \sum_{k=0}^{S-1} Q_k B_{k,\,3}\!\left(x_j^i\right) - P_i^{ma}\right)^2.$$

$$\Leftrightarrow \underset{Q \in \Re^S}{Min} \sum_{i=1}^{N} \left(\sum_{k=0}^{S-1} Q_k \sum_{j=1}^{ni} C_j^i B_{k,\,3}\!\left(x_j^i\right) - P_i^{ma}\right)^2$$

By defining:

$$a_k^{\,i} = \sum_{j-1}^{ni} C_j^i B_{k,\,3}\!\left(x_j^i\right) \tag{9.4}$$

the minimization problem can also be written as:

$$\underset{Q \in \Re^S}{Min} \sum_{i=1}^{N} \left(\sum_{k=0}^{S-1} Q_k a_k^{\,i} - P_i^{ma}\right)^2 \tag{9.5}$$

This is equivalent to looking for Q such that $\nabla F(Q) = 0$.

We express every component l of $\nabla F(Q)$ as:

$$(\nabla F(Q))_l = \partial_{Q_l} F(Q) \tag{9.6}$$

where

$$\delta_{Q_l} F(Q) = 2 \sum_{i=1}^{N} \left(\sum_{k=0}^{S-1} Q_k a_k^{\,i} - P_i^{ma}\right) a_l^{\,i}. \tag{9.7}$$

We are therefore looking for Q such that:

$$\sum_{i=1}^{N} \sum_{k=0}^{S-1} Q_k a_k^{\,i} a_k^{\,i} = \sum_{i=1}^{N} P_i^{ma} a_l^{\,i}. \tag{9.8}$$

This can also be written as:

$$\sum_{k=0}^{S-1} Q_k \sum_{i=1}^{N} a_k^{\,i} a_k^{\,i} = \sum_{i=1}^{N} P_i^{ma} a_l^{\,i}. \tag{9.9}$$

In conclusion then, the minimization problem we wish to solve is equivalent to solving the $S \times S$ linear system:

$$AQ = B \tag{9.10}$$

where

$$(A_{l, k})_{\substack{l = 0...S-1 \\ k = 0...S-1}} = \sum_{i=1}^{N} a_k^i a_l^i$$

and

$$(B_l)_{l = 0...S-1} = \sum_{i=1}^{N} P_i^{ma} a_l^i.$$

(A) is obviously symmetrical, which will allow the use of specific algorithms to solve the linear system of equations. For this illustration, however, we use the GMRES algorithm, described below.

Simplification

If all the bonds i under consideration pay a fixed coupon C^i and are redeemed at par, we have:

$$a_k^i = C^i \sum_{j=1}^{n_i-1} B_{k, 3}\left(x_j^i\right) + 100 B_{n_i}(x_{n_i}^i).$$

This assumes that prices are expressed as per cent of par.

A priori, the minimization problem described above is constraint-free. However, we wish to introduce the following constraints, as we know of two properties for discount curves that we wish to enforce in our methodology:

■ the discount factor for today is 1;

■ the discount factor curve tends to zero when time tends to infinity.

Ideally we want to have to deal with a constraint-free minimization problem. So we embed these two constraints in the definition of $F(Q)$ itself. This is carried out as follows.

For the constraint that Df for today is 1 we set:

$$\sum_{k=0}^{S-1} Q_k B_{k, 3}(Today) = 1. \tag{9.11}$$

By choosing the four first t_i equal to today ($t_0 = t_1 = t_2 = t_3 = Today$) and using properties of the B-splines (see the section later in this chapter), we only have one non-zero term in the above sum, which leaves us with:

$$Q_0 = 1. \tag{9.12}$$

Thus Q_0 is no longer an unknown in the problem; the linear system to solve becomes an $S - 1 \times S - 1$ system. Therefore the matrix A needs to be amended accordingly; the first row and first column disappear and the second member of the linear system becomes B' with:

$$\forall k = 1...S - 1 \; B'_k = B_k - A_{k,\,0}.$$

For the second constraint, by choosing t_{S+3} equal to a 'very big' number (in our example we chose 100,000 to 'approximate' to infinity), we ensure that the discount curve goes down smoothly to zero for this number. This is a satisfactory estimate for the purpose of having the discount curve going down to zero when time tends to infinity.

EXAMPLE   *9.3 Fitting the gilt zero-coupon yield curve*

In this example, we compute a zero curve on 30 June 1997 from UK gilt prices.[1] In it we use:

- 30 different bonds, so that N = 30;
- 21 dates to define the B-splines, so that S=17.

In Table 9.1 we show our choices for the t_i values.

TABLE 9.1 ■ t_i values

t0	30 June 1997	t11	7 June 2006
t1	30 June 1997	t12	7 August 2007
t2	30 June 1997	t13	7 December 2008
t3	30 June 1997	t14	7 June 2010
t4	7 September 1997	t15	7 June 2013
t5	30 March 1998	t16	7 June 2015
t6	7 June 1999	t17	25 August 2017
t7	7 June 2000	t18	25 August 2019
t8	7 December 2001	t19	8 June 2021
t9	7 June 2003	t20	100000
t10	7 December 2004		

---

1. Note that at that time gilt prices were quoted in 'ticks' or 32nds, similar to US Treasury price quotes.

Note the following:

■ On a daily basis, once the required bonds and the set of t_i are known, the matrix only needs to be computed once. As changes in market prices occur, the discount curve can be updated quickly by only computing again the second member of the linear system and then solving this.

■ The methodology can be enhanced to take into account the fact that some bonds are benchmarks whereas others are very illiquid. Investors usually ask for a yield premium to hold less liquid bonds. The direct effect when computing a discount curve is that it tends to distort the expected results. To cater for this, the original function can be changed by incorporating weights (w_i) in the model. $F(Q)$ then becomes:

$$F(Q) = \sum_{i=1}^{N} w_i \left(P_i^{th} - P_i^{ma} \right)^2.$$

The idea here is that when a bond is a benchmark issue, its corresponding weight is going to be high, whereas for a very illiquid bond, the weight is going to be low.

■ The choice of the t_i values will influence the accuracy of the model. Apart from the first four values and the last value, they must be connected to the maturity of the bonds used in the calculation. The more maturities we have in a given period, the more t_i we have to choose in that period. Of course, there is no need to choose many t_i values in a period when no bonds mature.

Table 9.2 shows the bonds that were used, together with their market price and the corresponding theoretical price for each bond, which has been computed using our methodology. The difference between the two prices is given in the column headed 'pence spread'.

TABLE 9.2 ■ UK gilt-observed market and theoretical prices

27 June 1997 for settlement 30 June 1997

Coupon	Maturity	Market price	Accrued	GRY	Theo. price	Theo. GRY	bp spread	pence spread
8.75%	1 Sep. 1997	100-11	2.901	6.411	100.315	6.576	−16.5	3
9.75%	19 Jan. 1998	101-21	4.327	6.705	101.704	6.616	8.8	−5
7.25%	30 Mar. 1998	100-09	1.827	6.798	100.218	6.885	−8.8	6
12.25%	26 Mar. 1999	108-14	3.222	6.972	108.486	6.944	2.8	−5
6.00%	10 Aug. 1999	98-08	2.301	6.913	98.163	6.958	−4.6	9
9.00%	3 Mar. 2000	104-20	2.934	7.052	104.649	7.042	1.0	−2

TABLE 9.2 ■ Continued

27 June 1997 for settlement 30 June 1997

Coupon	Maturity	Market price	Accrued	GRY	Theo. price	Theo. GRY	bp spread	Pence spread
13.00%	14 Jul. 2000	115-28	5.948	7.115	115.941	7.092	2.3	−7
8.00%	7 Dec. 2000	102-27	0.504	7.048	102.685	7.100	−5.2	16
10.00%	26 Feb. 2001	109-04	3.397	7.128	109.211	7.102	2.6	−9
7.00%	6 Nov. 2001	99-22	1.055	7.073	99.690	7.073	0.1	0
7.00%	7 Jun. 2002	99-27	0.441	7.034	99.652	7.081	−4.7	19
9.75%	27 Aug. 2002	111-04	3.286	7.139	111.346	7.091	4.8	−22
8.00%	10 Jun. 2003	104-10	0.438	7.095	104.249	7.108	−1.3	6
9.50%	25 Oct. 2004	113-14	1.718	7.108	113.528	7.093	1.5	−9
6.75%	26 Nov. 2004	98-05	0.647	7.068	98.006	7.094	−2.7	15
9.50%	18 Apr. 2005	114-02	1.900	7.115	114.167	7.098	1.6	−10
8.50%	7 Dec. 2005	108-23	0.536	7.105	108.654	7.115	−1.0	6
7.75%	8 Sep. 2006	104-04	2.421	7.124	104.155	7.119	0.4	−3
7.50%	7 Dec. 2006	102-21	0.473	7.106	102.594	7.115	−0.9	6
8.50%	16 Jul. 2007	109-22	3.842	7.137	109.893	7.109	2.7	−21
7.25%	7 Dec. 2007	101-06	0.457	7.085	100.995	7.111	−2.6	19
9.00%	13 Oct. 2008	114-08	1.923	7.136	114.271	7.134	0.2	−2
8.00%	25 Sep. 2009	106-24	2.126	7.157	106.775	7.154	0.3	−2
6.25%	25 Nov. 2010	92-02	0.616	7.178	92.095	7.174	0.4	−3
9.00%	12 Jul. 2011	116-01	4.167	7.173	115.987	7.177	−0.5	4
9.00%	6 Aug. 2012	116-19	3.551	7.184	116.574	7.186	−0.2	2
8.00%	27 Sep. 2013	107-24	2.082	7.179	107.786	7.175	0.4	−4
8.00%	7 Dec. 2015	108-23	0.504	7.140	108.702	7.142	−0.2	2
8.75%	25 Aug. 2017	116-18	2.997	7.184	116.569	7.183	0.1	−1
8.00%	7 Jun. 2021	109-31	0.504	7.125	109.968	7.125	0.0	0

The discount curve obtained and the corresponding zero curve are shown in Figure 9.1. For validation purposes, we have also included the three-month forward curve.

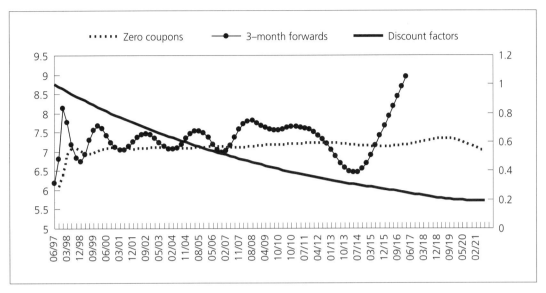

FIGURE 9.1 ■ Calculated discount function, spot and forward curves

Mathematical tools

In this chapter, we have used a pseudo-iterative method to solve a linear problem, known as GMRES, and a B-spline interpolation method for the discount factor curve. We now describe these two mathematical tools.

GMRES

GMRES is a methodology used to solve multi-dimensional linear problems; the acronym comes from General Minimum RESidual. GMRES has been used heavily in aeronautical engineering and aerodynamics since the early 1990s, because it has proven itself to be a very efficient solver. We have direct experience of using the method whilst at Dassault Aviation, to model flow behaviour around an airfoil and a rocket. Both applications were non-linear problems using the two-dimensional compressible potential equations and the two-dimensional Euler equations.

Remember that to solve a linear problem $Ax = b$, where A is a $n \times n$ matrix, x is the unknown n-vector and b is the second member n-vector, there are two families of algorithm we can use: direct methods, and iterative methods.

Direct methods include the intuitive one that readers will have learnt at school, when one has to invert the matrix A to obtain A^{-1}. The solution of the problem can then be directly obtained, by multiplying b by A^{-1}, that is:

$$x = A^{-1}b. \tag{9.13}$$

Direct methods have one main drawback: when the dimension of the problem increases, so that n goes up, the number of operations required to invert the matrix A goes up dramatically, as well as the computer memory required to store all the necessary data. Therefore in some cases the calculation cannot realistically be performed.

For this reason, mathematicians have introduced iterative methods. These consist of starting from an estimation of the solution, performing some operations to obtain a more precise solution and then performing the same kind of operation over and over again, until a predefined error is reached.

For example, assume the initial estimation of the solution is x_0. The initial error will then be:

$$||b - Ax_0|| \tag{9.14}$$

where $||.||$ is the norm of the vector $b - Ax_0$.

Then the following error will be $||b - Ax_1||$ where x_1 is the second estimation calculated, and so on.

The iterative algorithm will then certainly lead us to the solution when:

$$||b - Ax_0|| > ||b - Ax_1|| > ||b - Ax_2|| > ... > ||b - Ax_i|| > ||b - Ax_{i+1}|| > ... \tag{9.15}$$

because the error (the 'difference' between the solution and the estimation) is going down to zero.

In practice, the algorithm stops when the initial error is divided by 100, 1,000 or 10,000, depending on the overall problem to solve.

In general there is no need for x_0 to be an accurate estimation of the solution. If it is, then it usually increases the speed of the process, but if the user does not know what is required it should be set simply to the zero vector.

GMRES is in fact a direct method; by performing a defined number of operations the user will reach the exact solution. However, its algorithm looks like an iterative method, and to avoid using too much memory and reach a very good performance, it is used as an iterative method. For this reason it is called a *pseudo-iterative* method. In practice, GMRES has some practical advantages over other methods: it can solve non-symmetrical problems and there is no need to know precisely the A matrix. Only the result of the product of the matrix by a vector is required. For non-linear problems, where the matrix is not known but only approximated, it can be very useful.

Non-mathematicians and readers who are not interested in the derivation of the algorithm can go straight to the section on the GMRES algorithm later in this chapter. For the others, we now describe briefly the methodology.

GMRES is a minimum residual method, the objective of which is to obtain the vector x that minimizes the l^2 norm of the residual. So we seek the value x that fulfils:

$$\min_{x \in \Re^n} ||b - Ax||. \tag{9.16}$$

Assume $x = x_0 + z$ where z is a first estimation of x.

We then look for the value z that belongs to K_k, the Krylov vectorial space. This is the vectorial space whose base is:

$$\left(r_0, Ar_0,..., A^{k-1} r_0 \right)$$

where $r_0 = b - Ax_0$.

The minimization problem can then be written as the value of z that fulfils:

$$\min_{z \in K_k} ||r_0 - Az||. \tag{9.17}$$

Using a Gram-Schmidt orthogonalization process, we build an orthonormal base $U_k = (u_1, u_2,...u_k)$ of K_k as well as a rectangular Hessenberg matrix H whose dimensions are $(k + 1) \times k$.

H is defined by:

$$AU_k = U_{k + 1}H_k \tag{9.18}$$

Then $h_{i, j}$, the element of H that is on row i and column j, can be written as:

$$h_{i, j} = Au_j \bullet u_i \tag{9.19}$$

where $\bullet$ is the scalar product of two vectors.

By definition of U_k we have $h_{i, j} = 0$ when $i > j + 1$.

This explains why H is called a Hessenberg matrix; we extend their definition to rectangular matrices that have an upper triangular matrix in which we have an extra non-zero under-diagonal.

In addition we have:

$$h_{j + 1, j} = ||u_{j + 1}||. \tag{9.20}$$

z belongs to K_k and can therefore be written as:

$$z = \sum_{j=1}^{k} y_j u_j. \tag{9.21}$$

By defining $e \in \Re^{k + 1}$ $e = (||r_0||, 0,...,0)^t$, it can be shown that the original minimization problem can now be written as:

$$\min_{z \in K_k} ||r_0 - Az|| \Leftrightarrow \min_{y \in \Re^k} ||e - H_k y||. \tag{9.22}$$

The quasi-triangular structure of H_k eases the process to solve such problems; we use an algorithm based on a stable QR factorization. Above all, it gives the value of the minimal residual as a sub-product (so that there is no need for extra computation) at each iteration.

Therefore we build a matrix Q such that:

$$QH_k = R \tag{9.23}$$

where R is a $(k + 1) \times k$ 'upper triangular' matrix with its last row made only of zeros, as shown below.

$$R = \begin{vmatrix} x & x & x & x & x & x & x & x & x & x \\ 0 & x & x & x & x & x & x & x & x & x \\ 0 & 0 & x & x & x & x & x & x & x & x \\ 0 & 0 & 0 & x & x & x & x & x & x & x \\ 0 & 0 & 0 & 0 & x & x & x & x & x & x \\ 0 & 0 & 0 & 0 & 0 & x & x & x & x & x \\ 0 & 0 & 0 & 0 & 0 & 0 & x & x & x & x \\ 0 & 0 & 0 & 0 & 0 & 0 & 0 & x & x & x \\ 0 & 0 & 0 & 0 & 0 & 0 & 0 & 0 & x & x \\ 0 & 0 & 0 & 0 & 0 & 0 & 0 & 0 & 0 & x \\ 0 & 0 & 0 & 0 & 0 & 0 & 0 & 0 & 0 & 0 \end{vmatrix}$$

Q will be a unitary matrix, a product of k rotation matrices.

The problem can now be written as:

$$\min_{y \in \Re^k} ||e - H_k y| = \min_{y \in \Re^k} ||Qe - Ry||. \tag{9.24}$$

The solution of the problem is then obtained by solving the upper triangular system:

$$\tilde{R}y = \tilde{Q}e \tag{9.25}$$

where $\tilde{R}$ is the $(k \times k)$ matrix built using the first k rows of R, and where $\tilde{Q}e$ is the vector made of the k first components of Qe.

As we observe in the following, the error made is then given by e_{k+1}:

$$Qe - Ry = \begin{vmatrix} x \\ x \\ x \\ x \\ x \\ x \\ x \\ x \\ x \\ x \\ e_{k+1} \end{vmatrix} - \begin{vmatrix} x & x & x & x & x & x & x & x & x & x & x \\ 0 & x & x & x & x & x & x & x & x & x & x \\ 0 & 0 & x & x & x & x & x & x & x & x & x \\ 0 & 0 & 0 & x & x & x & x & x & x & x & x \\ 0 & 0 & 0 & 0 & x & x & x & x & x & x & x \\ 0 & 0 & 0 & 0 & 0 & x & x & x & x & x & x \\ 0 & 0 & 0 & 0 & 0 & 0 & x & x & x & x & x \\ 0 & 0 & 0 & 0 & 0 & 0 & 0 & x & x & x & x \\ 0 & 0 & 0 & 0 & 0 & 0 & 0 & 0 & x & x & x \\ 0 & 0 & 0 & 0 & 0 & 0 & 0 & 0 & 0 & x & x \\ 0 & 0 & 0 & 0 & 0 & 0 & 0 & 0 & 0 & 0 & x \end{vmatrix}$$

GMRES algorithm

We now describe in detail the GMRES algorithm, which will allow the reader to implement it reasonably quickly.

It has already been said that the only requirement for GMRES regarding the matrix A is to be able to compute the product of A with a vector. Therefore, it is advisable to implement a stand-alone sub-routine for GMRES that calls another routine to perform this multiplication. The algorithm will then be easily reusable to solve numerous different linear systems.

<u>Data</u>

A the matrix of the linear system to solve
b the second member of the system (vector)
k_0 the dimension of the Krylov space (set to 5 or 10)
ε the convergence parameter (set to 10^{-4} or 10^{-5}).

<u>Internal variable</u>

$TEST$:   Boolean

<u>Output</u>

x: solution of $Ax=b$

<u>Begin</u>
{Initialization of x and of the criteria to stop}

$x \leftarrow 0$
$TEST \leftarrow$ False
<u>While</u> $TEST$=False
      <u>Do</u>
      {Initialization of the GMRES loop}

      $u_1 \leftarrow b - Ax$
      $e \leftarrow (||u_1||,0,0,0,...,0)^t$
      $u_1 \leftarrow \dfrac{u_1}{||u_1||}$

      {Beginning of the GMRES loop}
      <u>For</u> i=1 <u>to</u> k_0

<u>Do</u>

{Building the Krylov vector number $i+1$}

$u_{i+1} \leftarrow Au_i$

<u>For</u> $j=1$ <u>To</u> i

    <u>Do</u>

$$\beta_{i+1,j} \leftarrow u_{i+1} \bullet u_j$$

$$u_{i+1} \leftarrow u_{i+1} - \beta_{i+1,j} u_j$$

<u>End For</u>

$$u_{i+1} \leftarrow \frac{u_{i+1}}{||u_{i+1}||}$$

{Building column number i of the Hessenberg Matrix H and update its QR factorization}

$$b_i \leftarrow (\beta_{i+1,1}, \beta_{i+1,2}, \ldots \beta_{i+1,i}, ||u_{i+1}||)^t$$

<u>For</u> $j=1$ <u>To</u> $i-1$

    <u>Do</u>

$$\begin{pmatrix} b_{j,i} \\ b_{j+1,i} \end{pmatrix} \leftarrow \begin{pmatrix} \cos\theta_j & \sin\theta j \\ -\sin\theta j & \cos\theta j \end{pmatrix} \begin{pmatrix} b_{j,i} \\ b_{j+1,i} \end{pmatrix}$$

<u>End For</u>

$$(\cos\theta_i \; \sin\theta_i) \leftarrow \frac{1}{\sqrt{b_{i,i}^2 + b_{i+1,i}^2}} \; (b_{i,i} \; b_{i+1,i})$$

$$(b_{i,i} \; b_{i+1,i}) \leftarrow \left(\sqrt{b_{i,i}^2 + b_{i+1,i}^2} \; \; 0 \right)$$

{update e, the error vector}

$$(e_i \; e_i+1) \leftarrow (\cos\theta_i e_i - \sin\theta_i e_i)$$

$TEST \leftarrow (|e_{i+1}| \leq \varepsilon)$

<u>If</u> $TEST$

    <u>Then</u>

        <u>GOTO</u> (**)

<u>End If</u>

<u>End For</u>

(**){compute x}
Solve the upper triangular linear system: $Hy=e$

$$x \leftarrow x + \sum_{j=1}^{i} y_j u_j$$

End While
End

B-splines

A key application of basis splines or *B-splines* in financial economics is when there is a need for interpolation of data. For instance, when using a bootstrapping methodology to compute zero rates from bond prices, the result is a set of rates for given dates. Obviously, if zero rates are required for other dates, an interpolation is then required to obtain these. The most popular methodology, as well as the simplest, is linear interpolation.

EXAMPLE   *9.4 Linear interpolation*

Consider the following scenario:

■   one-year zero rate of 10%;

■   two-year zero rate of 15%.

We require the 16-month rate Z16. Linear interpolation will give

Z16= 10%+ (15%-10%)*4/12=11.66%

However, using linear interpolation assumes that the zero-rate yield curve is linear by time bucket. This is not an accurate representation of reality because it does not take into account the smoothness and curvature of yield curves in the real world. Therefore if we require more realistic curves, for example for use when setting up arbitrage trading strategies, a B-spline can be used.

As observed earlier, B-splines are also used for defining discount curves as a linear combination of B-splines. The advantage of using them in this context is that it is straightforward to impose constraints on the curve itself. As we saw, the discount factor for the date of calculation (today) should be 1, and the discount factor at infinite should be zero (the discount curve should go down to zero when time goes by).

Definitions

We define the following:

▪ Let $(t_i)_{i=0..m}$ be a suite of $(m+1)$ points such as $\forall i,\ t_i \le t_{i+1}$. These points are called nodes. If r number of t_i are equal to τ, then τ is said to be an r-order node or of multiplicity r.

▪ For each (i,j) such as $1 \le j \le m + 1 - i$, we define $\omega_{i,j}(x)$ by:

$$\omega_{i,j}(x) = \begin{cases} \dfrac{x - t_i}{t_{i+j} - t_i} & \text{if } t_i < t_{i+j} \\ 0 \ \text{in all other cases} \end{cases}. \tag{9.26}$$

We can then define B-splines $B_{i,k}(x)$, $x \in \Re$ recursively on k as:

$\forall i,\ 0 \le i \le m - k - 1$

$$\begin{cases} B_{i,0}(x) = \begin{cases} 1 \ \text{if } t_i \le x \le t_{i+1} \\ 0 \ \text{in all other cases} \end{cases} \\ B_{i,k}(x) = \omega_{i,k}(x)B_{i,k-1}(x) + (1 - \omega_{i+1,k}(x))B_{i+1,k-1}(x),\ \forall k \ge 1. \end{cases} \tag{9.27}$$

It can be shown that $B_{i,k}(x)$ can be written as:

$$B_{i,k}(x) = \frac{x - t_i}{t_{i+k} - t_i} B_{i,k-1}(x) + \frac{t_{i+k+1} - x}{t_{i+k+1} - t_{i+1}} B_{i+1,k-1}(x),\ if\ t_i < t_{i+k}\ and\ t_{i+1} < t_{i+k+1}. \tag{9.28}$$

By definition of $\omega_{i,j}(x)$, those terms where the denominator would be nil are set to zero.

Properties

Assume k is given:

1. $B_{i,k}(x)$ is polynomial of degree k by bucket
2. $B_{i,k}(x) = 0$ *when* $x \notin [t_i, t_{i+k+1}]$
3. $B_{i,k}(x) > 0$ *when* $x \in [t_i, t_{i+k+1}]$
4. $B_{i,k}(t_i) = 0$ Except if $t_i = t_{i+1} = ... = t_{i+k} < t_{i+k+1}$. Then $B_{i,k}(t_i) = 1$
5. Given $[a, b]$ an interval such as $t_k \le a$ and $t_{m-k} \ge b$, then, $\forall x \in [a, b]$, we have:

    $$\sum_{i=0}^{m-k-1} B_{i,k}(x) = 1$$

6. Assume $x \in [t_i, t_{i+k+1}]$, then $B_{i,k}(x) = 1$ if and only if $x = t_{i+1} = ... = t_{i+k}$
7. $B_{i,k}(x)$ is infinitely right-differentiable for each $x \in \Re$.

First derivative

During the optimization process to compute a discount curve (see above), the first derivative of B-splines is required. This is:

$$B_{i,k}(x) = k \left[\frac{B_{i,k-1}(x)}{t_{i,+k} - t_i} - \frac{B_{i+1,k-1}(x)}{t_{i+k+1} - t_{i+1}} \right]. \qquad (9.29)$$

We retain the convention that if a denominator is equal to zero, this means that the term itself is equal to zero.

Generating curves using B-splines

As the basis has been described, we can move on to the main issue of curve generation using B-splines. In the following we deal with cubic splines (when $k = 3$). Although any number may be used in a polynomial spline application, generally cubic splines are the ones most commonly used in financial applications.

Definitions

▪ We set n points $(P_i)_{i=0...n-1}$ of $\mathfrak{R}^3$. γ is the parameterized B-spline curve associated to the polygon $P_0...P_{n-1}$, defined by:

$$S(t) = \begin{vmatrix} S_1(t) \\ S_2(t) \\ S_3(t) \end{vmatrix} = \sum_{i=0}^{n-1} P_i B_{i,3}(t) \ (a \leq t \leq b)$$

▪ The polygon $P_0...P_{n-1}$ is called the control polygon of the γ curve.

Properties

Properties from the B-spline functions trigger the following properties for B-spline curves:

1. In general, γ does not go through the points P_i, but if $a = t_0 = ... = t_3$, and $t_n = ... = t_{n+3} = b$ then $S(a) = P_0$ and $S(b) = P_{n-1}$. In this case, γ is tangent in P_0 and P_{n+1} to the edges (P_0, P_1) and (P_{n-2}, P_{n-1}) of the control polygon.

2. γ is in the convex envelope of the points $P_0,...P_{n-1}$. More precisely, if $t_i \leq t \leq t_{i+1}$ then $S(t)$ is in the convex envelope of the points $P_{i-k},...P_i$.

3. If for all i such as $4 \leq i \leq n-1$ the nodes t_i are simple (they are 1-order nodes), then γ is of class C^2 and is made of n parameterized polynomial arcs of degree equal to or less than 3.

This generates the curve.

Conclusion

We have described an advanced methodology by which one can extract a zero-coupon curve from market-observed bond prices. This is more reliable than the classic bootstrapping methodology because it smooths the discount curve, and therefore the zero curve, thanks to its B-spline definition. More importantly, it results in more realistic forward rates.

We also described the basic tools – that is the B-splines and the optimization method – so that non-mathematicians should be able to implement this methodology without undue complication, and perhaps on their own.

SELECTED BIBLIOGRAPHY AND REFERENCES

Brown, P.N., Saad, Y., 'Hybrid Krylov method for non linear systems of equations', Siam J., *Sci. STAT. COMPUT.* 11: 3, May 1990.

De Clermont-Tonnerre, A., Lévy, M.A, *Zero-coupon Bonds and Bond Stripping*, IFR Publishing 1995.

James, N., Webber, A., *Interest Rate Modelling*, Wiley 2000.

Joannas, D., *Optimisation de formes en aérodynamique*, PhD thesis, Université de Saint Étienne, France, 1992.

Martellini, L., Priaulet, P., *Fixed-Income Securities*, Wiley 2001, Chapter 3.

Riesler, J.J., *Méthodes mathématiques pour la C.A.O.*, Masson 1991.

Vasicek, O., Oldrich, A., and Gifford-Fong, H., 'Term structure modelling using exponential splines', *Journal of Finance*, XXXVII: 2, May 1982.

CHAPTER 10

Inflation-indexed bonds

In certain countries there is a market in bonds whose return, both coupon and final redemption payment, is linked to the consumer prices index. Investors' experience with inflation-indexed bonds differs across countries, since they were introduced at different times, and as a result the exact design of *index-linked bonds* varies across the different markets. This of course makes the comparison of issues such as yield difficult, and has in the past acted as a hindrance to arbitrageurs seeking to exploit real yield differentials. In this chapter we will highlight the basic concepts behind the structure of indexed bonds and show how this may differ from that employed in another market. Not all index-linked bonds link both coupon and maturity payments to a specified index; in some markets only the coupon payment is index-linked. Generally, the most liquid market available will be the government bond market in index-linked debt instruments.

The structure of index-linked bond markets across the world differs in various ways, including those noted below. Appendix 10.1 lists those countries that currently issue public-sector indexed securities.

Introduction and basic concepts

There are a number of reasons why investors and issuers alike are interested in inflation-indexed bonds. Before considering these, we look at some of the factors involved in security design.

Choice of index

In principle, bonds can be indexed to any number of variables, including various price indices, earnings, output, specific commodities or foreign currencies. Although ideally the chosen index would reflect the hedging requirements of both parties, these may not coincide. For instance, the overwhelming choice of retail investors is for indexation to consumer prices, whereas pension funds prefer linking to earnings levels, to offset earnings-linked pension liabilities. In practice, most bonds have been linked to an index of consumer prices such as the UK retail price index, since this is usually widely circulated and well understood and issued on a regular basis.

Indexation lags

To provide practically precise protection against inflation, interest payments for a given period would need to be corrected for actual inflation over the same period. However, there are unavoidable lags between the movements in the price index and the adjustment to the bond cash flows as they are paid (*see* Figure 10.1). This reduces the inflation-proofing properties of indexed bonds. Deacon and Derry (1998) state that there are two reasons why indexation lags are necessary. First, inflation statistics can only be calculated and published with a delay. The data for one month is usually known well into the next month, and there may be delays in publication. This calls for a lag of at least one month. Second, in some markets the size of the next coupon payment must be known before the start of the coupon period in order to calculate the accrued interest; this leads to a delay equal to the length of time between coupon payments.[1]

Coupon frequency

Index-linked bonds often pay interest on a semi-annual basis, but long-dated investors such as fund managers, whose liabilities may well include inflation-indexed annuities, are also – at least in theory – interested in indexed bonds that pay on a quarterly or even monthly basis.

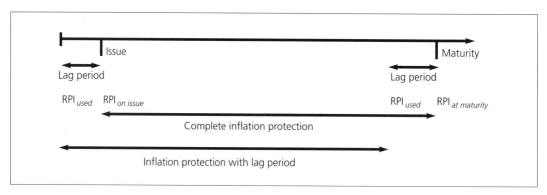

FIGURE 10.1 ■ The indexation lag

1. The same source cites various methods by which the period of the lag may be minimized; for example, the accrued interest calculation for Canadian Real Return Bonds is based on cumulative movements in the consumer prices index, which run from the last coupon date. This obviates the need to know with certainty the nominal value of the next coupon, unlike the arrangement for UK index-linked gilts. (See Deacon and Derry (1998), pp. 30–1.)

Indexing the cash flows

There are five basic methods of linking the cash flows from a bond to an inflation index. These are:

■ *Interest-indexed bonds*: These pay a fixed real coupon and an indexation of the fixed principal every period; the principal repayment at maturity is not adjusted. In this case all the inflation adjustment is fully paid out as it occurs and does not accrue on the principal. These type of bonds have been issued in Australia, although the most recent issue was in 1987.

■ *Capital-indexed bonds*: The coupon rate is specified in real terms. Interest payments equal the coupon rate multiplied by the inflation-adjusted principal amount. At maturity the principal repayment is the product of the nominal value of the bond multiplied by the cumulative change in the index. Compared with interest-indexed bonds of similar maturity, these bonds have higher duration and lower reinvestment risk. These type of bonds have been issued in Australia, Canada, New Zealand, the UK and the USA.

■ *Zero-coupon indexed bonds*: As their name implies, these pay no coupons but the principal repayment is scaled for inflation. They have the highest duration of all indexed bonds and have no reinvestment risk. These type of bonds have been issued in Sweden.

■ *Indexed annuity bonds*: The payments consist of a fixed annuity payment and a varying element to compensate for inflation. These bonds have the lowest duration and highest reinvestment risk of all index-linked bonds. They have been issued in Australia, although not by the central government.

■ *Current pay bond*: As with interest-indexed bonds, the principal cash flow on maturity is not adjusted for inflation. The difference with current pay bonds is that their term cash flows are a combination of an inflation-adjusted coupon and an indexed amount that is related to the principal. Thus in effect current pay bonds are an inflation-indexed floating-rate note. They have been issued in Turkey.

The choice of instrument will reflect the requirements of investors and issuers. Deacon and Derry (1998) cite duration, tax treatment and reinvestment risk as the principal factors that influence instrument design. Although duration for an indexed bond measures something slightly different to that for a conventional bond, being an indication of the bond price sensitivity due to changes in the real interest rate, as with conventional bonds it is higher for zero-coupon indexed bonds compared with coupon bonds. Indexed annuities will have the shortest duration. Longer-duration instruments will (in theory) be demanded by investors that have long-dated hedging liabilities. Again, as with conventional bonds, investors holding indexed bonds are exposed to reinvestment risk, which means that the true yield earned by holding a bond to maturity cannot be determined when it is purchased, because the rate at which interim cash flows can be invested is not known. Hence bonds that pay more of their return in the form of coupons are more exposed to this risk, which would be indexed annuities. Indexed zero-coupon bonds, like their conventional counterparts, do not expose investors to reinvestment risk.

The tax regime in individual markets will also influence investor taste. For instance, some jurisdictions tax the capital gain on zero-coupon bonds as income, with a requirement that any tax liability be discharged as current income. This is unfavourable treatment, because the capital is not available until maturity, which would reduce institutional investor demand for zero-coupon instruments. It should also be noted that in three countries, namely Canada, New Zealand and the USA, there exists a facility for investors to strip indexed bonds, thus enabling separate trading of coupon and principal cash flows.[2] Such an arrangement obviates the need for a specific issue of zero-coupon indexed securities, as the market can create them in response to investor demand.

Coupon-stripping feature

Allowing market practitioners to strip indexed bonds enables them to create new inflation-linked products that are more specific to investors' needs, such as indexed annuities or deferred-payment indexed bonds. In markets that allow stripping of indexed government bonds, a strip is simply an individual uplifted cash flow. An exception to this is in New Zealand, where the cash flows are separated into three components: the principal, the principal inflation adjustment and the set of inflation-linked coupons (that is, an indexed annuity).

Index-linked bond yields

Calculating index-linked yields

Inflation-indexed bonds have either or both of their coupon and principal linked to a price index such as the retail price index (RPI), a commodity price index (for example, wheat) or a stock market index. In the UK the reference is to the RPI, whereas in other markets the price index is the consumer price index (CPI). If we wish to calculate the yield on such bonds, it is necessary to make forecasts of the relevant index, which are then used in the yield calculation. In the UK both the principal and coupons on UK index-linked government bonds are linked to the RPI and are therefore designed to give a constant *real* yield. Most of the index-linked stocks that have been issued by the UK gov-

2. In the UK the facility of 'stripping' exists for conventional gilts but not index-linked gilts. The term originates in the US market, being an acronym for Separate Trading of Registered Interest and Principal.

ernment have coupons of 2% or $2\frac{1}{2}$%. This is because the return from an index-linked bond represents in theory *real* return, because the bond's cash flows rise in line with inflation. Historically, real rate of return on UK market debt stock over the long term has been roughly $2\frac{1}{2}$%.

Indexed bonds differ in their make-up across markets. In some markets only the principal payment is linked, whereas other indexed bonds link only their coupon payments and not the redemption payment. In the case of the former, each coupon and the final principal are scaled up by the ratio of two values of the RPI. The main RPI measure is the one reported for eight months before the issue of the gilt, and is known as the *base RPI*. The base RPI is the denominator of the index measure. The numerator is the RPI measure for eight months prior to the month coupon payment, or eight months before the bond maturity date.

The coupon payment of an index-linked gilt is given by:

$$(C/2) \times \frac{RPI_{C\text{-}8}}{RPI_0} . \tag{10.1}$$

Expression (10.1) shows the coupon divided by two before being scaled up, because index-linked gilts pay semi-annual coupons. The formula for calculating the size of the coupon payment for an annual-paying indexed bond is modified accordingly.

The principal repayment is given by:

$$100 \times \frac{RPI_{M\text{-}8}}{RPI_0} \tag{10.2}$$

where

C	is the annual coupon payment
RPI_0	is the RPI value eight months prior to the issue of the bond (the *base* RPI)
$RPI_{C\text{-}8}$	is the RPI value eight months prior to the month in which the coupon is paid
$RPI_{M\text{-}8}$	is the RPI value eight months prior to the bond redemption.

Price indices are occasionally 'rebased' which means that the index is set to a base level again. In the UK the RPI has been rebased twice, the last occasion being in January 1987, when it was set to 100 from the January 1974 value of 394.5.

EXAMPLE *10.1 Index-linked bond cash flows*

An index-linked gilt with a coupon of 4.625% was issued in April 1988 and matured in April 1998. The base measure required for this bond is the RPI for August 1987, which was 102.1. The RPI for August 1997 was 158.5. We can use these values to calculate the actual cash amount of the final coupon payment and principal repayment in April 1998:

$$\text{Coupon payment} = (4.625/2) \times \frac{158.5}{102.1} = \text{\textsterling}3.58992$$

$$\text{Principal repayment} = 100 \times \frac{158.5}{102.1} = \text{\textsterling}155.23996$$

We can determine the accrued interest calculation for the last six-month coupon period (October 1987 to April 1998) by using the final coupon payment, which is:

$$3.58992 \times \frac{\text{number of days accrued}}{\text{actual days in period}}.$$

The markets use two main yield measures for index-linked bonds, both of which are a form of yield to maturity. These are the *money* (or *nominal*) *yield* and the *real yield*.

In order to calculate a money yield for an indexed bond we require forecasts of all future cash flows from the bond. Since future cash flows from an index-linked bond are not known with certainty, we require a forecast of all the relevant future RPIs, which we then apply to all the cash flows. In fact the market convention is to take the latest available RPI and assume a constant inflation rate thereafter, usually $2\frac{1}{2}\%$ or 5%. By assuming a constant inflation rate we can set future RPI levels, which in turn allow us to calculate future cash flow values.

We obtain the forecast for the first relevant future RPI using (10.3):

$$RPI_1 = RPI_0 \times (1 + \tau)^{m/12} \tag{10.3}$$

where

RPI_1	is the forecast RPI level
RPI_0	is the latest available RPI
τ	is the assumed future annual inflation rate
m	is the number of months between RPI_0 and RPI_1.

Consider an indexed bond that pays coupons every June and December. For analysis we require the RPI forecast value for eight months prior to June and December, which will be for October and April. If we are now in February, we require a forecast for the RPI for the next April. This sets $m = 2$ in our equation at (10.3). We can then use (10.4) to forecast each subsequent relevant RPI required to set the bond's cash flows,

$$RPI_{j+1} = RPI_1 \times (1+\tau)^{j/2} \tag{10.4}$$

where j is the number of semi-annual forecasts after RPI_1 (which was our forecast RPI for April). For example, if the February RPI was 163.7 and we assume an annual inflation rate of 2.5%, then we calculate the forecast for the RPI for the following April to be:

$$RPI_1 = 163.7 \times (1.025)^{2/12}$$
$$= 164.4$$

and for the following October it would be:

$$RPI_3 = 164.4 \times (1.025)$$
$$= 168.5$$

Once we have determined the forecast RPIs we can calculate the yield. Under the assumption that the analysis is carried out on a coupon date, so that accrued interest on the bond is zero, we can calculate the money yield (ri) by solving equation (10.5):

$$P_d = \frac{(C/2)(RPI_1/RPI_0)}{\left(1 + \frac{1}{2}ri\right)} + \frac{(C/2)(RPI_2/RPI_0)}{\left(1 + \frac{1}{2}ri\right)^2} + \dots + \frac{([C/2] + M)(RPI_N/RPI_0)}{\left(1 + \frac{1}{2}ri\right)^N} \quad (10.5)$$

where
ri is the semi-annualized money yield to maturity
N is the number of coupon payments (interest periods) up to maturity.

Equation (10.5) is for semi-annual paying indexed bonds such as index-linked gilts. The equation for annual coupon indexed bonds is given at (10.6):

$$P_d = \frac{C(RPI_1/RPI_0)}{(1 + ri)} + \frac{C(RPI_2/RPI_0)}{(1 + ri)^2} + \dots + \frac{(C + M)(RPI_N/RPI_0)}{(1 + ri)^N} \quad (10.6)$$

The real yield ry is related to the money yield through equation (10.7), as it applies to semi-annual coupon bonds, which was first described by Fisher (1930).

$$(1 + \tfrac{1}{2}ry) = (1 + \tfrac{1}{2}ri) / (1 + \tau)^{\frac{1}{2}} \quad (10.7)$$

To illustrate this, if the money yield is 5.5% and the forecast inflation rate is 2.5%, then the real yield is calculated using (10.7), as shown below:

$$ry = \left\{ \frac{\left[1 + \frac{1}{2}(0.055)\right]}{[1 + (0.025)]^{\frac{1}{2}}} - 1 \right\} \times 2$$

$$= 0.0297 \text{ or } 2.97\%$$

We can rearrange equation (10.5) and use (10.7) to solve for the real yield, shown at (10.8) and applicable to semi-annual coupon bonds. Again, we use (10.8) where the calculation is performed on a coupon date.

$$P_d = \frac{RPI_a}{RPI_0} \left[\frac{(C/2)(1+\tau)^{\frac{1}{2}}}{\left(1+\frac{1}{2}ri\right)} + \frac{(C/2)(1+\tau)}{\left(1+\frac{1}{2}ri\right)^2} + \dots + \frac{(\{C/2\}+M)(1+\tau)^{\frac{N}{2}}}{\left(1+\frac{1}{2}ri\right)^N} \right]$$

$$= \frac{RPI_a}{RPI_0} \left[\frac{(C/2)}{\left(1+\frac{1}{2}ry\right)} + \dots + \frac{(C/2)+M}{\left(1+\frac{1}{2}ry\right)^N} \right]$$

(10.8)

where

$$RPI_a = \frac{RPI_1}{(1+\tau)^{\frac{1}{2}}}.$$

RPI_0 is the base index level as initially described. RPI_a/RPI_0 is the rate of inflation between the bond's issue date and the date the yield calculation is carried out.

It is best to think of the equations for money yield and real yield by thinking of which discount rate to employ when calculating a redemption yield for an indexed bond. Equation (10.5) can be viewed as showing that the money yield is the appropriate discount rate for discounting money or nominal cash flows. We then rearrange this equation as given in (10.8) to show that the real yield is the appropriate discount rate to use when discounting real cash flows.

The yield calculation for a US TIPS security is given in Appendix 10.2.

Assessing yield for index-linked bonds

Index-linked bonds do not offer *complete* protection against a fall in real value of an investment. That is, the return from index-linked bonds including index-linked gilts is not in reality a guaranteed real return, in spite of the cash flows being linked to a price index such as the RPI. The reason for this is the lag in indexation, which for index-linked gilts is eight months. The time lag means that an indexed bond is not protected against inflation for the last interest period of its life, which for gilts is the last six months. Any inflation occurring during this final interest period will not be reflected in the bond's cash flows and will reduce the real value of the redemption payment and hence the real yield. This can be a worry for investors in high inflation environments. The only way effectively to eliminate inflation risk for bondholders is to reduce the time lag in indexation of payments to something like one or two months.

Bond analysts frequently compare the yields on index-linked bonds with those on conventional bonds, because this implies the market's expectation of inflation rates. To compare returns between index-linked bonds and conventional bonds, analysts calculate the *break-even inflation* rate. This is the inflation rate that makes the money yield on an index-linked bond equal to the redemption yield on a conventional bond of the same maturity. Roughly speaking, the difference between the yield on an indexed bond and a conventional bond of the same maturity is what the market expects inflation during the life of the bond to be; part of the higher yield available on the conventional bond is therefore the inflation *premium*. In August 1999 the redemption yield on the $5\frac{3}{4}\%$ Treasury 2009, the ten-year benchmark gilt, was 5.17%. The real yield on the $2\frac{1}{2}\%$ index-linked 2009 gilt, assuming a constant inflation rate of 3%, was 2.23%. Using (10.5), this gives us an implied breakeven inflation rate of:

$$\tau = \left\{ \frac{[1 + \frac{1}{2}(0.0517)]}{[1 + \frac{1}{2}(0.0223)]} \right\}^2 - 1$$

$$= 0.029287 \text{ or } 2.9\%.$$

If we accept that an advanced, highly developed and liquid market such as the gilt market is of at least semi-strong form, if not strong form, then the inflation expectation in the market is built into these gilt yields. However, if this implied inflation rate understated what was expected by certain market participants, investors would start holding more of the index-linked bond rather than the conventional bond. This activity would then force the indexed yield down (or the conventional yield up). If investors had the opposite view and thought that the implied inflation rate overstated inflation expectations, they would hold the conventional bond. In our illustration above, the market is expecting long-term inflation to be at around 2.9% or less, and the higher yield of the $5\frac{3}{4}\%$ 2009 bond reflects this inflation expectation. A fund manager will take into account his view of inflation, amongst other factors, in deciding how much of the index-linked gilt to hold compared with the conventional gilt. It is often the case that investment managers hold indexed bonds in a portfolio against specific index-linked liabilities, such as pension contracts that increase their payouts in line with inflation each year.

The premium on the yield of the conventional bond over that of the index-linked bond is therefore compensation against inflation to investors holding it. Bondholders will choose to hold index-linked bonds instead of conventional bonds if they are worried by unexpected inflation. An individual's view on expected inflation will depend on several factors, including the current macroeconomic environment and the credibility of the monetary authorities, be they the central bank or the government. In certain countries, such as the UK and New Zealand, the central bank has explicit inflation targets and investors may feel that over the long term these targets will be met. If the track record of the monetary authorities is proven, investors may feel further that inflation is no longer a significant issue. In these situations the case for holding index-linked bonds is weakened.

The real-yield level on indexed bonds in other markets is also a factor. As capital markets around the world have become closely integrated in the last 20 years, global capital mobility means that high inflation markets are shunned by investors. Therefore over time expected returns, certainly in developed and liquid markets, should be roughly equal, so that real yields are at similar levels around the world. If we accept this premise, we would then expect the real yield on index-linked bonds to be at approximately similar levels, whatever market they are traded in. For example we would expect indexed bonds in the UK to be at a level near to that in, say, the US market. In fact in May 1999 long-dated index-linked gilts traded at just over 2% real yield, while long-dated indexed bonds in the USA were at the higher real-yield level of 3.8%. This was viewed by analysts as reflecting that international capital was not as mobile as had previously been thought, and that productivity gains and technological progress in the US economy had boosted demand for capital there to such an extent that real yield had had to rise. However, there is no doubt that there is considerable information content in index-linked bonds and analysts are always interested in the yield levels of these bonds compared with conventional bonds.

Further views on index-linked yields

The market analyzes the trading patterns and yield levels of index-linked gilts for their information content. The difference between the yield on index-linked gilts and conventional gilts of the same maturity is an indication of the market's view on future inflation; where this difference is historically low it implies that the market considers that inflation prospects are benign. So the yield spread between index-linked gilts and the same maturity conventional gilt is roughly the market's view of expected inflation levels over the long term. For example on 3 November 1999 the ten-year benchmark, the $5\frac{3}{4}$% Treasury 2009, had a gross redemption yield of 5.280%. The ten-year index-linked bond, the $2\frac{1}{2}$% I-L Treasury 2009,[3] had a *money yield* of 5.046% and a real yield of 2.041%, the latter assuming an inflation rate of 3%. Roughly speaking, this reflects a market view on inflation of approximately 3.24% in the ten years to maturity. Of course other factors drive both conventional and index-linked bond yields, including supply and demand, and liquidity. Generally, conventional bonds are more liquid than index-linked bonds. An increased demand will depress yields for the conventional bond as well.[4] However, the inflation expectation will also be built into the conventional bond yield and it is reasonable to assume the spread to be an approximation of the market's view on inflation over the life of the bond. A higher inflation expectation will result in a greater spread between the two bonds, which will be reflected by a premium to holders of the conventional issue as a compensation against the effects of inflation. This spread has declined slightly from May 1997 onwards, the point at which the government gave up control over monetary policy and the Monetary Policy Committee (MPC) of the Bank of England became responsible for setting interest rates.

---

3. This bond was issued in October 1982; as at October 1999 there was £2.625 billion nominal outstanding.

TABLE 10.1 ▪ Real yield on the $2\frac{1}{2}$% I-L 2009 *v.* the ten-year benchmark gilt

	Yields (%)							
Bonds	*Feb. 1997*	*June 1997*	*Feb. 1998*	*June 1998*	*Feb. 1999*	*June 1999*	*Sep. 1999*	*Nov. 1999*
2.5% I-L 2009 *	3.451	3.707	3.024	2.880	1.937	1.904	2.352	2.041
7.25% 2007	7.211	7.021	–	–	–	–	–	–
9% 2008	–	–	5.959	5.911	–	–	–	–
5.75% 2009	–	–	–	–	4.379	4.907	5.494	5.280
Spread	3.760	3.314	2.935	3.031	2.442	3.003	3.142	3.239

* Real yield, assuming 3% rate of inflation

Source: Bloomberg L.P.

Table 10.1 shows the real yield of the $2\frac{1}{2}$% I–L 2009 bond at selected points since the beginning of 1997, alongside the gross redemption yield of the ten-year benchmark conventional bond at the time (we use the same index-linked bond because there was no issue that matured in 2007 or 2008). Although the market's view on expected inflation rates over the ten-year period is on the whole stuck around the 3% level, there has been a downward trend in the period since the MPC became responsible for setting interest rates. As the MPC has an inflation target of 2.5%, the spread between the real yield on the ten-year linker and the ten-year conventional gilt implies that the market believes that the MPC will achieve its goal.[5]

The yield spread between index-linked and conventional gilts fluctuates over time and is influenced by a number of factors and not solely by the market's view of future inflation (the implied forward inflation rate). However, the market uses this yield spread to gauge an idea of future inflation levels. The other term used to describe the yield spread is *breakeven inflation*, that is the level of inflation required that would equate nominal yields on index-linked gilts with yields on conventional gilts. Figure 10.2 shows the implied forward inflation rate for the 15-year and 25-year terms to maturity as they fluctuated during 1998 and 1999. The data is from the Bank of England. For both maturity

4. For example two days later, following a rally in the gilt market, the yield on the conventional gilt was 5.069%, against a real yield on the index-linked gilt of 1.973%, implying that the inflation premium had been reduced to 3.09%. This is significantly lower than the premium just two days later, which may reflect the fact that the Monetary Policy Committee (MPC) of the Bank of England had just raised interest rates by $\frac{1}{4}$% the day before, but the rally in gilts would impact the conventional bond more than the linker.
5. In fact the MPC target centres on the RPIX measures of inflation, the 'underlying' rate. This is the RPI measure, but with mortgage interest payments stripped out.

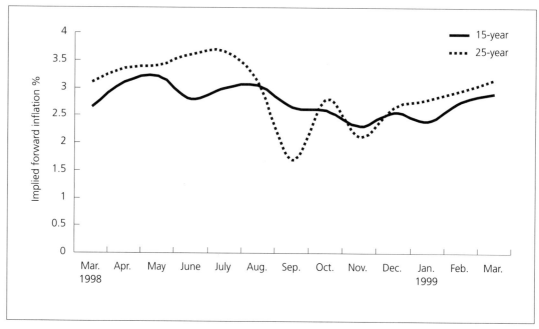

FIGURE 10.2 ■ UK implied forward inflation rates during 1998–9

Source: Bank of England

terms, the implied forward rate decreased significantly during the summer of 1998; analysts ascribed this to the rally in the conventional gilts, brought on by the 'flight to quality' after the emerging markets fall-out beginning in July that year. This rally was not matched by index-linked gilts performance. The 25-year implied forward inflation rate touched 1.66% in September 1999, which was considered excessively optimistic given that the Bank of England was working towards achieving a 2.5% rate of inflation over the long term! This suggested then that conventional gilts were significantly overvalued.[6] As we see in Figure 10.2, this implied forward rate for both maturity terms returned to more explainable levels later during the year – slightly above 3%. This is viewed as more consistent with the MPC's target, and can be expected to fall to just over 2.5% over the long term.

6. As we have noted, the yield spread between index-linked and conventional gilts reflects other considerations in addition to the forward inflation rate. As well as specific supply and demand issues, considerations include the inflation risk premium in the yield of conventional gilts, and distortions created when modelling the yield curve. There is also a liquidity premium priced into index-linked gilt yields that would not apply to benchmark conventional gilts. The effect of these is generally to overstate the implied forward inflation rate. Note also that the implied forward inflation rate applies to RPI, whereas the MPC's inflation objective targets the RPIX measure of inflation, which is the headline inflation rate minus the impact of mortgage interest payments.

Analysis of real interest rates[7]

Observing trading patterns in a liquid market in inflation-indexed bonds enables analysts to draw conclusions on nominal versus real interest indicators, and the concept of an inflation term structure. However, such analysis is often problematic because there is usually a significant difference between liquidity levels of conventional and indexed bonds. Nevertheless, as we discussed in the previous section, it is usually possible to infer market estimates of inflation expectations from the yields observed on indexed bonds, when compared with conventional yields.

Inflation expectations

Where an indexed bond incorporates an indexation lag there is an imperfect indexation and the bond's return will not be completely inflation-proof. Deacon and Derry (1998) suggest that this means an indexed bond may be regarded as a combination of a true indexed instrument (with no lag) and an unindexed bond. Where the lag period is exactly one coupon period, the price/yield relationship is given by:

$$P = \sum_{j=1}^{n} \frac{C \prod_{i=0}^{j-1} (1 + ri_i)}{(1 + rm_j)^j \prod_{i=1}^{j} (1 + ri_i)} + \frac{M \prod_{i=0}^{n-1} (1 + ri_i)}{(1 + rm_n)^n \prod_{i=1}^{n} (1 + ri_i)} \qquad (10.9)$$

where

ri is the rate of inflation between dates $i-1$ and i

rm is the redemption yield

and C and M are coupon and redemption payments as usual. If the bond has just paid the last coupon ahead of its redemption date, (10.9) reduces to:

$$P = \frac{C}{(1 + rm)(1 + ri)} + \frac{M}{(1 + rm)(1 + ri)}. \qquad (10.10)$$

In this situation the final cash flows are not indexed and the price/yield relationship is identical to that of a conventional bond. This fact enables us to quantify the indexation element, since the yields observed on conventional bonds can be compared to those on the non-indexed element of the indexed bond. This implies a true real yield measure for the indexed bond.

    The Fisher identity is used to derive this estimate. Essentially, this describes the relationship between nominal and real interest rates, and in one form is given as:

$$1 + y = (1 + r)(1 + i)(1 + \rho) \qquad (10.11)$$

7. This section follows the approach (with permission) adopted in Deacon and Derry (1998), Chapter 5.

where

    y is the nominal interest rate

    r is the real interest rate

    i is the expected rate of inflation

    ρ is a premium for the risk of future inflation.

Using (10.11), assuming a value for the risk premium ρ, we can link the two bond price equations, which can, as a set of simultaneous equations, be used to obtain values for the real interest rate and the expected inflation rate.

If they exist, one approach is to use two bonds of identical maturity, one conventional and one indexed, and ignoring lag effects use the yields on both to determine the expected inflation rate, given by the difference between the redemption yields of each bond. In fact, as we noted in the previous section, this measures the average expected rate of inflation during the period from now to the maturity of the bonds. This is at best an approximation. It is a flawed measure because an assumption of the expected inflation rate has been made when calculating the redemption yield of the indexed bond in the first place. The problem is exacerbated if the maturity of both bonds is relatively short, because the impact of the unindexed element of the indexed bond is greater the shorter its maturity. To overcome this flaw, a breakeven rate of inflation is used. This is calculated by first calculating the yield on the conventional bond, followed by the yield on the indexed bond using an assumed initial inflation rate. The risk premium ρ is set to an assumed figure, say 0. The Fisher identity is used to calculate a new estimate of the expected inflation rate i. This new estimate is then used to recalculate the yield on the indexed bond, which is then used to produce a new estimate of the expected inflation rate. The process is repeated iteratively until a consistent value for i is obtained.

The main drawback with this basic technique is that it is rare for there to exist a conventional and an index-linked bond of identical maturity, so approximately similar maturities have to be used, further diluting the results. The yields on each bond will also be subject to liquidity, taxation, indexation and other influences. There is also no equivalent benchmark (or *on-the-run*) indexed security. The bibliography cites some recent research that has investigated this approach.

An inflation term structure

Where a liquid market in indexed bonds exists, across a reasonable maturity term structure, it is possible to construct a term structure of inflation rates. In essence this involves fitting the nominal and real interest rate term structures, the two of which can then be used to infer an inflation term structure. This in turn can be used to calculate a forward

8. This is a term structure of *expected* inflation rates.

expected inflation rate for any future term, or a forward inflation curve, in the same way that a forward interest rate curve is constructed.

The Bank of England uses an iterative technique to construct a term structure of inflation rates.[8] First the nominal interest rate term structure is fitted using a version of the Waggoner model (1997, also described in James and Webber (2000)). An initial assumed inflation term structure is then used to infer a term structure of real interest rates. This assumed inflation curve is usually set flat at 3% or 5%. The real interest rate curve is then used to calculate an implied real interest rate forward curve. Second, the Fisher identity is applied at each point along the nominal and real interest rate forward curves, which produces a new estimate of the inflation term structure. A new real interest rate curve is calculated from this curve. The process is repeated until a single consistent inflation term structure is produced.

Appendix 10.1 Current issuers of public-sector indexed securities

TABLE 10.2 ■ Current issuers of public-sector inflation-indexed securities

Country	Date first issued	Index linking
Australia	1983	Consumer prices
	1991	Average weekly earnings
Austria	1953	Electricity prices
Brazil	1964–90	Wholesale prices
	1991	General prices
Canada	1991	Consumer prices
Chile	1966	Consumer prices
Colombia	1967	Wholesale prices
	1995	Consumer prices
Czech Republic	1997	Consumer prices
Denmark	1982	Consumer prices
France	1956	Average value of French securities
Greece	1997	Consumer prices
Hungary	1995	Consumer prices
Iceland	1964–80	Cost of building index
	1980–94	Credit terms index
	1995	Consumer prices
Ireland	1983	Consumer prices

TABLE 10.2 ■ Continued

Country	Date first issued	Index linking
Italy	1983	Deflator of GDP at factor cost
Mexico	1989	Consumer prices
New Zealand	1977–84	Consumer prices
	1995	Consumer prices
Norway	1982	Consumer prices
Poland	1992	Consumer prices
Sweden	1952	Consumer prices
	1994	Consumer prices
Turkey	1994–7	Wholesale prices
	1997	Consumer prices
UK	1981	Consumer prices
USA	1997	Consumer prices

Source: Deacon and Derry (1998). Used with permission of Prentice Hall Europe.

Appendix 10.2 US Treasury inflation-indexed securities

Indexation calculation

US Treasury inflation-indexed securities (TIPS) link their coupon and principal to an index ratio of the consumer prices index. The index ratio is given by

$$\frac{CPI_{\text{Settlement}}}{CPI_{\text{Issue}}} \tag{10.12}$$

where 'settlement' is the settlement date and 'issue' is the issue date of the bond. The actual CPI used is that recorded for the calendar month three months prior to the relevant date, this being the lag time. For the first day of any month, the reference CPI level is that recorded three months earlier, so for example on 1 May the relevant CPI measure would be that recorded on 1 February. For any other day in the month, linear interpolation is used to calculate the appropriate CPI level recorded in the reference month and the following month.

Cash flow calculation

The inflation adjustment for the security cash flows is given as the principal multiplied by the index ratio for the relevant date, minus the principal (ρ). This is termed the inflation compensation (IC), given as:

$$\text{Inflation compensation}_{\text{set date}} = (\text{principal} \times \text{index ratio}_{\text{set date}}) - \text{principal}$$

Coupon payments are given by:

$$Interest_{div\ date} = \frac{C}{2} \times (P + IC_{div\ date})$$ (10.13)

The redemption value of a TIPS is guaranteed by the Treasury to be a minimum of $100, whatever value has been recorded by the CPI during the life of the bond.

Settlement price

The price/yield formula for a TIPS security is given by the following expressions:

　　Price = inflation – adjusted price + inflation – adjusted accrued interest

　　Inflation – adjusted price = real price × index ratio$_{set\ date}$

The real price is given by:

$$\left[\frac{1}{1 + \frac{f}{d}\frac{r}{2}}\right]\left(\frac{C}{2} + \frac{C}{2}\sum_{j=1}^{n}\varnothing^{j} + 100\varnothing^{n}\right) - RAI$$ (10.14)

where

　　Inflation – adjusted accrued interest = $RAI \times IR_{set\ date}$

and where

$$\varnothing = \frac{1}{1 + \frac{r}{2}}$$

r　　is the annual real yield

RAI　is the unadjusted accrued interest, which is $\dfrac{C}{2} \times \dfrac{(d-f)}{d}$

f　　is the number of days from the settlement date to the next coupon date
d　　is the number of days in the regular semi-annual coupon period ending on the next coupon date
n　　is the number of full semi-annual coupon periods between the next coupon date and the maturity date.

SELECTED BIBLIOGRAPHY AND REFERENCES

Anderson, N., Breedon, F., Deacon, M., Derry, A., Murphy, J., *Estimating and Interpreting the Yield Curve*, Wiley 1996.
Arak, M., Kreicher, L., 'The real rate of interest: inferences from the new UK indexed gilts', *International Economic Review* 26:2, 1985, pp. 399–408.

Bootle, R., *Index-Linked Gilts: A Practical Investment Guide*, 2nd edition, Woodhead-Faulkner 1991.

Brown, R., Schaefer, S., 'The term structure of real interest rates and the Cox, Ingersoll and Ross model', *Journal of Financial Economics*, 35:1, 1994, pp. 3–42.

Brynjolfsson, J., Fabozzi, F., *Handbook of Inflation Indexed Bonds*, FJF Associates 1999.

Deacon, M., Derry, A., 'Deriving estimates of inflation expectations from the prices of UK government bonds', *Bank of England working paper* 23, July 1994.

Deacon, M., Derry, A., *Inflation Indexed Securities*, Prentice Hall 1998.

Fisher, I., *The Theory of Interests*, Macmillan 1930.

Foresi, S., Penati, A., Pennacchi, G., 'Reducing the cost of government debt: the role of index-linked bonds', in de Cecco, M., Pecchi, L., Piga, G. (eds), *Public Debt: Index-Linked Bonds in Theory and Practice*, Edward Elgar 1997.

James, J., Webber, N., *Interest Rate Modelling*, Wiley 2000.

Waggoner, D., 'Spline methods for extracting interest rate curves from coupon bond prices', *Federal Reserve Bank of Atlanta Working Paper* 97-10, 1997.

Wojnilower, A., *Inflation-Indexed Bonds: Promising the Moon*, Clipper Group 1997.

Part III

Structured financial products

The market in structured financial products is very large and diverse. In Part III we give readers a flavour of these instruments. After introducing the concept of securitization, we discuss mortgage-backed securities and collateralized debt obligations (CDOs). As usual, a number of recommended references are listed to enable readers to continue with their research.

CHAPTER 11

Structured financial products: mortgage-backed securities I

The process of securitization creates *asset-backed bonds*. These are debt instruments that have been created from a package of loan assets on which interest is payable, usually on a floating basis. The asset-backed market was developed in the USA and is a large, diverse market containing a wide range of instruments. The characteristics of asset-backed securities present additional features in their analysis, which are introduced in this chapter. Financial engineering techniques employed by investment banks today enable an entity to create a bond structure from any type of cash flow; the typical forms are high-volume loans, such as residential mortgages, car loans and credit card loans. The loans form assets on a bank or finance house balance sheet, which are packaged together and used as backing for an issue of bonds. The interest payments on the original loans form the cash flows used to service the new bond issue.

The development of the market in securitized bonds is such that these days an investment bank will not think it unusual to underwrite a bond issue secured against any type of cash flow, from the more traditional mortgages and loan assets to cash flows received by leisure and recreational facilities such as health clubs, public houses and other entities such as nursing homes. The asset class behind a securitized bond issue is significant, and there are distinct classes, each calling for their own methods of analysis and valuation. Traditionally mortgage-backed bonds are grouped in their own right as mortgage-backed securities (MBS) while other structured financial products are known as asset-backed securities (ABS) or collateralized debt obligations (CDO).

Introduction

Reasons for undertaking securitization

The driving force behind the growth of securitization was the need for banks to realize value from the assets on their balance sheet. Typically these assets were residential and commercial mortgages, corporate loans, and retail loans such as credit card debt. What factors might lead a financial institution to securitize a part of its balance sheet? A bank may wish to reduce the size of its balance sheet for the following reasons:

■ if revenues received from assets remain roughly unchanged but the size of assets has decreased, this will lead to an increase in the return on equity ratio;

■ the level of capital required to support the balance sheet will be reduced, which again can lead to cost savings or allows the institution to allocate the capital to other, perhaps more profitable, business;

■ to obtain cheaper funding: frequently the interest payable on ABS securities is considerably below the level payable on the underlying loans. This creates a cash surplus for the originating entity.

By entering into securitization, a lower-rated entity can access debt capital markets that would otherwise be the preserve of higher-rated institutions. The growth of the so-called 'credit card banks' in the USA, such as MBNA International, would have been severely restricted if a market for the securitized assets of these firms had not been in place.

Market participants

The securitization process involves a number of participants. In the first instance is the *originator*, the firm whose assets are being securitized. The most common process involves an *issuer*, acquiring the assets from the originator. The issuer is usually a company that has been specially set up for the purpose of the securitization and is known as a *special purpose vehicle* (SPV) and is usually domiciled offshore. The creation of an SPV ensures that the underlying asset pool is held separately from the other assets of the originator. This is done so that in the event that the originator is declared bankrupt or insolvent, the impact on the original assets is minimized.

This last is often the responsibility of a *trustee*. The issue trustee is responsible for looking after the interests of bondholders. Its roles include:

■ representing the interests of investors (note holders);

■ monitoring the transaction and issuer to see if any violation of the deal covenants has occurred;

■ enforcing the rights of the note holders in the event of bankruptcy.

The *security trustee* is responsible for:

■ holding the security interest in the underlying collateral pool;

■ liaising with the manager of the underlying collateral;

■ acting under the direction of the note trustee in the event of default.

By holding the assets within an SPV framework, defined in formal legal terms, the financial status and credit rating of the originator becomes almost irrelevant to the bond-holders. The process may also involve credit enhancements, in which a third-party guarantee of credit quality is obtained, so that notes issued under the securitization are often rated at investment grade and up to AAA grade.

There is also a third-party institution, often the same entity that provides the trustee service, which carries out the duties of *paying agent, cash manager* and *bond administrator.*

Figure 11.1 illustrates the process of securitization.

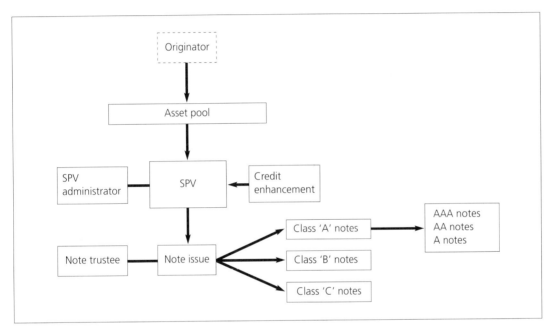

FIGURE 11.1 ■ The securitization process

Asset-backed bonds

Introduction

There is a well-developed market in bond instruments that trade under the overall heading of asset-backed bonds. These are bundled securities, so called because they are marketable instruments that result from the bundling or packaging together of a set of non-marketable assets. This process is known as *securitization*, when part of an institution's assets, such as commercial loans, is removed from its balance sheet and packaged together as one large loan, and then 'sold' on to an investor, or series of investors, who then receive the interest payments due on the assets until they are redeemed. The purchasers of the securitized assets often have no recourse to the original borrowers, in fact the original borrowers are not usually involved in the transaction or any of its processes.

Securitization was introduced in the US market, and this market remains the largest for asset-backed bonds. The earliest examples of such bonds were in the US mortgage market, where residential mortgage loans made by a *thrift* (building society) were packaged together and sold on to investors, who received the interest and principal payments made by the borrowers of the original loans. Market participants typically refer to asset-backed bonds as being securities backed by an underlying pool that includes commercial loans, credit card debt, car loans, lease receivables and so on, with *mortgage-backed bonds* considered to be a separate class, split into residential mortgage securities and commercial mortgage securities.

The process of securitization can benefit the originating institution in a number of ways. One key benefit is that removing assets from the balance sheet reduces risk exposure for a financial institution or bank and enhances its liquidity position. The effect of the numerous benefits is increased with the maturity of the original loans. For example in the case of mortgage loans, the term to maturity can be up to 25 years, perhaps longer. Most of these loans are financed out of deposits that can be withdrawn on demand, or at relatively short notice. In addition, it is often the case that as a result of securitization the packaged loans are funded at a lower rate than that charged by the original lending institution. This implies that the bundled loans can be sold off at a higher value than the level at which the lending institution valued them. Put another way, securitizing loans adds value to the loan book and it is the original lender that receives this value. Another benefit is that as a result of securitization, the total funding available to the lending institution may well increase due to its access to capital markets; in other words, the firm becomes less dependent on its traditional deposit base. And finally, by reducing the level of debt on the lending institution's balance sheet, securitization will improve the firm's gearing ratio.

The main advantage to the investor of securitization is that it offers a marketable asset-backed instrument in which to invest. Often the instrument offers two levels of protection: the original assets and credit enhancement. The original assets will provide good security if they are well diversified and equivalent in terms of quality, terms and conditions (for example, the repayment structure and maturity of assets). A diversified asset base reduces the risk of a single drastic failure, while homogeneous assets make it more straightforward to analyze the loan base. If there is little or no liquidity in the original loans (no secondary market), then investors will often require *credit enhancement* in the form of an insurance contract, letters of credit, subordination of a second tranche (which absorbs losses first), over-collateralization or a reserve fund (for the instrument to be sold at a price acceptable to the original lender). Ironically, by implementing one or more of the protection features described, securitization provides a better credit risk for the investor than the loans represented to the original lender.

Securitization began in the US housing market in 1970 after the Government National Mortgage Association (GNMA or 'Ginnie Mae') began issuing *mortgage pass-through certificates*. A pass-through is a security representing ownership in a pool of mortgages. The mortgages themselves are sold through a grantor trust and the certificates are sold in the capital markets. As with standard mortgages, the interest and amortized principal are paid monthly. Later on, *mortgage-backed bonds* were issued with semi-annual payments and maturities of up to 15 years, which were terms familiar to domestic bondholders. In 1983 *collateralized mortgage obligations* were issued, the collateral being provided by mortgages issued by the Federal Home Loans Mortgage Corporation. Being government agencies, the bonds that they issue are guaranteed and as such carry little additional risk compared with US Treasury securities. They can therefore be priced on the same basis as Treasuries. However, they present an additional type of risk, that of *prepayment risk*. This is the risk that mortgages will be paid off early, ahead of their term – a risk that increases when mortgages have been taken out at high fixed interest rates and rates have subsequently fallen. The existence of this risk therefore dictates that these bonds pay a higher return than corresponding Treasury bonds. The term *average life* is used to describe the years to maturity for asset-backed bonds that carry an element of prepayment risk, and is an estimate used by bond analysts.

Securitization was introduced in the UK market in 1985. A number of institutions were established for the purpose of securitizing mortgages and other assets such as car loans and credit card debt. These included the National Home Loans Corporation, Mortgage Funding Corporation and First Mortgage Securities.

Credit rating

Virtually all public mortgage-backed and asset-backed securities (MBS and ABS) are explicitly rated, often by one or both of the largest credit-rating agencies: Moody's and Standard & Poor's. In structured financings it is normal for the rating of the paper to be investment grade, with most issues at launch being rated Aaa and/or AAA. To suit investor requirements, issues are often structured as multi-tranche, with the highest-rated tranche (the 'class A' note) being AAA while the lowest-rated tranche may be, say, BB-rated. The rating of the issue is derived from a combination of factors. In so far as it cannot generally be expected that investors will be sufficiently protected by the performance of the collateral alone, the rating agencies look to minimize the risk of principal default and ensure timely payment of interest coupons by requiring additional enhancement. The percentage of additional enhancement is determined by analyzing the 'riskiness' of the collateral under a range of stress-tested environments. These seek to quantify the effect of various interest rate, foreclosure and loss scenarios, which are largely based on the expected performance of the collateral base in a recession. Much of the analysis is based on performance in the US markets, and the rating agencies try to establish criteria for each market and collateral type that is rated. The amount of enhancement required depends on the rating required at launch, for instance less is required for a lower rated issue. In many cases issues will be backed by a larger nominal value of collateral, known as a *float*; for example, an issue size of £480 million nominal is formed out of assets composed of, say, £550 million.

Enhancement levels are also determined by the agencies reviewing the legal risks in the transaction. The legal analysis examines the competing rights and interests in the assets, including those of the bondholders and various third parties. MBSs and ABSs are typically issued out of low capitalized SPV companies, established solely for the purpose of issuing the securities. The rating agencies need to be assured that there is no risk to the bondholders in the event of the originator – the seller of the assets to the SPV – becoming insolvent, and to be certain that a receiver or administrator cannot seize the assets or obtain rights to the SPV's cash flows. In the same way, the agencies need to be satisfied that the SPV will be able to meet its obligations to its investors in circumstances where the service body (the entity responsible for administering the collateral, usually the originator) becomes insolvent. Consequently, significant emphasis is placed on ensuring that all primary and supporting documentation preserves the rights of investors in the security. An independent trustee is appointed to represent the interests of investors.

A change in rating for an ABS or MBS issue may be due to deterioration in performance of the collateral, heavy utilization of credit enhancement, or downgrade of a supporting rating, for example an insurance company that was underwriting insurance on the pool of the assets.

Credit enhancement

To ensure investment-grade rating of issued notes where the quality of the underlying collateral pool is not AAA, credit enhancement is often arranged by the originator. Credit support enhancement for ABS and MBS issues is usually by one of the following methods:

- *Pool insurance*: An insurance policy provided by a composite insurance company to cover the risk of principal loss in the collateral pool. The claims-paying rating of the insurance company is important in determining the overall rating of the issue. In many cases in the past, the rating of the insurance company at launch proved to be insufficient to achieve the desired rating, and a reinsurance policy was entered into with a higher rated company in order to achieve the desired rating.

- *Senior/Junior note classes*: Credit enhancement is provided by subordinating a class of notes ('class B' notes) to the senior class notes ('class A' notes). The class B note's right to its proportional share of cash flows is subordinated to the rights of the senior note holders. Class B notes do not receive payments of principal until certain rating agency requirements have been met; specifically satisfactory performance of the collateral pool over a pre-determined period, or in many cases until all the senior note classes have been redeemed in full.

■ *Margin step-up*: A number of ABS issues incorporate a step-up feature in the coupon structure, which typically coincides with a call date. Although the issuer is usually under no obligation to redeem the notes at this point, the step-up feature was introduced as an added incentive for investors, to convince them from the outset that the economic cost of paying a higher coupon would be unacceptable and that the issuer would seek to refinance by exercising its call option.

■ *Substitution*: This feature enables the issuer to utilize principal cash flows from redemptions to purchase new collateral from the originator. This has the effect of lengthening the effective life of the transaction because the principal would otherwise have been used to redeem the notes. The issuer is usually under no obligation to substitute and it is an option granted by the investor.

Redemption mechanism

ABS and MBS issue terms incorporate one of two main methods through which redeeming principal can be passed back to investors:

■ *Drawing by lot*: The available principal from the relevant interest period is repaid to investors by the international clearing agencies (Euroclear and Cedel) drawing notes, at random, for cancellation. Notes will therefore trade at their nominal value.

■ *Pro rata*: The available principal for the interest period is distributed among all investors, dependent upon their holding in the security. A *pool factor* is calculated, which is the remaining principal balance of the note expressed as a factor of one. For instance, if the pool factor is 0.62557, this means that for each note of £10,000 nominal, £3,744.3 of principal has been repaid to date. A pool factor value is useful to investors since early repayment of, say, mortgages reduces the level of asset backing available for an issue; the outstanding value of such an issue is reduced on a pro-rata basis, like early redemption, by a set percentage, so that the remaining amount outstanding is adequately securitized.

Additional features

Some ABS structures will incorporate a *call option* feature. In some cases the terms of the issue prevent a call being exercised until a certain percentage of the issue remains outstanding, usually 10%, and a certain date has been passed.

It is common for ABS issues to have an *average life* quoted for them. This says that, based on the most recent principal balance for the security, it is assumed that a redemption rate is applied such that the resultant average life equals the number of months left from the last interest payment date, until 50% of the principal balance remains. Some issuers will announce the expected average life of their paper, and yield calculations are based on this average life.

Securitizing mortgages

Introduction

A mortgage is a loan made for the purpose of purchasing property, which in turn is used as the security for the loan itself. It is defined as a debt instrument giving conditional ownership of an asset, and secured by the asset that is being financed. The borrower provides the lender with a mortgage in exchange for the right to use the property during the term of the mortgage, and the borrower also agrees to make regular payments of both principal and interest. The mortgage lien is the security for the lender, and is removed when the debt is paid off. A mortgage may involve residential property or commercial property and is a long-term debt, normally 25 to 30 years; however, it can be drawn up for shorter periods if required by the borrower. If the borrower or *mortgagor* defaults on the interest payments, the lender or *mortgagee* has the right to take over the property and recover the debt from the proceeds of selling the property. Mortgages can be either fixed-rate or floating-rate interest. Although in the US mortgages are generally amortizing loans, known as *repayment* mortgages in the UK, there are also *interest-only* mortgages where the borrower pays only the interest on the loan; on maturity the original loan amount is paid off by the proceeds of a maturing investment contract taken out at the same time as the mortgage. These are known as *endowment* mortgages and are popular in the UK market, although their popularity has been waning in recent years.

A lending institution may have many hundreds of thousands of individual residential and commercial mortgages on its book. If the total loan book is pooled together and used as collateral for the issue of a bond, the resulting instrument is a *mortgage-backed security*. This process is known as *securitization*, which is the pooling of loan assets in order to use them as collateral for a bond issue. Sometimes an SPV is set up specifically to serve as the entity representing the pooled assets. This is done for administrative reasons and also sometimes to enhance the credit rating that may be assigned to the bonds. In the UK some SPVs have an AAA credit rating, although the majority of SPVs are below this rating, whilst retaining investment-grade status.

In the US market certain mortgage-backed securities are backed, either implicitly or explicitly, by the government, in which case they trade essentially as risk-free instruments and are not rated by the credit agencies. In the USA the GNMA and two other government-sponsored agencies, the Federal Home Loan Corporation and the Federal National Mortgage Association ('Freddie Mac' and 'Fannie Mae' respectively), purchase mortgages for the purpose of pooling them and holding them in their portfolios; they may then be securitized. Bonds that are not issued by government agencies are rated in the same way as other corporate bonds. On the other hand, non-government agencies sometimes obtain mortgage insurance for their issue, in order to boost its credit quality. When this happens the credit rating of the mortgage insurer becomes an important factor in the credit standing of the bond issue.

Growth of the market

One study[1] has suggested the following advantages of mortgage-backed bonds:

- Although many mortgage bonds represent comparatively high-quality assets and are collateralized instruments, the yields on them are usually higher than on corporate bonds of the same credit quality. This is because of the complexity of the instruments and the uncertain nature of the mortgage cash flows. In the mid-1990s mortgage-backed bonds traded at yields of around 100–200 basis points above Treasury bonds.

- The wide range of products offers investors a choice of maturities, cash flows and security to suit individual requirements.

- Agency mortgage-backed bonds are implicitly backed by the government and therefore represent a better credit risk than AAA-rated corporate bonds; the credit rating for non-agency bonds is often AAA or AA.

- The size of the market means that it is very liquid, with agency mortgage-backed bonds having the same liquidity as Treasury bonds.

- The monthly coupon frequency of mortgage-backed bonds makes them an attractive instrument for investors who require frequent income payments; this feature is not available for most other bond market instruments.

In the UK the asset-backed market has also witnessed rapid growth, and many issues are AAA rated because issuers create an SPV that is responsible for the issue. Various forms of insurance are also used. Most bonds are floating-rate instruments, reflecting the variable-rate nature of the majority of mortgages in the UK.

1. Hayre, L., *et al.*, 1989.

Mortgages

In the US market, the terms of a conventional mortgage, known as a *level-payment fixed-rate mortgage*, will state the interest rate payable on the loan, the term of the loan and the frequency of payment. Most mortgages specify monthly payment of interest. These are in fact the characteristics of a level-payment mortgage, which has a fixed interest rate and fixed term to maturity. This means that the monthly interest payments are fixed, hence the term 'level pay'.

The singular feature of a mortgage is that, even if it charges interest at a fixed rate, its cash flows are not known with absolute certainty. This is because the borrower can elect to repay any or all of the principal before the final maturity date. This is a characteristic of all mortgages, and although some lending institutions impose a penalty on borrowers who retire the loan early, this is a risk for the lender, known as *repayment risk*. The uncertainty of the cash flow patterns is similar to that of a callable bond, and as we shall see later this feature means that we may value mortgage-backed bonds using a pricing model similar to that employed for callable bonds.

Some mortgage contracts incorporate a *servicing fee*. This is payable to the mortgage provider to cover the administrative costs associated with collecting interest payments, sending regular statements and other information to borrowers, chasing overdue payments, maintaining the records and processing systems, and other activities. Mortgage providers also incur costs when repossessing properties after mortgagors have fallen into default. Mortgages may be serviced by the original lender, or another third-party institution that has acquired the right to service it, in return for collecting the fee. When a servicing charge is payable by a borrower, the monthly mortgage payment is comprised of the interest costs, the principal repayment and the servicing fee. The fee incorporated into the monthly payment is usually stated as a percentage, say 0.25%. This is added to the mortgage rate.

Another type of mortgage in the US market is the *adjustable-rate mortgage* (ARM). These loans allow interest payments to be reset at periodic intervals to a short-term interest rate index that has been specified beforehand. The resets are at periodic intervals depending on the terms of the loan, and can be on a monthly, six-monthly or annual basis, or even longer. The interest rate is usually fixed at a spread over the reference rate. The reference rate that is used can be a market-determined rate such as the prime rate, or a calculated rate based on the funding costs for US savings and loan institutions or *thrifts*. The cost of funds for thrifts is calculated using the monthly average funding cost on the thrifts' activities, and there are 'thrift indexes' that are used to indicate to the cost of funding. The two most common indices are the Eleventh Federal Home Loan Bank Board District Cost of Funds Index (COFI) and the National Cost of Funds Index. Generally, borrowers prefer to fix the rate they pay on their loans to reduce uncertainty, and this makes fixed-rate mortgages more popular than variable-rate mortgages. A common incentive used to entice borrowers away from fixed-rate mortgages is to offer a below-market interest rate on an ARM mortgage, usually for an introductory period. This comfort period may be from two to five years or even longer. ARM mortgages are usually issued with additional features such as an interest rate cap specified beforehand; such a cap limits the maximum rate that the borrower would have to pay in the event of market rates increasing dramatically. ARMs make up more than half the market share in the US domestic mortgage business.[2]

Mortgages in the UK are predominantly *variable-rate mortgages*, in which the interest rate moves in line with the clearing bank base rate. It is rare to observe fixed-rate mortgages in the UK market, although short-term fixed-rate mortgages are more common (the rate reverts to a variable basis at the termination of the fixed-rate period).

A *balloon mortgage* entitles a borrower to long-term funding, but, under its terms, at a specified future date the interest rate payable is renegotiated. This effectively transforms a long-dated loan into a short-term borrowing. The balloon payment is the original amount of the loan, minus the amount that is amortized. In a balloon mortgage, therefore, the actual maturity of the bonds is below that of the stated maturity.

A *graduated payment mortgage* (GPM) is aimed at lower-earning borrowers, since the mortgage payments for a fixed initial period, say the first five years, are set at lower than the level applicable for a level-paying mortgage with an identical interest rate. The later mortgage payments are higher as a result. Hence a GPM mortgage will have a fixed term and a mortgage rate, but the offer letter will also contain details on the number of years over which the monthly mortgage payments will increase and the point at which level payments will take over. There will also be information on the annual increase in the mortgage payments. As the initial payments in a GPM are below the market rate, there will be little or no repayment of principal at this time. This means that the outstanding balance may actually increase during the early stages, a process known as *negative amortization*. The higher payments in the remainder of the mortgage term are designed to pay off the entire balance in maturity. The opposite to the GPM is the *growing equity mortgage* (GEM). This mortgage charges fixed-rate interest but the payments increase over time; this means that a greater proportion of the principal is paid off over time, so that the mortgage itself is repaid in a shorter time than the level-paying mortgage.

In the UK market it is more common to encounter hybrid mortgages, which charge a combination of fixed-rate and variable-rate interest. For example, the rate may be fixed for the first five years, after which it will vary with changes in the lender's base rate. Such a mortgage is known as a *fixed/adjustable hybrid mortgage*.

---

2. Sundaresan (1997), p. 366.

Mortgage risk

Although mortgage contracts are typically long-term loan contracts, running usually for 20 to 30 years or even longer, there is no limitation on the amount of the principal that may be repaid at any one time. In the US market there is no penalty for repaying the mortgage ahead of its term, which is known as a mortgage prepayment. In the UK some lenders impose a penalty if a mortgage is prepaid early, although this is more common for contracts that have been offered at special terms, such as a discounted loan rate for the start of the mortgage's life. The penalty is often set as extra interest, for example six months' worth of mortgage payments at the time when the contract is paid off. As a borrower is free to prepay a mortgage at a time of his choosing, the lender is not certain of the cash flows that will be paid after the contract is taken out. This is known as *prepayment* risk.

A borrower may pay off the principal ahead of the final termination date for a number of reasons. The most common reason is when the property on which the mortgage is secured is subsequently sold by the borrower; this results in the entire mortgage being paid off at once. The average life of a mortgage in the UK market is eight years, and mortgages are most frequently prepaid because the property has been sold.[3] Other actions that result in the prepayment of a mortgage are when a property is repossessed after the borrower has fallen into default, if there is a change in interest rates making it attractive to refinance the mortgage (usually with another lender), or if the property is destroyed by accident or natural disaster.

An investor acquiring a pool of mortgages from a lender will be concerned at the level of prepayment risk, which is usually measured by projecting the level of expected future payments using a financial model. Although it would not be possible to evaluate meaningfully the potential of an individual mortgage to be paid off early, it is tenable to conduct such analysis for a large number of loans pooled together. A similar activity is performed by actuaries when they assess the future liability of an insurance provider who has written personal pension contracts. Essentially, the level of prepayment risk for a pool of loans is lower than that of an individual mortgage. Prepayment risk has the same type of impact on a mortgage pool's performance and valuation as a call feature does on a callable bond. This is understandable because a mortgage is essentially a callable contract, with the 'call' at the option of the borrower of funds.

The other significant risk of a mortgage book is the risk that the borrower will fall into arrears, or be unable to repay the loan on maturity (in the UK). This is known as *default risk*. Lenders take steps to minimize the level of default risk by assessing the credit quality of each borrower, as well as the quality of the property itself. A study has also found that

---

3. Source: Halifax plc.

Repackaged securities

Repackaged securities, also called *repackagings* or *repacks,* are a form of asset-backed security. The key feature of a repack is that the underlying asset is another bond or group of bonds, usually eurobonds. Restructuring a bond enables it to be taken out of an investor's portfolio, and this may be desired because the issue was not a great success initially, or if it subsequently becomes illiquid in the secondary market. By repackaging the bond, it can in effect be 'resold' to meet changing conditions and investor requirements. Repacks are conceptually similar to asset-backed securities, and in the same way require greater servicing than conventional bond issues. For instance, they are usually issued via an SPV and require a trustee, bond administrator and so on. In addition, the underlying bond or bonds are held by a third-party *custodian.*

Convertible securities are frequently subject to repackagings. Consider where a fall in the general level of the stock market makes the conversion terms of the convertible unattractive. Without this sweetener, the convertible coupon level is not sufficient reason for investors to hold it, so demand for the bond disappears. The issue's original underwriter may repackage the convertible, along with a number of other issues, so that the coupon payments are enhanced. With this higher coupon level, there should be some demand for the new structure and the issue can be sold again. To increase the level of interest payments, the underlying assets can include a conventional government or corporate bond with identical coupon dates, or a deposit of cash with interest payable on the same coupon dates.

---

the higher the deposit paid by the borrower, the lower the level of default.[4] Therefore lenders prefer to advance funds against a borrower's *equity* that is deemed sufficient to protect against falls in the value of the property. In the UK the typical deposit required is 25%, although certain lenders will advance funds against smaller deposits such as 10% or 5%.

Mortgage-backed securities

Mortgage-backed securities are bonds created from a pool of mortgages. They are formed from mortgages that are for residential or commercial property or a mixture of both. Bonds created from commercial mortgages are known as *commercial mortgage-backed*

---

4. Brown, S., *et al.*, 'Analysis of mortgage servicing portfolios', Financial Strategies Group, Prudential-Bache Capital Funding 1990.

securities. There are a range of different securities in the market, known in the US as *mortgage pass-through securities*. There also exist two related securities known as *collateralized mortgage securities* and *stripped mortgage-backed securities*. Bonds that are created from mortgage pools that have been purchased by government agencies are known as *agency mortgage-backed securities*, and are regarded as risk-free in the same way as Treasury securities.

A *collateralized mortgage obligation* (CMO) differs from a pass-through security in that the cash flows from the mortgage pool are distributed on a prioritized basis, based on the class of security held by the investor. In example 25.2 this might mean that three different securities are formed, say with a total nominal value of $100 million, each entitled to a pro rata amount of the interest payments but with different priorities for the repayment of principal. For instance, $60 million of the issue might consist of a bond known as 'class A' which may be entitled to receipt of all the principal repayment cash flows, after which the next class of bonds is entitled to all the repayment cash flow; this bond would be 'class B', of which, say, $25 million was created, and so on. If 300 class A bonds are created, they would have a nominal value of $200,000 and each would receive 0.33% of the total cash flows received by the class A bonds. Note that all classes of bonds receive an equal share of the interest payments; it is the principal repayment cash flows received that differ. What is the main effect of this security structure? The most significant factor is that, in our illustration, the class A bonds will be repaid earlier than any other class of bond that is formed from the securitization. They therefore have the shortest maturity. The last class of bonds will have the longest maturity. There is still a level of uncertainty associated with the maturity of each bond, but this is less than the uncertainty associated with a pass-through security.

Let us consider another type of mortgage bond, the *stripped mortgage-backed security*. As its name suggests, this is created by separating the interest and principal payments into individual distinct cash flows. This allows an issuer to create two very interesting securities: the IO bond and the PO bond. In a stripped mortgage-backed bond the interest and principal are divided into two classes, and two bonds are issued that are each entitled to receive one class of cash flow only. The bond class that receives the interest payment cash flows is known as an *interest-only* or IO class, while the bond receiving the principal repayments is known as a *principal-only* or PO class. The PO bond is similar to a zero-coupon bond in that it is issued at a discount to par value. The return achieved by a PO bondholder is a function of the rapidity at which prepayments are made; if prepayments are received in a relatively short time the investor will realize a higher return. This would be akin to the buyer of a zero-coupon bond receiving the maturity payment ahead of the redemption date, and the highest possible return that a

PO bondholder could receive would occur if all the mortgages were prepaid the instant after the PO bond was bought! A low return will be achieved if all the mortgages are held until maturity, so that there are no prepayments. Stripped mortgage-backed bonds present potentially less advantage to an issuer compared with a pass-through security or a CMO; however, they are liquid instruments and are often traded to hedge a conventional mortgage bond book.

The price of a PO bond fluctuates as mortgage interest rates change. As we noted earlier, in the US market the majority of mortgages are fixed-rate loans, so that if mortgage rates fall below the coupon rate on the bond, the holder will expect the volume of prepayments to increase as individuals refinance loans in order to gain from lower borrowing rates. This will result in a faster stream of payments to the PO bondholder as cash flows are received earlier than expected. The price of the PO rises to reflect this, and also because cash flows in the mortgage will now be discounted at a lower rate. The opposite happens when mortgage rates rise and the rate of prepayment is expected to fall, which causes a PO bond to fall in price.

An IO bond is essentially a stream of cash flows and has no par value. The cash flows represent interest on the mortgage principal outstanding, therefore a higher rate of prepayment leads to a fall in the IO price. This is because the cash flows cease once the principal is redeemed. The risk for the IO bond holder is that prepayments occur so quickly that interest payments cease before the investor has recovered the amount originally paid for the IO bond. The price of an IO is also a function of mortgage rates in the market, but exhibits more peculiar responses. If rates fall below the bond coupon, again the rate of prepayment is expected to increase. This would cause the cash flows for the IO to decline, as mortgages are paid off more quickly. This would cause the price of the IO to fall as well, even though the cash flows themselves would be discounted at a lower interest rate. If mortgage rates rise, the outlook for future cash flows will improve as the prepayment rate falls; however, there is also a higher discounting rate for the cash flows themselves, so the price of an IO may move in either direction. Thus IO bonds exhibit a curious characteristic for a bond instrument, in that their price moves in the same direction as market rates.

Both versions of the stripped mortgage bond are interesting instruments, and they have high volatilities during times of market rate changes. Note that PO and IO bonds could be created from the hypothetical mortgage pool described above; therefore the combined modified duration of both instruments must equal the modified duration of the original pass-through security.

The securities described so far are essentially plain vanilla mortgage-backed bonds. There are more complicated instruments currently trading in the market.

Cash flow patterns

We stated that the exact term of a mortgage-backed security cannot be stated with accuracy at the time of issue, because of the uncertain frequency of mortgage prepayments. This uncertainty means that it is not possible to analyze the bonds using the conventional methods used for fixed-coupon bonds. The most common approach used by the market is to assume a fixed prepayment rate at the time of issue and use this to project the cash flows – and hence the life span – of the bond. The choice of prepayment selected therefore is significant, although it is recognized also that prepayment rates are not stable and will fluctuate with changes in mortgage rates and the economic cycle. In this section we consider some of the approaches used in evaluating the prepayment pattern of a mortgage-backed bond.

Prepayment analysis

Some market analysts assume a fixed life for a mortgage pass-through bond based on the average life of a mortgage. In the US market traditionally, a '12-year prepaid life' has been used to evaluate the securities, as market data has suggested that the average mortgage has paid off after the twelfth year. This is not generally favoured because it does not take into account the effect of mortgage rates and other factors. A more common approach is to use a *constant prepayment rate* (CPR). This measure is based on the expected number of mortgages in a pool that will be prepaid in a selected period, and is an annualized figure. The measure for the monthly level of prepayment is known as the *constant monthly repayment*, and measures the expected amount of the outstanding balance, minus the scheduled principal, that will be prepaid in each month. Another name for the constant monthly repayment is the *single monthly mortality rate* or SMM. The SMM is given by 11.1 and is an expected value for the percentage of the remaining mortgage balance that will be prepaid in that month:

$$SMM = 1 - (1 - CPR)^{1/12}$$

(11.1)

EXAMPLE *11.1 Constant prepayment rate*

The constant prepayment rate for a pool of mortgages is 2% each month. The outstanding principal balance at the start of the month is £72,200, while the scheduled principal payment is £223. This means that 2% of £71,977, or £1,439, will be prepaid in that month. To approximate the amount of principal prepayment, the constant monthly prepayment is multiplied by the outstanding balance.

In the US market the convention is to use the prepayment standard developed by the Public Securities Association,[5] which is the domestic bond market trade association. The PSA benchmark, known as 100% PSA, assumes a steadily increasing constant prepayment rate each month until the 30th month, when a constant rate of 6% is assumed. The starting prepayment rate is 0.2%, increasing at 0.2% each month until the rate levels off at 6%.

For the 100% PSA benchmark we may set, if t is the number of months from the start of the mortgage, that:

if $t < 30$, the CPR = 6%.t / 30

while if t > 30, then CPR is equal to 6%.

This benchmark can be altered if required to suit changing market conditions, so for example the 200% PSA has a starting prepayment rate and an increase that is double the 100% PSA model, so the initial rate is 0.4%, increasing by 0.4% each month until it reaches 12% in the 30th month, at which point the rate remains constant. The 50% PSA has a starting (and increases by a) rate of 0.1%, remaining constant after it reaches 3%.

The prepayment level of a mortgage pool will have an impact on its cash flows. If the amount of prepayment is nil, the cash flows will remain constant during the life of the mortgage. In a fixed-rate mortgage the proportion of principal and interest payment will change each month as more and more of the mortgage amortizes. That is, as the principal amount falls each month, the amount of interest decreases. If we assume that a pass-through security has been issued today, so that its coupon reflects the current market level, the payment pattern will resemble the bar chart shown in Figure 11.2.

When there is an element of prepayment in a mortgage pool, for example as in the 100% PSA or 200% PSA model, the amount of principal payment will increase during the early years of the mortgages and then become more steady, before declining for the remainder of the term; this is because the principal balance has declined to such an extent that the scheduled principal payments become less significant. The example for a prepayment of a single loan at 100% PSA (for a 9% rate 30-year maturity loan) is shown in Figure 11.3.

The prepayment volatility of a mortgage-backed bond will vary according to the interest rate of the underlying mortgages. It has been observed that where the mortgages have interest rates of between 100 and 300 basis points above current mortgage rates, the prepayment volatility is the highest. At the bottom of the range, any fall in interest rates often leads to a sudden increase in refinancing of mortgages; while at the top of the range, an increase in rates will lead to a decrease in the prepayment rate.

5. Since renamed the Bond Market Association.

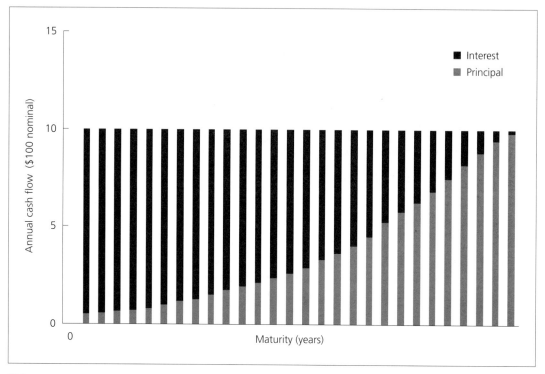

FIGURE 11.2 ■ Mortgage pass-through security with 0% constant prepayment rate

The actual cash flow of a mortgage pass-through is of course dependent on the cash flow patterns of the mortgages in the pool. The projected monthly mortgage payment for a level-paying fixed rate mortgage in any month is given by (11.2):

$$\overline{I}_t = \overline{M}_{mt-1}\left[\frac{r(1 + r)^{n-t+1}}{(1 + r)^{n-t+1} - 1}\right] \tag{11.2}$$

where

$\overline{I}_t$ is the projected monthly mortgage payment for month t

$\overline{M}_{mt-1}$ is the projected mortgage balance at the end of month t assuming that prepayments have occurred in the past.

To calculate the interest proportion of the projected monthly mortgage payment we use (11.3), where $\overline{i}_t$ is the projected monthly interest payment for month t.

$$\overline{i}_t = M_{mt-1}.i \tag{11.3}$$

Formula (11.3) states that the projected monthly interest payment can be obtained by multiplying the mortgage balance at the end of the previous month by the monthly inter-

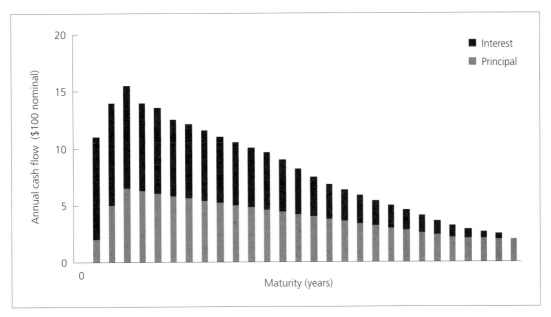

FIGURE 11.3 ▪ 100% PSA model

est rate. In the same way, the expression for calculating the projected monthly scheduled principal payment for any month is given by (11.4), where $-p_t$ is the projected scheduled principal payment for the month t.

$$\overline{p}_t = \overline{I}_t - \overline{i}_t \tag{11.4}$$

The projected monthly principal prepayment, which is an expected rate only and not a model forecast, is given by:

$$\overline{pp}_t = SMM_t(\overline{M}_{mt-1} - \overline{p}_t) \tag{11.5}$$

where $\overline{pp}_t$ is the projected monthly principal prepayment for month t.

The above relationships enable us to calculate values for:

▪ the projected monthly interest payment;

▪ the projected monthly scheduled principal payment;

▪ the projected monthly principal prepayment.

These values may be used to calculate the total cash flow in any month that a holder of a mortgage-backed bond receives, which is given by (11.6), where cf_t is the cash flow receipt in month t.

$$cf_t = \overline{i}_t + \overline{p}_t + \overline{pp}_t \tag{11.6}$$

The practice of using a prepayment rate is a market convention that enables analysts to evaluate mortgage-backed bonds. The original PSA prepayment rates were arbitrarily selected, based on the observation that prepayment rates tended to stabilize after the first 30 months of the life of a mortgage. A linear increase in the prepayment rate is also assumed. However, this is a market convention only, adopted by the market as a standard benchmark. The levels do not reflect seasonal variations in prepayment patterns, or the different behaviour patterns of different types of mortgages.

The PSA benchmarks can be (and are) applied to default assumptions to produce a default benchmark. This is used for non-agency mortgage-backed bonds only, because agency securities are guaranteed by one of the three government or government-sponsored agencies. Accordingly, the PSA *standard default assumption* (SDA) benchmark is used to assess the potential default rate for a mortgage pool. For example, the standard benchmark, 100SDA, assumes that the default rate in the first month is 0.02% and increases in a linear fashion by 0.02% each month until the 30th month, at which point the default rate remains at 0.60%. In month 60 the default rate begins to fall from 0.60% to 0.03% and continues to fall linearly until month 120. From that point the default rate remains constant at 0.03%. The other benchmarks have similar patterns.

Prepayment models

The PSA standard benchmark reviewed in the previous section uses an assumption of prepayment rates and can be used to calculate the prepayment proceeds of a mortgage. It is not, strictly speaking, a prepayment *model* because it cannot be used to estimate actual prepayments. A prepayment model, on the other hand, does attempt to predict the pre-payment cash flows of a mortgage pool, by modelling the statistical relationships between the various factors that have an impact on the level of prepayment. These factors are the current mortgage rate, the characteristics of the mortgages in the pool, seasonal factors and the general business cycle. Let us consider them in turn.

The prevailing mortgage interest rate is probably the most important factor in the level of prepayment. The level of the current mortgage rate and its spread above or below the original contract rate will influence the decision to refinance a mortgage; if the rate is materially below the original rate, the borrower will prepay the mortgage. As the mort-gage rate at any time reflects the general bank base rate, the level of market interest rates has the greatest effect on mortgage prepayment levels. The current mortgage rate also has an effect on housing prices, since if mortgages are seen as 'cheap' the general perception will be that now is the right time to purchase: this affects housing market turnover. The pattern followed by mortgage rates since the original loan also has an impact – a phenomenon known as *refinancing burnout*.

Observation of the mortgage market has suggested that housing market and mortgage activity follows a strong seasonal pattern. The strongest period of activity is during the spring and summer, while the market is at its quietest in the winter.

These various factors may be used to derive an expression that can be used to calculate expected prepayment levels. For example, a US investment bank uses the following model to calculate expected prepayments:[6]

Monthly prepayment rate =
(refinancing incentive) × (season multiplier) × (month multiplier) × (burnout)

Collateralized mortgage securities

In this section we review some of the newer structures of these instruments. A large number of the instruments in the US market are collateralized mortgage obligations, the majority of which are issued by government-sponsored agencies and so offer virtual Treasury bond credit quality but at significantly higher yields. This makes the paper attractive to a range of institutional investors, as does the opportunity to tailor the characteristics of a particular issue to suit the needs of a specific investor. The CMO market in the USA experienced rapid growth during the 1990s, with a high of $324 billion issued in 1993; this figure had fallen to just under $100 billion during 1998.[7] The growth of the market has brought with it a range of new structures; for example, bondholders who wished to have a lower exposure to prepayment risk have invested in *planned amortization classes* (PACs) and *targeted amortization classes* (TACs). The uncertain term to maturity of mortgage-backed bonds has resulted in the creation of bonds that were guaranteed not to extend beyond a stated date, which are known as *very accurately defined maturity* (VDAM) bonds. In the UK and certain overseas markets, mortgage-backed bonds pay a floating-rate coupon, and the interest from foreign investors in the US domestic market led to the creation of bonds with coupons linked to the Libor rate. Other types of instruments in the market include interest-only (IO) and principal-only (PO) bonds, also sometimes called strips, and inverse floating-rate bonds, which are usually created from an existing fixed-rate bond issue.

6. Bhattacharya and Fabozzi (1997).

7. The source for statistical data in this section is *Asset-Backed Alert* www.ABAlert.com. Used with permission.

The primary features of US-market CMOs are summarized as follows:

- *Credit quality*: CMOs issued by US government agencies have the same guarantee as agency pass-through securities, so may be considered risk-free. These bonds therefore do not require any form of credit insurance or credit enhancement. Whole-loan CMOs do not carry any form of government guarantee, and are rated by credit-rating agencies. Most bonds carry an AAA rating, either because of the quality of the mortgage pool or issuing vehicle, or because a form of credit enhancement has been used.

- *Interest frequency*: CMOs typically pay interest on a monthly basis, which is calculated on the current outstanding nominal value of the issue.

- *Cash flow profile*: The cash flow profile of CMOs is based on an assumed prepayment rate. This rate is based on the current market expectation of future prepayment levels and expected market interest rates, and is known as the *pricing speed*.

- *Maturity*: Most CMOs are long-dated instruments, and originally virtually all issues were created from underlying mortgage collateral with a 30-year stated maturity. During the 1990s issues were created from shorter-dated collateral, including 5–7-year and 15–20-year mortgages.

- *Market convention*: CMOs trade on a yield as opposed to a price basis and are usually quoted as a spread over the yield of the nearest maturity Treasury security. The yields are calculated on the basis of an assumed prepayment rate. Agency CMOs are settled on a T+3 basis via an electronic book-entry system known as 'Fedwire', the clearing system run by the Federal Reserve. Whole-loan CMOs also settle on a T+3 basis, and are cleared using either physical delivery or by electronic transfer. New issues CMOs settle from one to three months after the initial offer date.

Originally, mortgage-backed bonds were created from individual underlying mortgages. Agency CMOs are created from mortgages that have already been pooled and securitized, usually in the form of a pass-through security (*see* Chapter 25). Issuers of whole-loan CMOs do not therefore need to create a pass-through security from a pool of individual mortgages, but structure the notes based on cash flows from the entire pool. In the same way as agency pass-through securities, the underlying mortgages in a whole-loan pool are generally of the same risk type, maturity and interest rate. The other difference between whole-loan CMOs and agency pass-throughs is that the latter are comprised of mortgages of up to a stated maximum size, while larger loans are contained in CMOs. There are essentially two CMO structures: those issues that redirect the underlying pool interest payments, and issues redirecting both interest and principal. The main CMO instrument types pay out both interest and principal and are described below.

Whole-loan CMO structures also differ from other mortgage-backed securities in terms of what is known as *compensating interest*. Virtually all mortgage securities pay principal and interest on a monthly basis, on a fixed coupon date. The underlying mortgages, however, may be paid off on any day of the month. Agency mortgage securities guarantee their bondholders an interest payment for the complete month, even if the underlying mortgage has been paid off ahead of the coupon date (and so has not attracted any interest). Whole-loan CMOs do not offer this guarantee, and so any *payment interest shortfall* will be lost, meaning that a bondholder would receive less than one month's worth of interest on the coupon date. Some issuers, but not all, will pay a compensating interest payment to bondholders to make up this shortfall.

CMO structure

CMOs are usually rated AAA/Aaa by rating agencies, and this is because in practice the cash flows generated by the underlying mortgages or agency securities are well in excess of what is required to service the interest obligations of all tranches of the notes. As summarized in Sundaresan (1997, p. 389), the general characteristics of CMO structures include the following:

- The high credit rating is ensured by arranging credit insurance via a third-party provider, such as a specialist credit guarantee firm.
- There is always considerable excess of underlying collateral as against the nominal value of notes issued; this leads to a significant level of over-collateralization.
- Notes issued usually pay coupon on a semi-annual or quarterly basis, although the underlying mortgages pay interest more frequently, say monthly or almost daily. This surplus cash is reinvested in between coupon dates at a money market rate of interest. Issuers usually prefer a *guaranteed investment contract* (GIC) for their surplus cash, but these are only provided by a few banks and insurance companies, so most issuers have to settle for a money market account. However, the providers will usually accept funds at a much lower level than is usual for interbank deposits, sometimes down to $100,000.

The cash flows that originate from the underlying collateral are separated and allocated to more than one class of notes, known as *tranches*. Typically these tranches will pay different rates of interest to appeal to different classes of investors. The two basic CMO structures are *sequential* structure and *planned amortization class* structure.

Sequential structure

One of the requirements that CMOs were designed to meet was the demand for mortgage-backed bonds with a wider range of maturities. Most CMO structures redirect principal payments *sequentially* to individual classes of bonds within the structure, in accordance with the stated maturity of each bond. That is, principal payments are first used to pay off the class of bond with the shortest stated maturity, until it is completely redeemed, before being re-allocated to the next maturity band class of bond. This occurs until all the bonds in the structure are retired. Sequential-pay CMOs are attractive to a wide range of investors, particularly those with shorter-term investment horizons, since they are able to purchase only the class of CMO whose maturity terms meet their requirements. In addition, investors with more traditional longer-dated investment horizons are protected from prepayment risk in the early years of the issue, because principal payments are used to pay off the shorter-dated bonds in the structure.

The typical generic CMO sequential structure would have, say, four tranches, as suggested in Table 11.1. The collateral cash flows are allocated to each tranche in specified order, and the first tranche is allotted both its coupon and any prepayments. The remaining tranches do not receive any payments until the first one is fully retired, with the exception of their coupon payments. Essentially, each tranche receives successive payments as soon as its immediate predecessor is redeemed. The last tranche is usually known as a *Z-bond* and will receive no cash flows until all preceding tranches have been repaid. In the interim, the face amount of this note will accrue at the stated coupon.

TABLE 11.1 ■ Generic CMO sequential structure

Tranche	Principal	Coupon	Average life (years)	Yield
A	100	7%	2.5	2-year benchmark plus 80 bps
B	250	7%	5	5-year benchmark plus 100 bps
C	75	7%	10	10-year benchmark plus 120 bps
Z	75	7%	20	30-year benchmark plus 150 bps

Interest-only and principal-only class

Stripped coupon mortgage securities are created when the coupon cash flows payable by a pool of mortgages are split into interest-only and principal-only payments. The cash flows will be a function of the prepayment rate, since this determines the nominal value of the collateral pool. IO issues, also known as IO strips, gain whenever the prepayment rate falls, since interest payments are reduced as the principal amount falls. If there is a rise in the prepayment rate, PO bonds benefit because they are discount securities and a higher prepayment rate results in the redemption proceeds being received early. Early strip issues were created with an unequal amount of coupon and principal, resulting in a synthetic coupon rate that was different to the coupon on the underlying bond. These instruments were known as *synthetic coupon pass-throughs*. Nowadays it is more typical for all the interest to be allocated to one class, the IO issue, and all the principal to be allocated to the PO class.

The most common CMO structures have a portion of their principal stripped into IO and PO bonds, but in some structures the entire issue is made up of IO and PO bonds. The amount of principal used to create stripped securities will reflect investor demand. In certain cases, IO issues created from a class of CMO known as *real estate mortgage investment conduits* (REMICs) have quite esoteric terms. For example, the IO classes might be issued with an amount of principal attached, known as the nominal balance. The cash flows for bonds with this structure are paid through a process of amortizing and prepaying the nominal balance. The balance itself is a small amount, resulting in a very high coupon, so that the IO has a multi-digit coupon and very high price (such as 1183% and 3626–12).[8]

Strips created from whole-loan CMOs trade differently from those issued out of agency CMOs. Agency CMOs pay a fixed coupon, whereas whole-loan CMOs pay a coupon based on a weighted average of all the individual mortgage coupons. During the life of the whole-loan issue, this coupon value will alter as prepayments change the amount of principal. To preserve the coupon payments of all issues within a structure therefore, a portion of the principal and interest cash flows is stripped from the underlying mortgages, leaving collateral that has a more stable average life. This is another reason that IOs and POs may be created.

IO issue prices exhibit the singular tendency of moving in the same direction as interest rates in certain situations. This reflects the behaviour of mortgages and prepayment rates: when interest rates fall below the mortgage coupon rate, prepayment rates will increase. This causes the cash flow for an IO strip to fall, as the level of the underlying principal declines, which causes the price of the IO to fall as well. This is despite the fact that the issue's cash flows are now discounted at a lower rate. Figure 11.4 shows the price of a sensitivity of a 7% pass-through security compared with the prices of an IO and a PO that have been created from it. Note that the price of the pass-through is not particularly sensitive to a fall in the mortgage rate below the coupon rate of 7%. This illustrates the *negative convexity* property of pass-through securities. The price sensitivity of the two strip issues is very different. The PO experiences a dramatic fall in price as the mortgage rate rises above the coupon rate. The IO, on the other hand, experiences a rise in price in the same situation, while its price falls significantly if mortgage rates fall below the coupon rate.

---

8. Ames, 1997 (in Bhattacharya and Fabozzi, 1997).

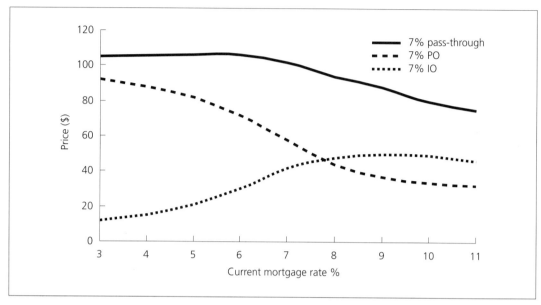

FIGURE 11.4 ■ Price sensitivity of pass-through security, IO and PO

Source: Bloomberg L.P.

Both PO and IO issues are extremely price volatile at times of moves in mortgage rates, and have much greater interest rate sensitivity than the pass-through securities from which they are created.

Non-agency CMO bonds

There are no significant differences in the structure and terms of non-agency CMOs compared with agency CMOs. The key feature of non-agency CMOs, however, is that they are not guaranteed by government agencies, and so carry an element of credit risk, in the same way that corporate bonds expose investors to credit risk. To attract investors, therefore, most non-agency CMOs incorporate an element of *credit enhancement,* designed to improve the credit standing of the issue. The use of credit enhancement usually results in an AAA rating, indeed a large majority of non-agency CMOs are AAA rated, with very few falling below an AA rating.

All of the four main private credit rating agencies are involved in credit analysis and rating of non-agency CMOs. The rating granted to a particular issue of CMOs is dependent on a range of factors, which include:

- the term of the underlying loans;
- the size of the loans, whether *conforming* or *jumbo* (agency mortgages do not include mortgages above a certain stated size, whereas non-agency issues are often made up of larger size loans known as *jumbo* loans);
- the interest basis for the loans, whether level-pay fixed-rate, variable or other type;
- the type of property;
- the geographical area within which the loans have been made;
- the purpose behind the loans, whether a first purchase or a refinancing.

In this section we discuss the credit enhancement facility that is used in non-agency CMOs.

Credit enhancements

CMOs are arranged with either an external or internal credit enhancement. An *external* credit enhancement is a guarantee made by a third party to cover losses on the issue. Usually a set amount of the issue is guaranteed, such as 25%, rather than the entire issue. The guarantee can take the form of a letter of credit, bond insurance or *pool insurance*. A pool insurance policy would be written to insure against losses that arose as a result of default, usually for a cash amount of cover that would remain in place during the life of the pool. Certain policies are set up so that the cash coverage falls in value during the life of the bond. Pool insurance is provided by specialized agencies. Note that only defaults and foreclosures are included in the policy, which forces investors to arrange further cover if they wish to be protected against any other type of loss. A CMO issue that obtains credit enhancement from an external party still has an element of credit risk, but now linked to the fortunes of the provider of insurance. That is, the issue is at risk from a deterioration in the credit quality of the provider of insurance. Investors who purchase non-agency CMOs must ensure that they are satisfied with the credit quality of the third-party guarantor, as well as with the quality of the underlying mortgage pool. Note that an external credit enhancement has no impact on the cash flow structure of the CMO.

Internal credit enhancements generally have more complex arrangements and sometimes also affect the cash flow structures of the instruments themselves. The two most common types of internal credit enhancement are *reserve funds* and a *senior/subordinated* structure.

Reserve funds

There are two types of reserve funds. A *cash reserve fund* is a deposit of cash that has been built up from payments arising from the issue of the bonds. A portion of the profits made when the bonds were initially issued is placed in a separate fund. The fund in turn places this cash in short-term bank deposits. The cash reserve fund is used in the event of default to compensate investors who have suffered capital loss. It is often set up in conjunction with another credit enhancement product, such as a letter of credit. An *excess servicing spread account* is also a separate fund, generated from excess spread after all the payments of the mortgage have been made – that is, the coupon, servicing fee and other expenses. For instance, if an issue has a gross weighted average coupon of 7.5%, and the service fee is 0.1% and the net weighted average coupon is 7.25%, then the excess servicing amount is 0.15%. This amount is paid into the spread account, and will grow steadily during the bond's life. The funds in the account can be used to pay off any losses arising from the bond that affect investors.

Senior/subordinated structure

This is the most common type of internal credit enhancement method encountered in the market. Essentially, it involves a bond ranking below the CMO that absorbs all the losses arising from default, or other cause, leaving the main issue unaffected. The subordinated bond clearly has the higher risk attached to it, so it trades at a higher yield. Most senior/subordinated arrangements also incorporate a 'shifting interest structure'. This arranges for prepayments to be redirected from the subordinated class to the senior class. Hence it alters the cash flow characteristics of the senior notes, irrespective of the presence of defaults or otherwise.

Commercial mortgage-backed securities

The mortgage-backed bond market includes a sector of securities that are backed by commercial, as opposed to residential, mortgages. These are known as *commercial mortgage-backed securities* (CMBSs). They trade essentially as other mortgage securities but there are differences in their structure, which are summarized in this section.

Issuing a CMBS

As with a residential mortgage security, a CMBS is created from a pool or 'trust' of commercial mortgages, with the cash flows of the bond backed by the interest and principal payments of the underlying mortgages. A commercial mortgage is a loan made to finance or refinance the purchase of a commercial (business) property. There is a market in direct purchase of a commercial loan book, in addition to the more structured CMBS transaction. An issue of a CMBS is rated in the same way as a residential mortgage security and usually has a credit enhancement arrangement to raise its credit rating. The credit rating of a CMBS takes into account the size of the issue as well as the level of credit enhancement support.

Classes of bonds in a CMBS structure are usually arranged in a sequential-pay series, and bonds are retired in line with their rating in the structure; the highest-rated bonds are paid off first.

Commercial mortgages impose a penalty on borrowers if they are redeemed early, usually in the form of an interest charge on the final principal. There is no such penalty in the US residential mortgage market, although early retirement fees are still a feature of residential loans in the UK. The early payment protection in a commercial loan can have other forms as well, such as a prepayment 'lock-out', which is a contractual arrangement that prevents early retirement. This early prepayment protection is repeated in a CMBS structure, and may be in the form of call protection of the bonds themselves. There is already a form of protection in the ratings of individual issues in the structure, because the highest-rated bonds are paid off first. That is, the AAA-rated bonds will be retired ahead of the AA-rated bonds, and so on. The highest-rated bonds in a CMBS structure also have the highest protection from default of any of the underlying mortgages, which means that losses of principal arising from default will affect the lowest-rated bond first.

As well as the early retirement protection, commercial mortgages differ from residential loans in that many of them are *balloon* mortgages. A balloon loan is one on which only the interest is paid, or only a small amount of the principal is paid as well as the interest, so that all or a large part of the loan remains to be paid off on the maturity date. This makes CMBSs potentially similar to conventional vanilla bonds (which are also sometimes called 'bullet' bonds) and so attractive to investors who prefer less uncertainty on term to maturity of a bond.

Types of CMBS structures[9]

In the US market there are currently six types of CMBS structures. They are:

■ liquidating trusts;

■ multi-property single-borrower;

■ multi-property conduit;

■ multi-property non-conduit;

■ single-property single-borrower;

■ multi-borrower/conduit.

We briefly describe the three most common structures here.

---

9. The structures described in this section are summarized from data contained in Dunlevy (1996), Chapter 30 in Fabozzi and Jacob (1996).

Liquidating trusts

This sector of the market is relatively small by value and represents bonds issued against non-performing loans, hence the other name of *non-performing CMBSs*. The market is structured in a slightly different way to regular commercial mortgage securities. The features include a *fast-pay structure*, which states that all cash flows from the mortgage pool be used to redeem the most senior bond first, and *overcollateralization*, which is when the value of bonds created is significantly lower than the value of the underlying loans. This overcollateralization results in bonds being paid off sooner. Due to the nature of the asset backing for liquidating CMBSs, bonds are usually issued with relatively short average lives, and will receive cash flows on only a portion of the loans. A target date for paying off is set and in the event that the target is not met, the bonds usually have a provision to raise the coupon rate. This acts as an incentive for the borrower to meet the retirement target.

Multi-property single-borrower

The single-borrower/multi-property structure is an important and large part of the CMBS market. The special features of these bonds include *cross-collateralization*, which is when properties that are used as collateral for individual loans are pledged against each loan. Another feature known as *cross-default* allows the lender to call each loan in the pool if any one of them defaults. Since cross-collateralization and cross-default link all the properties together, sufficient cash flow is available to meet the collective debt on all the loans. This influences the grade of credit rating that is received for the issue. A *property release provision* in the structure is set up to protect the investor against the lender removing or prepaying the stronger loans in the book. Another common protection against this risk is a clause in the structure terms that prevents the issuer from substituting one property for another.

Multi-borrower/conduit

A *conduit* is a commercial lending entity that has been set up solely to generate collateral to be used in securitization deals. The major investment banks have all established conduit arms. Conduits are responsible for originating collateral that meets requirements on loan type (whether amortizing or balloon, and so on), loan term, geographic spread of the properties and the time that the loans were struck. Generally, a conduit will want to have a diversified range of underlying loans, known as *pool diversification*, with a wide spread of location and size. A diversified pool reduces the default risk for the investor. After it has generated the collateral the conduit then structures the deal, on terms similar to CMOs but with the additional features described in this section.

Introduction to the evaluation and analysis of mortgage-backed bonds [10]

Term to maturity

The term to maturity cannot be given for certain for a mortgage pass-through security, since the cash flows and prepayment patterns cannot be predicted. To evaluate such a bond, therefore, it is necessary to estimate the term for the bond, and use this measure for any analysis. The maturity measure for any bond is important, because without it it is not possible to assess over what period of time a return is being generated; also, it will not be possible to compare the asset to any other bond. The term to maturity of a bond also gives an indication of its sensitivity to changes in market interest rates. If comparisons with other securities such as government bonds are made, we cannot use the stated maturity of the mortgage-backed bond because prepayments will reduce this figure. The convention in the market is to use other estimated values, which are *average life* and the more traditional duration measure.

The *average life* of a mortgage pass-through security is the weighted-average time to return of a unit of principal payment, made up of projected scheduled principal payments and principal prepayments. It is also known as the *weighted-average life*. It is given by (11.7):

$$\text{Average life} = \frac{1}{12} \sum_{t=1}^{n} \frac{t(\text{principal received at } t)}{\text{total principal received}} \tag{11.7}$$

where n is the number of months remaining. The time from the term measured by the average life to the final scheduled principal payment is the bond's *tail*.

We have seen that, to calculate duration (or Macaulay's duration) for a bond we require the weighted present values of all its cash flows. To apply this for a mortgage-backed bond, therefore, it is necessary to project the bond's cash flows, using an assumed prepayment rate. The projected cash flows, together with the bond price and the periodic interest rate, may then be used to arrive at a duration value. The periodic interest rate is derived from the yield. This calculation for a mortgage-backed bond produces a periodic duration figure, which must be divided by 12 to arrive at a duration value in years (or by 4 in the case of a quarterly-paying bond).

---

10. The pricing and hedging of mortgage-backed securities is a complex subject, and space does not permit any proper treatment of it here. The next chapter takes up the basic concepts with renewed vigour. Interested readers should consult Chapter 9 of Sundaresan (1997) or the other relevant references cited in the bibliography. Tuckman (1996) is also a good introduction to pricing models for mortgage securities (see his Chapter 18), while Chapter 2 of Golub and Tilman (2000) contains an excellent account of the interest rate risk aspects of mortgage-backed securities.

Calculating yield and price: static cash flow model

There are a number of ways that the yield on a mortgage-backed bond can be calculated. One of the most common methods employs the *static cash flow model*. This assumes a single prepayment rate to estimate the cash flows for the bond, and does not take into account how changes in market conditions might impact the prepayment pattern.

The conventional yield measure for a bond is the discount rate at which the sum of the present values of all the bond's expected cash flows will be equal to the price of the bond. The convention is usually to compute the yield from the *clean* price, that is excluding any accrued interest. This yield measure is known as the bond's *redemption yield* or *yield to maturity*. However, for mortgage-backed bonds it is known as a *cash flow yield* or *mortgage yield*. The cash flow for a mortgage-backed bond is not known with certainty, due to the effect of prepayments, and so must be derived using an assumed prepayment rate. Once the projected cash flows have been calculated, it is possible to calculate the cash flow yield. The formula is given as:

$$P = \sum_{n=1}^{N} \frac{C(t)}{(1 + ri/1200)^{t-1}} \qquad (11.8)$$

Note, however, that a yield so computed will be for a bond with monthly coupon payments,[11] so it is necessary to convert the yield to an annualized equivalent before any comparisons are made with conventional bond yields. In the US and UK markets, the bond-equivalent yield is calculated for mortgage-backed bonds and measured against the relevant government bond yield, which (in both cases) is a semi-annual yield. Although it is reasonably accurate simply to double the yield of a semi-annual coupon bond to arrive at the annualized equivalent,[12] to obtain the bond equivalent yield for a monthly paying mortgage-backed bond, we use (11.9):

$$rm = 2\left[\left(1 + ri_M\right)^6 - 1\right] \qquad (11.9)$$

where rm is the bond equivalent yield (we retain the designation that was used to denote yield to maturity in Chapter 4) and ri_M is the interest rate that will equate the present value of the projected monthly cash flows for the mortgage-backed bond to its current price. The equivalent semi-annual yield is given by (11.10):

$$rm_{s/a} = \left(1 + ri_M\right)^6 - 1 \qquad (11.10)$$

The cash flow yield calculated for a mortgage-backed bond in this way is essentially the redemption yield, using an assumption to derive the cash flows. As such, the measure

---

11. The majority of mortgage-backed bonds pay interest on a monthly basis, since individual mortgages usually do as well; certain mortgage-backed bonds pay on a quarterly basis.

12. *See* Chapter 2 for the formulae used to convert yields from one convention basis to another.

suffers from the same drawbacks as it does when used to measure the return of a plain vanilla bond, which are that the calculation assumes a uniform reinvestment rate for all the bond's cash flows and that the bond will be held to maturity. The same weakness will apply to the cash flow yield measure for a mortgage-backed bond. In fact, the potential inaccuracy of the redemption yield measure is even greater with a mortgage-backed bond because the frequency of interest payments is higher, which makes the reinvestment risk greater. The final yield that is returned by a mortgage-backed bond will depend on the performance of the mortgages in the pool, specifically the prepayment pattern.

Given the nature of a mortgage-backed bond's cash flows, the exact yield cannot be calculated; however, it is common for market practitioners to use the cash-flow yield measure and compare this to the redemption yield of the equivalent government bond. The usual convention is to quote the spread over the government bond as the main measure of value. When measuring the spread, the mortgage-backed bond is compared to the government security that has a similar duration, or a term to maturity similar to its average life.

As we noted in Chapter 4, it is possible to calculate the price of a mortgage-backed bond once its yield is known (or vice versa). As with a plain vanilla bond, the price is the sum of the present values of all the projected cash flows. It is necessary to convert the bond-equivalent yield to a monthly yield, which is then used to calculate the present value of each cash flow. The cash flows of IO and PO bonds are dependent on the cash flows of the underlying pass-through security, which is itself dependent on the cash flows of the underlying mortgage pool. Again, to calculate the price of an IO or PO bond, a prepayment rate must be assumed. This enables us to determine the projected level of the monthly cash flows of the IO and the principal payments of the PO. The price of an IO is the present value of the projected interest payments, while the price of the PO is the present value of the projected principal payments, comprising the scheduled principal payments and the projected principal prepayments.

Total return

To assess the value of a mortgage-backed bond over a given investment horizon it is necessary to measure the return generated during the holding period from the bond's cash flows. This is done using what is known as the *total return* framework. The cash flows from a mortgage-backed bond are comprised of (1) the projected cash flows of the bond (which are the projected interest payments and principal repayments and prepayments); (2) the interest earned on the reinvestment of all the payments; and (3) the projected price of the bond at the end of the holding period. The first sum can be estimated using an assumed prepayment rate during the period the bond is held, while the second cash flow requires an assumed reinvestment rate. To obtain (3) the bondholder must assume, first, what the bond equivalent yield of the mortgage bond will be at the end of the holding period, and second, what prepayment rate the market will assume at this point. The second rate is a function of the projected yield at the time. The total return during the time the bond is held, on a monthly basis, is then given by:

$$\left[\frac{\text{Total future cash flow amount}}{P_m} \right]^{1/n} - 1 \tag{11.11}$$

which can be converted to an annualized bond-equivalent yield using (11.9) or (11.10).

Note that the return calculated using (11.11) is based on a range of assumptions, which render it almost academic. The best approach to use is to calculate a yield for a range of different assumptions, which then gives some idea of the likely yield that may be generated over the holding period, in the form of a range of yields (that is, an upper and lower limit).

Price-yield curves of mortgage pass-through, PO and IO securities [13]

In this section we present an introduction to the yield behaviour of selected mortgage-backed securities under conditions of changing interest rates. To recap, in an environment of high interest rates the holders of mortgage-backed bonds prefer prepayments to occur. This is because the mortgage will be paying at a low interest rate relative to market conditions, and the likelihood of mortgage prepayment at par results in a higher value for the bond. In the same way when interest rates are low, note holders would prefer that there not be any prepayment, since the bond will be paying interest at a relatively high rate and will therefore be price valuable.

Figure 11.5 illustrates the price behaviour of pass-through securities, with a nominal coupon of 7%.

Under conditions of no prepayments, the bond cash flows are certain and the price-yield behaviour resembles that of a conventional bond. Under optimal prepayment, the bond will behave similarly to a callable bond: in a high interest rate environment the bond behaves much like a vanilla bond, while under lower rates the price of the bond is capped at par. However, under what Tuckman calls 'realistic payment' conditions the price behaviour is somewhat different, as illustrated in Figure 11.5. In an environment of very low rates, bond value is higher (with the realistic payments assumption) than it is with the other two scenarios. This is because there are always a number of mortgage borrowers who will repay their loans irrespective of the level of interest rates, whether rates are low or high. Remember that note holders desire prepayments when interest rates are high; the bond value under the realistic payments model is higher than those of the other two, which predict no prepayments under high interest rate conditions.

13. This section follows partly the Tuckman (1996), p. 254–60 in Chapter 18, which is a good introduction to the pricing and behaviour of mortgage-backed securities; and Sundaresan (1997), Chapter 9.

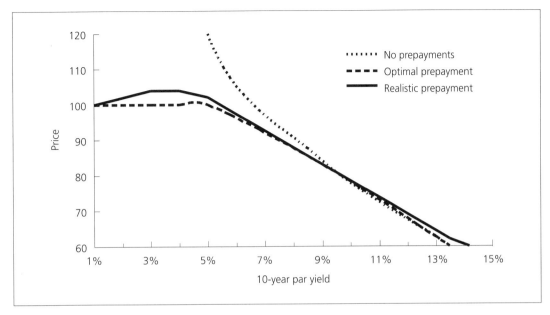

FIGURE 11.5 ■ Price behaviour of pass-through securities

As interest rates decrease, certain mortgage borrowers will prepay their loans, but by no means all. Since prepayment decreases the value of a mortgage under low interest rates, the fact that not all borrowers prepay under the 'optimal' scenario results in an increase in value of a mortgage to a level greater than its optimal prepaid value. This non-prepayment behaviour can lead to an increase in bond value above par. This is something of an anomaly, as the bond is then priced above the level at which it can theoretically be called. The scenario concludes when eventually all borrowers redeem their mortgages as rates have fallen far enough. This is why the realistic prepayments curve moves down to par at very low levels of rates. Figure 11.5 shows the existence of *negative convexity* as bond prices fall as interest rates decline, which reflects the behaviour of mortgage borrowers after a long enough period of very low rates. However, this does not mean that investors should not buy mortgage-backed bonds at that range of yields when negative convexity applies: as Tuckman notes, the mortgages will be earning rates at above-market levels. It is the total return of the bond over the holding period that is relevant, rather than its price behaviour.[14]

14. This is especially true when compared with the performance of other debt market investments. Investment reasoning on price behaviour alone is 'as bad as concluding that premium Treasuries should never be purchased because they will eventually decline in price to par' (Tuckman 1996, p. 256).

It is also worth commenting on the behaviour of IO and PO securities, which we described earlier. To recap, an IO receives the interest payments of the underlying collateral while the PO receives principal payments. Figure 11.6 illustrates the price behaviour of these instruments, based on a $100 nominal amount for both the underlying mortgage and the IO/PO.

Under very high interest rates and with prepayments unlikely, a PO will act as repayable at par on maturity, similar to a zero-coupon bond. As interest rates decline and the level of prepayments increases, the value of the PO will increase. However, other forces are at work which, as rates change further, make PO securities more interesting than vanilla strips. These are:

- the conventional price/yield effect, since lower interest rates cause higher prices;

- that the PO, again similarly to vanilla strips, is very sensitive to the price/yield effect;

- that as the level of prepayments increases, with the expectation of higher levels still, the effective maturity of the PO declines; this lower maturity raises the price of the PO even higher.

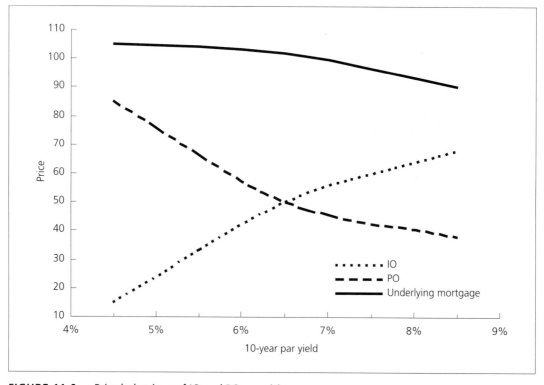

FIGURE 11.6 ■ Price behaviour of IO and PO securities

The impact of these factors is that PO securities are highly volatile.

The price/yield relationship of the IO is a function of that for the PO, and is obtained by subtracting the value of the latter from that of the underlying mortgage. A significant feature is the high price volatility of the IO under conditions of lower and falling interest rates. This is explained as follows: in a high interest rate environment, with very low pre-payment levels, IOs act as vanilla bonds with cash flows known with certainty. This changes as interest rates start to fall, and the cash flows of the IO effectively disappear. This is because as more principal is repaid, the nominal amount of the mortgage on which interest is charged decreases in amount. However, unlike pass-through or other mortgage securities, which receive some principal payment when interest payments decline or cease, IOs receive no cash flow. The impact of a vanishing cash flow is that, as interest rates fall, the price of the IO declines dramatically.

As well as purchases by investors, this negative duration property of IOs makes them useful as interest rate hedging instruments by market-makers in mortgage-backed securities.

The UK residential MBS market [15]

The mortgage-backed market in the UK was one of the earliest European securitization markets. Sterling residential MBSs (RMBSs) were introduced in significant volume from 1987, with National Home Loans Corporation and The Mortgage Corporation being amongst the largest originators. By 1990 there had been over 50 deals, with a total nominal value of £9 billion. Commercial banks began securitizing their loan books shortly after the mortgage corporations, for example the Gracechurch 1 and Lothbury transactions from Barclays Bank and National Westminster Bank. The latter (its full title is Lothbury Funding No.1 plc) was the first major mortgage-backed deal issued by a retail bank, in 1993. The Northern Rock Building Society issued the first RMBSs by such an institution in December 1994.

RMBS issuance now takes place in a liquid and sophisticated market. During 2000 the total volume issued in the UK was over £14 billion, from 15 different deals (*see* Table 11.2). The largest transaction was £4.7 billion of issuance from Abbey National plc, via its Holmes Funding Master Trust vehicle. Significant deals were also launched by Northern Rock plc (the Granite deal, over £2 billion) and Bradford & Bingley plc, which issued £1 billion of notes backed by buy-to-let mortgages via its Aire Valley No. 2 funding vehicle.

---

15. The volumes data source is ISR and Moody's Investors Service.

TABLE 11.2 ■ Selected UK RMBS transactions in 2000

Originator	Issuer name	Size (£m)	Date
Northern Rock	Granite Mortgages 00-1 plc	750	March 2000
Bank of Scotland	Mound Financing No.1 plc	750	May 2000
Bristol & West	Project Quayside	300	May 2000
Abbey National	Holmes Financing No.1 plc	2,256	July 2000
Northern Rock	Granite Mortgages 00-2 plc	1,300	September 2000
Abbey National	Holmes Financing No.2 plc	2,400	November 2000
Alliance & Leicester	Fosse Securities No.1 plc	250	November 2000

A number of innovations marked the UK market in 2000. One of the most significant was the introduction of the *master trust* structure, which was employed by both Abbey National and Bank of Scotland with their Holmes and Mound issues respectively. Master trusts were first used in the UK for credit card securitizations, and are a legal structure that facilitates repeat issues from the same originator much more quickly than before, because the legal documentation used for subsequent transactions is based on that used for the first deal. This enables second and subsequent issues to be brought to market more quickly than if a new funding vehicle is set up for each deal. The main attraction is that it enables the originator to issue soft bullet securities with short legal maturities.[16] This appeals to investors who wish to reduce reinvestment risk and cannot invest in long-dated paper. Issuers who wish to securitize on a regular basis benefit from a facility that allows them to issue on an ongoing basis. The master trust structure is illustrated in Figure 11.7.

Another innovation during 2000 was the emergence of a synthetic RMBS market. In a synthetic transaction the underlying assets are not actually transferred, however the issuer is able to transfer risk exposure without the cost or complexity of the traditional mechanism. This approach is used by originators that do not require funding but wish to put on some form of credit protection, or wish an off-balance sheet treatment for part of their regulatory capital calculation. The first public synthetic RMBS securitization in the UK was the £300 million Project Quayside deal, originated by Bristol & West plc

16. The previous convention was for a long legal maturity, say 25 or 30 years, similar to the theoretical maturity of the underlying loans. In practice, of course, the average maturity is much less due to prepayments.

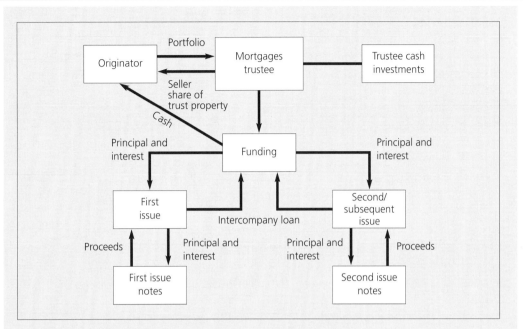

FIGURE 11.7 ▪ Master trust structure

in June 2000. This transaction enabled Bristol & West to arrange credit protection on a portfolio of buy-to-let mortgages, thereby transferring the credit risk of the assets to a counterparty bank. This was an example of a securitization carried out not for funding purposes but for balance sheet management.

SELECTED BIBLIOGRAPHY AND REFERENCES

Anderson, G., Barber, J., Chang, C., 'Prepayment risk and the duration of default-free mortgage-backed securities', *Journal of Financial Research* 16, 1993, pp. 1–9.

Arora, A., Heike, D., Mattu, R., 'Risk and return in the mortgage market: review and outlook', *Journal of Fixed Income*, June 2000, pp. 5–18.

Bartlett, W., *Mortgage-Backed Securities: Products, Analysis, Trading*, New York Institute of Finance 1989.

Bear Stearns, *Asset-Backed Securities Special Report*, 5 December 1994.

Bhattacharya, A., Fabozzi, F. (eds), *Asset-Backed Securities*, FJF Associates 1997.

Brown, S. *Analysis of Mortgage Servicing Portfolios*, Financial Strategies Group, Prudential-Bache Capital Funding 1990.

Fabozzi, F. (ed.), *Mortgage-Backed Securities: New Strategies, Applications and Research*, Probus Publishing 1987.

Fabozzi, F. (ed.), *The Handbook of Structured Financial Products*, FJF Associates 1998.

Fabozzi, F., *The Handbook of Mortgage-Backed Securities*, FJF Associates 2000.

Fabozzi, F., Jacob, D., *The Handbook of Commercial Mortgage-Backed Securities*, FJF Associates 1996.

Fabozzi, F., Ramsey, C., Ramirez, F., *Collateralized Mortgage Obligations*, FJF Associates 1994.

Golub, B., Tilman, L., *Risk Management: Approaches for Fixed Income Markets*, Wiley 2000.

Hayre, L., Chaudhary, S., Young, R., 'Anatomy of prepayments', *Journal of Fixed Income*, June 2000, pp. 19–49.

Hayre, L., Mohebbi, C., Zimmermann, T., 'Mortgage pass-through securities', in Fabozzi, F. (ed.), *Advances and Innovations in the Bond and Mortgage Markets*, Probus Publishing 1989, pp. 259–304.

Morris, D., *Asset Securitisation: Principles and Practices*, Executive Enterprise 1990.

Schwartz, E., Torous, W., 'Prepayment and valuation of mortgage pass-through securities', *Journal of Business* 15: 2, 1992, pp. 221–40.

Sundaresan, S., *Fixed Income Markets and Their Derivatives*, South-Western Publishing 1997, Chapter 9.

Tuckman, B., *Fixed Income Securities*, Wiley 1996, Chapter 18.

Waldman, M., Modzelewski, S., 'A framework for evaluating Treasury-based adjustable rate mortgages', in Fabozzi, F. (ed.), *The Handbook of Mortgage-Backed Securities*, Probus Publishing 1985.

CHAPTER 12

Mortgage-backed securities II

We continue the mortgage-backed theme in this chapter, describing the use of option-adjusted spread (OAS) analysis and measures of interest rate risk for mortgage-backed securities.

Prepayment and option-adjusted spread

Introduction

The OAS methodology was introduced in Chapter 6. Although it can be applied to any bond, the technique is primarily used in the analysis of bonds whose cash flow streams are contingent on the future direction of interest rates. As such, it is heavily used by participants in the MBS market.

The majority of mortgage contracts allow the borrower to repay the loan ahead of the planned maturity date without penalty. This means that the cash flow pattern of bonds issued against mortgage collateral cannot be predicted with certainty. In order to calculate fair value for these securities, it is necessary to project future cash flows by assuming a level of prepayment. Banks and thrifts (building societies) use econometric models that calculate prepayment rates as a function of general economic conditions, as well as more micro factors such as market interest rates, the age of the loan, the time of year, average earnings rates and so on. However, the most important determinant of prepayment rates is the level of mortgage interest rates in the market. Put simply, as these rates fall, the level of prepayment increases as borrowers seek to refinance their properties at lower interest rates. In modelling terms then, we would need to relate the possible paths of mortgage rates to those of short-term interest rates, and this can be done in a number of ways. A common method involves modelling the short-term interest rate and then modelling the mortgage rate as a separate random process, but correlated to the short rate. Another method involves formulating a statistical relationship between mortgage rates and a moving average of a short-term government yield. Whatever approach is used, once the range of paths of the mortgage rates has been produced, it is used to generate prepayment levels. The analyst will then be able to use the level of monthly prepayment to calculate a cash flow stream for a mortgage security.

Mortgage rates and repayment levels

In the US market there is a large and liquid market in mortgage-backed securities (MBSs) issued by government-sponsored agencies such as the GNMA and FNMA.[1] The first body carries an explicit guarantee from the US government, so its paper carries zero credit risk. The bonds issued by other agencies are implicitly guaranteed by the government and so carry a lower level of credit risk than, say, mortgage-backed bonds issued by bank origi-nators. However, all such bonds carry interest rate and prepayment risk. The effect of prepayment risk is conceptually similar to the effect of call risk on a callable bond issued by a corporate; namely, a certain degree of negative convexity as interest rates fall to a certain level. The call risk is to an extent greater on MBS issues however, due to the pre-payment factor, which can also be significant during a time of rising interest rates. This leads to lower convexity when prices are falling as well as rising.

The prepayment risk on an MBS is similar to the call risk on a callable bond, so it will influence the bond price at all times. The impact of this feature is dependent on the sensi-tivity of the prepayment level to changes in market interest rates. Fixed-coupon MBSs whose coupons are at current market levels or just above market levels will probably exhibit the highest prepayment risk. If market rates rise, there is always a decline in pre-payment rates as the level of refinancing falls. Therefore, when market rates are near either side to MBS coupon levels, the impact of the prepayment option on the bond's price is at its highest. If rates are far above or below MBS rates, the effect of the prepay-ment option is lowest.

The OAS methodology can be used for MBS analysis in a number of ways. To assess the impact of changes in prepayment levels, it is used to calculate the spread over the government rate that would be generated if prepayments were fixed at the rate used today. This is known as the *fixed cash flow* spread. By comparing this spread to the OAS calculated under varying prepayment and cash flow rates for each interest rate path, it is possible to determine the effect of prepayments on the value of the bond. This is some-times referred to as the *convexity cost* of prepayment levels, since it measures the impact of prepayment on the value of the MBS and hence its change in convexity.

In Figure 12.1 we illustrate the price/yield profile for a generic 8% MBS, similar to a GNMA security and so carrying no-default risk, when mortgage rates are 8%. The example indicates the extent of the convexity cost resulting from changes in prepayment levels.

---

1. Government National Mortgage Association and Federal National Mortgage Association, 'Ginnie Mae' and 'Fannie Mae' respectively.

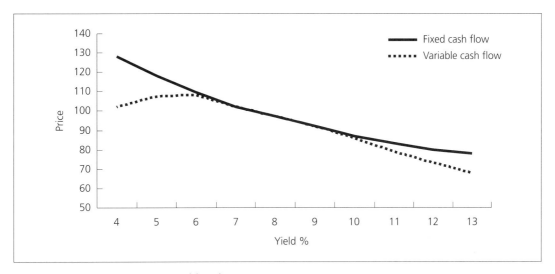

FIGURE 12.1 ▪ MBS 8% price/yield and prepayment

An introduction to analyzing prepayments

Prepayments occur generally as a result of three distinct events. These are:

▪ *Sale of the property*: A home sale results in the prepayment of the mortgage on the property. This is the major reason behind prepayments.

▪ *Refinancing of the mortgage*: The other major driver of prepayments is loan refinancing. This occurs typically in response to lower interest rates, but also takes place as homeowners access greater equity in the property or respond to an improvement in credit facilities.

▪ *Default on the mortgage.*

One other cause of prepayment is the occurrence of what is referred to as *curtailment* in the US market. This is the practice among homeowners of paying off a greater-than-required amount each month, as a means of building up equity in their home more quickly.

To accommodate the analysis of MBS securities, it is necessary to assume the level of prepayment when calculating cash flows. This is done using a *prepayment model*. Such models project the level of prepayment by making certain assumptions. Prepayment models are not discussed here, although the reader is directed to the bibliography for further study. Investors will sometimes eschew more sophisticated models and assume a single prepayment level or *speed* for the life of the deal. Even for short-dated securities however, this can lead to substantial inaccuracies. Hayre *et al.* (2000) suggest that for a prepayment model to be of reasonable value, it must incorporate the different effects of each of the four contributing prepayment factors. At any one time, the relative weight of each factor is dependent on the borrower's motivations, credit facilities, the level of the homeowner's equity and other factors. Hayre *et al.* suggest that each factor behind the prepayment of a mortgage be accounted for in a separate submodel, and these are then used to determine an aggregate prepayment rate.

We noted earlier that OAS analysis is used to assess the impact of prepayment variability in the overall return of MBS issues, by determining the spread over the risk-free yield that equates to the yield generated if prepayment levels were fixed at a specified rate. In some banks this is the *fixed cash flow* (FCF) spread. By varying the prepayment rates, and thus generating different OAS values, the FCF spread can be compared to each OAS, with the difference between the two being a measure of the convexity cost of holding the MBS bond. This is logical, since it is a measure of the effect of prepayment levels on the convexity of the MBS, and was illustrated in Figure 12.1.

As the cash flow profile of an MBS such as a GNMA bond is uncertain, the expected value of such a security is complex to measure. In falling interest rate environments the value of the bond will rise, unremarkably, to reflect lower interest rates. With MBS bonds though, this also leads to an increase in the level of prepayments as mortgage interest rates fall. As principal is paid off, the expected value declines. The effect is two-fold: first, coupon income, already of value as it is at a higher level than market rates, is reduced as the principal outstanding declines; second, the premium paid for the bond disappears. The impact on convexity is mirrored in an environment of rising interest rates. As prepayment levels decline, this counteracts the fall in price that results because the premium paid for the bond is received at a later date. In this situation the principal outstanding remains high but discounted at higher interest rates. The result is a decline in expected value, because the return of principal declines just at the time when reinvestment of these funds would be attractive, since interest rates are relatively high.

The level of prepayments is a function of the level of interest rates generally, so the extent of prepayment volatility reflects the volatility of interest rates. An environment of high interest rate volatility will result in high levels of prepayment volatility. Under these circumstances, the cost of convexity for MBS securities is higher, and hence the OAS is smaller.

Principal-only and interest-only strips

An established sector of the MBS market is that of interest-only and principal-only securities, which are created by stripping the interest and principal elements of the cash flows emanating from a pool of mortgage assets, and marketing these to investors as separate securities or *strips*. The cash flows of an IO are those of the mortgage interest payments only, and those of the PO are the principal payments only. The effect of this is that the upside impact of mortgage prepayments is reflected in the behaviour of the PO, while the downside impact is observed in the behaviour of the IO. For this reason, these instruments are used by market practitioners for interest rate hedging, as well as to reflect a view on future prepayment levels. Analysts use OAS in the analysis of IO and PO bonds.

Because of the nature of its cash flows, the impact of prepayments is particularly acute for PO and IO strips. The PO is similar to a discount instrument such as a zero-coupon bond, because no coupon interest is paid on the nominal amount. Investors' return achieved is completely in the form of repayment of principal. Therefore, return is highest if the principal is repaid as soon as possible. A longer time period to the return of principal will reduce investors' return. In other words, an increasing prepayment rate equates to higher return, while decreasing prepayment rates equate to lower return. A high level of prepayment volatility also leads to an increase in value. This is illustrated hypothetically in Figure 12.2 in the price/yield profile for a PO stripped from a generic agency 7% MBS bond.

The behaviour of the IO strip mirrors that of the PO. The IO exists only as long as there is principal balance outstanding, as this is charged interest. The higher the remaining balance, the greater the value of the interest payments on this balance. For IO holders therefore, an increasing level of prepayments reduces return, while return is enhanced as prepayment speeds decrease. IO strips exhibit negative convexity, and at certain interest rate levels there is an inverse price/yield relationship, as shown by Figure 12.3. The reason for this is that as interest rates fall, the conventional increase in bond price that one would expect is outweighed by the impact of rising prepayment levels. This price behaviour makes IOs suitable to hedge interest rate risk exposure.

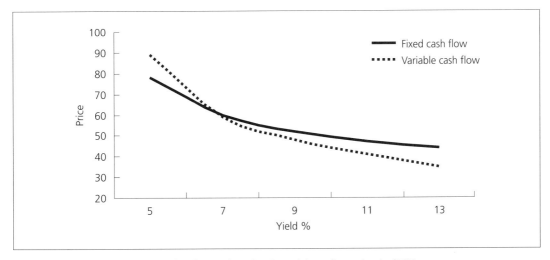

FIGURE 12.2 ■ Price/yield profile for PO bond stripped from hypothetical 7% coupon agency MBS security

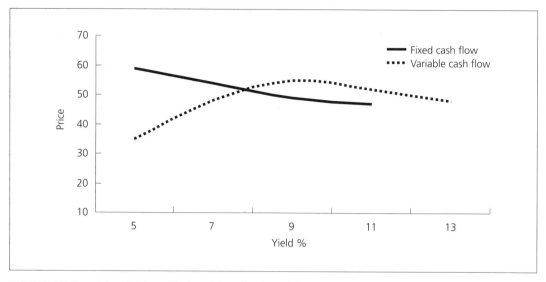

FIGURE 12.3 ■ Price/yield profile for IO bond stripped from hypothetical 7% coupon agency MBS security

PO and IO securities are perhaps the most sensitive instruments to interest rate movements and prepayment levels.

Collateralized mortgage obligations

Another well-established MBS product is the *collateralized mortgage obligation* or CMO. In a CMO structure the cash flow receipts are packaged into separate individual bond issues or *tranches*. The issue is structured in such a fashion so as to grant different credit ratings, and hence different coupons, to each tranche. This allows different issues to be placed with different types of investor. MBS issues may be comprised of tranches that pay fixed or floating coupons (with varying spreads over Libor in the case of the latter), with principal repayment schedules that differ, structured as POs or IOs, or in different combinations of these. In this section we consider a hypothetical MBS issue and discuss how OAS analysis can be applied.

Table 12.1 shows OAS analysis applied to the hypothetical MBS issue. We have assumed a projected 150PSA[2] and an expected average life across all the classes of 8.5 years. The A class notes are fixed coupon securities with amortization schedules that

---

2. A standard prepayment assumption, as initially described by the (since re-named) Public Securities Association.

TABLE 12.1 ■ Hypothetical MBS issue and results of OAS analysis

Issue   Residential MBS
Average life   8.6494 years
Volatility   10%

Share of issue (%)	Note	Coupon %	Expected average life (years)	Convexity	OAS
16	A1	6.5	2.9	4	41
16	A2	7.0	4.5	16	63
16	A3	7.0	7.0	18	67
14	B1	Libor + 50	8.9	7	39
12	B2	Libor + 100	10.2	11	44
11	C1	8.5	15.6	24	72
10	C2	9.5	21.4	31	88
5	D	9.5	3.1	12	54

are set so that the A1 note pays off the soonest and the A3 note pays off last. The B class notes pay off next in sequence. The C class notes only begin to pay interest after they begin to amortize; however, the interest payable accrues on the bond up until this point. As such they are also known as *accrual notes*. The A and B notes are less at risk from prepayment volatility compared with the C notes, and there is a range of average expected lives to suit investor requirements. In this structure the different tranches have redirected prepayment risk to different individual tranches. The A notes, for example, have reduced risk at the expense of the C notes. If, for instance, the D note amortized at 150PSA, its average life is considerably reduced; however, the C notes will accrue at the coupon rate of 8%, up to the point that the other bonds are redeemed. It then begins to pay down itself. This explains the longer expected average life for these notes. In practice there may be greater variability because prepayment speeds fluctuate over time.

Overall then, this RMBS issue presents investors with a choice of yields, spreads and average lives from which to choose. Investors who are prepared to accept prepayment risk may choose from average lives that range from 2.9 to 21.4 years. The OAS values for each class of note reflects the differing prepayment risks. The A and B notes have relatively low convexity cost, which results from the sequential order in which notes are paid off. Bonds that remain outstanding over a longer period of time are at greater risk that prepayment speeds will result in changes to the expected average life.

Interest rate risk

In the previous section we saw that the price/yield profile for MBSs differs from vanilla bonds. The traditional measures are not therefore as useful in capturing the interest rate risk of these bonds. One measure that is used is *coupon curve duration* (CCD).[3] The CCD is a measure of the price sensitivity of an MBS bond to a change in interest rates, and is relatively straightforward to understand because it is based on the coupon curve. This is the price sensitivity of other MBS bonds from the same issuer and with similar terms to maturity. The coupon curves for 20-year GNMA and FNMA securities as at January 2001 are shown in Figure 12.4.

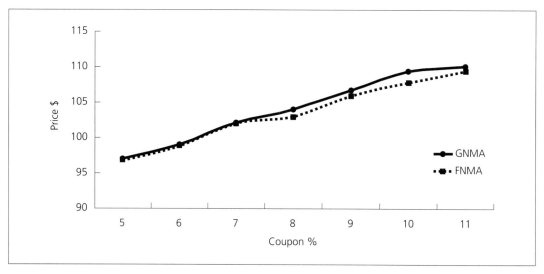

FIGURE 12.4 ■ Generic MBS coupon curves

Source: Bloomberg L.P.

CCD is the change in price given a 100 basis point change in interest rates. It is measured as a negative percentage change. Its premise is that as MBSs are very similar and differ only in terms of their coupon, when measuring the effect of the prepayment option, if there is a change in market interest rates by, say, 50 basis points, then the price of an 8% MBS should change to equal that of a 7.5% coupon MBS.

The CCD method described by Golub and Tilman (2000) is an important technique by which interest rate risk exposure may be measured. The two authors stress that it is only

---

3. See, for example, Golub and Tilman (2000), p. 48–56.

effective when used across a homogeneous set of MBS bonds with approximately identical expected average maturities. They also describe another approach that can be applied to MBS bonds, known as OAS curve duration. This method uses OAS curves to compare risk exposure across different bonds. So if there is a rise in interest rates of 50 basis points, the value of the prepayment option embedded in an 8% mortgage-backed bond behaves similarly to that of a 7.5% coupon MBS in the current interest rate environment. This means that we can describe the risk premium of the higher coupon bond in the higher interest rate environment as being equal to that of the lower coupon bond in the current environment. The OAS curves for the same bonds considered in Figure 12.4 are shown in Figure 12.5 as at January 2001.

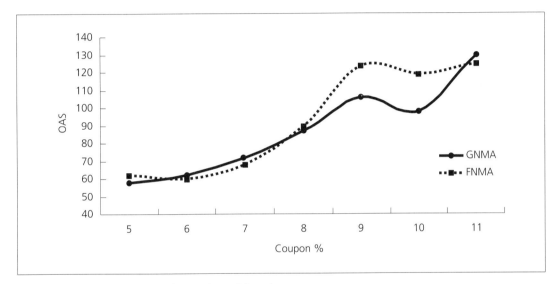

FIGURE 12.5 ■ OAS curves of generic MBS bonds

Source: Bloomberg L.P.

This method is an interesting approach, but space limits a fuller discussion and readers are encouraged to consider the Golub and Tilman reference for more details.

One other method worthy of consideration is the econometric approach. This is a means of measuring interest rate risk in terms of the empirical relationship between price and yield. Put this way, we set the change in price as the dependent variable and the change in yield as the independent variable. It is then possible to measure the statistical relationship between these two variables using standard regression techniques.

SELECTED BIBLIOGRAPHY AND REFERENCES

Arora, A., Heike, D., Mattu, R., 'Risk and return in the mortgage market: review and outlook', *Journal of Fixed Income*, June 2000, pp. 5–18.

Fabozzi, F. (ed.), *The Handbook of Mortgage-Backed Securities*, FJF Associates 2000.

Golub, B., Tilman, L., *Risk Management: Approaches for Fixed Income Markets*, Wiley 2000, Chapter 2.

Hayre, L., Chaudhary, S., Young, R., 'Anatomy of prepayments', *Journal of Fixed Income*, June 2000, pp. 19–49.

CHAPTER 13

Collateralized debt obligations

Introduction

The market in *collateralized bond obligations* (CBOs) and *collateralized loan obligations* (CLOs), which together make up *collateralized debt obligations* (CDOs), is one of the newest and most exciting developments in securitization (see Figure 13.1). The origins of the market are generally held to be the repackaging of high-yield debt or loans into higher-rated bonds, which began in the late 1980s, with the first CDO transaction believed to be by Kidder Peabody in 1989. This was a CBO, and the underlying asset pool was bonds off its balance sheet.[1] Today there is great diversity in the different CDO transactions, and the market has expanded into Europe and Asia from its origin in the USA (see Figure 13.2). Both CBOs and CDOs are notes or securities issued against an underlying collateral of assets, almost invariably a diverse pool of corporate bonds or loans, or a combination of both. A transaction with a corporate or sovereign bond asset pool is a CBO, while a CLO is backed by a portfolio of secured and/or unsecured corporate and commercial bank loans. CBOs and CDOs fall into two types; these are *arbitrage and balance sheet* CDOs. Some analysts also categorize a third variety known as *emerging market* CDOs.

A typical CDO structure involves the transfer of credit risk from an underlying asset pool to a special purpose vehicle (SPV) and this credit risk is then transferred to investors via the issue of credit-linked notes by the SPV. The objectives behind CDO transactions include:

▪ optimization of returns on regulatory capital by reducing the need for capital to support assets on the balance sheet;

▪ improvement of return on economic capital by managing risk effectively;

---

1. Thanks to Alicia Quinones at JP Morgan for this information.

■ credit risk management (for example, purchasing or transferring credit risk) and balance sheet management;

■ issue of securities as a means of funding;

■ provision of funding for the acquisition of assets;

■ increasing funds under management.

A typical conventional CDO structure is shown in Figure 13.4.

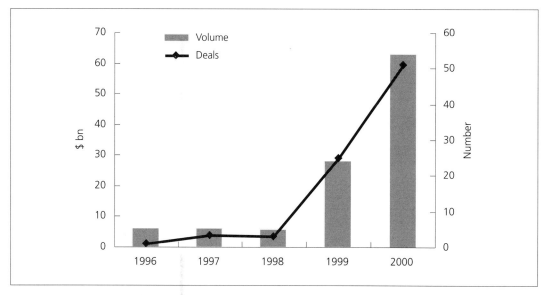

FIGURE 13.1 ■ CDO market volume

Source: Moody's Investors Service

The main distinction between a CLO and a CBO is the dominant investment class in the underlying asset pool. With a CLO, the underlying asset pool is a portfolio of bank loans, while a CBO series is issued against an underlying asset pool of a portfolio of bonds. So although they are grouped into a single generic form, there are key differences between CBOs and CLOs. In the first instance, assets such as bank loans have different features to bonds; the analysis of the two will therefore differ. In addition:

■ Loans are less uniform instruments, and their terms vary widely. This includes terms such as interest dates, amortization schedules, reference rate indices, reset dates, terms to maturity and so on, which impact the analysis of cash flows.

■ The legal documentation for loans is less standardized, in part reflecting the observation above, and this calls for more in-depth legal review.

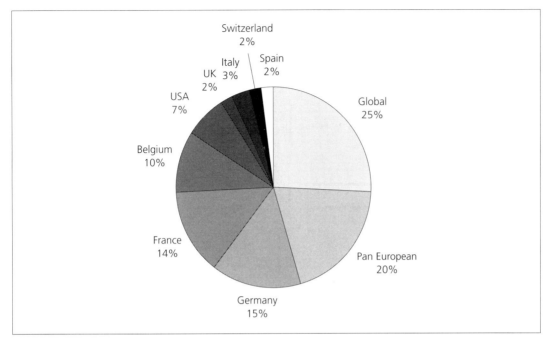

FIGURE 13.2 ■ Origin of assets

Source: Moody's Investors Service

■ It is often possible to restructure a loan portfolio to reflect changed or changing status of borrowers (for example, their ability to service the debt), a flexibility not usually afforded to participants in a CBO.

■ The market in bank loans is far less liquid than that in bonds.

These issues, among others, mean the analysis of CBOs often presents considerable differences from that used for CLOs.

This chapter briefly introduces CDOs, describes the motivation for an originator such as a commercial bank, and looks at some of the issues relating to the CDO structures.

CDO structures

CDO structures are classified into *conventional* CDO structures and *synthetic* CDO structures. The conventional CDO structures were the first to be widely used; however, synthetic CDOs have increasingly been used from the late 1990s onwards. The difference between these structures lies in the method of risk transfer from the originator to the SPV. In conventional CDO structures, the transfer of assets, known as a *true sale*, is how credit

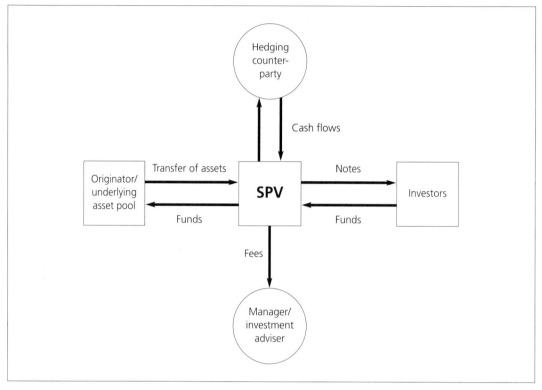

FIGURE 13.3 ■ Basic CDO structure

risk is transferred to the SPV. In synthetic CDO structures, credit derivative instruments, most commonly credit default swaps, are used to transfer credit risk.

In practice, the two structures are categorized by the reason behind their issue. There are two main motivations: issuer or *balance-sheet*-driven transactions and investor-driven or *market value* arbitrage transactions. To date, balance-sheet-driven transactions have been the main reason for structuring the majority of CDOs in Europe. However, investor-driven arbitrage CDO transactions are expected to experience strong growth as investment managers attempt to increase funds under management and attempt to release value through management expertise of the underlying asset portfolio.

The two structures are described in more detail below.

Conventional CDO structure

Conventional CDOs issue notes from an SPV to investors. SPVs are created to enable the effective transfer of risk from the originator. Most SPVs are set up so that they are bankruptcy-remote and isolated from the originator's credit risk. The creation of an SPV usually involves a nominal amount of equity, and the main funding comes from the issue of notes. SPVs are usually set up and registered in an off-shore location. The funds from the issue of the notes are used to 'acquire' the pool of underlying assets (the bonds or loans) from the originator. This will result in the 'true sale' of the assets to the SPV. In this way, the SPV has an asset and liability profile that must be managed during the term of the CDO.

The ownership of the assets is transferred into the SPV. This asset transfer, if performed and structured properly, may remove assets from the regulatory balance sheet of a bank originator. As a result, the securitized assets would not be included in the calculation of capital ratios. This provides regulatory capital relief and is the main motivation for some of the CDO structures in the market today.

The typical liability structure would include a senior tranche rated in the Aaa/AAA category, a junior tranche rated in the Baa/BBB category, and an unrated equity tranche. The equity tranche is the most risky, because first losses in the underlying portfolio are absorbed by the equity tranche. For this reason the equity tranche is often referred to as the 'first-loss' piece. The losses on the notes are said to 'indemnify' the SPV. The equity tranche offers investors a higher return to compensate for additional risk, but frequently is retained by the underwriting.

In the case of bank CLOs, the bank will continue to service the loans in the portfolio and usually also retains the first-loss interest.

Structuring a conventional CDO may give rise to significant other issues. The transfer of assets into the SPV in practice may have adverse tax, legal and regulatory implications. The impact will depend on the jurisdiction in which the transfer of assets takes place and the detailed legislation of that jurisdiction. Another practical issue is that the conventional CDO is a funded transaction because the originator receives cash. However, if the originator's main intention is to transfer credit risk or to acquire protection for credit risk, then the conventional CDO structure introduces reinvestment risk, because the cash received would need to be reinvested in other assets.

The SPV that issues the notes is generally an offshore bankruptcy-remote entity which isolates the underlying assets from the default risk of the originator. In most structures the transfer of credit risk to the investors is via the notes issued by the SPV. The return to investors in the issued notes will be dependent on the performance of the underlying asset pool.

Credit enhancement is provided via subordination (prioritization of cash flow payments to investors) of the tranches issued by the SPV. However, in addition to a multi-tranche structure, the bank may use other mechanisms to credit-enhance the senior notes. An example might include credit insurance on the underlying portfolio, known as a *credit wrap*, and the use of reserve accounts which assume a loss before the equity tranche.

Figure 13.4 illustrates a conventional CDO structure.

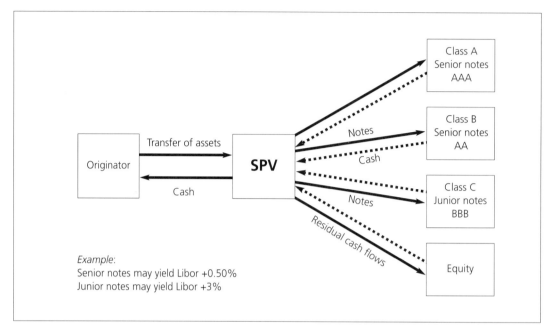

FIGURE 13.4 ■ Conventional CDO structure

Synthetic CDO structure

In a synthetic CDO no transfer of assets takes place, therefore the underlying reference pool of assets remains on the balance sheet of the originator. The originator buys credit protection from the SPV by entering into a credit default swap with the SPV, and the credit default swap covers any losses in the underlying asset pool on the originator's balance sheet. In this way, the credit default swap transfers the credit risk of the underlying asset portfolio to the SPV and this may allow the bank to release regulatory and economic capital, if the offset to the credit risk of the bank is recognized by its regulatory authority. The originator bank pays a premium, typically in the form of a regular fee, to the SPV for the credit protection and this contributes to the extra return to the investors for assuming the credit risk.

The SPV issues notes to investors, and the funds received are used to purchase high-quality (AAA) liquid securities which act as collateral. Examples of the type of collateral purchased include US Treasuries and AAA-rated German bonds such as Pfandbriefe. The collateral will provide the 'Libor-related' interest and principal cash flows into the SPV and the credit default swap premium pays the additional credit spread on the notes. The notes issued are linked to the credit risk of the portfolio via the credit default swap and to the credit derivative counterparty. Usually, the notes issued and the credit default swap will have the same term to maturity. The notes are therefore credit linked.

Any mismatch between the cash flows on the collateral and the payments on the issued notes, for example fixed receipts on the collateral versus floating payments on the notes issued, is usually managed by the use of a swap agreement between the SPV and a swap counterparty. The swap counterparty may also sell other derivative instruments, such as interest rate caps, to the SPV to manage possible cash flow risk. The management of the risk exposure in an SPV requires careful attention since the risk profile of the SPV is an important factor that may impact on the credit risk of notes issued. The amount of notes issued by the SPV to the investors will be equivalent to the credit protection it is offering on the reference pool of assets in an 'unleveraged' transaction. For example, if the credit default swap is on a nominal of $300 million then the nominal value of the notes issued will be $300 million.

The payout from the credit default swap will take place upon the occurrence of a credit event. The main credit events are usually defined as bankruptcy or failure to pay liabilities. The failure to pay definition may include a period of grace so that default is not triggered if the payment is delayed for technical reasons such as information technology

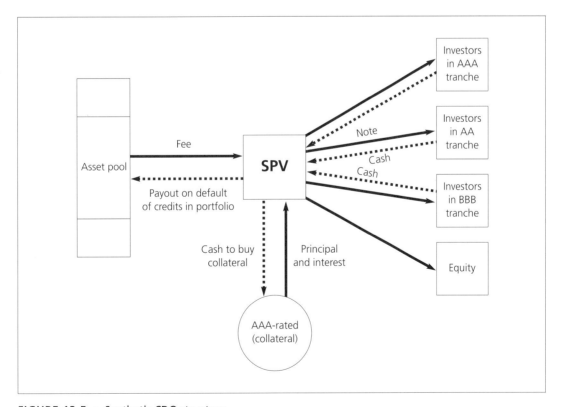

FIGURE 13.5 ▪ Synthetic CDO structure

issues. A precise definition of the credit event is important. Investors should understand the definition, as it may affect the return on the notes. The ISDA (International Swaps and Derivatives Association) definitions for a credit derivative transaction are market standard definitions for credit events.

If a credit event occurs then the SPV would usually make a payout of the cash amount equal to the par value of the underlying assets less the post default price. The alternative (which is less common) is for the SPV physically to settle the credit default swap payment, by purchasing the defaulted assets and paying par value. The credit loss is then passed on to the notes according to the priority of the notes.

The main motivation behind the issue of synthetic CDO structures remains the desire to hedge or transfer credit risk in order to achieve regulatory capital relief or effectively to obtain credit protection on an underlying asset pool. However synthetic transactions are now used in arbitrage driven transactions.

Figure 13.5 illustrates a synthetic CDO structure.

Motivation behind CDO issue

Balance-sheet-driven transactions

In a balance sheet CDO the motivation for the originator is usually to obtain capital relief by the transfer of credit risk on the pool of underlying assets. The transaction is intended to obtain off-balance sheet treatment for existing on-balance sheet assets to which bank capital has been allocated. The regulatory off-balance sheet treatment enables an originator bank to manage capital constraints and to improve the return on capital for the bank.

The originators of bank-balance-sheet CLOs are mainly commercial banks. The underlying asset pool may include commercial loans, both secured and unsecured, guarantees and revolving credits. The originator of the underlying assets usually acts as investment adviser so as to maintain the quality of the underlying asset pool. Although there is usually no trading intention for the underlying asset pool, over the life of the structure there may be changes such as substitutions or replenishments to the underlying asset pool. A form of protection to the note holders from these changes is usually that the quality of the underlying pool of assets does not significantly deteriorate. This may be via the maintenance of an average credit quality of the asset pool. Such a restriction is often required by the rating agencies.

The equity tranche in a CDO structure is commonly held by the originator for the following reasons:

- the bank has detailed information on the loans which will allow it to effectively manage the risk it retains;

- the bank retains economic interest in the performance of the loan portfolio and remains motivated to service the asset pool;

- the return required by a potential purchaser of the equity tranche may be too high, and this tranche may therefore be difficult to place if the risk/reward profile is not attractive to investors.

In some cases the lowest-rated debt tranche is also held by the originator.

Investor-driven arbitrage transactions

In an arbitrage CDO the underlying asset pool is more actively managed. The investment adviser is usually the manager of the CDO. The type of structure is driven by the opportunity to manage the portfolio actively with the intention of generating arbitrage profits from the spread differential between the investment and sub-investment grade markets. The underlying asset pool includes investments that not only provide investment income but may provide the opportunity to generate value from active trading strategies. The opportunity to generate arbitrage profits is often dependent on the quality and expertise of the manager of the CDO.

The underlying assets may be existing positions that are being managed or may be acquired for the CDO. In practice, when structuring the transaction the profitability of the transaction will depend on factors such as:

- the required return to the note holders of the issued tranches;

- the portfolio return of the underlying asset pool;

- the expenses (for example, management fee) of managing the SPV.

If the underlying portfolio performs well and the loss in the event of default profile is lower than expected, due to lower than expected default levels and higher levels of recovery, the required return to investors in the tranches of the CDO will be achieved and the return to the equity holder will be higher than expected. However, if the underlying portfolio performs poorly and the loss in the event of default is higher than expected (due to higher than expected default levels and lower levels of recovery rate, perhaps due to adverse economic conditions), then the return on the tranches issued will be lower than expected. Poor investment management performance will also adversely impact on the return to investors.

Fund managers use arbitrage CDOs in higher-yielding markets since the CDO structure may allow the manager to achieve a large size of funds under management for a comparatively small level of equity. This has been used effectively in the USA in the past few years. The objective is to set up the CDO so that the returns produced by the underlying pool of high-yielding assets will be enough to pay off investors and provide the originator/fund manager with a profit from the management fee and the return on the equity tranche.

Analysis and evaluation

Here we introduce some of the factors that are relevant when analyzing, evaluating or rating a CDO.

Portfolio characteristics

Credit quality

The credit quality of the underlying asset pool is critical because this is a source of credit risk in the structure. It is common to allocate an average rating to the initial reference asset pool. A constraint in the structuring of the transaction may be that any future changes to the asset pool that the structure allows should not reduce the average rating below the initial rating. The analysis of the portfolio's credit and the possible variability of the credit quality are used to determine the default frequency and the loss rates that may be experienced by the underlying asset pool. In some cases the originator's internal credit scoring system is a key part of the rating process. In particular, for unrated assets the rating process should involve a mapping process between the internal rating system and the agency's rating system to determine accuracy.

Diversity

The level of diversity within the reference portfolio directly influences the level of credit risk in the portfolio. Broadly, we would expect that the greater the level of diversification, the lower the level of credit risk. Diversity may be determined by considering concentrations by industry group, obligor and sovereign country. The level of diversity in the portfolio may be quantified by attributing a single diversity score to reflect the level of diversification of the underlying asset pool.

Broadly, the diversity score is a weighted average credit score for a portfolio of credit exposures. The marginal score allocated to each marginal credit exposure in the underlying asset pool depends on the existing credit portfolio. For example, if the portfolio has concentration in a category, for example an industry group, the marginal score attributed to the marginal credit is reduced to reflect this concentration (or lack of diversity). This has the effect that a higher diversity score is attributed to an asset pool where the range of credit exposure is wide. The higher the score, the better the level of diversification. All things being equal, the better the level of diversification, the more optimal the capital structure of the issued notes (or transactions).

A constraint may be placed on the level of change in the diversity as a result of a change to the underlying asset pool. For example, a minimum required diversity score for a transaction may need to be maintained.

Cash flow analysis and stress testing

The cash flow profile of a CDO structure depends on:

▪ the spread between the interest earned on the loans/collateral and the coupon paid on the securities issued by the CDO;

▪ the impact of default events, for example default frequency and severity (level of recovery rates) in the underlying asset pool and the impact of losses on the principal of investors;

▪ the principal repayment profile/expected amortization;

▪ the contingent payments in the event of default under the credit default swap which may be used to transfer credit risk from the originator to another party (such as the SPV or an OECD bank);

▪ contingent cash flows on any credit wrap or credit insurance on the underlying asset pool;

▪ cash flows receivable/payable with the hedge counterparty, for example under swap agreements or derivative contracts;

▪ the premium received from the credit default swap counterparty;

▪ fees and expenses.

The sensitivity of these cash flows is tested to understand the impact on the cash flow profile under stressed and normal scenarios. The relevant stress scenarios that are tested are dependent on the underlying asset pool.

Originator credit quality

The impact of the credit quality of the originator on the rating of the notes issued is dependent upon the structure. For example, where the underlying assets are transferred to the SPV (which is bankruptcy-remote) from the originator, in this case the credit quality of the CDO notes is only dependent on the portfolio performance and the credit enhancement. The credit performance of the CDO notes can be said to be 'de-linked' from the credit quality of the originator.

However, in some structures the underlying asset pool remains on the balance sheet of the originator, for instance as with credit-linked CDOs, as shown in Figure 13.6. In this case the notes issued by the SPV remain 'linked' to the credit of the originator. In this instance an investor in the CDO has exposure to both the credit quality of the bank and the portfolio performance. The rating of the credit-linked CDO is capped by the rating of the originator, because payment of interest and principal depends on the payment ability of the originator.

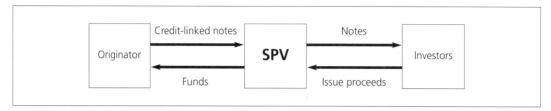

FIGURE 13.6 ■ Credit-linked CDO structure

However, for the senior tranches of a synthetic de-linked CDO, the portfolio may remain on the originator's balance sheet, but the senior tranches may be collateralized and de-linked from the bank's rating by using AAA-rated collateral and default swaps. The final rating is influenced by the credit rating of the default swap provider – the extent to which the cash flows to investors are exposed to the risk of default by the originator.

Operational aspects

In market value and cash flow transactions the abilities of the manager are a key aspect to consider, since the performance of the underlying portfolio is critical to the success of the structure. The review of the credit approval and monitoring process of the originator is another factor that may provide further comfort on the integrity and quality of the underlying asset portfolio. Better credit assessment and monitoring processes will lead to higher levels of comfort for both investors and the rating agencies.

Review of credit enhancement mechanisms

Credit enhancement may include the use of reserve accounts, subordinated tranches, credit wraps and liquidity facilities. These are briefly defined below. The impact of any credit enhancement methods should be considered and understood. This will usually be observed via stress scenarios, which are developed to determine the impact on the cash flows.

■ *Subordination*: The rights and priority of each tranche to interest and principal are set out in the offering circular for the issue. This is a detailed description of the notes, together with the legal structure. The cash flows are allocated according to priority of the notes. Typically, fees and expenses are paid first; the most senior tranches are then serviced, followed by the junior tranches and finally the equity tranche. The method by which excess cash flows can be allocated to remaining subordinated tranches is sometimes referred to as a *cash flow waterfall*.

■ *Credit wrap*: Credit protection of a debt instrument by an insurer or bank to improve the credit quality of the portfolio.

■ *Reserve accounts*: Cash reserves set up at the outset from note proceeds, which provide first-loss protection to investors. Such surplus funds are usually invested by the servicing agent or specialized cash management provider.

■ *Liquidity facility*: A liquidity facility may exist to ensure that short-term funding is available to pay any interest or principal obligations on the notes if there is a temporary cash shortfall.

Legal structure of the transaction

A typical CDO structure is described in a number of legal agreements. For example, the offering circular is the legal document that presents the transaction in detail to investors. The various legal agreements formalize the roles played in the CDO structure by the various counterparties to the deal. The documentation includes:

■ *Trustee agreements*: Provision of administrative duties and maintenance of books and records.

■ *Manager/servicer of the portfolio*: Manages the underlying portfolio and provides market expertise.

■ *Sale agreement or credit default swap agreements*: Used to transfer credit risk.

■ *Hedging agreements*: For example, interest rate or cross-currency swaps and other derivative contracts.

■ *Guarantees or insurance*: For example, credit wraps on the underlying asset pool.

Prior to the closure of the deal the SPV incorporation documents are also reviewed to ensure that it is bankruptcy-remote and that it is established in a tax-neutral jurisdiction.

Expected loss

The rating process for each transaction involves a detailed analysis of the CDO structure, including the points noted above. However, the actual process of assigning a rating to the notes issued in the CDO will include a quantitative assessment. This may be based on the expected loss (*EL*) to note holders, which is an important statistic when deciding on the quality of a tranche, according to Moody's Investors Service, a leading rating agency.[2]

The expected loss may be defined as:

$$EL = \sum_x p_x * L_x \tag{13.1}$$

where

L_x is the loss on the notes under scenario 'x'
p_x is the probability of the scenario 'x' occurring.

---

2. Other rating agencies – Fitch and S&P use different methodologies when determining the appropriate capital structure for a CDO.

The calculated expected loss statistic will be mapped to a table of ratings and their corresponding expected losses. In this way the rating can be allocated to each tranche. The loss to note holders is determined by considering the impact of credit losses on the cash flows to note holders that would occur under the various possible scenarios. This would involve the allocation of any credit loss to the various tranches in issue.

The cash flows to the note holders depend on whether or not a default has occurred, and the size of the loss in the event of default. The severity of the loss will depend on the par value of the note less the recovery rate. The calculated probability of default may be inferred from the rating of the underlying credit exposures. In practice, the calculation of the expected loss may be based on Monte Carlo simulation techniques in which thousands of scenarios and cash flows are simulated. This requires sophisticated computational models.

The expected losses on the tranches should be in line with the level of subordination. The expected losses on the tranche will be a key factor in the process of assigning a credit rating to the tranche. The credit rating of the tranche is a key determinant in the ultimate pricing and marketability of the tranche.

Pricing

Many CDO issues are often priced by reference to Libor, for example a spread over Libor. The level of the spread allocated to a tranche is largely dependent on the perceived credit quality of the stream of cash flows. As the rating of the notes reflects the credit quality, the spread over Libor is dependent on the rating. For instance, an issue may result in a senior tranche and a subordinated tranche. We would expect the subordinated tranche to provide the investor with a greater return than the senior tranche as a result of the higher credit risk associated with the cash flows. Additional factors that affect the pricing of the issued securities include a premium to reflect the new products or structures (a so-called 'novelty effect') and a premium for highly structured notes where the cash flows are not standardized.

The notes issued in a CDO transaction may be either fixed or floating coupon. The decision to issue fixed or floating depends on investor demand. For example, an investor may required fixed-rate CDO notes since these bonds would provide the investor with the required duration profile to match the liabilities it is managing. So an insurance company fund manager who is matching the medium to long-term fixed liabilities would opt for fixed coupon notes. Alternatively, the investor may prefer to hold floating rate notes so that the duration profile of their investment portfolio is not significantly affected by the additional investment.

The following case study uses Bloomberg screens to illustrate the notes issued from the CAST 2000–2 Deutsche Bank transaction. The screens show the following key information for each tranche: currency, term, rating, fixed rate or spread over Libor, the amount of the issue and the percentage of the whole issue for each note.

EXAMPLE *13.1 CAST 2000–2*

This transaction was underwritten by Deutsche Bank in August 2000. The issuer's objective in CAST 2000–2 was to transfer credit risk on a pool of corporate loans, bonds and guarantees. The risk transfer was achieved via the issue of several classes of credit-linked notes and unfunded credit default swaps between the issuer and swap counterparties. The issuer stated that proceeds from the funded notes would be used for banking purposes.

Structure type   Credit-linked notes
Issuer   Deutsche Bank Aktiengesellschaft

Reference portfolio criteria

Corporate loan, bond and guarantee claims (including syndicated loans) originated and held by the issuer or a consolidated European banking subsidiary of the issuer.

Maximum notional balance   2.5 billion euros (approx.)
Minimum rating agency diversity score   95
Weighted average rating   Baa3

TABLE 13.1 CAST 2000–2

Class	Amount (euros)	% of total	Spread over euribor	Maturity (scheduled maturity)	Maturity (legal final)	Rating
Senior swaps	2,225,000,000	89.00	Euribor +	Jan. 2008	Jan. 2010	NR
Sub senior swap	55,000,000	2.200	Euribor +	Jan. 2008	Jan. 2010	NR
A1	20,000,000	0.800	+0.7%	Jan. 2008	Jan. 2010	A1
A1A	9,000,000	0.360	6.05%	Jan. 2008	Jan. 2010	A1
A2	10,000,000	0.400	6.05%	Jan. 2008	Jan. 2010	A1
A3	11,000,000	0.440	6.05%	Jan. 2008	Jan. 2010	A1
B1	10,000,000	0.400	+1.5%	Jan. 2008	Jan. 2010	Baa1
B2	20,000,000	0.800	6.875%	Jan. 2008	Jan. 2010	Baa1
B3	21,200,000	0.848	6.875%	Jan. 2008	Jan. 2010	Baa1
C1	28,800,000	1.152	9.00%	Jan. 2008	Jan. 2010	Ba2
C2	10,000,000	0.400	9.00%	Jan. 2008	Jan. 2010	Ba2
D	80,000,000	3.200	+0.70%	Jan. 2008	Jan. 2010	NR

Source: Moody's Investors Services

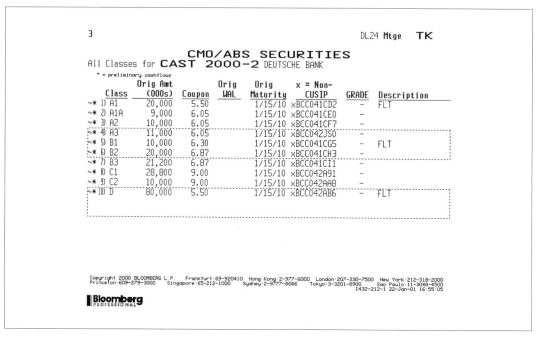

FIGURE 13.7 ■ CAST 2000–2 tranche structure

© Bloomberg L.P. Used with permission

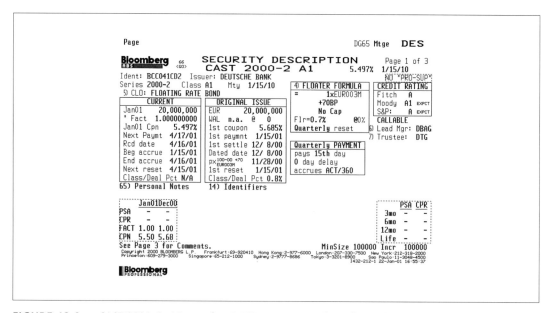

FIGURE 13.8 ■ CAST 2000–2, A1 tranche, 5.5% coupon, euribor plus 70 bps

© Bloomberg L.P. Used with permission

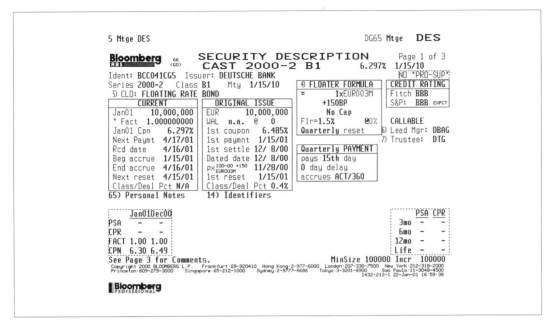

FIGURE 13.9 ■ CAST 2000–2, B1 tranche, 6.3% coupon, euribor plus 150 bps

© Bloomberg L.P. Used with permission

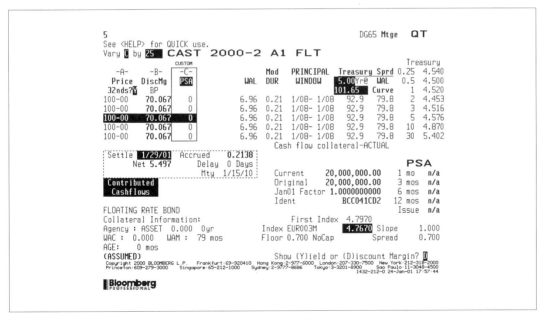

FIGURE 13.10 ■ CAST 2000–2, A1 tranche, price/yield table on 24 January 2001

© Bloomberg L.P. Used with permission

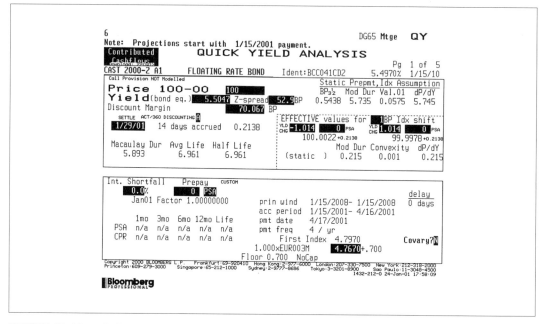

FIGURE 13.11 ■ CAST 2000–2, A1 tranche, yield analysis on 24 January 2001

SELECTED BIBLIOGRAPHY AND REFERENCES

Fabozzi, F., *Handbook of Structured Financial Products*, FJF Associates 1998.

Das, S., *Credit Derivatives and Credit-Linked Notes*, 2nd edition, Wiley 2000.

Part IV

Derivative instruments

Derivative instruments are another large and diverse product class. They are not securities, like the other products discussed in this book (although it is common to see them referred to as such), but are a vital part of the capital markets. The subject matter ordinarily demands several books in its own right. As usual, we aim to give readers a flavour of the diversity and introduce the basic techniques of analysis. Hence we discuss in Chapter 14 futures and forward rate agreements, and this is followed by a look at swaps. Three chapters are devoted to options, which reflects their complexity. Even so, the discussion on options is introductory, and readers are directed to a number of excellent textbooks in this area. The final chapter in Part IV looks at credit derivatives, one of the newest developments in the capital markets.

CHAPTER 14

Short-term interest rate derivatives

Introduction

The market in short-term interest rate derivatives is large and liquid, and the instruments involved are used for a variety of purposes. Here we review the two main contracts used in money markets trading: the short-term *interest rate future* and the *forward rate agreement*. In Chapter 4 we introduced the concept of the forward rate. Money market derivatives are priced on the basis of the forward rate, and are flexible instruments for hedging against or speculating on forward interest rates. The forward rate agreement and the exchange-traded interest rate future both date from around the same time, and although initially developed to hedge forward interest rate exposure, they now have a range of uses. In this chapter the instruments are introduced and analyzed, and there is a review of the main uses to which they are put.

Forward rate agreements

A *forward rate agreement* (FRA) is an over-the-counter (OTC) derivative instrument that trades as part of the money markets. An FRA is essentially a forward starting loan, dealt at a fixed rate, but with no exchange of principal – only the interest applicable on the notional amount between the rate dealt at and the actual rate prevailing at the time of settlement. So FRAs are *off-balance sheet* (OBS) instruments. By trading today at an interest rate that is effective at some point in the future, FRAs enable banks and corporates to hedge interest rate exposure. They are also used to speculate on the level of future interest rates.

An FRA is an agreement to borrow or lend a *notional* cash sum for a period of time lasting up to 12 months, starting at any point over the next 12 months, at an agreed rate of interest (the FRA rate). The 'buyer' of an FRA is borrowing a notional sum of money while the 'seller' is lending this cash sum. Note how this differs from all other money market instruments. In the cash market, the party buying a certificate of deposit (CD) or bill, or bidding for stock in the repo market, is the lender of funds. In the FRA market, to 'buy' is to 'borrow'. We use the term 'notional' because with an FRA no borrowing or lending of cash actually takes place, since it is an OBS product. The notional sum is simply the amount on which interest payment is calculated.

So when an FRA is traded, the buyer is borrowing (and the seller is lending) a specified notional sum at a fixed rate of interest for a specified period, the 'loan' to commence at an agreed date in the future. The *buyer* is the notional borrower, and so if there is a rise in interest rates between the date that the FRA is traded and the date that the FRA comes into effect, he will be protected. If there is a fall in interest rates, the buyer must pay the difference between the rate at which the FRA was traded and the actual rate, as a percentage of the notional sum. The buyer may be using the FRA to hedge an actual exposure, that is an actual borrowing of money, or simply speculating on a rise in interest rates. The counterparty to the transaction, the *seller* of the FRA, is the notional lender of funds, and has fixed the rate for lending funds. If there is a fall in interest rates the seller will gain, and if there is a rise in rates the seller will pay. Again, the seller may have an actual loan of cash to hedge or be a speculator.

In FRA trading only the payment that arises as a result of the difference in interest rates changes hands. There is no exchange of cash at the time of the trade. The cash payment that does arise is the difference in interest rates between that at which the FRA was traded and the actual rate prevailing when the FRA matures, as a percentage of the notional amount. FRAs are traded by both banks and corporates and between banks. The FRA market is very liquid in all major currencies and rates are readily quoted on screens by both banks and brokers. Dealing is over the telephone or over a dealing system such as Reuters.

The terminology quoting FRAs refers to the borrowing time period and the time at which the FRA comes into effect (or matures). Hence if a buyer of an FRA wished to hedge against a rise in rates to cover a three-month loan starting in three months' time, he would transact a 'three-against-six month' FRA, or more usually a 3 × 6 or 3 v 6 FRA. This is referred to in the market as a 'threes-sixes' FRA, and means a three-month loan in three months' time. So a 'ones-fours' FRA (1 v 4) is a three-month loan in one month's time, and a 'threes-nines' FRA (3 v 9) is six months of money in three months' time.

EXAMPLE   *14.1 FRA hedging*

A company knows that it will need to borrow £1 million in three months' time for a 12-month period. It can borrow funds today at Libor + 50 basis points. Libor rates today are at 5% but the company's treasurer expects rates to go up to about 6% over the next few weeks. So the company will be forced to borrow at higher rates unless some sort of hedge is transacted to protect the borrowing requirement. The treasurer

decides to buy a 3×15 ('threes-fifteens') FRA to cover the 12-month period beginning three months from now. A bank quotes $5\frac{1}{2}\%$ for the FRA which the company
buys for a notional £1 million.

Three months from now rates have indeed gone up to 6%, so the treasurer must
borrow funds at $6\frac{1}{2}\%$ (the Libor rate + spread). However he will receive a settlement
amount which will be the difference between the rate at which the FRA was bought
and today's 12-month Libor rate (6%) as a percentage of £1 million, which will compensate for some of the increased borrowing costs.

In virtually every market FRAs trade under a set of terms and conventions that are identical. The British Bankers Association (BBA) has compiled standard legal documentation to
cover FRA trading. The following standard terms are used in the market.

- *Notional sum*: The amount for which the FRA is traded.
- *Trade date*: The date on which the FRA is dealt.
- *Spot date*: The equivalent of the value date in the cash market.
- *Settlement date*: The date on which the notional loan or deposit of funds becomes
  effective, that is, is said to begin. This date is used, in conjunction with the notional
  sum, for calculation purposes only, since no actual loan or deposit takes place.
- *Fixing date*: The date on which the *reference rate* is determined, that is, the rate to
  which the FRA dealing rate is compared.
- *Maturity date*: The date on which the notional loan or deposit expires.
- *Contract period*: The time between the settlement date and maturity date.
- *FRA rate*: The interest rate at which the FRA is traded.
- *Reference rate*: The rate used as part of the calculation of the settlement amount,
  usually the Libor rate on the fixing date for the contract period in question.
- *Settlement sum*: The amount calculated as the difference between the FRA rate and
  the reference rate as a percentage of the notional sum, paid by one party to the other
  on the settlement date.

Some of these terms are illustrated in Figure 14.1.

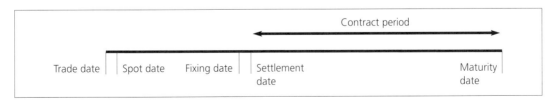

FIGURE 14.1 ■ Key dates in an FRA trade

The spot date is usually two business days after the trade date, however it can by agreement be sooner or later than this. The settlement date will be the time period after the spot date referred to by the FRA terms, for example a 1 × 4 FRA will have a settlement date one calendar month after the spot date. The fixing date is usually two business days before the settlement date. The settlement sum is paid on the settlement date, and as it refers to an amount over a period of time that is paid up front, at the start of the contract period, the calculated sum is discounted. This is because a normal payment of interest on a loan/deposit is paid at the end of the time period to which it relates; because an FRA makes this payment at the *start* of the relevant period, the settlement amount is a discounted figure.

With most FRA trades the reference rate is the Libor fixing on the fixing date. The settlement sum is calculated after the fixing date, for payment on the settlement date. We may illustrate this with a hypothetical example. Consider a case where a corporate has bought £1 million notional of a 1 v 4 FRA, and dealt at 5.75%, and that the market rate is 6.5% on the fixing date. The contract period is 90 days. In the cash market the extra interest charge that the corporate would pay is a simple interest calculation, and is:

$$\frac{6.50 - 5.75}{100} \times 1,000,000 \times \frac{91}{365} = £1869.86.$$

This extra interest that the corporate is facing would be payable with the interest payment for the loan, which (as it is a money market loan) is when the loan matures. Under an FRA then, the settlement sum payable should, if it was paid on the same day as the cash market interest charge, be exactly equal to this. This would make it a perfect hedge. As we noted above though, FRA settlement value is paid at the start of the contract period, that is, at the beginning of the underlying loan and not at the end. Therefore the settlement sum has to be adjusted to account for this, and the amount of the adjustment is the value of the interest that would be earned if the unadjusted cash value was invested for the contract period in the money market. The amount of the settlement value is given by (14.1):

$$\text{Settlement} = \frac{(r_{ref} - r_{FRA}) \times M \times \frac{n}{B}}{1 + (r_{ref} \times \frac{n}{B})} \tag{14.1}$$

where

r_{ref} is the reference interest fixing rate
r_{FRA} is the FRA rate or *contract rate*
M is the notional value
n is the number of days in the contract period
B is the day-count base (360 or 365).

The expression at (14.1) simply calculates the extra interest payable in the cash market, resulting from the difference between the two interest rates, and then discounts the amount because it is payable at the start of the period and not, as would happen in the cash market, at the end of the period.

In our hypothetical illustration, as the fixing rate is higher than the dealt rate, the corporate buyer of the FRA receives the settlement sum from the seller. This then compensates the corporate for the higher borrowing costs that it would have to pay in the cash market. If the fixing rate had been lower than 5.75%, the buyer would pay the difference to the seller, because the cash market rates will mean that he is subject to a lower interest rate in the cash market. What the FRA has done is hedge the corporate, so that whatever happens in the market, it will pay 5.75% on its borrowing.

A market-maker in FRAs is trading short-term interest rates. The settlement sum is the value of the FRA. The concept is exactly as with trading short-term interest rate futures; a trader who buys an FRA is running a long position, so that if on the fixing date $r_{ref} > r_{FRA}$, the settlement sum is positive and the trader realizes a profit. What has happened is that the trader, by buying the FRA, 'borrowed' money at an interest rate, which subsequently rose. This is a gain, exactly like a *short* position in an interest rate future, where if the price goes down (that is, interest rates go up), the trader realizes a gain. Equally, a 'short' position in an FRA, put on by selling an FRA, realizes a gain if on the fixing date $r_{ref} < r_{FRA}$.

FRA pricing

As their name says, FRAs are forward rate instruments and are priced using the forward rate principles we established earlier in the book.

We use the standard forward rate breakeven formula to solve for the required FRA rate. The relationship given at (14.2) connects simple (bullet) interest rates for periods of time up to one year, where no compounding of interest is required. As FRAs are money market instruments we are not required to calculate rates for periods in excess of one year,[1] where compounding would need to be built into the equation.

$$(1 + r_2 t_2) = (1 + r_1 t_1)(1 + r_f t_f) \qquad (14.2)$$

where

r_2 is the cash market interest rate for the long period
r_1 is the cash market interest rate for the short period
r_f is the forward rate for the gap period

---

1. Although it is of course possible to trade FRAs with contract periods greater than one year, for which a different pricing formula must be used.

t_2 is the time period from today to the end of the long period
t_1 is the time period from today to the end of the short period
t_f is the forward gap time period, or the contract period for the FRA.

This is illustrated diagrammatically in Figure 14.2.

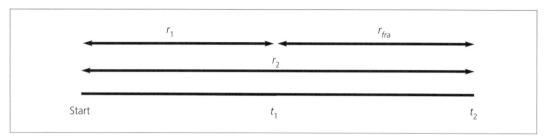

FIGURE 14.2 ■ Rates used in FRA pricing

The time period t_1 is the time from the dealing date to the FRA settlement date, while t_2 is the time from the dealing date to the FRA maturity date. The time period for the FRA (contract period) is t_2 minus t_1. We can replace the symbol t for time period with n for the actual number of days in the time periods themselves. If we do this and then rearrange the equation to solve for r_{fra} the FRA rate, we obtain (14.3):

$$r_{FRA} = \frac{r_2 n_2 - r_1 n_1}{n_{fra}\left(1 + r_1 \dfrac{n_1}{365}\right)} \tag{14.3}$$

where

n_1 is the number of days from the dealing date or spot date to the settlement date
n_2 is the number of days from dealing date or spot date to the maturity date
r_1 is the spot rate to the settlement date
r_2 is the spot rate from the spot date to the maturity date
n_{fra} is the number of days in the FRA contract period
r_{FRA} is the FRA rate.

If the formula is applied to, say, the US money markets, the 365 in the equation is replaced by 360, the day-count base for that market.

In practice, FRAs are priced off the exchange-traded short-term interest rate future for that currency, so that sterling FRAs are priced off LIFFE short sterling futures. Traders normally use a spreadsheet pricing model that has futures prices directly fed into it. FRA positions are also usually hedged with other FRAs or short-term interest rate futures.

FRA prices in practice

The dealing rates for FRAs are possibly the most liquid and transparent of any non-exchange-traded derivative instrument. This is because they are calculated directly from exchange-traded interest rate contracts. The key consideration for FRA market-makers, however, is how the rates behave in relation to other market interest rates. The forward rate calculated from two period spot rates must, as we have seen, be set such that it is arbitrage-free. If, for example, the six-month spot rate was 8.00% and the nine-month spot rate was 9.00%, the 6 v 9 FRA would have an approximate rate of 11%. What would be the effect of a change in one or both of the spot rates? The same arbitrage-free principle must apply. If there is an increase in the short-rate period, the FRA rate must decrease, to make the total return unchanged. The extent of the change in the FRA rate is a function of the ratio of the contract period to the long period. If the rate for the long period increases, the FRA rate will increase, by an amount related to the ratio between the total period to the contract period. The FRA rate for any term is generally a function of the three-month Libor rate generally, the rate traded under an interest rate future. A general rise in this rate will see a rise in FRA rates.

Forward contracts

A *forward* contract is an OTC instrument with terms set for delivery of an underlying asset at some point in the future. That is, a forward contract fixes the price and the conditions now for an asset that will be delivered in the future. As each contract is tailor-made to suit user requirements, a forward contract is not as liquid as an exchange-traded futures contract with standardized terms.

The theoretical textbook price of a forward contract is the spot price of the underlying asset plus the funding cost associated with holding the asset until forward expiry date, when the asset is delivered. More formally, it can be shown[2] that the price of a forward contract (written on an underlying asset that pays no dividends, such as a zero-coupon bond) is given by:

$$P_{fwd} = P_{und}e^{rn} \tag{14.4}$$

where

P_{und} is the price of the underlying asset of the forward contract
r is the continuously compounded risk-free interest rate for a period of maturity n
n is the term to maturity of the forward contract in days.

2. For instance, see Hull (1999), Jarrow and Turnbull (2000) or Kolb (2000).

The rule of no-arbitrage pricing states that (14.4) must be true. If $P_{fwd} < P_{und}e^{rn}$ then a trader could buy the cheaper instrument, the forward contract, and simultaneously sell the underlying asset. The proceeds from the short sale could be invested at r for n days; on expiry the short position in the asset is closed out at the forward price P_{fwd} and the trader will have generated a profit of $P_{und}e^{rn} - P_{fwd}$. In the opposite scenario, where $P_{fwd} > P_{und}e^{rn}$, a trader could put on a long position in the underlying asset, funded at the risk-free interest rate r for n days, and simultaneously sell the forward contract. On expiry, the asset is sold under the terms of the forward contract at the forward price and the proceeds from the sale used to close out the funding initially taken on to buy the asset. Again a profit would be generated, which would be equal to the difference between the two prices.

The relationship described here is used by the market to assume that forward rates implied by the price of short-term interest rate futures contracts are equal to forward rates given by a same-maturity forward contract. Although this assumption holds good for futures contracts with a maturity of up to three or four years, it breaks down for longer-dated futures and forwards. An accessible account of this feature is contained in Hull (1999).

Short-term interest rate futures

Description

A *futures* contract is a transaction that fixes the price today for a commodity that will be delivered at some point in the future. Financial futures fix the price for interest rates, bonds, equities and so on, but trade in the same manner as commodity futures. Contracts for futures are standardized and traded on exchanges. In London the main futures exchange is LIFFE, although commodity futures are also traded on, for example, the International Petroleum Exchange and the London Metal Exchange. The money markets trade short-term interest rate futures, which fix the rate of interest on a notional fixed-term deposit of money (usually for 90 days or three months) for a specified period in the future. The sum is notional because no actual sum of money is deposited when buying or selling futures; the instrument is off-balance sheet. Buying such a contract is equivalent to making a notional deposit, while selling a contract is equivalent to borrowing a notional sum.

The three-month interest rate future is the most widely used instrument used for hedging interest rate risk.

The LIFFE exchange in London trades short-term interest rate futures for major currencies, including sterling, euros, yen and Swiss francs. Table 14.1 summarizes the terms for the short sterling contract as traded on LIFFE.

TABLE 14.1 ■ Description of LIFFE short sterling future contract

Name	90-day sterling Libor future
Contract size	£500,000
Delivery months	March, June, September, December
Delivery date	First business day after last trading day
Last trading day	Third Wednesday of delivery month
Price	100 – yield
Tick size	0.005
Tick value	£6.25
Trading hours	0805–1757 (electronic screen trading)

The original futures contracts related to physical commodities, which is why we speak of *delivery* when referring to the expiry of financial futures contracts. Exchange-traded futures, such as those on LIFFE, are set to expire every quarter during the year. The short sterling contract is a deposit of cash, so as its price refers to the rate of interest on this deposit, the price of the contract is set as:

$$P = 100 - r$$

where P is the price of the contract and r is the rate of interest at the time of expiry implied by the futures contract. This means that if the price of the contract rises, the rate of interest implied goes down, and vice versa. For example, the price of the June 1999 short sterling future (written as Jun99 or M99, from the futures identity letters of H, M, U and Z for contracts expiring in March, June, September and December respectively) at the start of trading on 13 March 1999 was 94.88, which implied a three-month Libor rate of 5.12% on expiry of the contract in June. If a trader bought 20 contracts at this price and then sold them just before the close of trading that day, when the price had risen to 94.96, an implied rate of 5.04%, he would have made 16 ticks profit, or £2,000. That is, a 16-tick upward price movement in a long position of 20 contracts is equal to £2,000. This is calculated as follows:

Profit = ticks gained × tick value × number of contracts
Loss = ticks lost × tick value × number of contracts

The tick value for the short sterling contract is straightforward to calculate; since we know that the contract size is £500,000, there is a minimum price movement (tick movement) of 0.005% and the contract has a three-month 'maturity':

$$\text{Tick value} = 0.005\% \times \pounds500,000 \times \frac{3}{12}$$

$$= \pounds6.25$$

The profit made by the trader in our example is logical because if we buy short sterling futures we are depositing (notional) funds; if the price of the futures rises, it means the interest rate has fallen. We profit because we have 'deposited' funds at a higher rate before-hand. If we expected sterling interest rates to rise, we would sell short sterling futures, which is equivalent to borrowing funds and locking in the loan rate at a lower level.

Note how the concept of buying and selling interest rate futures differs from FRAs: if we buy an FRA we are borrowing notional funds, whereas if we buy a futures contract we are depositing notional funds. If a position in an interest rate futures contract is held to expiry, cash settlement will take place on the delivery day for that contract.

Short-term interest rate contracts in other currencies are similar to the short sterling contract and trade on exchanges such as Deutsche Terminbourse in Frankfurt and MATIF in Paris.

Pricing interest rate futures

The price of a three-month interest rate futures contract is the implied interest rate for that currency's three-month rate at the time of expiry of the contract. Therefore there is always a close relationship and correlation between futures prices, FRA rates (which are derived from futures prices) and cash market rates. On the day of expiry, the price of the future will be equal to the Libor rate as fixed that day. This is known as the *exchange delivery settlement price* (EDSP) and is used in the calculation of the delivery amount. During the life of the contract its price will be less closely related to the actual three-month Libor rate *today*, but closely related to the *forward rate* for the time of expiry.

Equation (14.2) was our basic forward rate formula for money market maturity forward rates, which we adapted to use as our FRA price equation. If we incorporate some extra terminology to cover the dealing dates involved, it can also be used as our futures price formula. Assume that:

T_0 is the trade date
T_M is the contract expiry date
T_{CASH} is the value date for cash market deposits traded on T_0
T_1 is the value date for cash market deposits traded on T_M
T_2 is the maturity date for a three-month cash market deposit traded on T_M.

We can then use equation (14.2) as our futures price formula to obtain P_{fut}, the futures price for a contract up to the expiry date:

$$P_{fut} = 100 - \left[\frac{r_2 n_2 - r_1 n_1}{n_f \left(1 + r_1 \frac{n_1}{365} \right)} \right] \tag{14.5}$$

where

P_{fut} is the futures price
r_1 is the cash market interest rate to T_1
r_2 is the cash market interest rate to T_2
n_1 is the number of days from TCASH to T_1
n_2 is the number of days from TCASH to T_2
n_f is the number of days from T1 to T_2.

The formula uses a 365-day-count convention, which applies in the sterling money markets; where a market uses a 360-day base this is used in the equation instead.

In practice, the price of a contract at any one time will be close to the theoretical price that would be established by (14.5) above. Discrepancies will arise for supply and demand reasons in the market, and also because Libor rates are often quoted only to the nearest sixteenth or 0.0625. The price between FRAs and futures is correlated very closely, in fact banks will often price FRAs using futures, and use futures to hedge their FRA books. When hedging an FRA book with futures, the hedge is quite close to being exact, because the two prices track each other almost tick for tick. However, the tick value of a futures contract is fixed, and uses (as we saw above) a 3/12 basis, while FRA settlement values use a 360 or 365-day base. The FRA trader will be aware of this when putting on his hedge.

In the discussion on forward rates we emphasized that they were the market's view on future rates using all information available today. Of course, a futures price today is very unlikely to be in line with the actual three-month interest rate that is prevailing at the time of the contract's expiry. This explains why prices for futures and actual cash rates will differ on any particular day. Up until expiry, the futures price is the implied forward rate; of course there is always a discrepancy between this forward rate and the cash market rate *today*. The gap between the cash price and the futures price is known as the *basis*. This is defined as:

Basis = cash price – futures price.

At any point during the life of a futures contract prior to final settlement – at which point futures and cash rates converge – there is usually a difference between current cash market rates and the rates implied by the futures price. This is the difference we have just explained; in fact the difference between the price implied by the current three-month interbank deposit and the futures price is known as *simple basis*, but it is what most market participants refer to as the basis. Simple basis consists of two separate components: *theoretical basis* and *value basis*. Theoretical basis is the difference between the price implied by the current three-month interbank deposit rate and that implied by the theoretical fair futures price based on cash market forward rates, given by (14.5) above. This basis may be either positive or negative depending on the shape of the yield curve. The value basis is the difference between the theoretical fair futures price and the actual futures price. It is a measure of how under or over-valued the futures contract is relative to its fair value. Value basis reflects the fact that a futures contract does not always trade at its mathematically calculated theoretical price, due to the impact of market sentiment and demand and supply. The theoretical and value bases can and do move independently of one another and in response to different influences. Both, however, converge to zero on the last trading day when final cash settlement of the futures contract is made.

Futures contracts do not in practice provide a precise tool for locking into cash market rates today for a transaction that takes place in the future, although this is what they are in theory designed to do. Futures do allow a bank to lock in a rate for a transaction to take place in the future, and this rate is the *forward rate*. The basis is the difference between today's cash market rate and the forward rate on a particular date in the future. As a futures contract approaches expiry, its price and the rate in the cash market will converge (the process is given the name *convergence*). As we noted earlier, this is given by the EDSP and the two prices (rates) will be exactly in line at the exact moment of expiry.

Hedging using interest rate futures

Banks use interest rate futures to hedge interest rate risk exposure in cash and OBS instruments. Bond trading desks also often use futures to hedge positions in bonds of up to two or three years' maturity, since contracts are traded up to three years' maturity. The liquidity of such 'far month' contracts is considerably lower than for near month contracts and the 'front month' contract (the current contract, for the next maturity month). When hedging a bond with a maturity of, say, two years', the trader will put on a *strip* of futures contracts that matches as nearly as possible the expiry date of the bond.

The purpose of a hedge is to protect the value of a current or anticipated cash market or OBS position from adverse changes in interest rates. The hedger will try to offset the effect of the change in interest rate on the value of his cash position with the change in value of his hedging instrument. If the hedge is an exact one, the loss on the main position should be compensated by a profit on the hedge position. If the trader is expecting a fall in interest rates and wishes to protect against such a fall, he will buy futures (known as a long hedge), and will sell futures (a short hedge) if wishing to protect against a rise in rates.

Bond traders also use three-month interest rate contracts to hedge positions in short-dated bonds; for instance, a market-maker running a short-dated bond book would find it more appropriate to hedge his book using short-dated futures rather than the longer-dated bond futures contract. When this happens it is important to calculate accurately the correct number of contracts to use for the hedge. To construct a bond hedge it will be necessary to use a *strip* of contracts, thus ensuring that the maturity date of the bond is covered by the longest-dated futures contract. The hedge is calculated by finding the sensitivity of each cash flow to changes in each of the relevant forward rates. Each cash flow is considered individually and the hedge values are then aggregated and rounded to the nearest whole number of contracts.

Examples 14.2 and 14.3 illustrate hedging with short-term interest rate contracts.

EXAMPLE *14.2 Hedging a forward three-month lending requirement*

On 1 June a corporate treasurer is expecting a cash inflow of £10 million in three months' time (1 December), which he will then invest for three months. The treasurer expects that interest rates will fall over the next few weeks and wishes to protect himself against such a fall. This can be done using short sterling futures. Market rates on 1 June are as follows:

Three-month Libor $6\frac{1}{2}\%$
September futures price   93.220

The treasurer buys 20 September short sterling futures at 93.22, this number being exactly equivalent to a sum of £10 million. This allows him to lock in a forward *lending* rate of 6.78%, if we assume there is no bid–offer quote spread.

Expected lending rate	=	rate implied by futures price
	=	$100 - 93.22$
	=	6.78%

On 1 September market rates are as follows:

Three-month Libor $6\frac{1}{4}\%$
September futures price   93.705

The treasurer unwinds the hedge at this price:

Futures p/l	=	+ 97 ticks ($93.705 - 93.22$), or 0.485%
Effective lending rate	=	three-month Libor + futures profit
	=	6.25% + 0.485%
	=	6.735%

The treasurer was quite close to achieving his target lending rate of 6.78% and the hedge has helped to protect against the drop in Libor rates from $6\frac{1}{2}\%$ to $6\frac{1}{4}\%$, due to the profit from the futures transaction.

In the real world, the cash market bid–offer spread will impact the amount of profit/loss from the hedge transaction. Futures generally trade and settle near the offered side of the market rate (Libor) whereas lending, certainly by corporates, will be nearer the Libid rate.

EXAMPLE *14.3 Hedging a forward six-month borrowing requirement* [3]

A treasury dealer has a six-month borrowing requirement for DEM30 million in three months' time, on 16 September. He expects interest rates to rise by at least $\frac{1}{2}\%$ before that date and would like to lock in a future borrowing rate. The scenario is detailed below.

Date	16 June
Three-month Libor	6.0625%
Six-month Libor	6.25%
September futures contract	93.66
December futures contract	93.39

In order to hedge a six-month DEM30 million exposure, the dealer needs to use a total of 60 futures contracts, as each has a nominal value of DEM1 million, and corresponds to a three-month notional deposit period. The dealer decides to sell 30 September futures contracts and 30 December futures contracts, which is referred to as a *strip* hedge. The expected forward borrowing rate that can be achieved by this strategy, where the expected borrowing rate is *rf*, is calculated as follows:

$$\left[1 + rf \times \frac{\text{days in period}}{360}\right] = \left[1 + \text{Sep. implied rate} \times \frac{\text{Sep. days period}}{360}\right]$$
$$\times \left[1 + \text{Dec. implied rate} \times \frac{\text{Dec. days period}}{360}\right]$$

Therefore we have:

$$\left[1 + rf \times \frac{180}{360}\right] = \left[1 + 0.0634 \times \frac{90}{360}\right] \times \left[1 + 0.0661 \times \frac{90}{360}\right]$$

3. This example pre-dates the introduction of the euro.

The rate *rf* is sometimes referred to as the 'strip rate'.

The hedge is unwound upon expiry of the September futures contract. Assume the following rates now prevail:

Three-month Libor	6.4375%
Six-month Libor	6.8125%
September futures contract	93.56
December futures contract	92.93

The futures profit and loss is:

September contract	+ 10 ticks
December contract	+ 46 ticks

This represents a 56 tick or 0.56% profit in three-month interest rate terms, or 0.28% in six-month interest rate terms. The effective borrowing rate is the six-month Libor rate minus the futures profit, or:

6.8125% – 0.28%, or 6.5325%.

In this case the hedge has proved effective because the dealer has realized a borrowing rate of 6.5325%, which is close to the target strip rate of 6.53%.

The dealer is still exposed to the basis risk when the December contracts are bought back from the market at the expiry date of the September contract. If, for example, the future was bought back at 92.73, the effective borrowing rate would be only 6.4325%, and the dealer would benefit. Of course, the other possibility is that the futures contract could be trading 20 ticks more expensive, which would give a borrowing rate of 6.6325%, which is 10 basis points above the target rate. If this happened, the dealer might elect to borrow in the cash market for three months, and maintain the December futures position until the December contract expiry date, and roll over the borrowing at that time. The profit (or loss) on the December futures position would compensate for any change in three-month rates at that time.

Refining the hedge ratio

A futures hedge ratio is calculated by dividing the amount to be hedged by the nominal value of the relevant futures contract and then adjusting for the duration of the hedge. When dealing with large exposures and/or a long hedge period, inaccuracy will result unless the hedge ratio is refined to compensate for the timing mismatch between the cash flows from the futures hedge and the underlying exposure. Any change in interest rates has an immediate effect on the hedge in the form of daily variation margin, but only affects the underlying cash position on maturity, that is, when the interest payment is due on the loan or deposit. In other words, hedging gains and losses in the futures position are realized over the hedge period while cash market gains and losses are deferred. Futures gains may be reinvested, and futures losses need to be financed.

The basic hedge ratio is usually refined to counteract this timing mismatch; this process is sometimes called 'tailing'.

EXAMPLE *14.4 Refining the hedge ratio*[4]

A dealer is hedging a three-month SFr100 million borrowing commitment commencing in two months' time and wishes to determine an accurate hedge ratio.

Two-month Libor	4.75%
Five-month Libor	4.875%
Implied 2 v 5 fwd-fwd rate	4.92%

The first part of the process to refine the hedge ratio involves measuring the sensitivity of the underlying position to a change in interest rates, that is the cost of a basis point move in Libor on the interest payment or receipt on maturity. We therefore calculate the basis point value as follows:

$$\text{Principal} \times 0.01\% \times \frac{\text{term (days)}}{360}$$

In this case the present value basis point (PVBP) is SFr2,500.

For every basis point increase (decrease) in three-month Libor, the dealer's interest rate expense at the maturity of the loan will increase (decrease) by SFr2,500. Correspondingly a SFr2,500 gain (loss) will be realized over the hedge period on the futures position. The present value of the futures gain (loss) is therefore greater than the present value of the loss (gain) on the loan. In other words, a hedge position consisting of short 100 lots is an over-hedge.

To calculate a more precise hedge ratio, the dealer needs to discount the nominal basis point value of the interest payments back from the maturity date of the loan to the start date of the loan. The discounting rate used in this calculation is the forward-forward rate over the loan period, that is, three months, implied by the current Libor market rates (given here as the 2 v 5 fwd-fwd rate). The discounting period may vary, depending on assumptions about the timing of cash flows. The formula for calculating the present value at the start date of the loan of a basis point move is calculated as:

---

4. This example is reproduced with permission from the LIFFE Technical Document.

$$\frac{\text{Nominal value of a basis point}}{1 + \text{fwd-fwd rate} \times \dfrac{\text{loan period (days)}}{360}}$$

For the dealer then the calculation is:

$$\frac{2500}{\left[1 + 4.92\% \times \dfrac{90}{360}\right]} = \text{SFr2,469.6}$$

To obtain the hedge ratio from this figure, the dealer would divide the PVBP value by the tick value of the futures contract, which for the LIFFE Euroswiss contract is SFr25:

$$\frac{\text{SFr2,470}}{\text{SFr25}} = 98.80$$

Therefore the correct number of contracts needed to hedge the SFr100 million exposure would be 99, rather than 100.

Appendix 14.1

The forward interest rate and futures-implied forward rate

The markets assume that the forward rate implied by the price of a futures contract is the same as the futures price itself for a contract with the same expiry date. This assumption is the basis on which futures contracts are used to price swaps and other forward rate instruments such as FRAs. In Appendix 14.2 we summarize a strategy first described by Cox, Ingersoll and Ross (1981) to show that under certain assumptions, namely that when the risk-free interest rate is constant and identical for all maturities (that is, in a flat-term structure environment), this assumption holds true. However, in practice, because the assumptions are not realistic under actual market conditions, this relationship does not hold for longer-dated futures contracts and forward rates.

In the first place, term structures are rarely flat or constant. The main reason, however, is because of the way futures contracts are settled, compared with forward contracts. Market participants who deal in exchange-traded futures must deposit daily margin with the exchange clearing house, reflecting their profit and loss with futures trading. Therefore a profit on a futures position will be received immediately, and in a positive-sloping yield curve environment this profit will be invested in a higher-than-average rate of interest. In the same way, a loss on futures trading would have to be funded straight away, and the funding cost would be at a lower-than-average rate of interest. However, the profit on a forward contract is not realized until the maturity of the contract, and so a position in a forward is not affected by daily profit or loss cash flows. Therefore, a long-dated futures contract will have more value to an investor than a long-dated forward contract, because of the opportunity to invest mark-to-market gains made during the life of the futures contract.

When the price of the underlying asset represented by a futures contract is positively correlated with interest rates, the price of futures contracts will be higher than the price of the same-contract forward contract. When the price of the underlying asset is negatively correlated with interest rates, which is the case with three-month interest rate futures like short sterling, forward prices are higher than futures prices. That is, the forward interest rate is lower than the interest rate implied by the futures contract price. This difference is not pronounced for short-dated contracts, and so is ignored by the market.

There are also other factors that will cause a difference in forward and futures prices, the most significant of these being transaction costs and liquidity: it is generally cheaper to trade exchange-traded futures and they tend to more liquid instruments. However, for longer-dated instruments, the difference in treatment between forwards and futures means that their rates will not be the same, and this difference needs to be taken into account when pricing long-dated forward instruments. The issue of *convexity bias* is discussed in a number of texts, the best known being Hull (1999); Choudhry (2001) carries an accessible introduction.

Appendix 14.2

Arbitrage proof of the futures price being equal to the forward price

Under certain assumptions it can be shown that the price of same-maturity futures and forward contracts is equal. The primary assumption is that interest rates are constant. The strategy used to prove this was first described by Cox, Ingersoll and Ross (1981).

Consider a futures contract with maturity of n days and with a price of P_i at the end of day i. Set r as the constant risk-free interest rate of interest per day. Assume a trading strategy that consists of:

- establishing a long position in the futures of e^r at the start of day 0;
- adding to the long position to make a total of e^{2r} at the end of day 1;
- adding to the long position to make a total of e^{3r} at the end of day 2;
- increasing the size of the position daily by the amount shown.

At the start of day i the long position is e^{ir}. The profit or loss from the position is given by:

$$P/L = (P_i - P_{i-1})e^{ir} \qquad (14.6)$$

If this amount is compounded on a daily basis using r, the final value on the expiry of the contract is given by:

$$(P_i - P_{i-1})e^{ir}\, e^{(n-i)r} = (P_i - P_{i-1})e^{nr} \tag{14.7}$$

so that the value of the position on the expiry of the contract at the end of day n is given by:

$$FV = \sum_{i=1}^{n} (P_i - P_{i-1})e^{nr}. \tag{14.8}$$

The expression at (14.8) may also be written as:

$$FV = [(P_n - P_{n-1}) + (P_{n-1} - P_{n-2}) + ... + (P_1 - P_0)]e^{nr}$$
$$= (P_n - P_0)e^{nr}. \tag{14.9}$$

In theory, the price of a futures contract on expiry must equal the price of the underlying asset on that day. If we set the price of the underlying asset on expiry as $P_{n-underlying}$, since P_n is equal to the final price of the contract on expiry, the final value of the trading strategy may be written as:

$$FV = (P_{n-underlying} - P_0)e^{nr}. \tag{14.10}$$

Investing P_0 in a risk-free bond and using the same strategy as that described above will therefore return:

$$P_0 e^{nr} + (P_{n-underlying} - P_0)e^{nr} \tag{14.11}$$

or an amount equal to $P_{n-underlying}e^{nr}$ at the expiry of the contract at the close of day n. Therefore this states that an amount P_0 may be invested to return a final amount of $P_{n-underlying}e^{nr}$ at the end of day n.

Assume that the forward contract price at the end of day 0 is $P_{0-forward}$. By investing this amount in a risk-free bond, and simultaneously establishing a long forward position of e^{nr} forward contracts, we are guaranteed an amount $P_{n-underlying}e^{nr}$ at the end of day n. We therefore have two investment strategies that both return a value of $P_{n-underlying}e^{nr}$ at the end of the same time period; one strategy requires an investment of P_0 while the other requires an investment of $P_{0-forward}$. Under the rule of no-arbitrage pricing, the price of both contracts must be equal, so that

$$P_0 = P_{0-fwd}. \tag{14.12}$$

That is, the price of the futures contract and the price of the forward contract at the end of day 0 are equal.

SELECTED BIBLIOGRAPHY AND REFERENCES

Chicago Board of Trade, *Interest Rate Futures for Institutional Investors*, CBOT 1987.
Choudhry, M., *The Bond and Money Markets*, Butterworth-Heinemann, 2001, Chapter 35.

Cox, J., Ingersoll, J., Ross, S., 'The relationship between forward prices and futures prices', *Journal of Financial Economics* 9, December 1981, pp. 321–46.

Figlewski, F., *Hedging with Financial Futures for Institutional Investors*, Probus Publishing 1986.

French, K., 'A comparison of futures and forwards prices', *Journal of Financial Economics* 12, November 1983, pp. 311–42.

Hull, J., *Options, Futures and Other Derivatives*, 4th edition, Prentice Hall 1999.

Jarrow, R., Oldfield, G., 'Forward contracts and futures contracts', *Journal of Financial Economics* 9, December 1981, pp. 373–82.

Jarrow, R., Turnbull, S., *Derivative Securities*, 2nd edition, South-Western Publishing 2000.

Kolb, R., *Futures, Options and Swaps*, 3rd edition, Blackwell 2000.

Veit, W., Reiff, W., 'Commercial banks and interest rate futures: a hedging survey', *Journal of Futures Markets* 3, 1983, pp. 283–93.

CHAPTER 15

Swaps

Swaps are off-balance sheet instruments involving combinations of two or more basic building blocks. Most swaps involve combinations of cash market securities, for example a fixed interest rate security combined with a floating interest rate security, possibly also combined with a currency transaction. The market has also seen swaps that involve a futures or forward component, as well as swaps that involve an option component. The main types of swap are interest rate swaps, asset swaps, basis swaps, fixed-rate currency swaps and currency coupon swaps. Swaps are one of the most important and useful instruments in the debt capital markets. They are used by a wide range of institutions, including banks, mortgage banks and building societies, corporates and local authorities. The demand for them has grown because the continuing uncertainty and volatility of interest rates and exchange rates has made it more important to hedge exposures. As the market has matured, the instrument has gained wider acceptance, and is regarded as a 'plain vanilla' product in the debt capital markets. Virtually all commercial and investment banks will quote swap prices for their customers, and as they are over-the-counter instruments, dealt over the telephone, it is possible for banks to tailor swaps to match the precise requirements of individual customers. There is also a close relationship between the bond market and the swap market, and corporate finance teams and underwriting banks keep a close eye on the government yield curve and the swap yield curve, looking out for interest rate advantages and other possibilities regarding new issue of debt.

We do not propose to cover the historical evolution of the swaps markets, nor the myriad swap products which can be traded today, all of which are abundantly covered in existing literature. Instead we review the use of interest rate swaps from the point of view of the bond market participant; this includes pricing and valuation and the use of swaps as a hedging tool. There is also an introduction to currency swaps and swaptions. The bibliography lists further reading on important topics such as pricing, valuation and credit risk.

Interest rate swaps

Introduction

Interest rate swaps are the most important type of swap in terms of volume of transactions. They are used to manage and hedge interest rate risk and exposure, while market-makers will also take positions in swaps that reflect their view on the direction of interest rates. An interest rate swap is an agreement between two counterparties to make periodic interest payments to one another during the life of the swap, on a pre-determined set of dates, based on a *notional* principal amount. One party is the fixed-rate payer, and this rate is agreed at the time of trade of the swap; the other party is the floating-rate payer, the floating rate being determined during the life of the swap by reference to a specific market index. The principal or notional amount is never physically exchanged, hence the term 'off-balance sheet', but is used merely to calculate the interest payments. The fixed-rate payer receives floating-rate interest and is said to be 'long' or to have 'bought' the swap. The long side has conceptually purchased a floating-rate note (because it receives floating-rate interest) and issued a fixed coupon bond (because it pays out fixed interest at intervals), that is, it has in principle borrowed funds. The floating-rate payer is said to be 'short' or to have 'sold' the swap. The short side has conceptually purchased a coupon bond (because it receives fixed-rate interest) and issued a floating-rate note (because it pays floating-rate interest). So an interest rate swap is:

- an agreement between two parties
- to exchange a stream of cash flows
- calculated as a percentage of a *notional* sum
- and calculated on different interest bases.

For example, in a trade between Bank A and Bank B, Bank A may agree to pay fixed semi-annual coupons of 10% on a notional principal sum of £1 million, in return for receiving from Bank B the prevailing six-month sterling Libor rate on the same amount. The known cash flow is the fixed payment of £50,000 every six months by Bank A to Bank B.

Interest rate swaps trade in a secondary market, so their value moves in line with market interest rates, in exactly the same way as bonds. If a five-year interest rate swap is transacted today at a rate of 5%, and five-year interest rates subsequently fall to 4.75%, the swap will have decreased in value to the fixed-rate payer, and correspondingly increased in value to the floating-rate payer, who has now seen the level of his interest payments fall. The opposite would be true if five-year rates moved to 5.25%. Why is this? Consider the fixed-rate payer in an interest rate swap to be a borrower of funds; if he fixes the interest rate payable on a loan for five years, and then this interest rate decreases shortly afterwards, is he better off? No, because he is now paying above the market rate for the funds borrowed. For this reason a swap contract decreases in value to the fixed-rate payer if there is a fall in rates. Equally, a floating-rate payer gains if there is a fall in rates, as he can take advantage of the new rates and pay a lower level of interest; hence the value of a swap increases to the floating-rate payer if there is a fall in rates.

A bank swaps desk will have an overall net interest rate position arising from all the swaps it has traded that are currently on the book. This position is an interest rate exposure at all points along the term structure, out to the maturity of the longest-dated swap. At the close of business each day all the swaps on the book will be *marked-to-market* at the interest rate quote for that day.

A swap can be viewed in two ways: either as a bundle of forward or futures contracts, or as a bundle of cash flows arising from the 'sale' and 'purchase' of cash market instruments. If we imagine a strip of futures contracts, maturing every three or six months out to three years, we can see how this is conceptually similar to a three-year interest rate swap. However, in our view it is better to visualize a swap as being a bundle of cash flows arising from cash instruments.

Let us imagine we have only two positions on our book:

■ a long position in £100 million of a three-year floating-rate note (FRN) that pays six-month Libor semi-annually, and is trading at par;

■ a short position in £100 million of a three-year gilt with a coupon of 6% that is also trading at par.

Being short a bond is the equivalent to being a borrower of funds. Assuming this position is kept to maturity, the resulting cash flows are shown in Table 15.1.

There is no net outflow or inflow at the start of these trades, as the £100 million purchase of the FRN is netted with receipt of £100 million from the sale of the gilt. The

TABLE 15.1 ■ Three-year cash flows

| Period (6-month) | Cash flows resulting from long position in FRN and short position in gilt | | |
	FRN	Gilt	Net cash flow
0	−£100m	+£100m	£0
1	+(Libor × 100)/2	−3	+(Libor × 100)/2 − 3
2	+(Libor × 100)/2	−3	+(Libor × 100)/2 − 3
3	+(Libor × 100)/2	−3	+(Libor × 100)/2 − 3
4	+(Libor × 100)/2	−3	+(Libor × 100)/2 − 3
5	+(Libor × 100)/2	−3	+(Libor × 100)/2 − 3
6	+[(Libor × 100)/2] + 100	−103	+(Libor × 100)/2 − 3

Note: The Libor rate is the six-month rate prevailing at the time of the setting, for instance the Libor rate at period 4 will be the rate actually prevailing at period 4.

resulting cash flows over the three-year period are shown in the last column of Table 15.1. This net position is exactly the same as that of a fixed-rate payer in an interest rate swap. As we had at the start of the trade, there is no cash inflow or outflow on maturity. For a floating-rate payer, the cash flow would mirror exactly a long position in a fixed-rate bond and a short position in an FRN. Therefore the fixed-rate payer in a swap is said to be short in the bond market, that is a borrower of funds; the floating-rate payer in a swap is said to be long the bond market.

Market terminology

Virtually all swaps are traded under the legal terms and conditions stipulated in the ISDA (International Swaps and Derivatives Association) standard documentation. The trade date for a swap is, not surprisingly, the date on which the swap is transacted. The terms of the trade include the fixed interest rate, the maturity and notional amount of the swap, and the payment bases of both legs of the swap. The date from which floating interest payments are determined is the *setting date*, which may also be the trade date. Most swaps fix the floating-rate payments to Libor, although other reference rates that are used include the US prime rate, euribor, the Treasury bill rate and the commercial paper rate. In the same way as for FRA and eurocurrency deposits, the rate is fixed two business days before the interest period begins. The second (and subsequent) setting date will be two business days before the beginning of the second (and subsequent) swap periods. The *effective date* is the date from which interest on the swap is calculated, and this is typically two business days after the trade date. In a *forward*-start swap the effective date will be at some point in the future, specified in the swap terms. The floating interest rate for each period is fixed at the start of the period, so that the interest payment amount is known in advance by both parties (the fixed rate is known, of course, throughout the swap by both parties).

Although for the purposes of explaining swap structures both parties are said to pay interest payments (and receive them), in practice only the net difference between both payments changes hands at the end of each interest payment. This eases the administration associated with swaps and reduces the number of cash flows for each swap. The counterparty that is the net payer at the end of each period will make a payment to the counterparty. The first payment date will occur at the end of the first interest period, and subsequent payment dates will fall at the end of successive interest periods. The final payment date falls on the maturity date of the swap. The calculation of interest is given by:

$$I = M \times r \times \frac{n}{B} \tag{15.1}$$

where

  I is the interest amount
  M is the nominal amount of the swap
  B is the interest day-base for the swap.

Dollar and euro-denominated swaps use an actual/360 day count, similar to other money market instruments in those currencies, while sterling swaps use an actual/365 day-count basis.

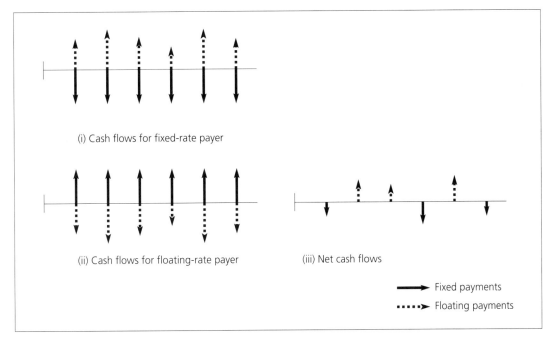

FIGURE 15.1 ■ Cash flows for typical interest rate swap

The cash flows resulting from a vanilla interest rate swap are illustrated in Figure 15.1, using the normal convention where cash inflows are shown as an arrow pointing up, while cash outflows are shown as an arrow pointing down. The counterparties in a swap transaction only pay across net cash flows however, so at each interest payment date only one actual cash transfer will be made, by the net payer. This is shown in Figure 15.1(iii).

Swap spreads and the swap yield curve

In the market, banks will quote two-way swap rates, on screens and on the telephone or via a dealing system such as Reuters. Brokers will also be active in relaying prices in the market. The convention in the market is for the swap market-maker to set the floating leg at Libor and then quote the fixed rate that is payable for that maturity. So for a five-year swap a bank's swap desk might be willing to quote the following:

Floating-rate payer: pay six-month Libor
receive fixed rate of 5.19%

Fixed-rate payer: pay fixed rate of 5.25%
receive six-month Libor

In this case the bank is quoting an offer rate of 5.25%, which the fixed-rate payer will pay, in return for receiving Libor flat. The bid price quote is 5.19% which is what a floating-rate payer will receive fixed. The bid–offer spread in this case is therefore 6 basis points. The fixed-rate quotes are always at a spread above the government bond yield curve. Let us assume that the five-year gilt is yielding 4.88%; in this case then the five-year swap bid rate is 31 basis points above this yield. So the bank's swap trader could quote the swap rates as a spread above the benchmark bond yield curve, say 37–31, which is his swap spread quote. This means that the bank is happy to enter into a swap paying fixed 31 basis points above the benchmark yield and receiving Libor, and receiving fixed 37 basis points above the yield curve and paying Libor. The bank's screen on, say, Bloomberg or Reuters might look something like Table 15.2, which quotes the swap rates as well as the current spread over the government bond benchmark.

The swap spread is a function of the same factors that influence the spread over government bonds for other instruments. For shorter duration swaps, say up to three years, there are other yield curves that can be used in comparison, such as the cash market curve or a curve derived from futures prices. For longer-dated swaps, the spread is determined mainly by the credit spreads that prevail in the corporate bond market. Because a swap is viewed as a package of long and short positions in fixed and floating-rate bonds, it is the credit spreads in these two markets that will determine the swap spread. This is logical; essentially it is the premium for greater credit risk involved in lending to corpo-

TABLE 15.2 ■ Swap quotes

1YR	4.50	4.45	+17
2YR	4.69	4.62	+25
3YR	4.88	4.80	+23
4YR	5.15	5.05	+29
5YR	5.25	5.19	+31
10YR	5.50	5.40	+35

rates that dictates that a swap rate will be higher than the same maturity government bond yield. Technical factors will be responsible for day-to-day fluctuations in swap rates, such as the supply of corporate bonds and the level of demand for swaps, plus the cost to swap traders of hedging their swap positions.

In essence, swap spreads over government bonds reflect the supply and demand conditions of both swaps and government bonds, as well as the market's view on the credit quality of swap counterparties. There is considerable information content in the swap yield curve, much like that in the government bond yield curve. During times of credit concerns in the market, such as the corrections in Asian and Latin American markets in the summer of 1998, the swap spread will increase, more so at longer maturities.

Zero-coupon swap pricing

Introduction

So far we have discussed how vanilla swap prices are often quoted as a spread over the benchmark government bond yield in that currency, and how this swap spread is mainly a function of the credit spread required by the market over the government (risk-free) rate. This method is convenient and also logical because banks use government bonds as the main instrument when hedging their swap books. However, because much bank swap trading is now conducted in non-standard, tailor-made swaps, this method can sometimes be unwieldy because each swap needs to have its spread calculated to suit its particular characteristics. Therefore banks use a standard pricing method for all swaps, known as *zero-coupon* swap pricing.

In Chapter 4 we referred to zero-coupon bonds and zero-coupon interest rates. Zero-coupon rates, or *spot rates*, are true interest rates for their particular term to maturity. In zero-coupon swap pricing, a bank will view all swaps, even the most complex, as a series of cash flows. The zero-coupon rates that apply now for each of the cash flows in a swap can be used to value these cash flows. Therefore to value and price a swap, each of the swap's cash flows is present-valued using known spot rates; the sum of these present values is the value of the swap.

In a swap the fixed-rate payments are known in advance and so it is straightforward to present-value them. The present value of the floating rate payments is usually estimated in two stages. First, the implied forward rates can be calculated using (15.2). We are quite familiar with this relationship from our reading of the earlier chapter.

$$rf_i = \left(\frac{df_i}{df_{i+1}} - 1\right) N \qquad (15.2)$$

where

rf_i is the one-period forward rate starting at time i
df_i is the discount factor for the maturity period i
df_{i+1} is the discount factor for the period $i + 1$
N is the number of times per year that coupons are paid.

By definition, the floating-payment interest rates are not known in advance, so the swap bank will predict what these will be, using the forward rates applicable to each payment date. The forward rates are those that are currently implied from spot rates. Once the size of the floating-rate payments has been estimated, these can also be valued by using the spot rates. The total value of the fixed and floating legs is the sum of all the present values, so the value of the total swap is the net of the present values of the fixed and floating legs.

While the term *zero-coupon* refers to an interest rate that applies to a discount instrument that pays no coupon and has one cash flow (at maturity), it is not necessary to have a functioning zero-coupon bond market in order to construct a zero-coupon yield curve. In practice, most financial pricing models use a combination of the following instruments to construct zero-coupon yield curves:

- money market deposits
- interest-rate futures
- FRAs
- government bonds.

Frequently an overlap in the maturity period of all instruments is used; FRA rates are usually calculated from interest rate futures so it is necessary to use only one of either FRA or futures rates.

Once a zero-coupon yield curve (*term structure*) is derived, this may be used to value a future cash flow maturing at any time along the term structure. This includes swaps: to price an interest rate swap, we calculate the present value of each of the cash flows using the zero-coupon rates and then sum all the cash flows. As we noted above, while the fixed-rate payments are known in advance, the floating-rate payments must be estimated, using the forward rates implied by the zero-coupon yield curve. The net present value of the swap is the net difference between the present values of the fixed and floating-rate legs.

Calculating the forward rate from spot rate discount factors

Remember that one way to view a swap is as a long position in a fixed-coupon bond that was funded at Libor, or against a short position in a floating rate bond. The cash flows from such an arrangement would be paying floating rate and receiving fixed rate. In the former arrangement, where a long position in a fixed-rate bond is funded with a floating-rate loan, the cash flows from the principals will cancel out, since they are equal and opposite (assuming the price of the bond on purchase was par), leaving a collection of cash flows that mirror an interest rate swap that pays floating and receives fixed. Therefore, as the fixed rate on an interest rate swap is the same as the coupon (and yield) on a bond priced at par, calculating the fixed rate on an interest rate swap is the same as calculating the coupon for a bond that we wish to issue at par.

The price of a bond paying semi-annual coupons is given by (15.3), which may be rearranged for the coupon rate r to provide an equation that enables us to determine the par yield, and hence the swap rate r, given by (15.4).

$$P = \frac{r_n}{2} df_1 + \frac{r_n}{2} df_2 + \dots + \frac{r_n}{2} df_n + M df_n \tag{15.3}$$

where r_n is the coupon on an n-period bond with n coupons and M is the maturity payment. It can be shown then that:

$$r_n = \frac{1 - df_n}{\dfrac{df_1}{2} + \dfrac{df_2}{2} + \dots + \dfrac{df_n}{2}}$$

$$= \frac{1 - df_n}{\displaystyle\sum_{i=1}^{n} \frac{df_i}{2}} \tag{15.4}$$

For annual coupon bonds there is no denominator for the discount factor, while for bonds paying coupons on a frequency of N we replace the denominator 2 with N.[1] The expression at (15.4) may be rearranged again, using F for the coupon frequency, to obtain an equation that may be used to calculate the nth discount factor for an n-period swap rate, given at (15.5):

$$df_n = \frac{1 - r_n \displaystyle\sum_{i=1}^{n-1} \frac{df_i}{N}}{1 + \dfrac{r_n}{N}}. \tag{15.5}$$

The expression at (15.5) is the general expression for the *bootstrapping* process that we first encountered in Chapter 4. Essentially, to calculate the n-year discount factor we use the discount factors for the years 1 to n-1, and the n-year swap rate or zero-coupon rate.

1. The expression also assumes an actual/365 day-count basis. If any other day-count convention is used, the 1/N factor must be replaced by a fraction made up of the actual number of days as the numerator and the appropriate year base as the denominator.

If we have the discount factor for any period, we may use (15.5) to determine the same period zero-coupon rate, after rearranging it, shown at (15.6):

$$rs_n = \sqrt[t_n]{\frac{1}{df_n}} - 1.$$

(15.6)

Discount factors for spot rates may also be used to calculate forward rates. We know that:

$$df_1 = \frac{1}{\left(1 + \frac{rs_1}{N}\right)}$$

(15.7)

where rs is the zero-coupon rate. If we know the *forward rate*, we may use this to calculate a second discount rate, shown by:

$$df_2 = \frac{df_1}{\left(1 + \frac{rf_1}{N}\right)}$$

(15.8)

where rf_1 is the forward rate. This is no use in itself; however we may derive from it an expression to enable us to calculate the discount factor at any point in time between the previous discount rate and the given forward rate for the period n to $n+1$, shown at (15.9), which may then be rearranged to give us the general expression to calculate a forward rate, given at (15.10).

$$df_{n+1} = \frac{df_n}{\left(1 + \frac{rf_n}{N}\right)}$$

(15.9)

$$rf_n = \left(\frac{df_n}{df_{n+1}} - 1\right)N$$

(15.10)

The general expression for an n-period discount rate at time n from the previous period forward rates is given by:

$$df_n = \frac{1}{\left(1 + \frac{rf_{n-1}}{N}\right)} \times \frac{1}{\left(1 + \frac{rf_{n-2}}{N}\right)} \times \ldots \times \frac{1}{\left(1 + \frac{rf_n}{N}\right)}$$

(15.11)

$$df_n = \prod_{i=0}^{n-1} \left[\frac{1}{\left(1 + \frac{rf_i}{N}\right)}\right].$$

From the above we may combine equations (15.4) and (15.10) to obtain the general expression for an n-period swap rate and zero-coupon rate, given by (15.12) and (15.13) respectively.

$$r_n = \frac{\sum_{i=1}^{n} \frac{rf_{i-1} \, df_i}{N}}{\sum_{i=1}^{n} \frac{df_i}{F}} \tag{15.12}$$

$$1 + rs_n = {}^{t_n}\!\sqrt{\prod_{i=0}^{n-1} \left(1 + \frac{rf_i}{N}\right)}. \tag{15.13}$$

The two expressions tell us that the swap rate, which we have denoted as r_n, is shown by (15.12) to be the weighted average of the forward rates. A strip of FRAs would constitute an interest rate swap, so a swap rate for a continuous period could be covered by a strip of FRAs. Therefore an average of the FRA rates would be the correct swap rate. As FRA rates are forward rates, we may be comfortable with (15.12), which states that the n-period swap rate is the average of the forward rates from rf_0 to rf_n. To be accurate, we must weight the forward rates, and these are weighted by the discount factors for each period. Note that although swap rates are derived from forward rates, interest payments under a swap are paid in the normal way at the end of an interest period, while payments for an FRA are made at the beginning of the period and must be discounted.

Equation (15.13) states that the zero-coupon rate is calculated from the geometric average of (1 +) the forward rates. The n-period forward rate is obtained using the discount factors for periods n and n-1. The discount factor for the complete period is obtained by multiplying the individual discount factors together, and exactly the same result would be obtained by using the zero-coupon interest rate for the whole period to obtain the discount factor.[2]

Illustrating the principles of an interest rate swap

The rate charged on a newly transacted interest rate swap is the one that gives its net present value as zero. The term *valuation* of a swap is used to denote the process of calculating the net present value of an existing swap, when marking-to-market the swap

---

2. Zero-coupon and forward rates are also related in another way. If we change the zero-coupon rate rs_n and the forward rate rf_i into their continuously compounded equivalent rates, given by $\ln(1 + rs_n)$ and $\ln(1 + rf_i)$, we may obtain an expression for the continuously compounded zero-coupon rate as being the simple average of the continuously compounded forward rates, given by:

$$rs_n' = \frac{1}{t_n} \sum_{i=0}^{n-1} \frac{rf_i'}{F}$$

against current market interest rates. Therefore, when we price a swap we set its net present value to zero, while when we value a swap we set its fixed rate at the market rate and calculate the net present value.

A vanilla interest rate swap calculator is included as part of the RATE applications software, part of this book.

To illustrate the basic principle, we price a plain vanilla interest rate swap with the terms set out below; for simplicity we assume that the annual fixed-rate payments are the same amount each year, although in practice there would be slight differences. Also assume we already have our zero-coupon yields as shown in Table 15.3.

We use the zero-coupon rates to calculate the discount factors, and then use the discount factors to calculate the forward rates. This is done using equation (15.10). These forward rates are then used to predict what the floating-rate payments will be at each interest period. Both fixed-rate and floating-rate payments are then present-valued at the appropriate zero-coupon rate, which enables us to calculate the net present value.

TABLE 15.3 ■ Generic interest rate swap

Period	Zero-coupon rate %	Discount factor	Forward rate %	Fixed payment	Floating payment	PV fixed payment	PV floating payment
1	5.5	0.947867298	5.5	689,625	550,000	653,672.9858	521,327.0142
2	6	0.88999644	6.502369605	689,625	650,236.9605	613,763.7949	578,708.58
3	6.25	0.833706493	6.751770257	689,625	675,177.0257	574,944.8402	562,899.4702
4	6.5	0.777323091	7.253534951	689,625	725,353.4951	536,061.4366	563,834.0208
5	7	0.712986179	9.023584719	689,625	902,358.4719	491,693.094	643,369.1194
		4.161879501				2,870,137	2,870,137

TABLE 15.4 ■ Generic interest rate swap (Excel formulae)

CELL	C	D	E	F	G	H	I	J
21			10000000					
22								
23	Period	Zero-coupon rate %	Discount factor	Forward rate %	Fixed payment	Floating payment	PV fixed payment	PV floating payment
24	1	5.5	0.947867298	5.5	689,625	"(F24*10,000,000)/100	"G24/1.055	"H24/(1.055)
25	2	6	0.88999644	"((E24/E25)-1)*100	689,625	"(F25*10,000,000)/100	"G24/(1.06)^2	"H25/(1.06)^2
26	3	6.25	0.833706493	"((E25/E26)-1)*100	689,625	"(F26*10,000,000)/100	"G24/(1.0625)^3	"H26/(1.0625^3)
27	4	6.5	0.777323091	"((E26/E27)-1)*100	689,625	"(F27*10,000,000)/100	"G24/(1.065)^4	"H27/(1.065)^4
28	5	7	0.712986179	"((E27/E28)-1)*100	689,625	"(F28*10,000,000)/100	"G24/(1.07)^5	"H28/(1.07)^5
			"SUM(E24:E28)				2,870,137	2,870,137

The fixed rate for the swap is calculated using equation (15.4) to give us:

$$\frac{1 - 0.71298618}{4.16187950}$$

or 6.8963%.

Nominal principal	£10,000,000
Fixed rate	6.8963%
Day count fixed	Actual/365
Day count floating	Actual/365
Payment frequency fixed	Annual
Payment frequency floating	Annual
Trade date	31 January 2000
Effective date	2 February 2000
Maturity date	2 February 2005
Term	Five years

For reference, the Microsoft Excel formulae are shown in Table 15.4. It is not surprising that the net present value is zero, because the zero-coupon curve is used to derive the discount factors which are then used to derive the forward rates, which are used to value the swap. As with any financial instrument, the fair value is its breakeven price or hedge cost, and in this case the bank that is pricing the five-year swap shown in Table 15.3 could hedge the swap with a series of FRAs transacted at the forward rates shown. If the bank is paying fixed and receiving floating rates, then the value of the swap to it will rise if there is a rise in market rates, and fall if there is a fall in market rates. Conversely, if the bank was receiving fixed and paying floating rates, the swap value to it would fall if there was a rise in rates, and vice versa.

This method is used to price any interest rate swap, even exotic ones.

Valuation using final maturity discount factor

A short-cut to valuing the floating-leg payments of an interest rate swap involves using the discount factor for the final maturity period. This is possible because, for the purposes of valuation, an exchange of principal at the beginning and end of the swap is conceptually the same as the floating-leg interest payments. This holds because, in an exchange of principal, the interest payments earned on investing the initial principal would be uncertain, as they are floating rate, while on maturity the original principal would be returned. The net result is a floating-rate level of receipts, exactly similar to the floating-leg payments in a swap. To value the principals then, we need only the final maturity discount rate.

To illustrate, consider Table 15.3, where the present value of both legs was found to be £2,870,137. The same result is obtained if we use the five-year discount factor:

$$PV_{floating} = (10,000,000 \times 1) - (10,000,000 \times 0.71298618) = 2,870,137$$

The first term is the principal multiplied by the discount factor 1; this is because the present value of an amount valued immediately is unchanged (or rather, it is multiplied by the immediate payment discount factor, which is 1.0000).

Therefore we may use the principal amount of a swap if we wish to value the swap. This is, of course, for valuation only, as there is no actual exchange of principal in a swap.

Summary of an interest rate swap

A plain vanilla interest rate swap has the following characteristics:

- one leg of the swap is fixed-rate interest, while the other will be floating rate, usually linked to a standard index such as Libor;
- the fixed rate is fixed through the entire life of the swap;
- the floating rate is set in advance of each period (quarterly, semi-annually or annually) and paid in arrears;
- both legs have the same payment frequency;
- the maturity can be standard whole years up to 30 years, or set to match customer requirements;
- the notional principal remains constant during the life of the swap.

To meet customer demand, banks can set up swaps that have variations on any or all of the above standard points. Some of the more common variations are discussed in the next section.

Non-vanilla interest rate swaps

The swap market is very flexible and instruments can be tailor-made to fit the requirements of individual customers. A wide variety of swap contracts have been traded in the market. Although the most common reference rate for the floating leg of a swap is six-month Libor, for a semi-annual paying floating leg other reference rates have been used, including three-month Libor, the prime rate (for dollar swaps), the one-month commercial paper rate, the Treasury bill rate and the municipal bond rate (again, for dollar swaps). The term of a swap need not be fixed; swaps may be *extendable* or *putable*. In an extendable swap, one of the parties has the right but not the obligation to extend the life of the swap beyond the fixed maturity date, while in a putable swap one party has the right to terminate the swap ahead of the specified maturity date. It is also possible to transact options on swaps, known as *swaptions*. A swaption is the right to enter into a swap agreement at some point in the future, during the life of the option. Essentially a swaption is an option to exchange a fixed-rate bond cash flow for a floating-rate bond cash flow structure. As a floating-rate bond is valued on its principal value at the start of a swap, a swaption may be viewed as the value on a fixed-rate bond, with a strike price that is equal to the face value of the floating-rate bond.

Constant maturity swap

A constant maturity swap is a swap in which the parties exchange a Libor rate for a fixed swap rate. For example, the terms of the swap might state that six-month Libor is exchanged for the five-year swap rate on a semi-annual basis for the next five years, or for the five-year government bond rate. In the US market the second type of constant maturity swap is known as a *constant maturity Treasury swap*.

Accreting and amortizing swaps

In a plain vanilla swap the notional principal remains unchanged during the life of the swap. However, it is possible to trade a swap where the notional principal varies during its life. An accreting (or *step-up*) swap is one in which the principal starts off at one level and then increases in amount over time. The opposite, an amortizing swap, is one in which the notional reduces in size over time. An accreting swap would be useful where, for instance, a funding liability that is being hedged increases over time. The amortizing swap might be employed by a borrower hedging a bond issue that featured sinking fund payments, where a part of the notional amount outstanding is paid off at set points during the life of the bond. If the principal fluctuates in amount, for example increasing in one year and then reducing in another, the swap is known as a *roller-coaster swap*. Another application for an amortizing swap is as a hedge for a loan that is itself an amortizing one. Frequently this is combined with a forward-starting swap, to tie in with the cash flows payable on the loan. The pricing and valuation of an amortizing swap are no different in principle to a vanilla interest rate swap; a single swap rate is calculated using the relevant discount factors, and at this rate the net present value of the swap cash flows will equal zero at the start of the swap.

Libor-in-arrears swap

In this type of swap (also known as a *back-set swap*) the setting date is just before the end of the accrual period for the floating-rate setting and not just before the start. Such a swap would be attractive to a counterparty who had a different view on interest rates than the market consensus. For instance, in a rising yield-curve environment, forward rates will be higher than current market rates, and this will be reflected in the pricing of a swap. A Libor-in-arrears swap would be priced higher than a conventional swap. If the floating-rate payer believed that interest rates would in fact rise more slowly than forward rates (and the market) were suggesting, he might wish to enter into an arrears swap as opposed to a conventional swap.

Basis swap

In a conventional swap one leg comprises fixed-rate payments and the other floating-rate payments. In a basis swap both legs are floating-rate, but linked to different money market indices. One leg is normally linked to Libor, while the other might be linked to the CD rate say, or the commercial paper rate. This type of swap would be used by a bank in the USA that had made loans that paid at the prime rate, and financed its loans at Libor. A basis swap would eliminate the *basis risk* between the bank's income and expense cash flows. Other basis swaps have been traded where both legs are linked to Libor, but at different maturities; for instance one leg might be at three-month Libor and the other at six-month Libor. In such a swap the basis is different and so is the payment frequency: one leg pays out semi-annually while the other would be paying on a quarterly basis. Note that where the payment frequencies differ, there is a higher level of counterparty risk for one of the parties. For instance, if one party is paying out on a monthly basis but receiving semi-annual cash flows, it would have made five interest payments before receiving one in return.

Margin swap

It is common to encounter swaps where there is a margin above or below Libor on the floating leg, as opposed to a floating leg of Libor flat. If a bank's borrowing is financed at Libor + 25 bps (basis points), it may wish to receive Libor + 25 bps in the swap so that its cash flows match exactly. The fixed-rate quote for a swap must be adjusted correspondingly to allow for the margin on the floating side, so in our example if the fixed-rate quote is, say, 6%, it would be adjusted to around 6.25%; differences in the margin quoted on the fixed leg might arise if the day-count convention or payment frequency were to differ between fixed and floating legs. Another reason why there may be a margin is if the credit quality of the counterparty demanded it, so that highly rated counterparties may pay slightly below Libor, for instance.

Differential swap

A differential swap is a basis swap but with one of the legs calculated in a different currency. Typically one leg is floating rate, while the other is floating rate but with the reference index rate for another currency, which is denominated in the domestic currency. For example, a differential swap may have one party paying six-month sterling

Libor, in sterling, on a notional principal of £10 million, and receiving euro-Libor, minus a margin, payable in sterling and on the same notional principal. Differential swaps are not very common and are the most difficult for a bank to hedge. The hedging is usually carried out using what is known as a *quanto* option.

Forward-start swap

A forward-start swap is one where the *effective date* is not the usual one or two days after the trade date but a considerable time afterwards, for instance six months after trade date. Such a swap might be entered into where one counterparty wanted to fix a hedge or cost of borrowing now, but for a point some time in the future. Typically this would be because the party considered that interest rates would rise or the cost of hedging would rise. The swap rate for a forward-starting swap is calculated in the same way as that for a vanilla swap.

Currency swaps

So far we have discussed swap contracts where the interest payments are both in the same currency. A *cross-currency* swap, or simply *currency swap*, is similar to an interest rate swap, except that the currencies of the two legs are different. Like interest rate swaps, the legs are usually fixed and floating rate, although again it is common to encounter both fixed-rate or both floating-rate legs in a currency swap. On maturity of the swap there is an exchange of principals, and usually (but not always) there is an exchange of principals at the start of the swap. Where currencies are exchanged at the start of the swap, at the prevailing spot exchange rate for the two currencies, the exact amounts are exchanged back on maturity. During the time of the swap, the parties make interest payments in the currency that they have *received* where principals are exchanged. It may seem that exchanging the same amount on maturity gives rise to some sort of currency risk; in fact, it is this feature that removes any element of currency risk from the swap transaction.

Currency swaps are widely used in association with bond issues by borrowers who seek to tap opportunities in different markets but have no requirement for that market's currency. By means of a currency swap, a company can raise funds in virtually any market and swap the proceeds into the currency that it requires. Often the underwriting bank that is responsible for the bond issue will also arrange for the currency swap to be transacted. In a currency swap therefore, the exchange of principal means that the value of the principal amounts must be accounted for, and it is dependent on the prevailing spot exchange rate between the two currencies.

Valuation of currency swaps

The same principles we established for the pricing and valuation of interest rate swaps may be applied to currency swaps. A generic currency swap with fixed-rate payment legs would be valued at the fair value swap rate for each currency, which would give a net present value of zero. The cash flows are illustrated in Figure 15.2. This shows that the two swap rates in a fixed-fixed currency swap would be identical to the same-maturity swap rate for each currency interest rate swap. So the swap rates for a fixed-fixed five-year sterling/dollar currency swap would be the five-year sterling swap rate and the five-year dollar swap rate.

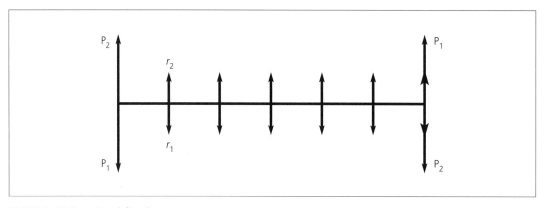

FIGURE 15.2 ■ Fixed-fixed rate currency swap

A floating-floating currency swap may be valued in the same way, and for valuation purposes the floating-leg payments are replaced with an exchange of principals, as we observed for the floating leg of an interest rate swap. A fixed-floating currency swap is therefore valued at the fixed-rate swap rate for that currency for the fixed leg, and at Libor or the relevant reference rate for the floating leg.

EXAMPLE *15.1 Bond issue and associated cross-currency swap*

A subsidiary of a US bank that invests in projects in the USA issues paper in markets around the world, in response to investor demand worldwide. The company's funding requirement is in US dollars, but it is active in issuing bonds in various currencies, according to where the most favourable conditions can be obtained. When an issue of debt is made in a currency other than dollars, the proceeds must be swapped into dollars for use in the USA, and interest payable on the swapped (dollar) proceeds. To facilitate this, the issuer will enter into a currency swap. One of the bank's issues was a Swiss franc step-up bond, part of an overall Euro-MTN programme. The details of the bond are summarized below.

Issue date   March 1998
Maturity   March 2003
Size   CHF15 million
Coupon   2.40% to 25 March 1999
               2.80% to 25 March 2000
               3.80% to 25 March 2001
               4.80% to 25 March 2002

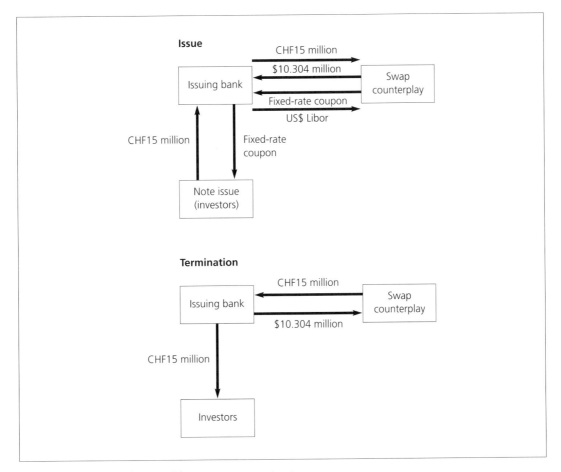

FIGURE 15.3 ■ Bond issue with currency swap structure

The bond was also callable on each anniversary from March 1999 onwards, and in fact was called by the issuer at the earliest opportunity. The issuing bank entered into a currency swap that resulted in the exchange of principals and the Swiss franc interest payments to be made by the swap counterparty; in return it paid US$ three-month Libor during the life of the swap. At the prevailing spot rate on the effective date, CHF15 million was exchanged for $10.304 million; these exact same amounts would be exchanged back on the maturity of the swap. When the issue was called, the swap was cancelled, and the swap counterparty paid a cancellation fee. The interest payment dates on the fixed leg of the swap matched the coupon dates of the bond exactly, as shown above. The floating leg of the swap paid US$ Libor on a quarterly basis, as required by the bond issuer.

The structure is shown in Figure 15.3. A currency swap structure enables a bank or corporate to borrow money in virtually any currency in which a liquid swap market exists, and swap this into a currency that is required. In our example the US bank was able to issue a bond that was attractive to investors. The swap mechanism also hedged the interest rate exposure on the Swiss franc note. The liability remaining for the issuer was quarterly floating rate interest on US dollars as part of the swap transaction.

Swaptions

Description

Swaptions are options on swaps. The buyer of a swaption has the right but not the obligation to enter into an interest rate swap agreement during the life of the option. The terms of the swaption will specify whether the buyer is the fixed or floating-rate payer; the seller of the option (the *writer*) becomes the counterparty to the swap if the option is exercised. The convention is that if the buyer has the right to exercise the option as the fixed-rate payer, he has traded a *call swaption*, also known as a *payer swaption*; while if, by exercising, the buyer of the swaption becomes the floating-rate payer, then he has bought a *put swaption*, also known as a *receiver swaption*. The writer of the swaption is the party to the other leg.

Swaptions are similar to forward-start swaps up to a point, but the buyer has the *option* of whether or not to commence payments on the effective date. A bank may purchase a call swaption if it expects interest rates to rise, and will exercise the option if indeed rates do rise as expected. A company will use swaptions as part of an interest rate hedge for a future exposure. For example, assume that a company will be entering into a five-year bank loan in three months' time. Interest on the loan is charged on a floating-rate basis, but the company intends to swap this to a fixed-rate liability after it has entered into the loan. As an added hedge, the company may choose to purchase a swaption that gives it the right to receive Libor and pay a fixed rate, say 10%, for a five-year period beginning in three months' time. When the time comes for the company to take out a swap and exchange its interest rate liability in three months' time (having entered into the loan), if the five-year swap rate is below 10%, the company will transact the swap in the normal way and the swaption will expire worthless. However, if the five-year swap rate is above 10%, the company will instead exercise the swaption, giving it the right to enter into a five-year swap and paying a fixed rate of 10%. Essentially, the company has taken out protection to ensure that it does not have to pay a fixed rate of more than 10%. Hence swaptions can be used to guarantee a maximum swap rate liability. They are similar to forward-starting swaps, but do not commit a party to enter into a swap on fixed terms. The swaption enables a company to hedge against unfavourable movements in interest rates but also to gain from favourable movements, although there is of course a cost associated with this, which is the premium paid for the swaption.

As with conventional put and call options, swaptions turn in-the-money under opposite circumstances. A call swaption increases in value as interest rates rise, and a put swaption becomes more valuable as interest rates fall. Consider a one-year European call swaption on a five-year semi-annual interest-rate swap, purchased by a bank counterparty. The notional value is £10 million and the 'strike price' is 6%, against Libor. Assume that the price (premium) of the swaption is 25 basis points, or £25,000. On expiry of the swaption, the buyer will either exercise it, in which case he will enter into a five-year swap paying 6% and receiving floating-rate interest, or elect to let the swaption expire with no value. If the five-year swap rate for counterparty of similar credit quality to the bank is above 6%, the swaption holder will exercise the swaption, while if the rate is below 6% the buyer will not exercise. The principle is the same for a put swaption, only in reverse.

Valuation

Swaptions are typically priced using the Black-Scholes or Black 76 option pricing models (*see* Chapter 17). These are used to value a European option on a swap, assuming that the appropriate swap rate at the expiry date of the option is lognormal. Consider a swaption with the following general terms:

Swap rate on expiry	rs
Swaption strike rate	rX
Maturity	T
Start date	t
Pay basis	F (say quarterly, semi-annual or annual)
Notional principal	M

If the actual swap rate on the maturity of the swaption is rs, the payoff from the swaption is given by:

$$\frac{M}{F} \max (r - r_n, 0).$$ (15.14)

The value of a swaption is essentially the difference between the strike rate and the swap rate at the time it is being valued. If a swaption is exercised, the payoff at each interest date is given by $(rs - rX) \times M \times F$. As a call swaption is only exercised when the swap rate is higher than the strike rate (that is, $rs > rX$), the option payoff on any interest payment in the swap is given by:

$$Swaption_{InterestPayment} = \text{Max}[0,(rs - rX) \times M \times F].$$ (15.15)

It can then easily be shown that the value of a call swaption on expiry is given by:

$$PV_{Swaption} = \sum_{n=1}^{n} Df_{(0, n)} (rs - rX) \times M \times F.$$ (15.16)

where $Df_{(0, n)}$ is the spot rate discount factor for the term beginning now and ending at time t. By the same logic, the value of a put swaption is given by the same expression, except that $(rX - rs)$ is substituted at the relevant point above.

A swaption can therefore be viewed as a collection of calls or puts on interest deposits or Libor, enabling us to use the Black model when valuing it. This means that we value each call or put on for a single payment in the swap, and then sum these payments to obtain the value of the swaption. The main assumption made when using this model is that the Libor rate follows a lognormal distribution over time, with constant volatility.

Consider a call swaption being valued at time t that matures at time T. We begin by valuing a single payment under the swap (assuming the option is exercised) made at time T_n. The point at time T_n is into the life of the swap, so that we have $T_n > T > t$. At the time of valuation, the option time to expiry is $T - t$ and there is $T_n - t$ until the nth payment. The value of this payment is given by:

$$C_t = MFe^{-r(T_n - t)}[rsN(d_1) - rXN(d_2)]$$ (15.17)

where

    C_t is the price of the call option on a single payment in the swap
    r is the risk-free instantaneous interest rate
    $N(.)$ is the cumulative normal distribution
    σ is the interest-rate volatility

and where

$$d_1 = \frac{\ln{(rs_t/rX)} + \frac{\sigma^2}{2}(T - t)}{\sigma \sqrt{T - t}}$$

$$d_2 = d_1 - \sigma \sqrt{T - t}.$$

The remaining life of the swaption $(T - t)$ governs the probability that it will expire in-the-money, determined using the lognormal distribution. On the other hand, the interest payment itself is discounted (using $e^{-r(T_n - t)}$) over the period $T_n - t$ because it is not paid until time T_n.

Having valued a single interest payment, viewing the swap as a collection of interest payments, we value the call swaption as a collection of calls. Its value is given therefore by:

$$PVSwaption_t = \sum_{n=1}^{n} MFe^{-r(T_n - t)}[rsN(d_1) - rXN(d_2)] \tag{15.18}$$

where t, T and n are as before.

If we substitute discrete spot rate discount factors instead of the continuous form given by (15.18) the expression becomes:

$$PVSwaption_t = MF[rsN(d_1) - rXN(d_2)]\sum_{n=1}^{n} Df_{t,\,T_n}. \tag{15.19}$$

EXAMPLE   *15.2 Swaption pricing[3]*

We present a new term structure environment in this example to illustrate the basic concepts. This is shown in Table 15.5. We wish to price a forward-starting annual interest swap starting in two years for a term of three years. The swap has a notional of £10 million.

The swap rate is given by:

$$rs = \frac{\sum_{t=1}^{N} rf_{(t-1),\,t} \times Df_{0,\,t}}{\sum_{t=1}^{N} Df_{0,\,t}}$$

where rf is the forward rate.

Using the above expression, the numerator in this example is:

$(0.0666 \times 0.8386) + (0.0672 \times 0.7861) + (0.0805 \times 0.7634)$ or 0.1701

---

3. This example follows the approach described in Kolb (2000), although here we use discount factors in the calculation whereas Kolb uses *zero-coupon factors* which are (1 + spot rate).

TABLE 15.5 ■ Interest rate data for swaption valuation

Date	Term (years)	Discount factor	Par yield	Zero-coupon rate	Forward rate
18 Feb 2001	0	1	5	5	5
18 Feb 2002	1	0.95238095	5.00	5	6.03015
18 Feb 2003	2	0.89821711	5.50	5.51382	7.10333
18 Feb 2004	3	0.83864539	6.00	6.04102	6.66173
18 Feb 2005	4	0.78613195	6.15	6.19602	6.71967
20 Feb 2006	5	0.73637858	6.25	6.30071	8.05230
19 Feb 2007	6	0.68165163	6.50	6.58946	8.70869
18 Feb 2008	7	0.62719194	6.75	6.88862	9.40246
18 Feb 2009	8	0.57315372	7.00	7.20016	10.18050
18 Feb 2010	9	0.52019523	7.25	7.52709	5.80396
18 Feb 2011	10	0.49165950	7.15	7.35361	6.16366

The denominator is:

0.8386 + 0.7861 + 0.7634 or 2.3881.

Therefore the forward-starting swap rate is 0.1701/2.3881 or 0.071228 (7.123%).

We now turn to the call swaption on this swap, the buyer of which acquires the right to enter into a three-year swap paying the fixed-rate swap rate of 7.00%. If the volatility of the forward swap rate is 0.20, the d_1 and d_2 terms are:

$$d_1 = \frac{\ln\left(\dfrac{rs}{rX}\right) + \dfrac{\sigma^2}{2}\,(T-t)}{\sigma\sqrt{T-t}} = \frac{\ln\left(\dfrac{0.071228}{0.07}\right) + \left(\dfrac{0.2^2}{2} \times 2\right)}{0.2\sqrt{2}}$$

or 0.2029068

$$d_2 = d_1 - \sigma\sqrt{T-t} = 0.20290618 - 0.2\,(1.4142)$$

or −0.079934.

The cumulative normal values are:

$N(d_1) = N(0.2029)$ which is 0.580397

$N(d_2) = N(-0.079934)$ which is 0.468145.[4]

---

4. These values may be found from standard normal distribution tables or using the Microsoft Excel formula =NORMSDIST().

From the above we know that $\sum Df_{t, T_n}$ is 2.3881. So using (15.19) we calculate the value of the call swaption to be:

$$PVSwaption_t = MF\,[rsN\,(d_1) - rXN(d_2)]\sum_{n=1}^{N} Df_{t, T_n}$$
$$= 10,000,000 \times 1 \times [0.07228 \times 0.580397 - 0.07 \times 0.468145] \times 2.3881$$
$$= 219,250$$

or £219,250. Option premiums are frequently quoted as basis points of the notional amount, so in this case the premium is (219,250/10,000,000) or 219.25 basis points.

Overview of interest rate swap applications

In this section we review some of the principal uses of swaps as a hedging tool.

Corporate applications

Swaps are part of the over-the-counter market and so they can be tailored to suit the particular requirements of the user. It is common for swaps to be structured so that they match particular payment dates, payment frequencies and Libor margins, which may characterize the underlying exposure of the customer. As the market in interest rate swaps is so large, liquid and competitive, banks are willing to quote rates and structure swaps for virtually all customers.

Swap applications can be viewed as being one of two main types: *asset-linked* swaps and *liability-linked* swaps. Asset-linked swaps are created when the swap is linked to an asset such as a bond in order to change the characteristics of the income stream for investors. Liability-linked swaps are traded when borrowers of funds wish to change the pattern of their cash flows. Of course, just as with repo transactions, the designation of a swap in such terms depends on whose point of view is looking at the swap. An asset-linked swap hedge is a liability-linked hedge for the counterparty, except in the case of swap market-making banks which make two-way quotes in the instruments.

A straightforward application of an interest rate swap is when a borrower wishes to convert a floating-rate liability into a fixed-rate one, usually in order to remove the exposure to upward moves in interest rates. For instance, a company may wish to fix its financing costs. Let us assume a company currently borrowing money at a floating rate, say six-month Libor + 100 basis points, fears that interest rates may rise in the remaining three years of its loan. It enters into a three-year semi-annual interest rate swap with a bank, as the fixed-rate payer, paying 6.75% against receiving six-month Libor. This fixes the company's borrowing costs for three years at 7.75% (7.99% effective annual rate). This is shown in Figure 15.4.

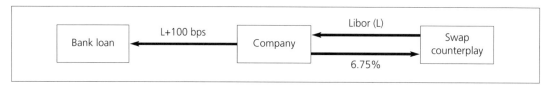

FIGURE 15.4 ■ Changing liability from floating to fixed rate

EXAMPLE *15.3 Liability-linked swap: fixed, to floating, to fixed-rate exposure*

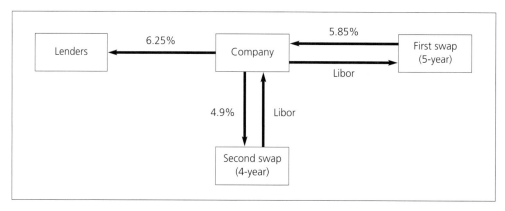

FIGURE 15.5 ■ 'Changing swap basis'

A corporate borrows for five years at a rate of 6.25% and shortly after enters into a swap paying floating rate, so that its net borrowing cost is Libor + 40 basis points. After one year swap rates have fallen such that the company is quoted four-year swap rates at 4.90%. The company decides to switch back into fixed-rate liability in order to take advantage of the lower interest rate environment. It enters into a second swap paying fixed at 4.9% and receiving Libor. The net borrowing cost is now 5.3%. The arrangement is illustrated in Figure 15.5. The company has saved 95 basis points on its original borrowing cost, which is the difference between the two swap rates.

Asset-linked swap structures might be required when, for example, investors require a fixed-interest security when floating-rate assets are available. Borrowers often issue FRNs, the holders of which may prefer to switch the income stream into fixed coupons. As an example, consider a local authority pension fund holding two-year floating-rate gilts. This is an asset of the highest quality, paying Libid minus 12.5 basis points. The pension fund wishes to swap the cash flows to create a fixed-interest asset. It obtains a quote for a tailor-made swap where the floating leg pays Libid, the quote being 5.55–50%. By entering into this swap, the pension fund has in place a structure that pays a fixed coupon of 5.375%. This is shown in Figure 15.6.

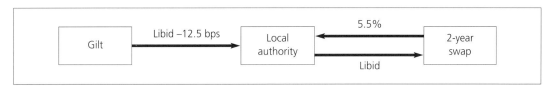

FIGURE 15.6 ▪ Transforming a floating-rate asset to fixed rate

Hedging bond instruments using interest rate swaps

We illustrate here a generic approach to the hedging of bond positions using interest rate swaps. The bond trader has the option of using other bonds, bond futures or bond options, as well as swaps, when hedging the interest rate risk exposure of a bond position. However, swaps are particularly efficient instruments to use because they display positive convexity characteristics; that is, the increase in value of a swap for a fall in interest rates exceeds the loss in value with a similar magnitude rise in rates. This is exactly the price/yield profile of vanilla bonds.

The primary risk measure we require when hedging using a swap is its present value of a basis point (PVBP).[5] This measures the price sensitivity of the swap for a basis point change in interest rates. The PVBP measure is used to calculate the hedge ratio when hedging a bond position. The PVBP can be given by:

$$PVBP = \frac{\text{change in swap value}}{\text{rate change in basis points}} \qquad (15.20)$$

which can be written as:

$$PVBP = \frac{dS}{dr} \qquad (15.21)$$

Using the basic relationship for the value of a swap, which is viewed as the difference between the values of a fixed-coupon bond and equivalent-maturity floating-rate bond (*see* Table 15.1) we can also write:

$$PVBP = \frac{d\text{Fixed bond}}{dr} - \frac{d\text{Floating bond}}{dr} \qquad (15.22)$$

5. This is also known as DVBP, or dollar value of a basis point, in the US market.

which essentially states that the basis point value of the swap is the difference in the basis point values of the fixed-coupon and floating-rate bonds. The value is usually calculated for a notional £1 million of swap. The calculation is based on the duration and modified duration calculations used for bonds[6] and assumes that there is a parallel shift in the yield curve.

Table 15.6 illustrates how equations (15.21) and (15.22) can be used to obtain the PVBP of a swap. Hypothetical five-year bonds are used in the example. The PVBP for a bond can be calculated using Bloomberg or the MDURATION function on Microsoft Excel. Using either of the two equations above, we see that the PVBP of the swap is £425. This is shown below.

TABLE 15.6 ■ PVBP for interest rate swap

Interest rate swap

Term to maturity	5 years
Fixed leg	6.5%
Basis	Semi-annual, actual/365
Floating leg	6-month Libor
Basis	Semi-annual, actual/365
Nominal amount	£1,000,000

		Present value £	
	Rate change −10 bps	0 bps	Rate change +10 bps
Fixed-coupon bond	1,004,940	1,000,000	995,171
Floating-rate bond	1,000,640	1,000,000	999,371
Swap	4,264	0	4,236

Calculating the PVBP using (15.21) we have:

$$PVBP_{swap} = \frac{dS}{dr} = \frac{4264 - (-4236)}{20} = 425$$

while using (15.22) we obtain the same result using the bond values:

$$PVBP_{swap} = PVBP_{fixed} - PVBP_{floating}$$

$$= \frac{1004940 - 995171}{20} - \frac{1000640 - 999371}{20}$$

$$= 488.45 - 63.45$$

$$= 425.00$$

6. *See* Chapter 5.

The swap basis point value is lower than that of the five-year fixed-coupon bond, that is £425 compared with £488.45. This is because of the impact of the floating-rate bond risk measure, which reduces the risk exposure of the swap as a whole by £63.45. As a rough rule of thumb, the PVBP of a swap is approximately equal to that of a fixed-rate bond that has a maturity similar to the period from the next coupon reset date of the swap through to the maturity date of the swap. This means that a ten-year semi-annual paying swap would have a PVBP close to that of a 9.5-year fixed-rate bond, and a 5.5-year swap would have a PVBP similar to that of a five-year bond.

When using swaps as hedge tools, we bear in mind that over time the PVBP of swaps behaves differently to that of bonds. Immediately preceding an interest reset date, the PVBP of a swap will be near-identical to that of the same-maturity fixed-rate bond, because the PVBP of a floating-rate bond at this time has essentially nil value. Immediately after the reset date, the swap PVBP will be near-identical to that of a bond that matures at the next reset date. This means that at the point (and this point only) right after the reset, the swap PVBP will decrease by the amount of the floating-rate PVBP. In between reset dates the swap PVBP is quite stable, because the effects of the fixed and floating-rate PVBP changes cancel each other out. Contrast this with the fixed-rate PVBP, which decreases in value over time in stable fashion.[7] This feature is illustrated in Figure 15.7. A slight anomaly is that the PVBP of a swap actually increases by a small amount between reset dates; this is because the PVBP of a floating-rate bond decreases at a slightly faster rate than that of the fixed-rate bond during this time.

Hedging bond instruments with interest rate swaps is conceptually similar to hedging with another bond or with bond futures contracts. If one is holding a long position in a vanilla bond, the hedge requires a long position in the swap: remember that a long position in a swap is to be paying fixed (and receiving floating). This hedges the receipt of fixed from the bond position. The change in the value of the swap will match the change in value of the bond, but in the opposite direction.[8] The maturity of the swap should match as closely as possible that of the bond. As swaps are OTC contracts, it should be possible to match interest dates as well as maturity dates. If one is short the bond, the hedge is to be short the swap, so the receipt of fixed then matches the pay-fixed liability of the short bond position.

The correct nominal amount of the swap to put on is established using the PVBP hedge ratio. This is given as:

---

7. This assumes no large-scale sudden yield movements.

8. The change will not be an exact mirror. It is very difficult to establish a precise hedge for a number of reasons, which include differences in day-count bases, maturity mismatches and basis risk.

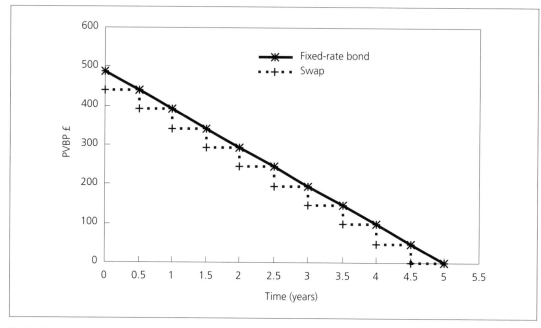

FIGURE 15.7 ■ PVBP of a five-year swap and fixed-rate bond maturity period

$$\frac{PVBP_{bond}}{PVBP_{swap}} \qquad\qquad (15.23)$$

This technique is still used in the market but suffers from the assumption of parallel yield curve shifts and can therefore lead to significant hedging error at times. However such techniques are still used by banks when hedging books using swaps.

SELECTED BIBLIOGRAPHY AND REFERENCES

Bicksler, J., Chen, A., 'An economic analysis of interest rate swaps', *Journal of Finance* 41: 3, 1986, pp. 645–55.

Brotherton-Ratcliffe, R., Iben, B., 'Yield curve applications of swap products', in Schwartz, R., Smith, C. (eds), *Advanced Strategies in Financial Risk Management*, New York Institute of Finance 1993.

Choudhry, M., *Bond Market Securities*, FT Prentice Hall 2001, Chapter 11.

Das, S., *Swaps and Financial Derivatives*, 2nd edition, IFR Publishing 1994.

Decovny, S., *Swaps*, 2nd edition, FT Prentice Hall 1998.

Dunbar, N., 'Swaps volumes see euro wane', *Risk*, September 2000.

Eales, B., *Financial Risk Management*, McGraw-Hill 1995, Chapter 3.

Fabozzi, F. (ed.), *Perspectives on Interest Rate Risk Management for Money Managers and Traders*, FJF Associates 1998.

Gup, B., Brooks, R., *Interest Rate Risk Management*, Irwin 1993.

Henna, P., *Interest-rate Risk Management Using Futures and Swaps*, Probus Publishing 1991.

International Swaps and Derivatives Association, *Code of Standard Working, Assumptions and Provisions for Swaps*, ISDA 1991.

Jarrow, R., Turnbull, S., *Derivative Securities*, 2nd edition, South-Western Publishing 2000.

Khan, M., 'Online platforms battle for business', *Risk*, September 2000.

Kolb, R., *Futures, Options and Swaps*, 3rd edition, Blackwell 2000.

Li, A., Raghavan, V.R., 'LIBOR-in-arrears swaps', *Journal of Derivatives* 3, spring 1996, pp. 44–8.

Lindsay, R., 'High wire act', *Risk*, August 2000.

Marshall, J., Kapner, K., *Understanding Swap Finance*, South-Western Publishing 1990.

Turnbull, S., 'Swaps: a zero sum game', *Financial Management* 16, spring 1987, pp. 15–21.

CHAPTER 16

Options I

As a risk management tool, options allow banks and corporates to hedge market exposure but also to gain from upside moves in the market; this makes them unique amongst hedging instruments. Options have special characteristics that make them stand apart from other classes of derivatives. As they confer a right to conduct a certain transaction, but not an obligation, their payoff profile is different from other financial assets, both cash and off-balance sheet. This makes an option more of an insurance policy rather than a pure hedging instrument, as the person who has purchased the option for hedging purposes need only exercise it if required. The price of the option is in effect the insurance premium that has been paid for peace of mind. Options are also used for purposes other than hedging. They form part of speculative and arbitrage trading, and option market-makers generate returns from profitably managing the risk on their option books.

The range of combinations of options that can be dealt today, and the complex structured products of which they form a part, is constrained only by imagination and customer requirements. Virtually all participants in capital markets will have some requirement that may be met by the use of options. The subject is a large one, and there are a number of specialist texts devoted to them. In this chapter we introduce the basics of options; subsequent chapters will review option pricing, the main sensitivity measures used in running an option book, and the uses to which options may be put. Key reference articles and publications are also listed in the bibliography.

Introduction

An option is a contract in which the buyer has the right, but not the obligation, to buy or sell an underlying asset at a pre-determined price during a specified period of time. The seller of the option, known as the *writer*, grants this right to the buyer in return for receiving the price of the option, known as the *premium*. An option that grants the right to buy an asset is a *call* option, while the corresponding right to sell an asset is a *put* option. The option buyer has a long position in the option and the option seller has a short position in the option.

Before looking at the other terms that define an option contract, we will discuss the main feature that differentiates an option from all other derivative instruments, and from cash assets. Because options confer on a buyer the right to effect a transaction, but not the obligation (and correspondingly on a seller the obligation, if requested by the buyer, to effect a transaction), their risk/reward characteristics are different from other financial products. The payoff profile from holding an option is unlike that of any other instrument.

Let us consider the payoff profiles for a vanilla call option and a gilt futures contract. Suppose that a trader buys one lot of the gilt futures contract at 114.00 and holds it for one month before selling it. On closing the position the profit made will depend on the contract sale price: if it is above 114.00 the trader will have made a profit and if below 114.00 he will have made a loss. On one lot this represents a £1,000 gain for each point above 114.00. The same applies to someone who had a short position in the contract and closed it out – if the contract is bought back at any price below 114.00 the trader will realize a profit. The profile is shown in Figure 16.1. This profile is the same for other derivative instruments such as FRAs and swaps, and of course for cash instruments such as bonds or equity. The payoff profile therefore has a *linear* characteristic, and it is linear whether one has bought or sold the contract.

The profile for an option contract differs from the conventional one. Because options confer a right to one party but not an obligation (to the buyer), and an obligation but not a right to the seller, the profile will differ according to whether one is the buyer or seller. Suppose now that our trader buys a call option that grants the right to buy a gilt futures

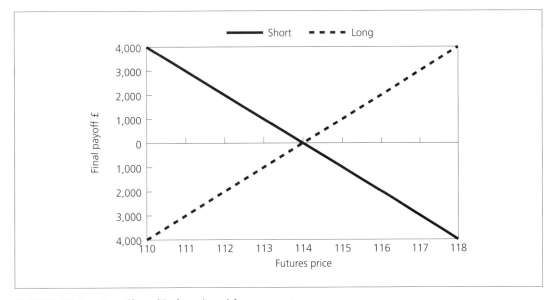

FIGURE 16.1 ▪ Payoff profile for a bond futures contract

contract at a price of 114.00 at some point during the life of the option. His resulting payoff profile will be like that shown in Figure 16.2. If during the life of the option the price of the futures contract rises above 114, the trader will exercise his right to buy the future, under the terms of the option contract. This is known as *exercising* the option. If, on the other hand, the price of the future falls below 114.00, the trader will not exercise the option and, unless there is a reversal in price of the future, it will eventually expire worthless, on its maturity date. In this respect it is exactly like an equity or bond warrant. The seller of this particular option has a very different payout profile. If the price of the future rises above 114.00 and the option is exercised, the seller will bear the loss equal to the profit from which the buyer is now benefiting. The seller's payoff profile is also shown in Figure 16.2, as the dashed line. If the option is not exercised and expires, for the seller the trade will have generated premium income, which is revenue income that contributes to the profit and loss account.

This illustrates how, unlike every other financial instrument, the holders of long and short positions in options do not have the same symmetrical payoff profile. The buyer of the call option will benefit if the price of the underlying asset rises, but will not lose if the price falls (except losing the funds paid for purchasing the rights under the option). The seller of the call option will suffer loss if the price of the underlying asset rises, but will not benefit if it falls (except realizing the funds received for writing the option). The buyer has a right but not an obligation, while the seller has an obligation if the option is exercised. The premium charged for the option is the seller's compensation for granting such a right to the buyer.

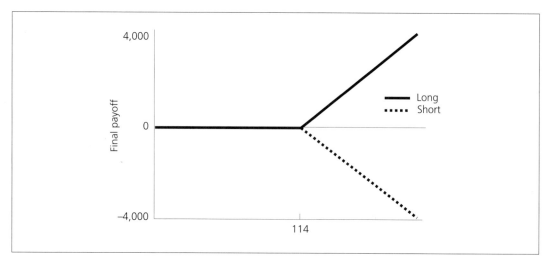

FIGURE 16.2 ■ Payoff profile for a call option contract

Let us recap on the basic features of the call option. A call option is the right to buy, without any obligation, a specified quantity of the underlying asset at a given price on or before the expiry date of the option. A long position in a call option allows the holder, as shown in Figure 16.2, to benefit from a rise in the market price of the underlying asset. If our trader wanted to benefit from a fall in the market level, but did not want to short the market, he would buy a *put* option. A put option is the right to sell, again without any obligation, a specified quantity of the underlying asset at a given price on or before the expiry date of the option. Put options have the same payoff profile as call options, but in the opposite direction. Remember also that the payoff profile is different for the buyer and seller of an option. The buyer of a call option will profit if the market price of the underlying asset rises, but will not lose if the price falls (at least, not with regard to the option position). The writer of the option will not profit whatever direction the market moves in, and will lose if the market rises. The compensation for taking on this risk is the premium paid for writing the option, which is why we likened options to insurance policies at the start of the chapter.

Originally, options were written on commodities such as wheat and sugar. Nowadays these are referred to as *options on physicals*, while options on financial assets are known as *financial options*. Today one is able to buy or sell an option on a wide range of underlying instruments, including financial products such as foreign exchange, bonds, equities and commodities, and derivatives such as futures, swaps, equity indices and other options.

Option terminology

Let us now consider the basic terminology used in the options markets.

A *call* option grants the buyer the right to buy the underlying asset, while a *put* option grants the buyer the right to sell the underlying asset. There are therefore four possible positions that an option trader may put on: long a call or put, and short a call or put. The payoff profiles for each type are shown in Figure 16.3.

The *strike price* describes the price at which an option is exercised. For example, a call option to buy ordinary shares of a listed company might have a strike price of £10. This means that if the option is exercised, the buyer will pay £10 per share. Options are generally either *American* or *European* style, which defines the times during the option's life when it can be exercised. There is no geographic relevance to these terms, since both styles can be traded in any market. There is also another type, *Bermudan*-style options, which can be exercised at pre-set dates.[1] For reasons that we shall discuss later, it is very rare for an American option to be exercised ahead of its expiry date, so this distinction has little impact in practice, although of course the pricing model being used to value

1. Perhaps because Bermuda is midway between Europe and America. There are also 'Asian' average-rate options, because these originated in Japanese commodity markets.

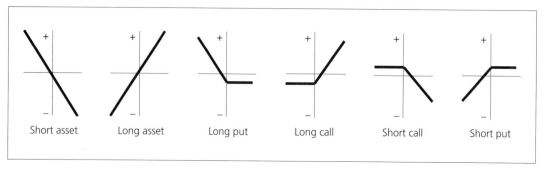

| Short asset | Long asset | Long put | Long call | Short call | Short put |

FIGURE 16.3 ■ Basic option payoff profiles

European options must be modified to handle American options. The holder of a European option cannot exercise it prior to expiry; however, if he wishes to realize its value he will sell it in the market.

The *premium* of an option is the price at which the option is sold. Option premium is made up of two constituents: *intrinsic value* and *time value*. The intrinsic value of an option is the value of the option if it is exercised immediately, and it represents the difference between the strike price and the current underlying asset price. If a call option on a bond futures contract has a strike price of 100.00 and the future is currently trading at 105.00, the intrinsic value of the option is 5.00, as this would be the immediate profit gain to the option holder if it were exercised. Since an option will only be exercised if there is benefit to the holder from so doing, its intrinsic value will never be less than zero. So in our example if the bond future was trading at 95.00 the intrinsic value of the call option would be zero, not –5.00. For a put option the intrinsic value is the amount by which the current underlying price is below the strike price. When an option has intrinsic value it is described as being *in-the-money*. When the strike price for a call option is higher than the underlying price (or for a put option is lower than the underlying price) and has no intrinsic value it is said to be *out-of-the-money*. An option for which the strike price is equal to the current underlying price is said to be *at-the-money*. This term is normally used at the time the option is first traded, in cases where the strike price is set to the current price of the underlying asset.

The time value of an option is the amount by which the option value exceeds the intrinsic value. An option writer will almost always demand a premium that is higher than the option's intrinsic value, because of the risk that the writer is taking on. This reflects the fact that over time the price of the underlying asset may change sufficiently to produce a much higher intrinsic value. During the life of an option, the option writer has nothing more to gain over the initial premium at which the option was sold; however until expiry there is a chance that the writer will lose if the markets move against him, hence the inclusion of a time value element. The value of an option that is out-of-the-money is composed entirely of time value.

Table 16.1 summarizes the main option terminology.

TABLE 16.1 ■ Basic option terminology

Call	The right to buy the underlying asset
Put	The right to sell the underlying asset
Buyer	The person who has purchased the option and has the right to exercise it if he wishes
Writer	The person who has sold the option and has the obligation to perform if the option is exercised
Strike price	The price at which the option may be exercised, also known as the exercise price
Expiry date	The last date on which the option can be exercised, also known as the maturity date
American	The style of option; an American option can be exercised at any time up to the expiry date
European	An option that may be exercised on the maturity date only, and not before
Premium	The price of the option, paid by the buyer to the seller
Intrinsic value	The value of the option if it was exercised today, which is the difference between the strike price and the underlying asset price
Time value	The difference between the current price of the option and its intrinsic value
In-the-money (ITM)	The term for an option that has intrinsic value
At-the-money (ATM)	An option for which the strike price is identical to the underlying asset price
Out-of-the-money (OTM)	An option that has no intrinsic value

Option instruments

Options are traded both on recognized exchanges and in the over-the-counter market. The primary difference between the two types is that exchange-traded options are standardized contracts and essentially plain vanilla instruments, while OTC options can take on virtually any shape or form. Options traded on an exchange are often options on a futures contract, so for example a gilt option on LIFFE in London is written on the exchange's gilt futures contract. The exercise of a futures option will result in a long position in a futures contract being assigned to the party that is long the option, and a short position in the future to the party that is short the option. Note that exchange-traded options on US Treasuries are quoted in option ticks that are half the bond tick, that is 1/64th rather than 1/32nd. The same applied to gilt options on LIFFE until gilts themselves switched to decimal pricing at the end of 1998.

Like OTC options, those traded on an exchange can be either American or European style. For example, on the Philadelphia Currency Options Exchange both versions are available, although on LIFFE most options are American style. Exchange-traded options are available on the following:

- *Ordinary shares*: Major exchanges, including the New York Stock Exchange, LIFFE, Eurex, the Chicago Board Options Exchange (CBOE), and SIMEX in Singapore, trade options on corporation ordinary shares.

- *Options on futures*: Most exchanges trade an option contract written on the futures that are traded on the exchange, which expires one or two days before the futures contract itself expires. In certain cases, such as those traded on the Philadelphia exchange, cash settlement is available, so that if, for example, the holder of a call exercises, he will be assigned a long position in the future as well as the cash value of the difference between the strike price and the futures price. One of the most heavily traded exchange-traded options contracts is the Treasury bond option, written on the futures contract, traded on the Chicago Board of Trade Options Exchange.

- *Stock index options*: These are equity market instruments that are popular for speculating and hedging, for example the FTSE-100 option on LIFFE and the S&P500 on CBOE. Settlement is in cash and not the shares that constitute the underlying index, much like the settlement of an index futures contract.

- *Bond options*: Options on bonds are invariably written on the bond futures contract, for example the Treasury bond option or LIFFE's gilt option. Options written on the cash bond must be traded in the OTC market.

- *Interest rate options*: These are also options on futures, as they are written on the exchange's 90-day interest rate futures contract.

- *Foreign currency options*: These are rarer among exchange-traded options, and the major exchange is in Philadelphia. The sterling option contract, for example, is for an underlying amount of £31,250.

Option trading on an exchange is similar to that for futures, and involves transfer of margin on a daily basis. Individual exchanges have their own procedures; for example on LIFFE the option premium is effectively paid via the variation margin. The amount of variation margin paid or received on a daily basis for each position reflects the change in the price of the option. So if, for example, an option were to expire on maturity with no intrinsic value, the variation margin payments made during its life would be equal to the change in value from the day it was traded to zero. The option trader does not pay a separate premium on the day the position is put on. On certain other exchanges, however, it is the other way around, and the option buyer will pay a premium on the day of purchase but then pay no variation margin. Some exchanges allow traders to select either method. Margin is compulsory for a party that writes options on the exchange.

The other option market is the OTC market, where there is a great variety of instruments traded. As with products such as swaps, the significant advantage of OTC options is that they can be tailored to meet the specific requirements of the buyer. Hence they are ideally suited as risk management instruments for corporate and financial institutions, because they can be used to structure hedges that match perfectly the risk exposure of the buying party. Some of the more ingenious structures are described in Chapter 18 on exotic options.

Option pricing: setting the scene

The price of an option is a function of six different factors, which are:

■ the current price of the underlying asset;

■ the strike price of the option;

■ the time to expiry;

■ the volatility of the underlying asset's price returns;

■ the risk-free rate of interest that applies to the life of the option;

■ the value of any dividends or cash flows paid by the underlying asset during the life of the option.

Pricing inputs

Let us consider the parameters of option pricing. Possibly the two most important are the current price of the underlying asset and the strike price of the option. The intrinsic value of a call option is the amount by which the strike price is below the price of the underlying asset, as this is the payoff if the option is exercised. Therefore the value of the call option will increase as the price of the underlying asset increases, and will fall as the underlying price falls. The value of a call will also decrease as the strike price increases. All this is reversed for a put option.

Generally, for bond options a higher time to maturity results in higher option value. All other parameters being equal, a longer-dated option will always be worth at least as much as one that had a shorter life. Intuitively we would expect this because the holder of a longer-dated option has the same benefits as someone holding a shorter-dated option, in addition to a longer time period in which the intrinsic may increase. This rule is always true for American options, and usually true for European options. However, certain factors, such as the payment of a coupon during the option life, may cause a longer-dated option to have only a slightly higher value than a shorter-dated option.

The risk-free interest rate is the rate applicable to the period of the option's life, so for our table of gilt options in the previous section, the option value reflected the three-month rate. The most common rate used is the T-bill rate, although for bond options it is more common to see the government bond repo rate being used. A rise in interest rates will increase the value of a call option, although not always for bond options. A rise in rates lowers the price of a bond, because it decreases the present value of future cash flows. However in the equity markets it is viewed as a sign that share price growth rates will increase. Generally, however, the relationship is the same for bond options as equity options. The effect of a rise in interest rates for put options is the reverse: they cause the value to drop.

A coupon payment made by the underlying asset during the life of the option will reduce the price of the underlying asset on the ex-dividend date. This will result in a fall in the price of a call option and a rise in the price of a put option.

Bounds in option pricing

The upper and lower limits on the price of an option are relatively straightforward to set because prices must follow the rule of no-arbitrage pricing. A call option grants the buyer the right to buy a specified quantity of the underlying asset, at the level of the strike price, so therefore it is clear that the option could not have a higher value than the underlying asset itself. Therefore the upper limit or *bound* to the price of a call option is the price of the underlying asset. Therefore:

$$C \leq S \tag{16.1}$$

where C is the price of a call option and S is the current price of the underlying asset. A put option grants the buyer the right to sell a specified unit of the underlying asset at the strike price X, therefore the option can never have a value greater than the strike price X. So we may set:

$$P \leq X \tag{16.2}$$

where P is the price of the put option. This rule will still apply for a European put option on its expiry date, so therefore we may further set that the option cannot have a value greater than the present value of the strike price X on expiry. That is:

$$P \leq Xe^{-rT} \tag{16.3}$$

where r is the risk-free interest for the term of the option life and T is the maturity of the option in years.

The minimum limit or bound for an option is set according to whether the underlying asset is a dividend-paying security or not. For a call option written on a non-dividend-paying security the lower bound is given by:

$$C \geq S - Xe^{-rT}. \tag{16.4}$$

In fact, as we noted early in this chapter, a call option can only ever expire worthless, so its intrinsic value can never be worth less than zero. Therefore $C > 0$ and we then set the following:

$$C \geq \max [S - Xe^{-rT}, 0] \tag{16.5}$$

This reflects the law of no-arbitrage pricing. For put options on a non-dividend-paying stock, the lower limit is given by:

$$P \geq Xe^{-rT} - S \tag{16.6}$$

and again the value is never less than zero, so we may set:

$$P \geq \max [Xe^{-rt} - S, 0] \tag{16.7}$$

As we noted above, payment of a dividend by the underlying asset affects the price of the option. In the case of dividend paying stocks, the upper and lower bounds for options are as follows:

$$C \geq S - D - Xe^{rT} \tag{16.8}$$

and

$$P \geq D + Xe^{-rT} - S \tag{16.9}$$

where D is the present value of the dividend payment made by the underlying asset during the life of the option.

We can now look at option pricing in the Black-Scholes model, and this is considered in the next chapter.

SELECTED BIBLIOGRAPHY AND REFERENCES

Chance, D., *An Introduction to Options and Futures Markets*, Dryden Press 1989.

Galitz, L., *Financial Engineering*, FT Pitman 1993.

Grabbe, J.O., *International Financial Markets*, 2nd edition, Elsevier 1991.

Hull, J., *Options, Futures and Other Derivatives*, 4th edition, Prentice Hall 1999.

Jarrow, R., Turnbull, S., *Derivative Securities*, 2nd edition, South-Western Publishing 1999.

Levy, H., *Introduction to Investments*, 2nd edition, South-Western Publishing 1999, Chapters 22–5.

Livingstone, M., *Money and Capital Markets*, 2nd edition, New York Institute of Finance 1993, Chapter 19.

London International Financial Futures and Options Exchange, *LIFFE Options*, LIFFE 1999.

McMillan, L., *Options as a Strategic Investment*, New York Institute of Finance 1986.

CHAPTER 17

Options II

In this chapter we present an overview of option pricing. There is a vast literature in this field and space constraints allow us to consider only the basic concepts here. Readers are directed to the bibliography for further recommended texts.

Option pricing

Previous interest rate products described in this book so far, both cash and derivatives, can be priced using rigid mathematical principles, because on maturity of the instrument there is a defined procedure that takes place such that one is able to calculate a fair value. This does not apply to options because there is uncertainty as to what the outcome will be on expiry; an option seller does not know whether the option will be exercised or not. This factor makes options more difficult to price than other financial market instruments. In this section we review the parameters used in the pricing of an option, and introduce the Black-Scholes pricing model.

Pricing an option is a function of the probability that it will be exercised. Essentially the premium paid for an option represents the buyer's *expected profit* on the option. Therefore, as with an insurance premium, the writer of an option will base his price on the assessment that the payout on the option will be equal to the premium, and this is a function on the probability that the option will be exercised. Option pricing therefore bases its calculation on the assessment of the probability of exercise, and deriving from this is an expected outcome, and hence a fair value for the option premium. The expected payout, as with an insurance company premium, should equal the premium received.

The following factors influence the price of an option:

■ *The behaviour of financial prices*: One of the key assumptions made by the Black-Scholes (B-S) model is that asset prices follow a lognormal distribution. Although this is not strictly accurate, it is a close enough approximation to allow its use in option pricing. In fact observation shows that while prices themselves are not normally distributed, asset returns are, and we define returns as $\ln \left[\dfrac{P_{t+1}}{P_t} \right]$ where P_t is the market price at time t and P_{t+1} is the price one period later. The distribution of prices is called a lognormal distribution because the logarithm of the prices is normally distributed; the asset returns are defined as the logarithm of the price relatives and are assumed to follow the normal distribution. The expected return as a result of assuming this distribution is given by $E\left[ln\left(\dfrac{P_t}{P_0}\right)\right] = rt$ where $E[\ ]$ is the expectation operator and r is the annual rate of return. The derivation of this expression is given in Appendix 17.2.

■ *The strike price*: The difference between the strike price and the underlying price of the asset at the time the option is struck will influence the size of the premium, since this will impact on the probability that the option will be exercised. An option that is deeply in-the-money has a greater probability of being exercised.

■ *Volatility*: The volatility of the underlying asset will influence the probability that an option is exercised, because a higher volatility indicates a higher probability of exercise. This is considered in detail below.

■ *The term to maturity*: A longer-dated option has greater time value and a greater probability of eventually being exercised.

■ *The level of interest rates*: The premium paid for an option in theory represents the expected gain to the buyer at the time the option is exercised. It is paid up-front, so it is discounted to obtain a present value. The discount rate used therefore has an effect on the premium, although it is less influential than the other factors presented here.

The volatility of an asset measures the variability of its price returns. It is defined as the annualized standard deviation of returns, where variability refers to the variability of the returns that generate the asset's prices, rather than the prices directly. The standard deviation of returns is given by:

$$\sigma = \sqrt{\sum_{i=1}^{N} \frac{(x_i - \mu)^2}{N - 1}}$$

(17.1)

where

x_i is the i'th price relative
μ is the arithmetic mean of the observations
N is the total number of observations.

The value is converted to an annualized figure by multiplying it by the square root of the number of days in a year, usually taken to be 250 working days. Using this formula, from market observations it is possible to calculate the *historic volatility* of an asset. The volatility of an asset is one of the inputs to the B-S model. Of the inputs to the B-S model, the variability of the underlying asset, or its volatility, is the most problematic. The distribution of asset prices is assumed to follow a lognormal distribution, because the logarithm of the prices is normally distributed (we assume lognormal rather than normal distribution to allow for the fact that prices cannot – as could be the case in a normal distribution – have negative values): the range of possible prices starts at zero and cannot assume a negative value.

Note that it is the asset price *returns* on which the standard deviation is calculated, and not the actual prices themselves. This is because using prices would produce inconsistent results, since the actual standard deviation itself would change as price levels increased.

However, calculating volatility using the standard statistical method gives us a figure for *historic volatility*. What is required is a figure for *future volatility*, since this is relevant for pricing an option expiring in the future. Future volatility cannot be measured directly, by definition. Market-makers get around this by using an option pricing model 'backwards'. An option pricing model calculates the option price from volatility and other parameters. Used in reverse, the model can calculate the volatility implied by the option price. Volatility measured in this way is called *implied volatility*. Evaluating implied volatility is straightforward using this method and generally more appropriate than using historic volatility, because it provides a clearer measure of an option's fair value. Implied volatilities of deeply in-the-money or out-of-the-money options tend to be relatively high.

The Black-Scholes option model

Most option pricing models are based on one of two methodologies, although both types employ essentially identical assumptions. The first method is based on the resolution of the partial differentiation equation of the asset price model, corresponding to the expected payoff of the option security. This is the foundation of the B-S model. The second type of model uses the martingale method, and was first introduced by Harrison and Kreps (1979) and Harrison and Pliska (1981), where the price of an asset at time 0 is given by its discounted expected future payoffs, under the appropriate probability measure, known as the risk-neutral probability. There is a third type of option pricing model that assumes lognormal distribution of asset returns but follows the two-step binomial process.

In order to employ the pricing models, we accept a state of the market that is known as a *complete market*,[1] one where there is a viable financial market. This is where the rule of no-arbitrage pricing exists, so that there is no opportunity to generate risk-free arbitrage due to the presence of, say, incorrect forward interest rates. The fact that there is no opportunity to generate risk-free arbitrage gains means that a zero-cost investment strategy that is initiated at time t will have a zero maturity value. The martingale property of the behaviour of asset prices states that an accurate estimate of the future price of an asset

1. First proposed by Arrow and Debreu (1953, 1954).

may be obtained from current price information. Therefore the relevant information used to calculate forward asset prices is the latest price information. This was also a property of the semi-strong and strong-form market efficiency scenarios described by Fama (1965).

In this section we describe the B-S option model in accessible fashion; more technical treatments are given in the relevant references listed in the bibliography.

Assumptions

The B-S model describes a process to calculate the fair value of a European call option under certain assumptions. Apart from the price of the underlying asset S and the time t, all the variables in the model are assumed to be constant, including most crucially the volatility. The following assumptions are made:

■ there are no transaction costs, and the market allows short selling;

■ trading is continuous;

■ underlying asset prices follow geometric Brownian motion, with the variance rate proportional to the square root of the asset price;

■ the asset is a non-dividend-paying security;

■ the interest rate during the life of the option is known and constant;

■ the option can only be exercised on expiry.

The B-S model is neat and intuitively straightforward to explain, and one of its many attractions is that it can be readily modified to handle other types of options such as foreign exchange or interest rate options. The assumption of the behaviour of the underlying asset price over time is described by (17.2), which is a generalized Weiner process, and where a is the expected return on the underlying asset and b is the standard deviation of its price returns.

$$\frac{dS}{S} = adt + bdW \qquad (17.2)$$

The Black-Scholes model and pricing derivative instruments

We assume a financial asset is specified by its terminal payoff value; therefore when pricing an option we require the fair value of the option at the initial time when the option is struck, and this value is a function of the expected terminal payoff of the option, discounted to the day when the option is struck. In this section we present an intuitive explanation of the B-S model, in terms of the normal distribution of asset price returns.

From the definition of a call option, we can set the expected value of the option at maturity T as:

$$E(C_T) = E[\max(S_T - X, 0)] \tag{17.3}$$

where

S_T is the price of the underlying asset at maturity T
X is the strike price of the option.

From (17.3) we know that there are only two possible outcomes that can arise on maturity: either the option will expire in-the-money and the outcome will be $S_T - X$, or the option will be out-of-the-money and the outcome will be 0. If we set the term p as the probability that on expiry $S_T > X$, equation (17.3) can be rewritten as:

$$E(C_T) = p \times (E[S_T \mid S_T > X] - X) \tag{17.4}$$

where $E[S_T \mid S_T > X]$ is the expected value of S_T given that $S_T > X$. Equation (17.4) gives us an expression for the expected value of a call option on maturity. Therefore to obtain the fair price of the option at the time it is struck, the value given by (17.4) must be discounted back to its present value, and this is shown as:

$$C = p \times e^{-rt} \times (E[S_T \mid S_T > X] - X) \tag{17.5}$$

where r is the continuously compounded risk-free rate of interest, and t is the time from valuation date until maturity. Therefore, to price an option we require the probability p that the option expires in-the-money, and we require the expected value of the option given that it does expire in-the-money, which is the last term of (17.5). To calculate p we assume that asset prices follow a stochastic process, which enables us to model the probability function.

The B-S model is based on the resolution of the following partial differential equation:

$$\frac{1}{2} \sigma^2 S^2 \left(\frac{\partial^2 C}{\partial S^2} \right) + rS \left(\frac{\partial C}{\partial S} \right) + \left(\frac{\partial C}{\partial t} \right) - rC = 0 \tag{17.6}$$

under the appropriate parameters. We do not demonstrate the process by which this equation is arrived at. The parameters refer to the payoff conditions corresponding to a European call option, which we considered above. We do not present a solution to the differential equation at (17.6), since this is beyond the scope of the book, but we can consider now how the probability and expected value functions can be solved. For a fuller treatment readers may wish to refer to the original account by Black and Scholes (1973); other good accounts are given in Ingersoll (1987), Neftci (1996) and Nielsen (1999), among others.

The probability p that the underlying asset price at maturity exceeds X is equal to the probability that the return over the time period the option is held will exceed a certain critical value. Remember that we assume normal distribution of asset price returns. As asset returns are defined as the logarithm of price relatives, we require p such that:

$$p = prob[S_T > X] = prob\left[return > \ln\left(\frac{X}{S_0}\right)\right] \tag{17.7}$$

where S_0 is the price of the underlying asset at the time the option is struck. Generally, the probability that a normal distributed variable x will exceed a critical value x_c is given by:

$$p[x > x_c] = 1 - N\left(\frac{x_c - \mu}{\sigma}\right) \tag{17.8}$$

where μ and σ are the mean and standard deviation of x respectively and $N(\ )$ is the cumulative normal distribution. We know from our earlier discussion of the behaviour of asset prices that an expression for μ is the natural logarithm of the asset price returns; we already know that the standard deviation of returns is $\sigma \sqrt{t}$. Therefore, with these assumptions, we may combine (17.7) and (17.8) to give us (17.9):

$$prob[S_T > X] = prob\left[return > \ln\left(\frac{X}{S_0}\right)\right] = 1 - N\left(\frac{\ln\left(\frac{X}{S_0}\right) - \left(r - \frac{\sigma^2}{2}\right)t}{\sigma \sqrt{t}}\right). \tag{17.9}$$

Under the conditions of the normal distribution, the symmetrical shape of the normal distribution means that we can obtain the probability of an occurrence based on $1-N(d)$ being equal to $N(-d)$. Therefore we are able to set the following relationship:

$$p = prob[ST > X] = N\left(\frac{\ln\left(\frac{S_0}{X}\right) + \left(r - \frac{\sigma^2}{2}\right)t}{\sigma \sqrt{t}}\right). \tag{17.10}$$

Now we require a formula to calculate the expected value of the option on expiry, the second part of the expression at (17.5). This involves the integration of the normal distribution curve over the range from X to infinity. This is not shown here, however the result is given at (17.11):

$$E[S_T \mid S_T > X] = S_0 e^{rt}\frac{N(d_1)}{N(d_2)} \tag{17.11}$$

where

$$d_1 = \frac{\ln\left(\frac{S_0}{X}\right) + \left(r + \frac{\sigma^2}{2}\right)t}{\sigma \sqrt{t}}$$

and

$$d_2 = \frac{\ln\left(\frac{S_0}{X}\right) + \left(r - \frac{\sigma^2}{2}\right)t}{\sigma \sqrt{t}} = d_1 - \sigma \sqrt{t}.$$

We now have expressions for the probability that an option expires in-the-money as well as the expected value of the option on expiry, and we incorporate these into the expression at (17.5), which gives us:

$$C = N(d_2) \times e^{-rt} \times \left(S_0 e^{rt} \frac{N(d_1)}{N(d_2)} - X \right). \tag{17.12}$$

Equation (17.12) can be rearranged to give (17.13), which is the famous and well-known Black-Scholes option pricing model for a European call option:

$$C = S_0 N(d_1) - Xe^{-rt} N(d_2) \tag{17.13}$$

where

S_0 is the price of the underlying asset at the time the option is struck

X is the strike price

r is the continuously compounded risk-free interest rate

t is the maturity of the option.

What the expression at (17.13) states is that the fair value of a call option is the expected present value of the option on its expiry date, assuming that prices follow a lognormal distribution.

$N(d_1)$ and $N(d_2)$ are the cumulative probabilities from the normal distribution of obtaining the values d_1 and d_2, given above. $N(d_1)$ is the *delta* of the option. The term $N(d_2)$ represents the probability that the option will be exercised. The term e^{-rt} is the present value of one unit of cash received t periods from the time the option is struck. Where $N(d_1)$ and $N(d_2)$ are equal to 1, which is the equivalent of assuming complete certainty, the model is reduced to:

$$C = S - Xe^{-rt} \tag{17.14}$$

which is the expression for Merton's lower bound for continuously compounded interest rates, and which we introduced in intuitive fashion in the previous chapter. Therefore, under complete certainty, the B-S model reduces to Merton's bound.

The put–call parity relationship

Up to now we have concentrated on calculating the price of a call option. However, the previous section introduced the boundary condition for a put option, so it should be apparent that this can be solved as well. In fact the price of a call option and a put option are related via what is known as the *put–call parity theorem*. This is an important relationship and obviates the need to develop a separate model for put options.

Consider a portfolio Y that consists of a call option with a maturity date T and a zero-coupon bond that pays X on the expiry date of the option. Consider also a second portfolio Z that consists of a put option also with maturity date T and one share. The value of portfolio A on the expiry date is given by:

$$MV_{Y, T} = \max[S_T - X, 0] + X = \max[X, S_T].$$ (17.15)

The value of the second portfolio Z on the expiry date is:

$$MV_{Z, T} = \max[X - S_T, 0] + S_T = \max[X, S_T].$$ (17.16)

Both portfolios have the same value at maturity. Therefore they must also have the same initial value at start time t, otherwise there would be an arbitrage opportunity. Prices must be arbitrage-free, therefore the following put–call relationship must hold:

$$C_t - P_t = S_t - Xe^{-r(T - t)}.$$ (17.17)

If the relationship at (17.17) did not hold, then arbitrage would be possible. So, using this relationship, the value of a European put option is given by the B-S model as shown, at (17.18):

$$P(S, T) = -SN(-d_1) + Xe^{-rT} N(-d_2).$$ (17.18)

EXAMPLE   *17.1 The Black-Scholes model*

Here we illustrate a simple application of the B-S model. Consider an underlying asset, usually assumed to be non-dividend-paying equity, with a current price of 25, and volatility of 23%. The short-term risk-free interest rate is 5%. An option is written with strike price 21 and a maturity of three months. Therefore we have:

$S = 25$
$X = 21$
$r = 5\%$
$T = 0.25$
$\sigma = 23\%$

To calculate the price of the option, we first calculate the discounted value of the strike price, as follows:

$$Xe^{-rT} = 21e^{-0.05(0.25)} = 20.73913$$

We then calculate the values of d_1 and d_2:

$$d_1 = \frac{\ln(25/21) + [0.05 + (0.5)(0.23)^2]\,0.25}{0.23\,\sqrt{0.25}} = \frac{0.193466}{0.115} = 1.682313$$

$$d_s = d_1 - 0.23\,\sqrt{0.25} = 1.567313$$

We now insert these values into the main price equation:

$$C = 25N(1.682313) - 21e^{-0.05(0.25)}\,N(1.567313).$$

Using the approximation of the cumulative normal distribution at the points 1.68 and 1.56, the price of the call option is:

$$C = 25(0.9535) - 20.73913(0.9406) = 4.3303$$

or 4.3303

What would be the price of a put option on the same stock?

The values of $N(d_1)$ and $N(d_2)$ are 0.9535 and 0.9406, therefore the put price is calculated as:

$$P = 20.7391\,(1 - 0.9406) - 25\,(1 - 0.9535) = 0.06943$$

If we use the call price and apply the put–call parity theorem, the price of the put option is given by:

$$
\begin{aligned}
P &= C - S + Xe^{-rT} \\
&= 4.3303 - 25 + 21e^{-0.05(0.25)} \\
&= 0.069434
\end{aligned}
$$

This is exactly the same price that was obtained by the application of the put option formula in the B-S model above.

As we noted early in this chapter, the premium payable for an option will increase if the time to expiry, the volatility or the interest rate is increased (or any combination is increased). Thus if we maintain all the parameters constant but price a call option that has a maturity of six months or $T = 0.5$, we obtain the following values:

$$d_1 = 1.3071, \text{ giving } N(d_1) = 0.9049$$
$$d_2 = 1.1445, \text{ giving } N(d_2) = 0.8740$$

The call price for the longer-dated option is 4.7217.

The Black-Scholes model as an Excel spreadsheet

In Appendix 17.3 we show the spreadsheet formulae required to build the B-S model into Microsoft Excel. The user must ensure that the Analysis Tool-Pak add-in is available, otherwise some of the function references may not work. By setting up the cells in the way shown, the fair value of a vanilla call or put option may be calculated. The put–call parity is used to enable calculation of the put price.

The Black-Scholes model and the valuation of bond options

In this section we illustrate the application of the B-S model to the pricing of an option on a zero-coupon bond and a plain vanilla fixed-coupon bond.

For a zero-coupon bond the theoretical price of a call option written on the bond is given by:

$$C = PN(d_1) - Xe^{-rT} N(d_2) \tag{17.19}$$

where P is the price of the underlying bond and all other parameters remain the same. If the option is written on a coupon-paying bond, it is necessary to subtract the present value of all coupons paid during the life of the option from the bond's price. Coupons sometimes lower the price of a call option because a coupon makes it more attractive to hold a bond rather than an option on the bond. Call options on bonds are often priced at a lower level than similar options on zero-coupon bonds.

EXAMPLE *17.2 The Black-Scholes model and bond option pricing*

Consider a European call option written on a bond that has the following characteristics:

Price	£98
Coupon	8% (semi-annual)
Time to maturity	Five years
Bond price volatility	6.02%
Coupon payments	£4 in three months and nine months
Three-month interest rate	5.6%
Nine-month interest rate	5.75%
One-year interest rate	6.25%

The option is written with a strike price of £100 and has a maturity of one year. The present value of the coupon payments made during the life of the option is £7.78, as shown below:

$$4e^{-0.056 \times 0.25} + 4e^{-0.0575 \times 0.75} = 3.9444 + 3.83117 = 7.77557$$

This gives us $P = 98 - 7.78 = £90.22$

Applying the B-S model we obtain:

$d_1 = [\ln(90.22/100) + 0.0625 + 0.001812]/0.0602 = -0.6413$

$d_2 = d_1 - (0.0602 \times 1) = -0.7015$

$C = 90.22N(-0.6413) - 100e - 0.0625\ N(-0.7015)$
$\quad = 1.1514$

Therefore the call option has a value of £1.15, which will be composed entirely of time value. Note also that a key assumption of the model is constant interest rates, yet the model is being applied to a bond price – which is essentially an interest rate – that is considered to follow stochastic price processes.

Interest rate options and the Black model

In 1976 Fisher Black presented a slightly modified version of the B-S model, using similar assumptions, to be used in pricing forward contracts and interest rate options. The Black model is used in banks today to price instruments such as swaptions, as well as bond and interest rate options like caps and floors.

In the Black 76 model the spot price $S(t)$ of an asset or a commodity is the price payable for immediate delivery today (in practice, up to two days forward) at time t. This price is assumed to follow a geometric Brownian motion. The theoretical price for a futures contract on the asset $F(t,T)$ is defined as the price agreed today for delivery of the asset at time T, with the price agreed today but payable on delivery. When $t = T$, the futures price is equal to the spot price. A futures contract is cash settled every day via the clearing mechanism, whereas a forward contract is a contract to buy or sell the asset where there is no daily mark-to-market and no daily cash settlement.

We set f as the value of a forward contract, u as the value of a futures contract and C as the value of an option contract. Each of these contracts is a function of the futures price $F(t,T)$, as well as additional variables. So we may write at time t the values of all three contracts as $f(F,t)$, $u(F,t)$ and $C(F,t)$. The value of the forward contract is also a function of the price of the underlying asset S at time T and can be written $f(F,t,S,T)$. Note that the value of the forward contract f is not the same as the price of the forward contract. The forward price at any given time is the delivery price that would result in the contract having a zero value. At the time the contract is transacted, the forward value is zero. Over time both the price and the value will fluctuate. The futures price, on the other hand, is the price at which a forward contract has a zero current value. Therefore at the time of the trade the forward price is equal to the futures price F, which may be written as:

$$f(F, tF, T) = 0 \tag{17.20}$$

Equation (17.20) simply states that the value of the forward contract is zero when the contract is taken out and the contract price S is always equal to the current futures price,

$F(t, T).^2$

The principal difference between a futures contract and a forward contract is that a futures contract may be used to imply the price of forward contracts. This arises from the fact that futures contracts are repriced each day, with a new contract price that is equal to the new futures price. Hence when F rises, such that $F > S$, the forward contract has a positive value and when F falls the forward contract has a negative value. When the transaction expires and delivery takes place, the futures price is equal to the spot price and the value of the forward contract is equal to the spot price minus the contract price or the spot price:

$$f(F, T, S, T) = F - S. \tag{17.21}$$

On maturity, the value of a bond or commodity option is given by the maximum of zero, and the difference between the spot price and the contract price. Since at that date the futures price is equal to the spot price, we conclude that:

$$C(F, T) = \begin{cases} F - S & \text{if } F \geq S_T \\ 0 & \text{else} \end{cases}. \tag{17.22}$$

The assumptions made in the Black model are that the prices of futures contracts follow a lognormal distribution with a constant variance, and that the capital asset pricing model (*see* Chapter 21) applies in the market. There is also an assumption of no transaction costs or taxes. Under these assumptions, we can create a risk-free hedged position that is composed of a long position in the option and a short position in the futures contract. Following the B-S model, the number of options put on against one futures contract is given by $[\partial C(F, t)/\partial F]$, which is the derivative of $C(F, t)$ with respect to F. The change in the hedged position resulting from a change in price of the underlying asset is given by:

$$\partial C(F, t) - [\partial C(F, t)/\partial F]\partial F. \tag{17.23}$$

Due to the principle of arbitrage-free pricing, the return generated by the hedged portfolio must be equal to the risk-free interest rate, and this together with an expansion of $\partial C(F, t)$ produces the following partial differential equation:

$$\left[\frac{\partial C(F, t)}{\partial t}\right] = r C(F, t) - \tfrac{1}{2} \sigma^2 F^2 \left[\frac{\partial^2 C(F, t)}{\partial F^2}\right]. \tag{17.24}$$

which is solved by setting the following:

2. This assumption is held in the market but does not hold good over long periods, due chiefly to the difference in the way futures and forwards are marked-to-market, and because futures are cash-settled on a daily basis while forwards are not.

$$\tfrac{1}{2}\sigma^2 \, F^2 \left[\frac{\partial^2 C(F, t)}{\partial F^2} \right] - r \, C(F, t) + \left[\frac{\partial C(F, t)}{\partial t} \right] = 0. \tag{17.25}$$

The solution to the partial differential equation (17.24) is not presented here.

The result, by denoting $T = t - T$ and using (17.23) and (17.24), gives the fair value of a commodity option or option on a forward contract as shown below:

$$C(F, t) = e^{-rT}[FN(d_1) - S_T N(d_2)] \tag{17.26}$$

where

$$d_1 = \frac{1}{\sigma \sqrt{T}} \left[\ln \left(\frac{F}{S_T} \right) + \left(\tfrac{1}{2} \sigma^2 \right) T \right]$$

$$d_2 = d_1 - \sigma \sqrt{T}$$

There are a number of other models that have been developed for specific contracts, for example the Garman and Kohlhagen (1983) and Grabbe (1983) models, used for currency options, and the Merton, Barone-Adesi and Whaley or BAW model (1987) used for commodity options. For the valuation of American options, on dividend-paying assets, another model has been developed by Roll, Geske and Whaley. More recently the Black-Derman-Toy model (1990)[3] has been used to price exotic options. A detailed discussion of these, though very interesting, is outside the scope of this book.

Comment on the Black-Scholes model

The introduction of the B-S model was one of the great milestones in the development of the global capital markets, and it remains an important pricing model today. Many of the models introduced later for application to specific products are still based essentially on the B-S model. Subsequently, academics have presented some weaknesses in the model that stem from the nature of the main assumptions behind the model itself, which we will summarize here. The main critique of the B-S model centres on the following assumptions:

- *Frictionless markets*: This is at best only approximately true for large market counterparties.

- *Constant interest rate*: This is possibly the most unrealistic assumption. Interest rates over even the shortest time frame (the overnight rate) fluctuate considerably. In addition to a dynamic short rate, the short-end of the yield curve often moves in the opposite direction to moves in underlying asset prices, particularly so with bonds and bond options.

3. Cited in a collected edition (Hughston, 1996) in the references.

▪ *Lognormal distribution*: This is accepted by the market as a reasonable approximation but not completely accurate, and also missing out most extreme moves or market shocks.

▪ *European option only*: Although it is rare for American options to be exercised early, there are situations when it is optimal to do so, and the B-S model does not price these situations.

▪ *Continuous constant dividend yield*: For stock options, this assumption is clearly not realistic, although the trend in the US markets is for ordinary shares to cease paying dividends altogether.

These points notwithstanding, the Black-Scholes model paved the way for the rapid development of options as liquid tradeable products, and it is widely used today.

Stochastic volatility

The B-S model assumes a constant volatility; for this reason – and because it is based on mathematics – it often fails to pick up on market 'sentiment' when there is a large downward move or shock. This is not a failing limited to the B-S model. But for this reason the B-S model undervalues out-of-the-money options, and to compensate for this, market-makers push up the price of deep in-the-money or out-of-the-money options, giving rise to the volatility *smile*. This is considered in the next chapter.

The effect of stochastic volatility not being catered for is to introduce mispricing, specifically the undervaluation of out-of-the-money options and the overvaluation of deeply in-the-money options. This is because when the price of the underlying asset rises, its volatility level also increases. The effect of this is that assets priced at relatively high levels do not tend to follow the process described by geometric Brownian motion. The same is true for relatively low asset prices and price volatility, but in the opposite direction. To compensate for this stochastic volatility, other models have been developed, such as the Hull-White model (1987).

Implied volatility

The volatility parameter in the B-S model, by definition, cannot be observed directly in the market, because it refers to volatility going forward. It is different to historic volatility, which can be measured directly, and this value is sometimes used to estimate implied volatility of an asset price. Banks therefore use the value for *implied volatility*, which is the volatility obtained using the prices of exchange-traded options. Given the price of an option and all the other parameters, it is possible to use the price of the option to determine the volatility of the underlying asset implied by the option price. The B-S model, however, cannot be rearranged into a form that expresses the volatility measure as a function of the other parameters. Generally, therefore, a numerical iteration process is used to arrive at the value for σ, given the price of the option; this is usually the Newton-Raphson method.

The market uses implied volatilities to gauge the volatility of individual assets relative to the market. Volatility levels are not constant, and fluctuate with the overall level of the market, as well as for stock-specific factors. When assessing volatilities with reference to exchange-traded options, market-makers will use more than one value, because an asset will have different implied volatilities depending on how in-the-money the option itself is. The price of an at-the-money option will exhibit greater sensitivity to volatility than the price of a deeply in-the-money or out-of-the-money option. Therefore market-makers will take a combination of volatility values when assessing the volatility of a particular asset.

A final word on option models

We have only discussed the B-S model and the Black model in this chapter. Other pricing models have been developed that follow on from the pioneering work done by Black and Scholes. The B-S model is essentially the most straightforward and the easiest to apply, and subsequent research has focused on easing some of the restrictions of the model in order to expand its applicability. Areas that have been focused on include a relaxation of the assumption of constant volatility levels for asset prices, as well as work on allowing for the valuation of American options and options on dividend-paying stocks. However, often in practice some of the newer models require input of parameters that are difficult to observe or measure directly, which limits their application as well. Often there is a difficulty in calibrating a model due to the lack of observable data in the marketplace. The issue of calibration is an important one in the implementation of a pricing model, and involves inputting actual market data and using this as the parameters for calculation of prices. So, for instance, a model used to calculate the prices of sterling market options would use data from the UK market, including money market, futures and swaps rates to build the zero-coupon yield curve, and volatility levels for the underlying asset or interest rate (if it is valuing options on interest rate products, such as caps and floors). What sort of volatility is used? In some banks actual historical volatilities, more usually volatilities implied by exchange-traded option prices. Another crucial piece of data for multi-factor models (following Heath-Jarrow-Morton and other models based on this) is the correlation coefficients between forward rates on the term structure. This is used to calculate volatilities using the model itself.

The issue of calibrating the model is important, because incorrectly calibrated models will produce errors in option valuation. This can have disastrous results, which may be discovered only after significant losses have been suffered. If data is not available to calibrate the model, it may be that a simpler one needs to be used. The lack of data is not an issue for products priced in, say, dollars, sterling or euros, but may be in other currency products if data is not so readily available. This might explain why the B-S model is still widely used today, although markets observe an increasing use of models such as the Black-Derman-Toy (1990) and Brace-Gatarek-Musiela (1994)[4] for more exotic option products.

Many models, because of the way that they describe the price process, are described as Gaussian interest rate models. The basic process is described as an Itô process of the form:

$$dP_T/P_T = \mu_T d + \sigma_T dW \tag{17.27}$$

where P_T is the price of a zero-coupon bond with maturity date T, and W is a standard Weiner process. The basic statement made by Gaussian interest rate models is that:

$$P_T(t) = E_T \exp\left(-\int_t^T r(s)ds\right). \tag{17.28}$$

Models that capture the process in this way include those of Cox, Ingersoll and Ross (1985) and Harrison and Pliska (1981). We are summarizing here only, but essentially such models state that the price of an option is equal to the discounted return from a risk-free instrument. This is why the basic B-S model describes a portfolio of a call option on the underlying stock and a cash deposit invested at the risk-free interest rate. This was reviewed in this chapter. We then discussed how the representation of asset prices as an expectation of a discounted payoff from a risk-free deposit does not capture the real-world scenario presented by many option products. Hence the continuing research into developments of the basic model.

Following on from the B-S model, under the assumption that the short-term spot rate drives bond and option prices, the basic model can be used to model an interest rate term structure, as given by Vasicek (1977) and Cox, Ingersoll and Ross (1985). The short-term spot rate is assumed to follow a diffusion process:

$$dr = \mu dt + \sigma dW \tag{17.29}$$

which is a standard Weiner process. From this it is possible to model the complete term structure based on the short-term spot rate and the volatility of the short-term rate. This approach is modified by Heath, Jarrow and Morton (1992), which was reviewed earlier as an interest rate model.

Appendix 17.1

Summary of basic statistical concepts

The arithmetic mean μ is the average of a series of numbers. The *variance* is the sum of the squares of the difference of each observation from the mean, and from the variance we obtain the standard deviation σ, which is the square root of the variance. The *probability density* of a series of numbers is the term for how likely any of them is to occur. In a normal probability density function, described by the normal distribution, the probability density is given by:

---

4. Cited in a collected edition (Hughston, 1996) in the references.

$$\frac{1}{\sqrt{2\pi}e^{\frac{x^2}{2}}}. \tag{17.30}$$

Most option pricing formulae assume a normal probability density function, specifically that movements in the natural logarithm of asset prices follow this function. That is:

$$\ln\left(\frac{\text{today's price}}{\text{yesterday's price}}\right) \tag{17.31}$$

is assumed to follow a normal probability density function. This relative price change is equal to:

$$\left(1 + r \times \frac{days}{year}\right) \tag{17.32}$$

where r is the rate of return being earned on an investment in the asset. The value:

$$\ln\left(1 + r \times \frac{days}{year}\right)$$

is equal to $r \times \frac{days}{year}$ where r is the continuously compounded rate of return. Therefore the value

$$\ln\left(\frac{\text{today's price}}{\text{yesterday's price}}\right)$$

is equal to the continuously compounded rate of return on the asset over a specified holding period.

Appendix 17.2

Lognormal distribution of returns

In the distribution of asset price returns, returns are defined as the logarithm of price relatives and are assumed to follow the normal distribution, given by:

$$\ln\left(\frac{P_t}{P_0}\right) \sim N\left(rt, \sigma\sqrt{t}\right) \tag{17.33}$$

where

P_t is the price at time t
P_0 is the price at time 0
$N(m,s)$ is a random normal distribution with mean m and standard deviation s
r is the annual rate of return
σ is the annualized standard deviation of returns.

From (17.33) we conclude that the logarithm of the prices is normally distributed, due to (17.34) where P_0 is a constant:

$$\ln\left(P_t\right) \sim \ln\left(P_0\right) + N\left(rt, \sigma\sqrt{t}\right). \tag{17.34}$$

We conclude that prices are normally distributed and are described by the relationship:

$$\frac{P_t}{P_0} \sim e^{N(rt,\ \sigma\sqrt{t})} \tag{17.35}$$

and from this relationship we may set the expected return as rt.

Appendix 17.3

The Black-Scholes model in Microsoft Excel

To value a vanilla option under the following parameters, we can use Microsoft Excel to carry out the calculation, as shown in Table 17.1.

Price of underlying	100
Volatility	0.0691
Maturity of option	Three months
Strike price	99.5
Risk-free rate	5%

TABLE 17.1 ▪ Microsoft Excel calculation of a vanilla option price

Cell	C	D	
8	Underlying price, S	100	
9	Volatility %	0.0691	
10	Option maturity years	0.25	
11	Strike price, X	99.50	
12	Risk-free interest rate %	0.05	
13			
14			
15			Cell formulae:
16	ln (S/X)	0.005012542	=LN (D8/D11)
17	Adjusted return	0.0000456012500	=((D12-D9)^2/ 2)*D10
18	Time-adjusted volatility	0.131434394	=(D9*D10)^0.5
19	d_2	0.038484166	=(D16+D17)/D18
20	$N(d_2)$	0.515349233	=NORMSDIST(D19)
21			
22	d_1	0.16991856	=D19+D18
23	$N(d_1)$	0.56746291	=NORMSDIST(D22)
24	e^{-rt}	0.9875778	=EXP(–D10*D12)
25			
26	CALL	6.106018498	=D8*D23-D11*D20*D24
27	PUT	4.370009648	* =D26-D8+D11*D24

$\ast$ By put–call parity,

$$P = C - S + Xe^{-rt}$$

SELECTED BIBLIOGRAPHY AND REFERENCES

Arrow, K., Debreu, G., 'Existence of an equilibrium for a competitive economy', *Econometrica* 22, 1954, pp. 265–90.

Black, F., Derman, E., Toy, W., 'A one-factor model of interest rates and its application to Treasury bond options', in Hughston, L. (ed.), *Vasicek and Beyond*, Risk Publications 1996.

Black, F., 'Pricing of commodity contracts', *Journal of Financial Economics 3*, 1976.

Black, F., Scholes, M., 'The pricing of options and corporate liabilities', *Journal of Political Economy* 81, May–June 1973, pp. 637–59.

Bookstaber, R., *Option Pricing and Strategies in Investing*, Addison-Wesley 1982.

Boyle, P., 'Option valuation using a three jump process', *International Options Journal* 3, 1986, pp. 7–12.

Brace, A., Gatarek, D., Musiela, M. 'The market model of interest rate dynamics', in Hughston, L. (ed.), *Vasicek and Beyond*, Risk Publications 1996.

Briys, E., *et al.*, *Options, Futures and Exotic Derivatives*, John Wiley & Sons 1998.

Choudhry, M., *The Bond and Money Markets: Strategy, Trading, Analysis*, Butterworth-Heinemann 2001, Chapters 42–9.

Cox, D., Miller, H., *The Theory of Stochastic Processes*, Chapman & Hall 1965.

Cox, J., Ingersoll, J., Ross, S., 'An inter-temporal general equilibrium model of asset prices', *Econometrica* 53, 1985.

Cox, J., Ross, S., 'The valuation of options for alternative stochastic processes', *Journal of Financial Economics* 3, 1976, pp. 145–66.

Cox, J., Ross, S., Rubinstein, M., 'Option pricing: a simplified approach', *Journal of Financial Economics* 7, October 1979, pp. 229–64.

Debreu, G., 'Representation of a preference ordering by a numerical function', in Thrall, R., Coombs, C., Davis, R. (eds), *Decision Processes*, Wiley 1954.

Fama, E., 'The behaviour of stock prices', *Journal of Business* 38, January 1965, pp. 34–105.

Harrison, J., Kreps, D., 'Martingales and arbitrage in multi-period securities markets', *Journal of Economic Theory* 20, 1979, pp. 381–408.

Harrison, J., Pliska, S., 'Martingales and stochastic integrals in the theory of continuous trading', *Stochastic Processes and Their Applications* 11, 1981, pp. 216–60.

Haug, E. G., *The Complete Guide to Option Pricing Formulas*, McGraw-Hill 1998.

Heath, D., Jarrow, R., Morton A., 'Bond pricing and the term structure of interest rates: a new methodology for contingent claims valuation', *Econometrica* 60, January 1992, pp. 77–105.

Heston, S., 'A closed form solution for options with stochastic volatility with application to bond and currency options', *Review of Financial Studies* 6, 1993, pp. 327–43.

Heston, S., 'Invisible parameters in option prices', *Journal of Finance* 48: 3, 1993, pp. 933–47.

Hull, J., White, A., 'The pricing of options on assets with stochastic volatilities', *Journal of Finance* 42, 1987, pp. 281–300.

Hull, J., White, A., 'An analysis of the bias caused by a stochastic volatility in option pricing', *Advances in Futures and Options Research* 3, 1988, pp. 29–61.

Ingersoll, J., *Theory of Financial Decision Making*, Rowman & Littlefield 1987.

Ito, K., 'On stochastic differential equations', *American Mathematical Society* 4, 1951, pp. 1–51.

Klemkosky, R., Resnick, B., 'Put-call parity and market efficiency', *Journal of Financial Economics* 34, December 1979, pp. 1141–55.

Merton, R., 'Theory of rational option pricing', *Bell Journal of Economics and Management Science* 4, spring 1973, pp. 141–183.

Merton, R., 'Option pricing when underlying stock returns are discontinuous', *Journal of Financial Economics* 3, Jan.–Mar. 1976, pp. 125–44.

Merton, R., *Continuous-Time Finance*, Blackwell 1990.

Neftci, S., *An Introduction to the Mathematics of Financial Derivatives*, Academic Press 1996.

Nielsen, L. T., *Pricing and Hedging of Derivative Securities*, Oxford University Press 1999.

Rendleman, R., Bartter, B., 'Two-state option pricing', *Journal of Finance* 34, 1979, pp. 1092–110.

Rubinstein, M., 'Nonparametric tests of alternative option pricing models', *Journal of Financial Economics* 40, 1985, pp. 455–80.

Scott, L., 'Option pricing when the variance changes randomly', *Journal of Financial and Quantitative Analysis* 22, 1987, pp. 419–38.

Stein, E., Stein, J., 'Stock price distributions with stochastic volatility: an analytic approach', *Review of Financial Studies* 4, 1991, pp. 113–35.

Vasicek, O., 'An equilibrium characterization of the term structure', *Journal of Financial Economics* 5, 1977, pp. 177–88.

Whaley, R., 'On the valuation of American call options on stocks with known dividends', *Journal of Financial Economics* 9, 1981, pp. 207–11.

CHAPTER 18

Options III

We continue with options in this chapter with a look at how they behave in response to changes in market conditions. To start, we consider the main issues that a market-maker in options must consider when writing options. We then review the 'Greeks': the measures by which the sensitivity of an option book is calculated. We conclude with a discussion on an important set of interest rate options in the market: *caps and floors*.

Behaviour of option prices

As we noted in Chapter 16, the value of an option is a function of six factors:

- the price of the underlying asset;
- the strike price of the option;
- the time to expiry of the option;
- the volatility level of the underlying asset price returns;
- the risk-free interest rate applicable to the life of the option;
- the value of any dividends or cash flows paid by the underlying asset during the life of the option.

The Black-Scholes (B-S) model assumes that the levels of volatility and interest rates stay constant, so that changes in these will impact on the value of the option. On the expiry date, the price of the option will be a function of the strike price and the price of the underlying asset. However, for pricing purposes an option trader must take into account all the factors above. From Chapter 16 we know that the value of an option is composed of intrinsic value and time value; intrinsic value is apparent straight away when an option is struck, and a valuation model is essentially pricing the time value of the option. This is considered next.

Assessing time value

The time value of an option reflects the fact that it is highest for at-the-money options and also higher for an in-the-money option than an out-of-the-money option. This can be demonstrated by considering the hedge process followed by a market-maker in options. An out-of-the-money call option, for instance, presents the lowest probability of exercise for the market-maker; therefore he may not even hedge such a position. There is a risk, of course, that the price of the underlying asset will rise sufficiently to make the option in-the-money, in which case the market-maker would have to purchase the asset in the market, thereby suffering a loss. This must be considered by the market-maker, but deeply out-of-the-money options are often not hedged. So the risk to the market-maker is lowest for this type of option, which means that the time value is also lowest for such an option.

An in-the-money call option carries a greater probability that it will be exercised. A market-maker writing such an option will therefore hedge the position, either with the underlying asset, with futures contracts or via a *risk reversal*. This is a long or short position in a call that is reversed to the same position in a put by selling or buying the position forward (and vice versa). The risk with hedging using the underlying asset is if its price falls, causing the option not to be exercised and forcing the market-maker to dispose of the underlying at a loss. However, this risk is lowest for a deeply in-the-money option, and this is reflected in the time value for such options, which diminishes the more in-the-money the option is.

The highest risk lies in writing an at-the-money option. In fact, the majority of over-the-counter options are struck at-the-money. The risk level reflects the fact that there is greatest uncertainty with this option, because there is an even chance of it being exercised. The decision on whether to hedge is therefore not as straightforward. As an at-the-money option carries the greatest risk for the market-maker in terms of hedging it, the time value for it is the highest.

American options

In the previous chapter we discussed the B-S and other models in terms of European options, and also briefly referred to a model developed for American options on dividend-paying securities. In theory, an American option will have greater value than an equivalent European option, because of the early-exercise option. This added feature implies a higher value for the American option. In theory this is correct, but in practice it carries lower weight because American options are rarely exercised ahead of expiry. A holder of an American option must assess whether it is ever optimal to exercise it ahead of the expiry date, and usually the answer to this is 'no'. This is because, by exercising an option, the holder realizes only the intrinsic value of the option. However, if the option is traded in the market – that is, sold – then the full value will be realized, including the time value. Therefore it is rare for an American option to be exercised ahead of the expiry date; rather, it will be sold in the market to realize full value.

As the chief characteristic that differentiates American options from European options is rarely employed, in practical terms American options do not have greater value than European ones. Therefore they have similar values to equivalent European options. However, an option pricing model, calculating the probability that an option will be exercised, will determine under certain circumstances that the American option has a higher probability of being exercised and assign it a higher price.

Under certain circumstances it is optimal to exercise American options early. The most significant is when an option has negative time value. An option can have negative time value when, for instance, a European option is deeply in-the-money and very near to maturity. The time value will be small positive, however the potential value in deferring cash flows from the underlying asset may outweigh this, leading to a negative time value. The best example of this is for a deeply in-the-money option on a futures contract. By deferring exercise, the opportunity to invest the cash proceeds from the profit on the futures contract (remember, futures are cash settled daily via the margin process) is lost, and this is potential interest income foregone. In such circumstances, it would be optimal to exercise an option ahead of its maturity date, assuming it is an American one. Therefore when valuing an American option, the probability of it being exercised early is considered, and if it is deeply in-the-money this probability will be at its highest.

Measuring option risk: the Greeks

It is apparent from a reading of the previous chapter that the price sensitivity of options is different to that of other financial market instruments. This is clear from the variables that are required when pricing an option, which we presented by way of recap at the start of this chapter. The value of an option is sensitive to changes in one or any combination of the six variables that are used in the valuation.[1] This makes risk managing an option book more complex compared with other instruments. For example, the value of a swap is sensitive to one variable only, the swap rate. The relationship between the change in value of the swap and the change in the swap rate is also a linear one. A bond futures contract is priced as a function of the current spot price of the cheapest-to-deliver bond and the current money market repo rate. Options, on the other hand, react to moves in any of the

---

1. Of course, the strike price for a plain vanilla option is constant.

variables used in pricing them; more importantly the relationship between the value of the option and the change in a key variable is not a linear one. The market uses a measure for each of the variables, and in some cases for a derivative of these variables, which are termed the 'Greeks' as they are called after letters in the ancient Greek alphabet.[2] In this section we introduce these sensitivity measures and how they are used.

Delta

The *delta* of an option is a measure of how much the value or premium of the option changes with changes in the price of the underlying asset. That is:

$$\delta = \frac{\Delta C}{\Delta S}.$$

Mathematically the delta of an option is the partial derivative of the option premium with respect to the underlying, given by:

$$\delta = \frac{\partial C}{\partial S}$$

or   (18.1)

$$\partial = \frac{\partial P}{\partial S}.$$

In fact the delta of an option is given by the $N(d1)$ term in the B-S equation. It is closely related to but not equal to the probability that an option will be exercised. If an option has a delta of 0.6 or 60%, this means that a £100 increase in the value of the underlying asset will result in a £60 increase in the value of the option. Delta is probably the most important sensitivity measure for an option, because it measures the sensitivity of the option price to changes in the price of the underlying asset, and this is very important for option market-makers. It is also the main hedge measure. When an option market-maker wishes to hedge a sold option, he may do this by buying a matching option, by buying or selling another instrument with the same but opposite value as the sold option, or by buying or selling the underlying asset. If the hedge is put on with the underlying asset, the amount is governed by the delta. So, for instance, if the delta of an option written on one ordinary share is 0.6 and a trader writes 1,000 call options, the hedge would be a

....

2. All but one; the term for the volatility sensitivity measure, *vega*, is not a Greek letter. In certain cases one will come across the use of the term *kappa* to refer to volatility, and this is a Greek letter. However, it is more common for volatility to be referred to by the term vega.

long position in 600 of the underlying shares. This means that if the value if the shares rises by £1, the £600 rise in the value of the shares will offset the £600 loss in the option position. This is known as *delta hedging*. As we shall see later on, this is not a static situation; in addition, the fact that delta changes, and is also an approximation, means that hedges must be monitored and adjusted – so-called *dynamic hedging*.

The delta of an option measures the extent to which the option moves with the underlying asset price; at a delta of zero the option does not move with moves in the underlying asset, while at a delta of 1 it will behave identically to the underlying asset.

A positive delta position is equivalent to being long the underlying asset, and can be interpreted as a bullish position. A rise in the asset price results in profit, because in theory a market-maker could sell the underlying asset at a higher price, or in fact sell the option. The opposite is true if the price of the underlying asset falls. With a positive delta, a market-maker would be over-hedged if running a delta-neutral position. Table 18.1 shows the effect of changes in the underlying price on the delta position in the option book; to maintain a delta-neutral hedge, the market-maker must buy or sell delta units of the underlying asset, although in practice futures contracts may be used.

TABLE 18.1 ■ Delta-neutral hedging for changes in the underlying price

Option	Rise in underlying asset price	Fall in underlying asset price
Long call	Rise in delta: sell underlying	Fall in delta: buy underlying
Long put	Fall in delta: sell underlying	Rise in delta: buy underlying
Short call	Rise in delta: buy underlying	Fall in delta: sell underlying
Short put	Fall in delta: buy underlying	Rise in delta: sell underlying

Gamma

In a similar way that the modified duration measure becomes inaccurate for larger yield changes, due to the nature of its calculation, there is an element of inaccuracy with the delta measurement and with delta hedging an option book. This is because the delta itself is not static, and changes with changes in the price of the underlying. A book that is *delta neutral* at one level may not be so as the underlying price changes. To monitor this, option market-makers calculate *gamma*. The gamma of an option is a measure of how much the delta value changes with changes in the underlying price. It is given by:

$$\Gamma = \frac{\Delta\delta}{\Delta S}$$

Mathematically, gamma is the second partial derivative of the option price with respect to the underlying price, that is:

$$\frac{\partial^2 C}{\partial S^2} \quad \text{or} \quad \frac{\partial^2 P}{\partial S^2}$$

and is given by:

$$\Gamma = \frac{N(d_1)}{S\sigma\sqrt{T}}. \tag{18.2}$$

The delta of an option does not change rapidly when an option is deeply in-the-money or out-of-the-money, so that in these cases the gamma is not significant. However, when an option is close to or at-the-money, the delta can change very suddenly and at that point the gamma is very large. The value of gamma is positive for long call and put options, and negative for short call and put options. An option with high gamma causes the most problems for market-makers, since the delta hedge must be adjusted constantly, which will lead to high transaction costs. The higher the gamma, the greater is the risk that the option book is exposed to loss from sudden moves in the market. A negative gamma exposure is the highest risk, and this can be hedged only by putting on long positions in other options. A perfectly hedged book is gamma neutral, which means that the delta of the book does not change.

When gamma is positive, a rise in the price of the underlying asset will result in a higher delta. Adjusting the hedge will require selling the underlying asset or futures contracts. The reverse applies if there is a fall in the price of the underlying asset. As the hedge adjustment is made in the same direction in which the market is moving, this adjustment is possibly easier to conceptualize for newcomers to a market-making desk. When adjusting a hedge in a rising market, underlying assets or futures are sold, which in itself may generate profit. In a falling market, the delta hedge is insufficient and must be rebalanced through purchase of the underlying asset.

However, with a negative gamma, an increase in the price of the underlying asset will reduce the value of the delta, so therefore to adjust the delta hedge the market-maker must buy more of the underlying asset or futures equivalents. However, when the underlying asset price falls, the delta will rise, necessitating selling of the underlying asset to rebalance the hedge. In this scenario, irrespective of whether cash or off-balance sheet instruments are being used, the hedge involves selling assets in a falling market, which will generate losses even as the hedge is being put on. Negative gamma is, therefore, a high-risk exposure in a rising market. Managing an option book that has negative gamma is more risky if the underlying asset price volatility is high. In a rising market the market-maker becomes short and must purchase more of the underlying asset, which may produce losses. The same applies in a falling market. If the desk is pursuing a delta-neutral strategy, running a positive gamma position should enable generation of profit in volatile market conditions. Under the same scenario, a negative gamma position would be risky and would be excessively costly in terms of dynamically hedging the book.

Gamma is the only one of the major Greeks that does not measure the sensitivity of the option premium; instead, it measures the change in delta. The delta of an option is its hedge ratio, and gamma is a measure of how much this hedge ratio changes with changes in the price of the underlying assets. This is why a gamma value results in problems in hedging an option book, since the hedge ratio is always changing. This ties in with our earlier comment that at-the-money options have the highest value, because they present the greatest uncertainty and hence the highest risk. The relationship is illustrated by the behaviour of gamma, which follows that of the delta.

To adjust an option book so that it is gamma neutral, a market-maker must put on positions in an option on the underlying asset or on the future. This is because the gamma of the underlying asset and the future is zero. It is common for market-makers to use exchange-traded options. Therefore a book that needs to be made gamma neutral must be rebalanced with options; however, by adding to its option position, the book's delta will alter. Therefore to maintain the book as delta neutral, the market-maker will have to rebalance it using more of the underlying asset or futures contracts. The calculation made to adjust gamma is a snapshot in time, and since the gamma value changes dynamically with the market, the gamma hedge must be continually rebalanced, like the delta hedge, if the market-maker wishes to maintain the book as gamma neutral.

Theta

The *theta* of an option measures the extent of the change in value of an option with changes in the time to maturity. That is, it is:

$$\Theta = \frac{\Delta C}{\Delta T}$$

or

$$-\frac{\partial C}{\partial T} \text{ or } -\frac{\partial P}{\partial T}$$

and, from the formula for the B-S model, mathematically it is given for a call option as:

$$\Theta = -\frac{S\sigma}{2\sqrt{2\pi T}} e^{-\frac{d_1^2}{2}} - Xre^{-rT} N(d_2). \tag{18.3}$$

Theta is a measure of time decay for an option. A holder of a long option position suffers from time decay because, as the option approaches maturity, its value is made up increasingly of intrinsic value only, which may be zero as the option approaches expiry. For the writer of an option, the risk exposure is reduced as a result of time decay, so it is favourable for the writer if the theta is high. There is also a relationship between theta and gamma however; when an option gamma is high, its theta is also high, and this results in the option losing value more rapidly as it approaches maturity. Therefore a high theta option, while welcome to the writer, has a downside because it is also high gamma. There is therefore in practice no gain to be high theta for the writer of an option. The theta value impacts certain option strategies. For example, it is possible to write a short-dated option and simultaneously purchase a longer-dated option with the same strike price. This is a play on the option theta; if the trader believes that the time value of the longer-dated option will decay at a slower rate than the short-dated option, the trade will generate a profit.

Vega

The *vega* of an option measures how much its value changes with changes in the volatility of the underlying asset. It is also known as *epsilon* (ε), *eta* (η) or *kappa* (κ).

We define vega as:

$$v = \frac{\Delta C}{\Delta \sigma}$$

or

$$v = \frac{\partial C}{\partial \sigma} \quad \text{or} \quad \frac{\partial P}{\partial \sigma}$$

and mathematically from the B-S formula it is defined as (18.4) for a call or put:

$$v = \frac{S\sqrt{\dfrac{T}{2\pi}}}{e^{\frac{d_1^2}{2}}} . \qquad (18.4)$$

It may also be given by:

$$v = S\sqrt{\Delta T}N(d_1). \qquad (18.5)$$

An option exhibits its highest vega when it is at-the-money, and decreases as the underlying and strike prices diverge. Options with only a short time to expiry have a lower vega compared with longer-dated options. An option with positive vega generally has positive gamma. Vega is also positive for a position composed of long call and put options, and an increase in volatility will then increase the value of the options. A vega of 12.75 means that for a 1% increase in volatility, the price of the option will increase by 0.1275. Buying options is the equivalent of buying volatility, while selling options is equivalent to selling volatility. Market-makers generally like volatility and set up their books so that they are positive vega. The basic approach for volatility trades is that the market-maker will calculate the implied volatility inherent in an option price, and then assess whether this is accurate compared with his own estimation of volatility. Just as positive vega is long call and puts, if the trader feels the implied volatility in the options is too high, he will put on a short vega position of short calls and puts, and then reverse the position out when the volatility declines.

Table 18.2 shows the response to a delta hedge following a change in volatility.

TABLE 18.2 ■ Dynamic hedging as a result of changes in volatility

Option position	Rise in volatility	Fall in volatility
Long call		
ATM	No adjustment to delta	No adjustment to delta
ITM	Rise in delta, buy underlying	Rise in delta, sell underlying
OTM	Fall in delta, sell underlying	Fall in delta, buy underlying
Long put		
ATM	No adjustment to delta	No adjustment to delta
ITM	Fall in delta, sell underlying	Rise in delta, buy underlying
OTM	Rise in delta, buy underlying	Fall in delta, sell underlying
Short call		
ATM	No adjustment to delta	No adjustment to delta
ITM	Fall in delta, sell underlying	Rise in delta, buy underlying
OTM	Rise in delta, buy underlying	Fall in delta, sell underlying
Short put		
ATM	No adjustment to delta	No adjustment to delta
ITM	Rise in delta, buy underlying	Rise in delta, sell underlying
OTM	Fall in delta, sell underlying	Fall in delta, buy underlying

Managing an option book involves trade-offs between the gamma and the vega, much like there are between gamma and theta. A long in options means long vega and long gamma, which is not conceptually difficult to manage; however, if there is a fall in volatility levels, the market-maker can either maintain positive gamma, depending on his view of whether the fall in volatility can be offset by adjusting the gamma in the direction of the market, or he can sell volatility (that is, write options) and set up a position with negative gamma. In either case, the costs associated with rebalancing the delta must compensate for the reduction in volatility.

Rho

The *rho* of an option is a measure of how much its value changes with changes in interest rates. Mathematically this is:

$$\frac{\partial C}{\partial r} \quad \text{or} \quad \frac{\partial P}{\partial r}$$

and the formal definition, based on the B-S model formula, is given at (18.6) for a call option:

$$\rho = Xte^{-rT}N(d_2). \tag{18.6}$$

The level of rho tends to be higher for longer-dated options. It is probably the least used of the sensitivity measures because market interest rates are probably the least variable of all the parameters used in option pricing.

Lambda

The *lambda* of an option is similar to its delta in that it measures the change in option value for a change in underlying price. However, lambda measures this sensitivity as a percentage change in the price for a percentage change in the price of the underlying asset. Hence lambda measures the gearing or leverage of an option. This in turn gives an indication of expected profit or loss for changes in the price of the underlying asset. From Figure 18.1 we note that in-the-money options have a gearing of a minimum of five, and sometimes the level is considerably higher. This means that if the underlying asset was to rise in price, the holder of the long call could benefit by a minimum of five times more than if he had invested the same cash amount in the underlying asset instead of in the option.

This has been a brief review of the sensitivity measures used in managing option books. They are very useful to market-makers and portfolio managers because they enable them to see what the impact of changes in market rates is on an entire book. A market-maker need take only the weighted sum of the delta, gamma, vega and theta of all the options on the book to see the impact of changes on the portfolio. Therefore, the combined effect of changes can be calculated, without having to reprice all the options on the book. The Greeks are also important to risk managers and those implementing value-at-risk systems.

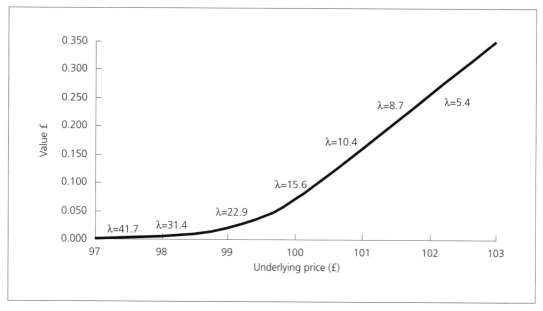

FIGURE 18.1 ■ Option lambda, nine-month bond option

The option smile

Our discussion of the behaviour and sensitivity of options prices will conclude with an introduction to the option *smile*. Market-makers calculate a measure known as the volatility smile, which is a graph that plots the implied volatility of an option as a function of its strike price. The general shape of the smile curve is given in Figure 18.2. What the smile tells us is that out-of-the-money and in-the-money options both tend to have higher implied volatilities than at-the-money options. We define an at-the-money option as one whose strike price is equal to the forward price of the underlying asset.

Under the B-S model assumptions, the implied volatility should be the same across all strike prices of options on the same underlying asset and with the same expiry date. However, implied volatility is usually observed in the market as a convex function of exercise price, shown in generalized form in Figure 18.2 (in practice, it is not a smooth line or even often a real smile). The observations confirm that market-makers price options with strikes that are less than *S*, and those with strikes higher than *S*, with higher volatilities than options with strikes equal to *S*. The existence of the volatility smile curve indicates that market-makers make more complex assumptions about the behaviour of asset prices than can be fully explained by the geometric Brownian motion model. As a result, market-makers attach different probabilities to terminal values of the underlying asset price than those that are consistent with a lognormal distribution.

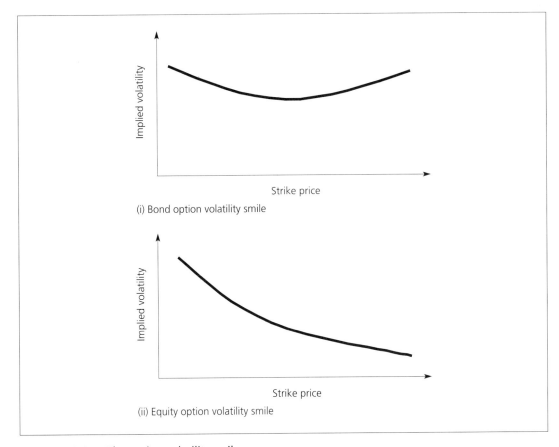

FIGURE 18.2 ■ The option volatility smile curve

The extent of the convexity of the smile curve indicates the degree to which the market price process differs from the lognormal function contained in the B-S model. In particular, the more convex the smile curve, the greater the probability the market attaches to extreme outcomes for the price of the asset on expiry, S_T. This is consistent with the observation that in reality asset price returns follow a distribution with 'fatter tails' than that described by the lognormal distribution. In addition, the direction in which the smile curve slopes reflects the skew of the price process function; a positively sloped implied volatility smile curve results in a price returns function that is more positively skewed than the lognormal distribution. The opposite applies for a negatively sloping curve. The existence of the smile suggests asset price behaviour that is more accurately described by non-standard price processes, such as the jump diffusion model, or a stochastic volatility, as opposed to constant volatility model.

Considerable research has gone into investigating the smile. The book references in this and the previous chapter are good starting points on this subject.

Caps and floors

Caps and *floors* are options on interest rates. They are commonly written on Libor or another interest rate such as euribor, the US prime rate or a commercial paper rate. In this section we review caps, which are essentially calls on an interest rate, while a floor is a put on an interest rate.

A cap is an option contract in which an upper limit is placed on the interest rate payable by the borrower on a cash loan. The limit is known as the *cap level*. The seller of the cap, which is the market-making bank, agrees to pay to the buyer the difference between the cap rate and the higher rate, should interest rates rise above the cap level. The buyer of the cap is long the option and will have paid the cap premium to the seller. Hence a cap is a call option on interest rates. The cash loan may have been taken out before the cap, or indeed with another counterparty, or the cap may have been set up alongside the loan as a form of interest rate risk management. If a cap is set up in conjunction with a cash loan, the notional amount of the cap will be equal to the amount of the loan. Caps can be fairly long-dated options, for example ten-year caps are not uncommon.

In a typical cap, the cap rate is measured alongside the indexed interest rate at the specified fixing dates. So during its life a cap may be fixed semi-manually with the six-month Libor rate. At the fixing date, if the index interest rate is below the cap level, no payment changes hands, and if there is a cash loan involved the borrower will pay the market interest rate on the loan. If the index rate is fixed above the cap level, the cap seller will pay the difference between the index interest rate and the cap level, calculated for the period of the fix (quarterly, semi-annually, etc.) on the notional amount of the cap. Individual contracts, that is each fixing, during the life of the cap are known as *caplets*. The interest payment on each caplet is given by:

$$Int = \frac{\max[r - rX, 0] \times (N/B) \times M}{1 + r(N/B)} \tag{18.7}$$

where

r is the interest rate fixing for the specified index
rX is the cap level
M is the notional amount of the cap
B is the day base (360 or 365)
N is the number of days in the interest period (days to the next rate fix).

Similarly to FRAs, any payment made is an up-front payment for the period covered, and so is discounted at the index rate level.

As a cap is a call option on a specified interest rate, the premium charged by a cap market-maker will be a function of the probability that the cap is exercised, based on the volatility of the forward interest rate. Caps are frequently priced using the Black 76 model.

The strike rate is the cap level, while the forward rate is used as the 'price' of the underlying. Using Black's model then, the option premium is given by:

$$C = \frac{\phi M}{1 + \phi rf} \times e^{-rT} \times [rfN(d_1) - rXN(d_2)] \qquad (18.8)$$

where

$$d_1 = \frac{\ln(rf/rX)}{\sigma_f\sqrt{T}} + \frac{\sigma_f}{2}\sqrt{T}$$

$$d_2 = d_1 - \sigma_f\sqrt{T}$$

and

rf is the forward rate for the relevant term (three-month, six-month, etc.)
ϕ is the rate fixing frequency, such as semi-annually or quarterly
σ_f is the forward rate volatility
T is the time period from the start of the cap to the caplet payment date.

Each caplet can be priced individually and the total premium payable on the cap is the sum of the caplet prices. The Black model assumes constant volatility, and so banks use later models to price products when this assumption is considered to be materially unrealistic.

A vanilla cap pricing calculator is part of the RATE application software included in this book.

In the same way as caps and caplets, a *floorlet* is essentially a put option on an interest rate, with a sequence of floorlets being known as a *floor*. This might be used, for example, by a lender of funds to limit the loss of income should interest rate levels fall. If a firm buys a call and sells a floor, this is known as buying a *collar* because the interest rate payable is bound on the upside at the cap level and on the downside at the floor level. It is possible to purchase a *zero-cost collar* where the premiums of the cap and floor elements are identical. This form of interest rate risk management is very popular with corporates.

SELECTED BIBLIOGRAPHY AND REFERENCES

Briys, E. *et al.*, *Options, Futures and Exotic Derivatives*, Wiley 1999.

Galitz, L., *Financial Engineering*, revised edition, FT Pitman 1995.

Hull, J., *Options, Futures and Other Derivatives*, 4th edition, Prentice Hall 2000.

Kolb, R., *Futures, Options and Swaps*, 3rd edition, Blackwell 2000.

Marshall, J., Bansal, V., *Financial Engineering*, New York Institute of Finance 1992.

Tucker, A., *Financial Futures, Options and Swaps*, West Publishing 1991.

CHAPTER 19

Credit derivatives

Introduction

Credit derivatives are a recent addition to the range of financial instruments used by banks and financial institutions. In 2000 the British Bankers Association estimated that the global credit derivatives market could be worth more than $1.5 trillion in notional outstanding by the end of 2002. The increase in credit derivative activity is related to the increased focus of investors on credit as an asset class in its own right.

Terminology and definitions in credit derivative contracts have been a discussion area over the last few years. The need for suitable 'credit derivatives definitions' have been considered by the International Swaps and Derivatives Association. The ISDA has released standard definitions to be used in the confirmations of individual credit derivative transactions. Although the definitions are in the context of a credit default product, we expect that as the market develops most credit derivative contracts will be based on standard ISDA definitions.

Credit derivative instruments

The most common credit derivatives include:

- credit default swaps
- total return swaps
- credit spread derivatives
- asset swaps
- credit-linked notes.

Credit derivative products are defined by reference to underlying reference assets, which include corporate bonds, bank loans, sovereign debt, Brady bonds and eurobonds. Credit derivatives are now used increasingly in structured transactions. For example, synthetic collateralized loan obligations (*see* Chapter 13) often use credit default swaps to transfer credit risk from the originator to the special purpose vehicle. Currently the most common products are credit default products and total return swaps. Credit derivative transactions involve both a protection buyer and a protection seller.

Banks currently act as either buyers or sellers of credit protection in a transaction. Insurance companies are also active in the credit derivatives market as sellers of credit protection.

Credit default swaps

Credit default swaps are flexible instruments which can be structured to the needs of the protection buyer. Default swaps involve the exchange of periodic payments (usually expressed as basis points multiplied by the notional amount of the swap) by the protection buyer for a contingent payment from the protection seller for losses (e.g. par minus recovery rate (R)) on a reference asset following a credit event.

The cash flows of a typical credit default swap are set out in Figure 19.1. The payout to the protection buyer is zero if there is no default, or in the event of a credit event such as default, par value less the recovery rate.

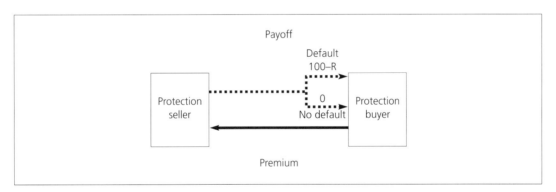

FIGURE 19.1 ■ Credit default swap

More complex default swap products can also be structured, for example a *first to default basket swap*. In this product the buyer makes periodic payments for a contingent default payment on the first default of a group of securities. A diagrammatic representation is shown in Figure 19.2

Total return swaps

A *total return swap* (TRS) is a derivative instrument that allows the protection buyer to swap the total economic return of an asset (for example, loans or securities) for fixed or floating interest payments. A typical TRS may have the following cash flows:

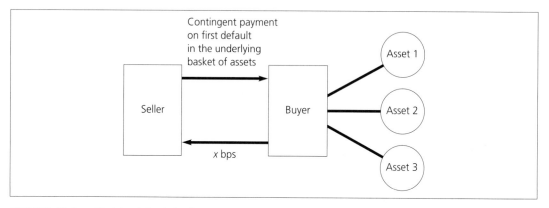

FIGURE 19.2 ■ First to default basket

Protection buyer payout:

■ coupons on the bond

■ positive return to the protection seller.

Protection seller payout:

■ Libor +/– spread

■ negative return to the protection buyer.

In the event of default, the protection buyer would be compensated for any loss in value as a result of a credit event affecting the market value of the reference asset. The total return swap allows the protection buyer to transfer economic exposure of the underlying asset to the protection seller.

EXAMPLE *19.1 Total Return Swap*

An investor enters into a TRS to obtain economic exposure to a five-year Ba1-rated corporate bond. The terms of the TRS are:

Reference asset	$200 million nominal value of 7% Ba1 corporate bond
Term of TRS	Six months
TRS payer	Bank
Floating payer	Investor
Six-month Libor fixing	6%
Spread	30 bps
Clean bond price at inception of contract	105
Clean bond price at termination of contract	108

What are the cash flows of the TRS?

Coupon	$200m × 0.07/2 =$7 million
Capital movement	(price at termination – price at inception) × nominal value = (108 – 105)/100 × $200 million = $6 million
Floating interest payment	Nominal × (Libor + spread) × fraction of year = $200m × (0.06 + 0.003) × 1/2= $6.3 million

Therefore the net cash flow to investor is: $7 million + $6 million – $6.3 million or $6.7 million.

We note that the return to the investor is influenced by the return on the underlying reference asset.

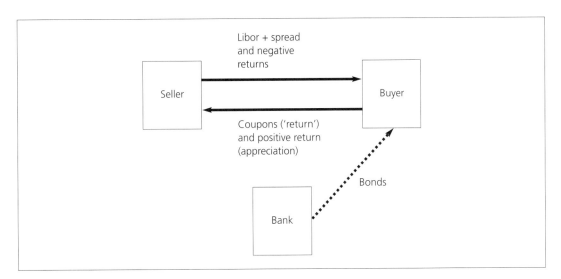

FIGURE 19.3 ■ Total return swap

Credit spread derivatives

Credit spread derivatives are forwards and options that reflect views on the credit spread movements of underlying credit assets. Therefore credit spread derivatives may be used to isolate the credit spread risk of reference assets.

Forward credit spread

Forward credit spreads are based on the risky forward rate less the risk-free forward rate. The forward credit spread can be estimated as the difference between the forward yield for a benchmark bond and the yield on the reference credit asset.

Spread forwards may be used by investors who wish to implement an investment strategy based on its view on movements in spreads.

EXAMPLE *19.2 Forward credit spread*

An investor has the view that credit spread on the corporate issue ABC plc maturing in 2008 will narrow from today's level of 80 bps (basis points) in six months. Therefore the investor enters into a six-month credit spread forward with the counterparty (for example, a bank) with strike level at the 80 bps level. The payout of the contract is structured so that:

- as the spread narrows the counterparty pays the investor a sum calculated as the nominal multiplied by (strike spread less final spread);
- as the spread widens the investor pays the counterparty a sum calculated as the nominal multiplied by (final spread less strike).

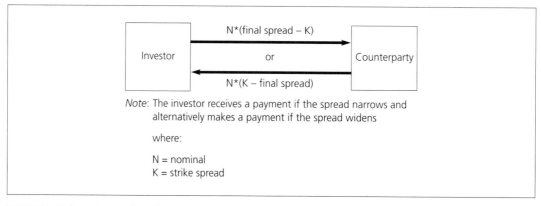

Note: The investor receives a payment if the spread narrows and alternatively makes a payment if the spread widens

where:

N = nominal
K = strike spread

FIGURE 19.4 ■ Forward credit spread

Credit spread options

Credit spread options are options whose payout is linked to the credit spread of the reference credit. This product can be used to manage the credit risk on corporate bond and corporate bond option positions. It isolates credit spread risk, which is an important factor in the underlying corporate bond pricing.

- *Call options*: The buyer has the right to buy the spread and benefits from the spread decreasing in value. The payoff is calculated as max (strike–spread,0). This option pays out if the spread tightens below the strike level; a tightening spread would result in an increasing bond price. Therefore the credit spread call option provides a payout should the underlying bond position increase in value due to credit spread tightening.

■ *Put options*: The buyer has the right to sell the spread and benefits from the spread increasing in value. The payoff is calculated as max (spread–strike,0). This option pays out if the spread widens above the strike level; a widening spread would result in a decreasing bond price. Therefore the credit spread put option provides a payout should the underlying bond position decrease in value due to credit spread widening.

The payoffs from credit spread derivatives may be multiplied by a leverage or duration factor to relate the spread changes to price changes of the underlying instrument. However in our examples we have ignored this factor.

EXAMPLE *19.3 Credit spread option*

An investor follows a strategy that involves going long of Latin American sovereign bond. The bond is currently yielding 350 bps over the benchmark US Treasury bond. If the sovereign bond falls in price then the investor will purchase it. The investor expects that the target price for the purchase should be when the spread is 400 bps.

In this case let us assume that the premium for a credit spread put option is 30 bps. The credit spread put option will be sold by the investor to the counterparty (for example a bank) with a strike level of 370 bps. The option will provide the following payout:

■ If the spread rises above 370 bps then the bank can put the bond to the investor at the strike level of 370 bps. The investor will pay out under the option in this case. For example, if the spread is 450 bps, then the payout under the option is 80 bps. Therefore the total cost is –80 + 30 bps = –50 bps. The cost of the bond position is therefore 50 bps. The effect in basis points is similar to the effect had the investor bought the bond at 400 bps and the price had moved to 450 bps. Alternatively, the investor may be able to purchase the bond of the counterparty at the strike rate.

■ If the spread is below 370 bps then the option expires. The investor has earned a premium of 30 bps multiplied by the nominal value of the contract; this can be used to buy the bond at a price below market value.

Asset swaps

Asset swaps enable an investor to hedge the interest rate risk of a fixed rate bond by swapping fixed cash flow into floating. The asset swap market is an important segment of the credit derivatives market since it explicitly sets out the price of credit as a spread over Libor.[1]

1. Asset swaps are used in debt capital markets. Although it is not a 'true' credit derivative instrument it is closely   associated with the credit derivatives market.

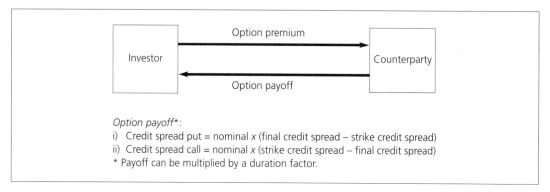

FIGURE 19.5 ▪ Credit spread option

Pricing a bond by reference to Libor is commonly used and the spread over Libor is a measure of credit risk in the cash flow of the underlying bond. Asset swaps can be thought of as a combination of a fixed rate bond and an interest rate swap. The swap is used to convert the fixed cash flows from the bond into floating cash flows. However, the spread to libor is usually chosen so that the asset swap package is priced at par.

An example would be that of an investor in a fixed rate risky bond who wishes to create a floating rate note (par) to increase the liquidity of the holding. By means of an asset swap, the investor will use an interest rate swap to repackage the fixed rate bond into the floating rate note which is priced at par. In the event of default, the interest rate swap cash flows will continue even if the underlying bond defaults, thus the investor retains the credit exposure to the fixed rate bond in an asset swap package.

Credit-linked notes

A credit-linked note (CLN) is a structured note that combines both a debt instrument and a credit derivative. The structured note includes an embedded credit derivative that isolates the credit risk of the reference asset; in this way an investor in this type of structured note may be able to transform its credit risk exposure. The investor in this note makes a cash investment in a bond-like instrument and receives a return that is related to the payout from the embedded derivative. Therefore the return from this cash investment in a CLN is dependent on the credit performance of an underlying reference asset. CLNs may be structured for investors who wish to gain exposure to various credit risks. CLNs allow investors to take a view on credit without directly buying or selling derivatives and without purchasing the underlying credits.

A variety of credit-linked structures may be created to suit the various risk/reward profiles of investors. For example, some CLNs may protect the principal amount, and credit events may only affect the interest cash flow from the CLN, whereas others may link the redemption of principal to the performance of reference credit instruments.

For example, if we have a CLN that pays out a reduced amount on the event of default of a reference asset then this CLN may be similar to a straightforward cash investment, plus the sale of a credit default swap (CDS). Then the return to this CLN investor may be:

■ 100 if there is no default; or

■ recovery rate (R) of the reference asset on default (that is, 100 received and (100 – R) paid).

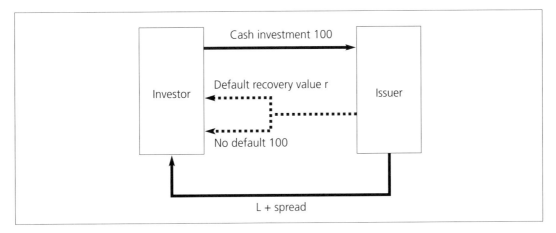

FIGURE 19.6 ■ Credit-linked note

In this way the investor in this CLN receives a credit-linked return and is compensated for the credit risk he has assumed by the increased returns from the CLN (that is, the embedded CDS premium which is paid to the investor in the CLN).

Pricing of credit derivatives

Introduction

The pricing of credit derivatives should aim to provide a 'fair value' for the credit derivative instrument. In the sections below we discuss and provide a brief overview of the pricing models currently proposed by the industry. The effective use of pricing models requires an understanding of the models' assumptions, the key pricing parameters and a clear understanding of the limitations of a pricing model. The pricing of credit derivatives has become more sophisticated and the developments in pricing of credit derivatives over the last few years have been significant.

TABLE 19.1 Credit derivative swap products

	Asset swaps	Total return swaps	Credit default swaps
Advantages	Allow the repackaging of fixed rate bonds into par bonds	Manage credit risk without selling the bond; this may be useful in managing economic and regulatory capital	Manage credit risk and both economic and regulatory capital
	Create synthetic exposure for time periods that are not present in the market	Gain economic returns without directly holding the security	Reduce exposure to default risks in a portfolio
	Transfer exposure to the credit risk of the underlying asset without sale of the bond	Provide access to credits that cannot be efficiently (e.g. tax reasons/regulatory) held by the investor	Used in structured products to synthetically transfer credit risk to a special purpose vehicle or counterparty
	Flexible instruments that transform the nature of cash flows of an underlying credit	Reference asset may include bonds, loans or a basket of bonds or loans	Reference asset may be selected from a range of securities (i.e. bonds and loans)
	Clearly price credit as a spread over Libor	Hedge the risk of assets that the investor does not wish to sell for tax reasons	Hedge the risk of assets that the investor does not wish to sell for tax or commercial reasons (e.g. the client relationship)
Disadvantages	Exposure to the credit risk of the underlying bond and the swap counterparty	Illiquidity: the liquidity is related to the liquidity of the underlying reference asset	Illiquidity: the liquidity is related to the liquidity of the underlying reference asset
	Pricing can be complicated by the existence of illiquid markets for the reference credit or structured notes	Require the development of an appropriate pricing model to capture the risks of the product and provide a fair value	Require the development of an appropriate pricing model to provide the fair value for exotic credit default swap products
	Documentation has to be carefully prepared – it should be clear and consistent with ISDA recommendations	Documentation has to be carefully prepared – it should be clear and consistent with ISDA recommendations	Documentation has to be carefully prepared – it should be clear and consistent with ISDA recommendations

Summary

Table 19.1 presents a summary of the main characteristics of credit derivative swap products.

Issues to consider when carrying out credit derivative pricing include:

■ implementation and selection of appropriate modelling techniques;

■ parameter estimation;

■ quality and quantity of data to support parameters and calibration;

■ calibration to market instruments for risky debt.

For credit derivative contracts in which the payout is on credit events other than default, the modelling of the credit evolutionary path is critical. If, however, a credit derivative contract does not pay out on intermediate stages between the current state and default then the important factor is the probability of default from the current state.

Pricing models

Pricing models for credit derivatives fall into the following classes: *structural* models, *transition* (migration) models and *reduced-form* models. We discuss these models below.

Structural models

Structural models are characterized by modelling the firm's value in order to provide the probability of a firm default. The Black-Scholes and Merton option pricing framework is the foundation of the structural model approach. The default event is assumed to occur when the firm's assets fall below the book value of the debt. Merton applied option pricing techniques to the valuation of corporate debt. By extension, the pricing of credit derivatives based on corporate debt may in some circumstances be treated as an option on debt (which is therefore analogous to an option on an option model).

Merton models have the following features:

■ default events occur predictably when a firm has insufficient assets to pay its debt;

■ firm's assets evolve randomly (the probability of a firm default is determined using the Black-Scholes-Merton option pricing theory).

Some practitioners argue that Merton models are more appropriate than reduced-form models when pricing default swaps on high-yield bonds, due to the higher correlation of high-yield bonds with the underlying equity of the issuer firm.

The constraint of structural models is that the behaviour of the value of assets and the parameters used to describe the process for the value of the firm's assets are not directly observable and the method does not consider the underlying market information for credit instruments.

Reduced-form models

Reduced-form models are a form of no-arbitrage model. These models can be fitted to the current term structure of risky bonds to generate no-arbitrage prices. In this way the pricing of credit derivatives using these models will be consistent with the market data on the credit risky bonds traded in the market. These models allow the default process to be separated from the asset value and are more commonly used to price credit derivatives.

Some key features of reduced-form models include:

- complete and arbitrage-free credit market conditions are assumed;
- recovery rate is an input into the pricing model;
- use of credit spread data to estimate the risk-neutral probabilities;
- use of transition probabilities from credit agencies can be accommodated in some of these models; the formation of the risk-neutral transition matrix from the historical transition matrix is a key step;
- default can take place randomly over time and the default probability can be determined using the risk-neutral transition matrix.

When implementing reduced-form models it is necessary to consider issues such as the illiquidity of underlying credit-risky assets. Liquidity is often assumed to be present when we develop pricing models. However in practice there may be problems when calibrating a model to illiquid positions, and in such cases the resulting pricing framework may be unstable and provide the user with spurious results. Another issue is the relevance of using historical credit transition data, used to project future credit migration probabilities. In practice, it is worthwhile reviewing the sensitivity of price to the historical credit transition data when using the models.

Examples of reduced-form models and migration models

Recent models that provide a detailed modelling of default risk include those presented by Jarrow, Lando and Turnbull (1997), Das and Tufano (1996) and Duffie and Singleton (1999).We consider these models in this section.

The Jarrow-Lando-Turnbull (JLT) model

This model focuses on modelling default and credit migration. Its data and assumptions include the use of:

■ a statistical rating transition matrix which is based on historic data;

■ risky bond prices from the market used in the calibration process;

■ a constant recovery rate assumption; the recovery amount is assumed to be received at the maturity of the bond;

■ a credit spread assumption for each rating level.

It also assumes no correlation between interest rates and credit rating migration.

The statistical transition matrix is adjusted by calibrating the expected risky bond values to the market values for risky bonds. The adjusted matrix is referred to as the risk-neutral transition matrix. The risk-neutral transition matrix is key to the pricing of several credit derivatives.

The JLT model allows the pricing of default swaps, because the risk-neutral transition matrix can be used to determine the probability of default. The JLT model is sensitive to the level of the recovery rate assumption and the statistical rating matrix. It has a number of advantages. Because the model is based on credit migration, it allows the pricing of derivatives for which the payout depends on such credit migration. In addition, the default probability can be explicitly determined and may be used in the pricing of credit default swaps.

The disadvantages of the model include the fact that it depends on the selected historical transition matrix. The applicability of this matrix to future periods needs to be considered carefully; whether, for example, it adequately describes future credit migration patterns. In addition, the model assumes all securities with the same credit rating have the same spread, which is restrictive. For this reason the spread levels chosen in the model are a key assumption in the pricing model. Finally, the constant recovery rate is another practical constraint, as in practice the level of recovery will vary.

The Das-Tufano model

The Das-Tufano (DT) model is an extension of the JLT model. The model aims to produce the risk-neutral transition matrix in a similar way to the JLT model, however this model uses stochastic recovery rates. The final risk-neutral transition matrix should be computed from the observable term structures. The stochastic recovery rates introduce more variability in the spread volatility. Spreads are a function of factors that may not only be dependent on the rating level of the credit, since in practice credit spreads may change even though credit ratings have not changed. Therefore to some extent the DT model introduces this additional variability into the risk-neutral transition matrix.

Various credit derivatives may be priced using this model; for example, credit default swaps, total return swaps and credit spread options. The pricing of these products requires the generation of the appropriate credit-dependent cash flows at each node on a lattice of possible outcomes. The fair value may be determined by discounting the probability-weighted cash flows. The probability of the outcomes would be determined by reference to the risk-neutral transition matrix.

The Duffie-Singleton model

The Duffie-Singleton modelling approach considers the three components of risk for a credit-risky product, namely the risk-free rate, the hazard rate and the recovery rate.

The *hazard rate* characterizes the instantaneous probability of default of the credit-risky underlying exposure. Since each of the components above may not be static over time, a pricing model may assume a process for each of these components of risk. The process may be implemented using a lattice approach for each component. The constraint on the lattice formation is that this lattice framework should agree to the market pricing of credit-risky debt.

Here we demonstrate that the credit spread is related to risk of default (as represented by the hazard rate) and the level of recovery of the bond. We assume that a zero-coupon risky bond maturing in a small time element Δt where

λ is the annualized hazard rate
φ is the recovery rate as a percentage of market value
r is the risk-free rate
s is the credit spread

and where its price P is given by:

$$P = e^{-r\Delta t}((1-\lambda\Delta t) + (\lambda\Delta t)\varphi) \tag{19.1}$$

Alternatively P may be expressed as:

$$P \cong e^{-\Delta t(r + \lambda(1 - \varphi))} \tag{19.2}$$

However as the usual form for a risky zero-coupon bond is:

$$P = e^{-\Delta t(r + s)} \tag{19.3}$$

we have shown that:

$$s \cong \lambda(1-\varphi) \tag{19.4}$$

This would imply that the credit spread is closely related to the hazard rate (that is, the likelihood of default) and the recovery rate.

This relationship between the credit spread, hazard rate and recovery rate is intuitively appealing. The credit spread is perceived to be the extra yield (or return) the investor requires for credit risk assumed. For example:

■ as the hazard rate (or instantaneous probability of default) rises then the credit spread increases;

■ as the recovery rate decreases the credit spread increases.

A hazard rate function may be determined from the term structure of credit. The hazard rate function has its foundation in statistics and may be linked to the instantaneous default probability.

The hazard rate function (λ(s)) can then be used to derive a probability function for the survival function S(t):

$$S(t) = \exp^{-\int_0^t \lambda(s)ds} \tag{19.5}$$

The hazard rate function may be determined by using the prices of risky bonds. The lattice for the evolution of the hazard rate should be consistent with the hazard rate function implied from market data. An issue when performing this calibration is the volume of relevant data available for the credit.

The *recovery rate* usually takes the form of the percentage of the par value of the security recovered by the investor. The key elements of the recovery rate include:

■ the level of the recovery rate;

■ the uncertainty of the recovery rate based on current conditions specific to the reference credit;

■ the time interval between default and the recovery value being realized.

Generally, recovery rates are related to the seniority of the debt. Therefore as the seniority of debt changes then the recovery value of the debt may change. In practice, the recovery rates actually achieved can exhibit significant volatility.

Credit spread modelling

Although spreads may be viewed as a function of default risk and recovery risk, spread models do not attempt to break down the spread into its default risk and recovery risk components.

The pricing of credit derivatives that pay out according to the level of the credit spread would require that the credit spread process is adequately modelled. In order to achieve this a stochastic process for the distribution of outcomes for the credit spread is an important consideration.

An example of the stochastic process for modelling credit spreads,[2] which may be assumed,[3] includes a mean-reverting process such as:

$$ds = k\,(\mu - s)dt + \sigma\,sdw \tag{19.6}$$

where

ds is the change in the value of the spread over an element of time (dt)
dt is the element of time over which the change in spread is modelled
s is the credit spread
k is the rate of mean reversion
μ is the mean level of the spread
dw is Weiner increment (sometimes written dW, dZ or dz)
σ is the volatility of the credit spread.

In this model when s rises above a mean level of the spread, the drift term ($\mu - s$) will become negative and the spread process will drift towards (revert) to the mean level. The rate of this drift towards the mean is dependent on k, the rate of mean reversion.

The pricing of a European spread option requires the distribution of the credit spread at the maturity (T) of the option. The choice of model affects the probability assigned to each outcome. The mean-reversion factor reflects the historic economic features over time of credit spreads, to revert to the average spreads after larger than expected movements away from the average spread.

Therefore the European option price may be reflected as:

$$E\left[e^{-rT}(\text{payoff}(s, X))\right] = e^{-rT}\int_0^\infty f(s, X)p(s)ds \tag{19.7}$$

where

X is the strike price of the spread option
$p(s)$ is the probability function of the credit spread
$E[\,]$ denotes the expected value
$f(s, X)$ is the payoff function at maturity of the credit spread.

More complex models for the credit spread process may take into account factors such as the term structure of credit and possible correlation between the spread process and the interest process.

---

2. For illustration and examples in this book.
3. In practice a lognormal process for credit spreads may be assumed to ensure positive credit spreads.

TABLE 19.2 ■ Comparison of valuation results

Expiry in six months Risk free rate = 10% Strike = 70 bps Credit spread = 60 bps Volatility = 20%	Mean-reversion model price	Standard Black- Scholes* price	% difference between standard Black-Scholes and mean-reversion model price
Mean level = 50 bps K = 0.2			
Put	0.4696	0.5524	17.63%
Call	10.9355	9.7663	11.97%
Mean level = 50 bps K = 0.3			
Put	0.3510	0.5524	57.79%
Call	11.2031	9.7663	14.12%
Mean level = 80 bps K = 0.2			
Put	0.8729	0.5524	58.02%
Call	8.4907	9.7663	15.02%
Mean level = 80 bps K =.3			
Put	0.8887	0.5524	60.87%
Call	7.5411	9.7663	29.51%

*The Black-Scholes price is only shown so that difference between the assumed underlying process and the impact on pricing is clearly seen. The Black-Scholes model is not used to price credit spread options in practice.

The pricing of a spread option is dependent on the underlying process. As an example, we compare the pricing results for a spread option model, including mean reversion, to the pricing results from a standard Black-Scholes model in Tables 19.2 and 19.3. These tables show the sensitivity on the pricing of a spread option to changes to the underlying process. Comparing Table 19.3 to Table 19.2 shows the impact of time to expiry increasing by six months. In a mean-reversion model the mean level and the rate of mean reversion are important parameters that may significantly affect the probability distribution of outcomes for the credit spread, and hence the price.

Credit default swaps

The pricing of a credit default swap that has a payout referenced to the debt obligations issued by company ABC plc involves the following key factors when pricing:

TABLE 19.3 ■ Comparison of valuation results (ii)

Expiry in 12 months Risk free rate = 10% Strike = 70 bps Credit spread = 60 bps Volatility = 20%	Mean-reversion model price	Standard Black- Scholes price	% difference between standard Black-Scholes and mean-reversion model price
Mean level = 50 bps K = 0.2			
Put	0.8501	1.4331	68.58%
Call	11.2952	10.4040	8.56%
Mean level = 50 bps K = 0.3			
Put	0.7624	1.4331	87.97%
Call	12.0504	10.4040	15.82%
Mean level = 80 bps K = 0.2			
Put	1.9876	1.4331	38.69%
Call	7.6776	10.4040	35.51%
Mean level = 80 bps K = 0.3			
Put	2.4198	1.4331	68.85%
Call	6.7290	10.4040	54.61%

■ risk-free interest rate term structure;

■ risky term structure: ideally we would determine this by considering the term of the bonds issued by company ABC; however, if a wide term is not available then the bonds of similar credit-risky companies may be used to create a more complete term structure of credit;

■ the recovery rate.

For the risk-free interest rate term structure, the observable money market and swap curve may be best choice; however, a risk-free interest term structure may also be built from government bond prices.

The CD-ROM in this book sets out examples of curve-building techniques, while Chapter 3 discusses how the discount function can be implied from the term structure of interest rates.

The risky term structure and the recovery rate can be used to estimate the risk-neutral probability of default:

$$rs_{risky} = rs_{riskfree}*[((1 - p)*1) + (p*R)] \tag{19.8}$$

where:

rs_{risky} is the risky zero-coupon rate (from the risky term structure)
$rs_{riskfree}$ is the risk-free zero-coupon rate (from the risk-free term structure)
p is the risk-neutral default probability
R is the recovery rate.

The unknown p can be implied out of equation (19.8):

$$p = [1/(1 - R)]*[1 - (rs_{risky}/rs_{riskfree})] \tag{19.9}$$

Equation (19.9) shows that the probability of default is related to the risky term structure, risk-free term structure and the recovery rate. In order to determine p we will make assumptions for a suitable recovery value to be used in the above equation.

The expected value of a single period credit swap may take the form of the expected payout:

$$CDS_1 = rs_{riskfree}*[(0*(1-p)) + (p*(1-R)] \tag{19.10}$$

This reflects the fact that there is no payout on survival of the credit; that is, in the event of no default.

Key issues in the pricing of credit default swaps include:

■ determining an appropriate assumption for the recovery rate;

■ selecting an appropriate risky debt required for calibration and the necessary adjustments to allow for liquidity and embedded options of the risky debt;

■ selecting an appropriate risk-free curve;

■ allowing for the credit risk of the counterparty and correlation of the underlying credit with the counterparty; we would expect that the cost of credit protection is cheaper if it is purchased from a 'high-risk' counterparty.

The level of sensitivity of the pricing of credit default swaps (for example, a one-period credit default swap pricing analysis) is examined in Table 19.4. The table compares the

TABLE 19.4 ■ Comparison of pricing outputs

	A	B	C	D
rs_{risky}	0.95	0.949	0.95	0.95
$rs_{riskfree}$	0.97	0.97	0.969	0.97
R	0.5	0.5	0.5	0.3
p	0.041237	0.043299	0.039216	0.029455
Credit default swap (CDS) price	0.02	0.021	0.019	0.02

pricing of a default swap based on the inputs in the table. The discussion below compares the pricing outputs and identifies sensitivities of the pricing to changes in the inputs.

'Pricing analysis'

Credit default swap price column A/column B = 0.02/0.021 = 0.952381

As a result of changing the risky zero-coupon price by approximately 0.1% (compare column A inputs to column B inputs) we have a CDS price change of approximately 5%. Clearly this shows the sensitivity of the CDS price to a change in the risky zero-coupon price. This emphasizes the risk in the estimates of the zero-coupon risky price and the impact of possible adjustments relating to illiquidity and embedded options.

Credit default swap price column A/column C = 0.02/0.019 = 1.052632

As a result of changing the risk-free zero-coupon price by approximately 0.1% (compare column A to column C) we have a CDS price change of approximately 5%. This shows the sensitivity of the CDS price to a change in the risk-free zero-coupon price; however, given the technology and existing research into yield curves, this is perhaps a smaller risk than (i).

Credit default swap price column A/column D = 0.02/0.02 = 1

The CDS pricing is relatively insensitive to the change in recovery price (column D's recovery is 0.3). However we note that the risk-neutral default probability (p) is sensitive to the change in the recovery price assumption. This shows that there is a compensating effect in the pricing of a CDS between the probability of default and the level of recovery for a given risky zero coupon price. However, care should be taken if the default payoff is fixed (for example, a digital swap) since then this compensating effect is removed.

Credit spread products

The forward credit spread

The forward credit spread can be determined by considering the spot prices for the risky security and risk-free benchmark security, while the forward yield can be derived from the forward price of these securities. The forward credit spread is the difference between the forward risky security yield and the forward yield on a risk-free security. The forward credit spread is calculated by using yields to the forward date and the yield to the maturity of the risky assets.

EXAMPLE *19.4 Determining the forward credit spread*

Current date	1 February 1998
Forward date	1 August 1998
Maturity	1 August 2006
Time period from current date to maturity	Eight years and six months
Time period from current date to forward date	Six months

Yield to forward date

Risk-free security	6.25%
Risky security	6.5%

Yield to maturity

Risk-free security	7.8%
Risky security	8.2%

Forward yields (calculated from inputs above; see below for detailed derivation)

Risk-free security	7.8976 %
Risky security	8.3071%

The details of the calculation of forward rates are as follows.

Risk-free security:

$$(1.0780)^{8^{6/12}} = ((1.0625)^{6/12}*(1 + rf_{riskfree})^8$$

where $rf_{riskfree}$ is the forward risk-free rate implied by the yields on a risk-free security. This equation implies that $rf_{riskfree}$ is 7.8976 %.

Similarly for the risky security we have:

$$(1.082)^{8^{6/12}} = ((1.065)^{6/12}*(1 + rf_{risky})^8$$

where rf_{risky} is the forward risky rate implied by the yields on a risky security. This equation implies that rf_{risky} is 8.3071%.

Therefore the forward credit spread is the difference between the forward rate implied by the risky security less the forward rate implied by the yields on a risk-free security. In the example above this is:

$$rf_{risky} - rf_{riskfree} = 8.3071 - 7.8976 = 0.4095\%$$

The current spread is equal to 8.20–7.80 = 0.40% = 40 bps.

The difference between the forward credit spread and the current spread is:

0.4095 – 0.40 = 0.0095% = 0.95 bps

The calculation of the forward credit spread is critical to the valuation of credit spread products, while the payoff of spread forwards is highly sensitive to the implied forward credit spread.

Credit spread options

First-generation pricing models for credit spread options may use models as described in the section on spread models. The key market parameters in a spread option model include the forward credit spread and the volatility of the credit spread.

The volatility of the credit spread is a difficult parameter to determine. It may be approached in different ways, including:

- the historical volatility of the difference between the reference asset yield and the yield on a risk-free benchmark;

- an estimation of the historical volatility by considering the components: historic volatility of the reference asset yield, historic volatility of the benchmark yield, correlation of the returns between the reference asset yield and the benchmark yield;

- by using the implied volatility of the reference asset yield, implied volatility of the benchmark yield and a suitable forward looking estimate of the correlation between the returns on the reference asset yield and benchmark asset yield.

If the model incorporates mean reversion then other key inputs will include the mean reversion level and the rate of mean reversion. These inputs cannot be observed directly and the choice should be supported by the model developers and constantly reviewed to ensure that they remain relevant. Other inputs include:

- the strike price
- the time to expiry
- the risk-free rate for discounting.

A key issue with credit spread options is ensuring that the pricing models used will calibrate to the market prices of credit-risky reference assets. The recovery of forward prices of the reference asset would be a constraint to the evolution of the credit spread. More complex spread models may allow for the correlation between the level of the credit spread and the interest rate level. The reduced-form models described earlier are a new generation of credit derivative pricing model which are now increasingly being used to price spread options.

Asset swaps

The value of an asset swap is the spread an investor pays over or under Libor in an asset swap package. This is based on the following components:

- the value of the coupons of the underlying asset compared to the market swap rate;

- the accrued interest and the clean price premium or discount compared to par value. Thus when pricing the asset swap it is necessary to compare the par value to the underlying bond price.

The spread above Libor reflects the credit spread difference between the bond and the swap rate.

The Bloomberg asset swap calculator pricing screen in Figure 19.7 shows these components in the analysis of the swapped spread details.

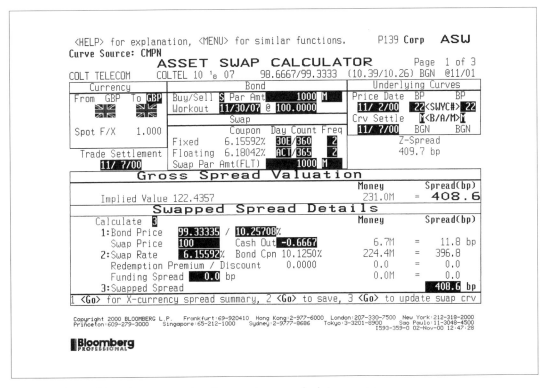

FIGURE 19.7 ■ Bloomberg example of an asset swap calculator screen

EXAMPLE   *19.5 Asset swap spread*

Let us assume that we have a credit-risky bond with the following details:

Currency	EUR
Issue date	31 March 2000
Maturity	31 March 2007
Coupon	5.5% per annum
Price (dirty)	98.3%
Price (clean)	97%
Yield	5%
Accrued interest	4.1%
Rating	A1

To buy this bond the investor would pay 98.3% of par value. The investor would receive the fixed coupons of 5.5% of par value. Let us assume that the swap rate is 5%. The investor in this bond wishes to asset swap the bond.

The asset swap price (that is, spread) on this bond has the following components:

■ The value of the excess value of the fixed coupons over the market swap rate. Let us assume that in this case this is approximately 0.5% when spread into payments over the life of the asset swap.

■ The difference between the bond price and par value is another factor in the pricing of an asset swap. In this case the price discount, which is expressed in present value terms, should be spread over the term of the swap and treated as a payment by the investor in the asset swap (if a dirty price is at a premium to the par value then the payment is made to the investor). For example, in this case let us assume that this results in a payment from the investor under the asset swap of approximately 0.23% when spread over the term of the swap.

These two elements result in a net spread of 0.5% + 0.23% = 0.73%. Therefore the asset swap would be quoted as Libor + 0.73% (or Libor + 73 bps).

Total return swap

The present value of the two legs of the TRS should be equivalent. This would imply that the level of the spread is therefore dependent on the following factors:

- the credit quality of the underlying asset;

- the credit quality of the TRS counterparty;

- capital costs and target profit margins;

- the funding costs of the TRS provider, who will hedge the swap by holding the position in the underlying asset.

The fair value for the TRS will be the value of the spread for which the present value of the Libor +/– spread leg equals the present value of the returns on the underlying reference asset. The present value of the returns on the underlying reference asset may be determined by evolving the underlying reference asset. The expected value of the TRS payoff at maturity should be discounted to the valuation date.

The reduced-form models described earlier are a new generation of credit derivative pricing models which are now increasingly being used to price total return swaps.

Appendix 19.1

Terms and definitions

Credit spread: The difference (in basis points) between the yield of a credit (reference) asset and that of a benchmark security such as a US Treasury or UK gilts. The credit spread is: yield of risky bond – yield on 'risk-free' bond.

Reference asset: A security or loan in a derivatives contract to which the cash flows in the contract are linked.

Protection buyer: This is the party purchasing or receiving protection from the credit risk of a reference asset.

Protection seller: This party takes on the credit risk of a position and is compensated by the protection buyer.

Recovery rate: The percentage of notional value of an asset that a creditor will be able to recover in the event of default.

SELECTED BIBLIOGRAPHY AND REFERENCES

Das, S., Tufano, P., 'Pricing credit sensitive debt when interest rates, credit ratings and credit spreads are stochastic', *Journal of Financial Engineering* 5, 1996, pp. 161–98.

Das, S., *Credit Derivatives and Credit-Linked Notes*, 2nd Edition, Wiley 2000.

Duffie, D., Singleton, K., 'Modelling term structure models of defaultable bonds', *Review of Financial Studies* 12, 1999, pp. 687–720.

Jarrow, R., Lando, D., Turnbull, S., 'A Markov model for the term structure of credit spreads', *Review of Financial Studies* 10, 1997, pp. 481–523.

Part V

Equity instrument analysis

In Part V we present an overview of the basic concepts in equity valuation and analysis. Analysis of the equity instrument is different to that of the debt instrument, for a number of fundamental reasons. These are touched on at the start of Chapter 20. We then discuss the basic concepts of the dividend valuation model and dividend growth model. Chapter 21 looks at fundamentals of ratio analysis and the cost of capital.

Introduction to equity instrument analysis

Equity instruments call for a different approach in their analysis compared with debt securities. This reflects the different nature of the asset. Compared with conventional bonds, shares do not pay a fixed cash flow during their life and do not have a fixed maturity date. Instead, the future cash flows of shares cannot be determined with certainty and must be assumed, and since they are in effect perpetual securities they have no redemption value. In addition, they represent a higher form of risk for their holders. The analysis and valuation of shares therefore calls for different techniques to that of bonds. Furthermore, the interests of shareholders and bondholders often sit at opposite ends of the risk spectrum. While a firm's bondholders are to some extent primarily concerned with financial probity and the maintenance (or upgrade) of the firm's credit rating, shareholders gain, at least in the short term, from high-risk and high-return strategies where favourable perceptions lead to a short-term rise in the share price.

In this chapter we present basic concepts in investment analysis for equities, beginning with the financial structure of the firm. We then consider the fair pricing of an equity and dividend policy. In the following chapter we introduce ratio analysis and basic concepts in assessing the cost of capital.

The financial structure of a firm, and company accounts

A corporate entity or *firm* is governed by the types of equity capital it can issue as stipulated in its *memorandum* and *articles of association*. In the past, in the UK market at least, firms would issue different classes of shares including 'A' shares that carried restricted voting rights. However this was not encouraged by the London Stock Exchange and the most common form of share in the market is the *ordinary share*, which is known as *common stock* in the US market. The holders of ordinary shares are entitled to certain privileges, including the right to vote in the running of the company, the right to dividend payments and the right to subscribe for further shares ahead of non-shareholders, in the event of a new issue. Dividends are payable only after liabilities to all other parties with a claim on the company – including bondholders – have been discharged. Shares are issued with a par value, but this has no relevance to their analysis and is frequently for a token amount such as £0.10 or £0.25. Firms also issue *preference shares* which are a type of hybrid between shares and bonds, but these are less common and we will ignore them in this chapter. An introduction to preference shares is given in Choudhry (2001).

We begin by considering the financial structure of the firm, which traditionally was of vital importance to shareholders. We say 'traditionally' because many of the accepted tenets of fundamental investment analysis were in effect ignored by investors during the so-called 'dot.com' bull market of the late 1990s. However, since then the various technology indices have been falling dramatically and it is perhaps a good time to reacquaint ourselves with the basic concepts.

We can consider the importance to shareholders of the financial structure of a firm by comparing the interests of shareholders with those of bondholders. Unlike shareholders, bondholders have a prior contractual claim on the firm. This means that as and when the contractual claim is covered, bondholders have no further interest in the firm. Put another way, as long as the firm is able to meet its contractual commitments, which are interest and principal payments owing to creditors, bondholders will be satisfied.[1] On the other hand, shareholders have what is known as a *residual* claim on the firm. As the owners of the firm, they will be concerned about the overall value of the firm and that this is being maximized. Hence they are (in theory) keenly concerned with the financial structure of their firm, as well as its long-term prospects.

We begin, therefore, with a review of company accounts. Firms are required by law to produce accounts, originally under the belief that owners should be kept informed about how the directors are managing the company. In the UK, for example, this is stipulated in section 226 of the Companies Act 1985, which updated previous versions of the Act.

The balance sheet

The balance sheet is a snapshot in time of the asset value of a company. We are familiar with the two sources of corporate financing in a developed economy: debt finance sourced from lenders, including banks, finance houses, and directly from the market through bond issues; and equity finance sourced from shareholders and retained profits. Put simply, once a corporate entity has repaid all its debt financing, remaining funds are the property of the shareholders. Hence we may state:

---

1. This is perhaps too simplistic; bondholders will also be concerned if any developments affect the *perceived* ability of the firm to meet its future liabilities, such as a change of credit rating. Such events will affect the value of the bonds issued by the firm, which is why they will be of concern to bondholders.

Assets – liabilities = shareholders' funds.

Again in simple terms, the valuation of one share in the company is a function of the total assets of the company less the liabilities. So, as a firm's assets decrease in value, shareholders will experience a decrease in their share value, while the opposite occurs if there is an increase in firm assets. This explains why a corporate balance sheet always balances.

A company balance sheet may be put together using one of three different approaches, namely *historic cost book value*, *current cost* or *market value*. Equity analysts' preference is for the market value basis, which records the value of assets and liabilities in the balance sheet using current market values. For liabilities this is relatively straightforward to undertake if the firm is listed on an exchange and there is a liquid market in its shares; the net value of the firm can be taken to be the difference between the market value of the firm's ordinary shares and the *book value* of the shares. The latter is the par value of the shares together with the share premium and accumulated retained earnings. It is more problematic to determine a market value for firm assets, however; for instance, what is the market value of two-year-old photocopying machines? In fact, the majority of incorporated institutions do not have their shares traded on an exchange and so a market value balance sheet is rarely released.

The most common balance sheet approach uses the historic cost book value approach, in which assets and liabilities are valued at their original cost, known as historic cost. The net worth of the company is calculated as the sum of the share capital and retained profits (reserves). It is rare to observe balance sheets presented using the current cost book value approach, which values assets at current replacement cost.

A hypothetical company balance sheet is shown in Table 20.1.

Note that the balance sheet orders assets and liabilities in terms of their maturity. Fixed assets are recorded first, followed by current assets less current liabilities. This value, the net current assets, indicates whether the company is able to cover its short-term liabilities with its current assets. The net current asset value is added to the fixed assets value, resulting in the value of the firm's assets less current liabilities. The balance sheet then records long-term liabilities, and these are then subtracted from the previous figure, showing the total value of the company once all liabilities have been discharged. This is also known as shareholders' funds, and would be distributed to them in the event that the firm was wound up at this point.

Shareholders' funds are represented by the capital and reserves entries. Share capital is the sum of the issued share par value and the share premium. These are defined as follows:

■ *Paid-up share capital*: the nominal value of the shares, which represents the total liabilities of the shareholders in the event of winding up, and which has been paid by shareholders.

■ *Share premium*: the difference between market value of the shares and the nominal or par value.

TABLE 20.1 ■ Hypothetical corporate balance sheet

Balance sheet as at 31 December 2001

	£m	£m
Fixed assets		675
Long-term investments		98
		773
Current assets		
Stock	365	
Debtors	523	
Cash	18	
	906	
Short-term liabilities		
Creditors	355	
Short-dated loans	109	
Bank overdraft	88	
Corporation tax	91	
Planned dividend	66	
	709	
Net current assets		197
Total assets less current liabilities		970
Liabilities falling due after 12 months		
Creditors	28	
Long-dated debt, bonds	400	(428)
Net assets		542
Share capital		
Ordinary shares issued		170
Preference shares		30
		200
Capital and reserves		
Paid-up capital	25	
Share premium	109	
Profit and loss account (reserves)	208	342
Shareholders' funds		542

Notes: Fixed assets include items such as factory buildings, property holdings, etc.
Short-term liabilities are those falling due within 12 months

The entry for 'profit and loss account' sometimes appears as *retained earnings*. This is the accumulated profit over the life of the company that has not been paid out as dividend to shareholders, but has been reinvested back into the company. The profit and loss account is part of the firm's reserves, and its calculation is arrived at via a separate financial statement.

The profit and loss account

The profit and loss account, also known as the *income statement*, shows the profit generated by a firm, separating out the amount paid to shareholders and that retained in the company. Hence the profit and loss account is also a statement of retained earnings. Unlike the balance sheet, which is a snapshot in time, the income statement is a rolling total of retained profit from the last accounting period to the current one. Generally this period is one year.

The calculation of the profit and loss account[2] is relatively straightforward, recording income less expenses. A firm's income is that generated from its business activities, and so excludes share capital or loan funding. The expenses are daily costs of running the business, and so exclude items such as plant and machinery, which are considered 'capital' expenditure and recorded as fixed assets in the balance sheet. Due to the different accounting conventions and bases in use, it is possible for two identical companies to produce very different profit and loss statements. This is a complex and vast subject, well outside of the scope of this book, and so we will not enter into it. A good overview of accounting principles in the context of corporate finance is given in Higson (1995).

A hypothetical profit and loss statement is shown in Table 20.2.

In the context of a profit and loss statement the *net profit* is the gross profit minus business operating expenses. This is an accurate measure of the profit that the firm's managers have generated. The more efficiently managers run the business, the lower its expenses will be, and correspondingly the higher the net profit will be. Tax expenses are outside the control of the firm's managers and so appear afterwards. *Extraordinary items* are deemed to be those generating income that are outside the ordinary business activities of the company, and expected to be one-off or rare occurrences. These might include the disposal of a subsidiary, for example.

Consolidated accounts

Consolidated accounts are produced when a company has one or more subsidiaries: the accounts of the individual undertakings are combined into a single consolidated account for shareholders. In the UK this is required under the Companies Act 1985, based on the belief

---

2. Strictly speaking, it is a profit *or* loss account, as the firm would have made one or the other in the accounting period.

TABLE 20.2 ▪ Hypothetical corporate profit and loss statement

	£m	£m	£m
Operating revenue	737		
Operating costs	(389)		
Gross operating profit		348	
Expenses			
Administration	(19)		
Sales	(67)		
Financial	(27)		
		(113)	
Net profit		235	
Taxation		(78)	
Profit on ordinary activities after tax		157	
Extraordinary items		–	
		157	
Dividends			30
Retained profit			127
Retained profit brought forward			81
Retained profit carried forward			208

that a company's business will be closely linked to that of any subsidiary that it owns, and therefore its shareholders require financial statements on the combined entity. At the same time, the subsidiaries also produce their balance sheet and profit and loss account.

Valuation of shares

In this section we present some fundamental concepts in equity valuation. The approaches described seek to determine a share's *fair value*, which would then be compared against its market value. We consider first dividend valuation methods and then the *expected earnings* method.

Dividend valuation model

We assume a corporate entity that pays an annual dividend. An investor thinking of purchasing a number of shares of this company, and holding them for one year, will expect to receive the annual dividend payment during the time he holds them, as well as the share proceeds on disposal. The fair value that the investor would be prepared to pay today for the shares is given by:

$$P_t = \frac{E(DV_{t+1})}{1+r} + \frac{E(P_{t+1})}{1+r} \tag{20.1}$$

where

P_t is the price of the shares at time t

r is the required rate of return

$E(DV_{t+1})$ is the expected annual dividend one year after t

$E(P_{t+1})$ is the expected price of the share one year after t.

The rate of return r may be related to the company's cost of capital plus a spread, or some other market-determined discount rate. The return generated by the shareholding is split between the income element, given by the dividend amount (DV_{t+1}), and the capital-gain element, given by $(P_{t+1} - P_t)$.

Following (20.1) we may say that:

$$E(P_{t+1}) = \frac{E(DV_{t+2})}{1+r} + \frac{E(P_{t+2})}{1+r} \tag{20.2}$$

and by using substitution and continuing for successive years we obtain:

$$P_0 = \sum_{t=1}^{T} \frac{E(DV_t)}{(1+r)^t} + \frac{E(P_T)}{(1+r)^T} \tag{20.3}$$

for the period beginning now (at $t = 0$) and where DV_t is the dividend per share in year t. If we extend T to the limiting factor as it becomes close to infinity, the share price element will disappear, and so (20.3) transforms to:

$$P_0 = \sum_{t=1}^{\infty} \frac{E(DV_t)}{(1+r)^t}. \tag{20.4}$$

Expression (20.4) is the dividend discount model and one can observe its similarity to the bond price/redemption yield expression straight away. However, the comparison of share and bond values using this method is fraught with complications, and so is rarely undertaken. This reflects problems with the approach. First, the model assumes a constant discount rate or cost of capital over time, which is unrealistic; for this reason the appropriate t-period zero-coupon interest rate is sometimes used as the discount rate, with a spread added to the government rate to reflect additional risk associated with holding the share. Other problems associated with the model include:

■ problems of divergence associated with the infinite time period implied by (20.4);

■ an expectation of infinite dividend payments.

These issues may be resolved in practice by introducing further assumptions, considered in the next section as part of corporate dividend policy.

Dividend growth model

Following the dividend valuation model, let us assume a constant growth rate in dividend payments given by c. The dividend valuation model is then given by:

$$P_0 = \sum_{t=0}^{\infty} \frac{DV_t}{(1 + r)^t} = \sum_{t=0}^{\infty} \frac{DV_0(1 + c)^t}{(1 + r)^t}.$$ (20.5)

Assuming further that $r > c$, then it can be shown[3] that the sum of this infinite series is given by:

$$P_0 = \frac{DV_1}{r - c}.$$ (20.6)

What (20.6) states is that, under a constant dividend growth rate c that is less than the required rate of return r, the value of a company's share is the year 1 dividend divided by the dividend yield of $r - c$, which itself is the required rate of return minus the dividend growth rate.

We can rearrange (20.6) to give:

$$r = \frac{DV_1}{P_0} + c$$ (20.7)

which states that the share's fair value is the dividend yield together with the expected dividend growth rate. The expression at (20.7) is known as the Gordon growth model after its first presentation in Gordon (1962).

Expected earnings valuation model

In the expected earnings model, again the cash flow stream of the expected earnings are discounted at the required rate of return or market-determined discount rate r. To ensure consistency, the values given by the earnings model and the dividend model must be identical. This is achieved by using what are known as *economic earnings* rather than reported earnings when undertaking the valuation. Economic earnings of a share are defined as the maximum quantity of resources that may be withdrawn from the share and consumed before the share becomes unable to provide real consumption at a future date.

---

3. For instance, see the appendix in Chapter 5 of Higson (1995).

A *cash flow statement* is used to convert reported earnings into economic earnings. Put simply for sources this is:

Reported earnings + new external funds = total sources

while for uses this is:

Dividends + net investment = total uses

The relationship just given describes a *net* cash flow statement. If stated per share issued, the cash flow statement is given by:

$$y_t + F_t \equiv DV_t + x_t \qquad (20.8)$$

where

y_t is the reported earnings per share in year t
F_t are the new external funds per share in year t
DV_t is the dividend per share in year t
x_t is the net investment per share in year t.

The relationship at (20.8) illustrates that if the firm raises new external finance, so that $F_t \neq 0$, a company can make the decision to proceed with new investment independently of the funding decision. However, if all the new investment in the company is sourced from retained earnings, an increase in dividends will decrease net investment, which will then reduce the company's ability to generate further real income in the future. By reinvesting a portion of its earnings and guaranteeing financial health, a company's retained earnings do not represent genuine economic income that is available to shareholders. From this reasoning, economic earnings per share are defined as:

$$y_t + F_t - x_t$$

where

$$\sum_{t=1}^{\infty} F_t/(1 + r)^t = 0 \qquad (20.9)$$

We therefore reason that the present value of externally sourced funds must be equal to zero, and as we assume this funding to be debt, all its debt is required to be repaid during the life of the company.

Therefore we say that:

Economic earnings = reported earnings + new external funds – net investment.

From this relationship and the expression above, we can value shares on the basis of economic earnings using the expression at (20.10):

$$P_0 = \sum_{t=0}^{\infty} \frac{E(y_t + F_t - x_t)}{(1 + r)^t} = \sum_{t=0}^{\infty} \frac{E(y_t - x_t)}{(1 + r)^t}. \qquad (20.10)$$

Identical valuations will be produced irrespective of the method used. This would be expected from no-arbitrage principles, but also because, as (20.8) shows, the value of dividends would be equal to that of economic earnings.

Dividend policy

Some companies have never paid a dividend, a well-known example being Microsoft. However, dividends analysis and dividend policy are fundamental tenets of corporate finance theory and so for this reason we consider it briefly here.

Classical finance writing such as Modigliani and Miller (1961) holds that a firm's dividend policy will not impact its valuation. The relationship at (20.8) would suggest that if a company can raise funds externally, its dividend policy will not affect its value. In theory and in practice, though, it can be shown to have some impact. Consider the dividend valuation model: under its approach a firm that did not pay dividends, generating return for its shareholders purely in the form of capital gain, would have a share value of zero. This is seen immediately by entering the DV_t value as zero. This is clear because under this model the entire value of the share would be contained at the infinity time point, which results in a present value of zero. So the conventional analysis states that the value of a share derives from its ability to cover dividend payments.[4] If no dividends are currently being paid, in order for shareholders to realize its value the firm will eventually have to pay dividends.

In practice the dividend policy adopted by a firm is analyzed for its supposed information content. We summarize here the three conventional explanations why a firm might pay dividends.

Signalling policy

This explanation was first presented by Ross (1976). It suggests that dividend announcements are signals to the market of a company's intentions. As managers are privy to inside information on the true financial health of a company, it is logical for managers to signal this state of affairs by means of the dividend. So a company in good health might announce a dividend increase over last year's level. This would be a 'good' signal. However, an increased dividend might also be a ruse by managers wishing to conceal the

4. As we noted, some well-known companies have never paid a dividend and have exhibited spectacular share price gains during their life; witness also the extraordinary bull run in 'dot.com' companies and the technology sector generally during the second half of the 1990s. However, as there is as yet no formal model explaining this price behaviour, we confine ourselves to a review of the traditional approach.

fact that their company is in parlous health. This is termed as 'false' good signal. The occurrence of false signals can be prevented by incentivizing managers in an appropriate way, so that the penalty for sending false good signals is severe enough to prevent such signals, and leads instead to a true 'bad' signal being sent instead. A bad signal would be an unchanged dividend or a reduction in the dividend. For this to be effective, signals also must be correlated with actual corporate performance, such that bad signals are associated with future insolvency. In this scenario a company that sent out false good signals would be faced with a greater chance of going bankrupt compared with if it had sent out a true bad signal. If these conditions exist, dividend levels and changes in these levels can be viewed as possessing significant information content on the state of the firm.

Principal-agent concern

This was presented by Rozeff (1977). Although shareholders are the owners of a firm, in practice they delegate the daily running of the firm to managers who run the company on the shareholders' behalf. Thus the shareholders are principals while the managers are agents. The interests of the two may conflict however, leading to managers acting in ways that do not maximize shareholder value, while being in their own short-term interest. To guard against this, the owners undertake monitoring that has attendant *agency costs*. Such costs are minimized when funds are raised externally, because outside investors subject the firm to considerable inspection and scrutiny whenever this occurs. At the same time, there are costs incurred when raising funds in such a way. In this scenario then, the payment of an annual dividend is viewed as a trade-off between agency costs and the costs of flotation. If dividends are at higher levels, externally sourced funds will have to be raised on a more frequent basis and the average cost of so doing is raised as well. However, the average agency costs decrease in this environment. So the 'optimum' dividend level for any company is that which minimizes the sum of the two different costs.

Tax clientele effect

This was first presented by Modigliani and Miller (1961). A dividend policy might be used by a firm to dictate which class of investor ends up buying a company's shares. So investors liable to the top rate of tax will prefer to hold shares of low-dividend-paying companies, while investors with low or zero marginal tax rates will prefer to hold the shares of high-dividend-paying companies. Therefore if a company wishes particular classes of investor to hold its shares, it can tailor its dividend policy to effect this.

Under the supposed new paradigm, dividends are viewed as important to traditional 'bricks and mortar' companies, and considered unfashionable for, say, technology companies. It is too early to state with certainty whether there has been such a paradigm shift, and so we conclude for the moment that a dividend policy is important and firms are likely to adopt one of the policies we have summarized here.

SELECTED BIBLIOGRAPHY AND REFERENCES

Choudhry, M., *The Bond and Money Markets: Strategy, Trading, Analysis*, Butterworth-Heinemann 2001, Chapter 23.

Gordon, M., *The Investment, Financing and Valuation of the Corporation*, Irwin 1962.

Higson, C., *Business Finance*, 2nd edition, Butterworths 1995.

Mills, R., Robertson, J., *Fundamentals of Managerial Accounting and Finance*, Mars Business Associates 1995.

Modigliani, F., Miller, M., 'Dividend policy, growth and the valuation of shares', *Journal of Business* 34, 1961, pp. 411–33.

Ross, S., 'The arbitrage theory of capital pricing', *Journal of Economic Theory*, December 1976, pp. 343–62

Rozeff, M., 'The dividend discount model', *Journal of Portfolio Management*, Winter 1977.

Sharpe, W., Alexander G., Bailey, J., *Investments*, Prentice Hall 1995.

Van Horne, J., *Financial Management and Policy*, 10th edition, Prentice Hall 1995.

Introduction to financial ratio analysis

The second chapter in our brief look at equity analysis considers some key concepts in finance, followed by an introduction to financial ratio analysis.

Key concepts in finance

The cornerstone of financial theory is the concept of the time value of money, which we introduced early in the book. This principle underpins discounted cash flow analysis, which is long established as a key element in financial analysis. The academic foundation of the *present value rule* as a corporate finance project appraisal technique is the Fisher-Hirshleifer model, generally quoted as first being presented by Fisher (1930) and Hirshleifer (1958). The present value rule established that in order to maximize shareholder wealth, a firm would be on safe ground accepting all projects with a positive net present value. The milestones in finance that followed this landmark are generally cited as being the *efficient market hypothesis*, *portfolio theory* and the *capital asset pricing model* (CAPM). Without going into the mathematics and derivation, we briefly introduce these topics in this section.

The efficient market hypothesis is attributed to Fama (1965). Its primary message is that it is not possible to outperform the market. Investors who find they beat the market in the short term will not be able to sustain this over time because information reaches the market very quickly and other investors will react to this information immediately. This reaction to buy or sell assets will in turn impact share prices so that shares rapidly become fully valued; after this only unexpected events will influence these prices. These events may have either a negative or positive impact on share prices, so that it becomes impossible to discern a clear trend in the movement of prices.

The key aspects of the efficient markets hypothesis are that:

■ the current price of a stock reflects all that is known about the stock and the issuing company, as well as relevant market and economic information;

■ if we accept market efficiency, share prices can be accepted to be fair value, and – given all *publicly available* information – neither under nor over-valued;

- it is not possible for an investor to beat the market, unless he is privy to information ahead of the market;

- only unpredictable relevant news can cause share prices to change, and all previously released news has already been incorporated into the share price;

- since unpredictable news is, by its nature, unpredictable, changes in share prices are also unpredictable and follow what is known as a *random walk*.

The key assumptions underlying the efficient market hypothesis are that investors are rational operators, and that being rational they will undertake dealing only on the receipt of new information, and not using intuition. The assumption of rationality later gave rise to the CAPM.

Portfolio theory was first presented by Markowitz (1959), and suggests that an investor who diversifies will achieve superior returns compared with one who does not. It also follows naturally from the efficient market hypothesis; since it is not possible to outperform the market, the most logical investment decision would be to hold the market itself in the form of a basket of shares that represent the entire market. The two main assumptions of the theory are that:

- investment appraisal risk is given by the amount of variation in the returns over time;
- the overall risk level may be reduced if the assets are combined into a portfolio.

The CAPM was developed from portfolio theory, and assumes that rational investors require a premium when holding risk-bearing assets. The model defines the risk premium of an individual share in relation to the market, and can be used as a project appraisal tool. The risk premium is measured by quantifying the volatility of an individual share in relation to the market as a whole, by means of the share's *beta*. Assuming that markets absorb all relevant information efficiently, share prices will react to information rapidly, and their adjusted price will then fully reflect all information received to date, as well as all expectations of the company's future prospects. Individual shares are more or less risky than the average of the market as a whole, and this is captured by its beta. Regression techniques are commonly used to measure beta, using historical share price data. For example, the London Business School's *Risk Measurement Service* uses monthly share price movements of the previous five years to estimate beta values for liquid securities.

The CAPM is attributed to Sharpe (1964) and it states that:

- the return on a risk-bearing asset is the sum of the *risk-free* interest rate together with a risk *premium*, which is a multiple of the beta and the premium of the market itself;

- the constituents of share prices include their perceived risk-bearing level, and discounts built into them explain the higher returns achieved by certain investors;

- a portfolio of shares with high volatility will have a lower price for a specified return, so in order to generate higher returns, investors must accept higher risk.

An overview discussion of the CAPM is given in Appendix 21.1.

Under the CAPM the market itself has a beta value of 1. An individual share exhibiting price movements identical to the market therefore also has a beta of 1. A share that was three times as volatile as the market[1] would have a beta of 3.

A good practical example in the application and use of beta is in regard to the South African gold market. Gold mining companies can have significantly different production costs. In the late 1980s and early 1990s a number of gold companies had production costs of over $400 per ounce. At current gold prices that would make those mines unprofitable, and some mines have in fact closed. All the mines that operate today do so at a much reduced cost per ounce.

For example, with a gold price hovering around $270 per ounce, a mining company (Company A) which is able to produce gold at $240 per ounce will make a profit of $30 per ounce. But a company (Company B) that is able to run at a lower cost of, say, $170 would in turn make a $100 profit per ounce. If the gold price were to increase by $20 that would increase Company A's profit by $20 or 67%. On the other hand, Company B's profit per ounce would increase by only 20%. This makes Company A much more sensitive or 'marginal' to movements in the gold price. In this case, Company A would have a higher beta against gold than Company B.[2]

The beta is the covariance of the securities return against the return of the market index (in our case gold), divided by the variance of the market index, or:

$$\beta = \frac{Cov(r_s, r_m)}{Var(r_m)}. \tag{21.1}$$

To provide a practical working example we calculated the beta of Roodepoort Deep over the period August 1998 to February 2001. As a comparison we also calculated the beta of Anglo Gold. The Anglo group of companies is the world's largest gold producer and Anglo Gold Ltd has historically had a lower cost of production. Although the calculation is simple, the method used to determine the return on the security or market could change the beta. To conceal any daily random movements we decided to use a 20-day moving average. It turns out that whether using the daily return or a 20-day moving average, the beta of Roodepoort Deep is approximately 1.5 times the beta of Anglo Gold.

This beta measure can be dependent on factors other than a mine's margin. Offshore mining will give rise to higher or lower currency exposure and therefore a different

---

1. So that if the market rose by 10% the share price would rise by 30%, and a fall in the market of 10% would equally observe a fall in the share price of 30%.
2. This is discussed in the South African *Business Times,* in an article published in August 1998 entitled 'Gold fever hits Durban Roodepoort Deep at last'. It says: 'Where a mine operates right at the margin and often at a loss, an uptick in gold leads to big jumps in profitability.'

return, and diversification in mining activities, for example base and ferrous metals, would have an effect. To a certain extent, a company can even manage its own beta through effective treasury management. Companies that trade in gold forwards and options stand a much better chance of managing their beta in a way that suits management's and share-holders' objectives.

A critique of the CAPM and review of its strengths and weaknesses is outside the scope of this book. Comments about the effectiveness of beta as a measure of risk later led to the development of *arbitrage pricing theory* (APT), first presented by Ross (1976). This states that:

- two assets possessing identical risk exposures must offer investors identical returns, otherwise an arbitrage opportunity will arise;

- the various elements of market risk can be measured in terms of a number of economic factors, including inflation levels, interest rates, production figures and so on, which influence all share prices;

- by using regression techniques it is possible to calculate an estimate of the impact of each of these economic factors on the overall level of risk.

There have been a number of criticisms of both the CAPM and APT,[3] and the valuation of companies that have yet to make a profit illustrates how analysts can no longer apply the traditional techniques to all companies. Essentially, the CAPM and APT assume that the past is a good representation of the future, which may be unrealistic for companies that have undergone or which are undergoing significant changes, or which operate in rapidly changing or developing industries. As beta is measured by a regression of past returns over a relatively long period of time, any impact on the level of beta will be felt only slowly. Hence the historical beta of a company that has, say, changed its view on risk exposure will not be a reliable estimate of its future beta. Finally, it is difficult to use either method for firms that no have publicly traded shares, or for divisions within companies. However, generally both the CAPM and APT and the efficient market hypothesis are still considered because no alternative models have been presented, which explains why these approaches are still used in the markets.

Ratio analysis

Ratio analysis is used heavily in financial analysis. In this section we present a review of the general application of ratio analysis and its use in peer group analysis.

---

3. Most significantly, in Fama and French (1992). However, see Roll and Ross (1992) for an argument that the CAPM and APT can still be applied.

Overview of ratio analysis

A number of performance measures are used as management information in the financial analysis of corporations. Generally they may be calculated from published accounts. The following key indicators are used by most listed companies to monitor their performance:

▪ return on capital employed;

▪ profit on sales;

▪ sales multiple on capital employed;

▪ sales multiple of fixed assets;

▪ sales per employee;

▪ profit per employee.

These indicators are all related and it is possible to measure the impact of an improvement in one of them on the others. Return on capital employed (ROCE) is defined in a number of ways, the two most common being return on net assets (RONA) and return on

TABLE 21.1 ▪ Constructa plc balance sheet for the year ended 31 December 2000

	Notes	2000	1999	1998
		£m	£m	£m
Fixed assets		97.9	88.2	79.4
Current assets				
Stock		80.6	67.3	65.4
Debtors	(2)	44.3	40.5	39.6
Cash		2.4	2.7	1.4
		127.3	110.5	106.4
Creditors: amounts due within one year	(3)	104.8	85.8	70.0
Net current assets		22.5	24.7	36.4
Total assets less current liabilities		120.4	112.9	115.8
Creditors: amounts due after one year	(3)	31.4	36.9	35.5
		89.0	76.0	80.3
Capital and reserves				
Paid-up share capital	(4)	15.0	15.0	15.0
Share premium account		45.5	37.2	46.1
Profit and loss account		28.5	23.8	19.2
Shareholders' funds		89.0	76.0	80.3

equity (ROE). RONA measures the overall return on capital irrespective of the long-term source of that capital, while ROE measures return on shareholders' funds only, thereby ignoring interest payments to providers of debt capital. Focusing on RONA, which gives an indication of the return generated from net assets (that is, fixed assets and current assets minus current liabilities), analysts frequently split this into return on sales and sales multiples. Such measures are commonly calculated for quoted and unquoted companies, and are used in the comparison of performance between different companies.

We illustrate the calculation and use of these ratios in the next section.

Using ratio analysis

In Tables 21.1 and 21.2 we show the published accounts for a fictitious manufacturing company, Constructa plc. These are the balance sheet and profit and loss account. From the information in the accounts we are able to calculate the RONA, return on sales and sales multiples ratios, shown in Table 21.4.

TABLE 21.2 ■ Constructa plc profit and loss account for the year ended 31 December 2000

	Notes	2000 £m	1999 £m	1998 £m
Turnover		251.6	233.7	211.0
Cost of sales		118.2	109.3	88.7
Gross profit		133.4	124.4	122.3
Operating expenses		109.0	102.7	87.9
Operating profit		24.4	21.7	34.4
Interest payable	(1)	7.6	6.2	7.1
Profit before tax		16.8	15.5	27.3
Tax liability		5.04	4.65	8.19
Shareholders' profit		11.8	10.9	19.1
Dividends		7.1	6.2	8.5
Reserves		4.7	4.6	10.6
Earnings per share		7.87	7.27	12.7

TABLE 21.3 ■ Constructa plc: notes to the accounts

	2000 £m	1999 £m	1998 £m
(1) Interest payable			
Bank loans and short-term loans	5.8	4.1	5.4
Hire purchase	1.0	1.0	1.0
Leases and other loans	0.8	1.1	0.7
	7.6	6.2	7.1
(2) Debtors			
Trade debtors	34.3	31.8	32.1
Other debtors	10	8.7	7.5
	44.3	40.5	39.6
(3) Creditors: amounts due within one year			
Bank loans	31.7	26	21.1
Bond	7	7	7
Trade creditors	30.6	28.4	19.4
Tax and national insurance	10.8	6.8	3.8
Leases	3.5	2.6	11.7
Other creditors	8.9	4.1	1.4
Accruals	6.8	5.8	1.6
Dividend	5.5	5.1	4
	104.8	85.8	70.0
(3) Creditors: amounts due after one year			
Bank loans	12.1	11.8	10.2
Bond	7	7	7
Leases	8.9	9.4	9.1
Other creditors	3.4	8.7	9.2
	31.4	36.9	35.5

(4) Paid-up share capital
10p ordinary shares, 150 million

From Table 21.4 we see that Constructa's RONA measure was 20.3% in 2000; however on its own this figure is meaningless. To gauge the relative importance of this measure we would have to compare it to previous years' figures, to see if any trend was visible. Other useful comparisons would be to the same measure for Constructa's competitor companies, as well as industry sector averages. From the information available here, it is possible only to make a historical comparison. We see that the measure has fallen considerably from the 29.7% figure in 1998, but that the most recent year has improved from the year before. The sales margin shows exactly the same pattern; however, the sales generation figure has not decreased. During a period of falling return such as this, which is

TABLE 21.4 ■ Constructa plc RONA ratio measures

Ratio	Calculation	2000	1999	1998
RONA %	(3) / (5) × 100	20.3%	19.2%	29.7%
Return on sales %	(3) / (4) × 100	9.7%	9.3%	16.3%
Sales multiple (×)	(4) / (5)	2.1×	2.1×	1.8×
	Source	£m	£m	£m
(1) Profit before tax	P&L account	16.8	15.5	27.3
(2) Interest payable	P&L account	7.6	6.2	7.1
(3) Profit before interest and tax	(1) + (2)	24.4	21.7	34.4
(4) Sales ('turnover')	P&L account	251.6	233.7	211.0
(5) Net assets	Balance sheet	120.4	112.9	115.8

commonly encountered during a recession, a company would analyze its asset base, with a view to increasing the sales generation ratio and countering the decrease in decreasing margin ratio.

This illustration is a very basic one. Any management-level ratio analysis would need to look at a higher level if it was to provide any meaningful insight. We consider this in the next section.

Management-level ratio analysis

Return on equity

We now consider a number of performance measures that are used in corporate-level analysis. Table 21.5 shows performance for a UK-listed company in terms of return on equity (ROE). The terms we have considered, together with a few we have not, are shown as a historical trend. 'Asset turnover' refers to the sales generation or sales multiple, while 'leverage factor' is a measure of the *gearing* level, which we consider shortly.

TABLE 21.5 ■ UK plc corporate performance 1995–9

Performance measure	1999	1998	1997	1996	1995
Asset turnover (sales generation)	2.01	1.97	1.85	1.91	1.79
Return on net sales	4.26%	4.43%	3.99%	4.77%	4.12%
Return on net assets (1)	8.56%	8.73%	7.38%	9.11%	7.37%
Leverage factor (gearing)	2.43	2.54	2.83	2.95	2.71
Return on equity (2)	20.80%	22.17%	20.89%	26.87%	19.97%

(1) Asset turnover × return on net sales
(2) Return on net assets × leverage factor

TABLE 21.6 ■ Constructa plc corporate-level ratios

Ratio	Calculation	2000	1999	1998
RONA %	See Table 21.4	20.3%	19.2%	29.7%
Return on sales %	See Table 21.4	9.7%	9.3%	16.3%
Sales multiple (×)	See Table 21.4	2.1×	2.1×	1.8×
ROE %	(6) / (7) × 100	13.26%	14.21%	23.78%
Gearing (×)	(5) / (7)	1.35×	1.49×	1.44×
	Source	£m	£m	£m
(1) Profit before tax	P&L account	16.8	15.5	27.3
(2) Interest payable	P&L account	7.6	6.2	7.1
(3) Profit before interest and tax	(1) + (2)	24.4	21.7	34.4
(4) Sales ('turnover')	P&L account	251.6	233.7	211.0
(5) Net assets	Balance sheet	120.4	112.9	115.8
(6) Shareholders' profit	P&L account	11.8	10.8	19.1
(7) Shareholders' funds	Balance sheet	89.0	76.0	80.3

Our analysis of the anonymous UK plc shows how ROE is linked to RONA which we illustrated in the earlier analysis. How do the figures turn out for the hypothetical Constructa plc? These are listed in Table 21.6.

Unlike our actual examples from the anonymous UK plc, the ratios for Constructa plc do not work out as a product of lower-level ratios. This is because different profit measures have been used to calculate the RONA and ROE; this is deliberate. With RONA we wish to measure the profit generated by the business irrespective of the source of funds used in generating this profit. ROE, on the other hand, measures profit attributable to shareholders, so we use the profit after tax and interest figure. The actual results illustrate a downtrend in the ROE and senior management will be concerned about this. However, this is outside the scope of this chapter.

Gearing

In Table 21.5 we encountered a leverage ratio, known as gearing in the UK. We also observed that gearing combined with RONA results in ROE. Put simply, gearing is the ratio of debt capital to equity capital, and measures the extent of indebtedness of a company. Gearing ratios are used by analysts and investors because they indicate the impact on ordinary shareholders'

4. A good illustration of this was the experience of telecommunications companies after they borrowed heavily in the debt capital market to pay for so-called 'third generation' mobile phone licences, which were auctioned off by respective European governments. As a result of the multi-billion dollar sums involved in the purchase of each licence, some of the telecoms companies saw their credit ratings downgraded by Moody's and S&P (in the case of BT plc, to one level above non-investment grade) as concerns were raised about their resulting high gearing levels.

earnings of a change in operating profit. For a company with high gearing, such change in profit can have a disproportionate impact on shareholders' earnings because more of the profit has to be used to service debt. There is no one 'right' level of gearing, but at some point the level will be high enough to raise both shareholders' and rating agency concerns, as doubts creep in about the company's ability to meet its debt interest obligations.[4]

The acceptable level of gearing for any company is dependent on a number of issues, including the type of business it is involved in, the average gearing level across similar companies, the stage of the business cycle (companies with high gearing levels are more at risk if the economy is heading into recession), the level of and outlook for interest rates, and so on. The common view is that a firm with a historically good track record and less prone to the effects of changes in the business cycle can afford to be more highly geared than a company that does not boast these features.

As the values for debt and equity capital can be measured in more than one way, so a company's gearing level can take more than one value. We illustrate this below. Table 21.7 shows hypothetical company results.

TABLE 21.7 ■ Hypothetical company results

	£m
Short-term debt	190
Long-term debt	250
Preference shares	35
Shareholders' funds	500
Cash at bank	89
Market value of long-term debt	276
Market value of shareholders' funds	2,255

TABLE 21.8 ■ Gearing ratios

Measure	Gearing
Long-term debt/Equity [250/(35 + 595)]	39.7%
Short-term and long-term debt/Shareholders' funds [(190 + 250)/595]	74.0%
Short-term and long-term debt less cash at bank/Shareholders' funds [(190 + 250 – 89)/595	59.0%
Market value of long-term debt/Market value of equity [276/1,977]	14.0%

From the data in Table 21.7 it is possible to calculate a number of different gearing ratios. These are shown in Table 21.8. So any individual measure of gearing is essentially meaningless unless it is also accompanied by a note of how it was calculated.

Market-to-book and price–earnings ratio

The remaining performance measures we wish to consider are the market-to-book ratio (MB) and the price–earnings or p/e ratio. It was not possible to calculate these for the hypothetical Constructa plc because we do not have a publicly quoted share price for it.[5] However, these ratios are widely used and quoted by analysts and investors. For valuation purposes, they are used to obtain an estimated value of a company or subsidiary. Provided we have data for shareholders' earnings and shareholders' funds, as well as MB and p/e figures for comparable companies, it is possible to calculate an approximation of fair market value for an unquoted company.

The p/e ratio is considered to be an important performance indicator and for Stock-Exchange listed companies it is quoted in, for example, the London *Financial Times*. It is given by:

$$p/e = \frac{P_{share}}{EPS} \qquad (21.2)$$

where P_{share} is the market price of the company's shares and *EPS* is the earnings per share. For quoted companies both these values may be obtained with ease.

The p/e ratio is an indication of the price that investors are prepared to pay for a company's shares in return for its current level of earnings. It relates shareholder profit to the market value of the company. Companies that are in 'high-growth' sectors, such as (during the late 1990s) the 'dot.com' or technology sector, are observed generally to have high p/e ratios, while companies in low-growth sectors will have lower p/e ratios. This illustrates one important factor of p/e ratio analysis: an individual figure on its own is of no real use, rather, it is the sector average as well as the overall level of the stock market that are important considerations for the investor. In the *Financial Times* the company pages list the p/e ratio for each industry sector, thus enabling investors to compare specific company p/e ratios with the sector level and the market level.[6] The *p/e relative* is calculated by comparing specific and industry-level p/e ratios, given at (21.3), which is an indication of where investors rate the company in relation to the industry it is operating in, or the market as a whole.

----

5. Not every 'public listed company' (plc) actually has its shares quoted on the Sstock Eexchange. It is possible for a company to be a plc without having quoted shares.
6. These figures are not listed in the Monday edition of the *FT*, which contains other relevant data.

$$p/e \ relative = \frac{p/e_{company}}{p/e_{market}}. \tag{21.3}$$

A very high p/e relative for a specific company may indicate a highly rated company and one that is a sector leader. However it may also indicate a 'glamour' company that is significantly overvalued and so overdue for a correction and decline in its share price.

The MB ratio relates a company's market value to shareholder funds value. If we see the p/e ratio as emanating from the profit and loss (P & L) account, then the MB ratio emanates from the balance sheet. It is given by:

$$MB = ROE \% \times p/e \ ratio. \tag{21.4}$$

We consider the MB and p/e ratios in the context of business valuation in the next section.

Corporate valuation

We have noted how, for a company listed on a stock exchange, it is straightforward to know its market value: its share price. However for subsidiaries and divisions of quoted companies or unquoted companies, a proper market value is not so simple to obtain. In this section we provide an introduction of how analysis from within a 'peer group' of companies may be used to obtain an estimated valuation for unquoted companies.

We wish to calculate an estimated market share price for Constructa plc, our hypothetical manufacturing company. Assume that we are fortunate to observe a peer group that consists of three other manufacturing companies of comparable size and performance, operating in a similar line of business as Constructa plc. The three companies are known as 'X', 'Y' and 'Z'. Table 21.9 shows financial data and key performance indicators for the year 2000 for each of these three companies.

The next step is to use this observed data in conjunction with Constructa plc data to obtain a range of possible values for the latter's market value. First, we calculate the mean p/e and MB ratios of the three peer group companies, and then from the range of ratios for these companies calculate the estimated Constructa plc values, using that company's own earnings per share value. In this way, we obtain a highest and lowest possible market valuation and a mean valuation. We have not previously calculated a book value per share for Constructa plc, so this is done now; the result is 59.3 pence, obtained by dividing the shareholders' funds figure of £89 million by the number of shares (150 million).

The mean value p/e and MB ratios are shown in Table 21.10, together with the range of possible market values for Constructa plc using each method.

Using this approach we obtain a mean value for the Constructa plc share price of £1.53 or £2.79, depending on which method we use. It is a subjective issue as to which

TABLE 21.9 ■ Comparable company financial indicators, 2000

		X plc	Y plc	Z plc
Turnover (£m)		821.4	369.7	211.3
Profit before interest and tax (£m)		97.6	41.9	18.7
Net profit (profit after interest and tax) (£m)		56.2	26.7	15.4
Book value of shareholders' funds (£m)		331.2	219.6	46.9
Shares in issue		167m	55m	48m
Share market price		712p	408p	926p
Return on sales %	(1)	11.88	11.33%	8.85%
Earnings per share	(2)	33.7p	48.5p	32.1p
p/e ratio	(3)	21.1	8.4	28.8
Book value per share	(4)	198p	399p	97.7p
MB ratio	(5)	3.6	1.02	9.5

(1) Return on sales is [profit before interest and tax/turnover]
(2) EPS is [net profit/number of shares in issue]
(3) p/e ratio is [share price/earnings per share]
(4) Book value per share is [book value of shareholders' funds/number of shares in issue]
(5) MB ratio is [share market price/book value per share]

TABLE 21.10 ■ Peer group company ratios, mean values and Constructa plc market valuation

	Mean value	X plc	Y plc	Z plc
p/e ratio	19.4	21.1	8.4	28.8
MB ratio	4.7	3.6	1.02	9.5

Constructa plc		Mean value	High value	Low value
Valuation using p/e ratio				
EPS	7.87			
p/e ratio		19.4	28.8	8.4
Share market value (1)		152.7p	226.7p	66.1p
Valuation using MB ratio				
Book value per share	59.3p			
MB ratio		4.7	9.5	1.02
Share market value (2)		278.7p	563.4p	60.5p

(1) EPS × p/e ratio
(2) Book value per share × MB ratio

approach is the better one, and the motivation of the analyst undertaking the calculation is key. In practice, analysts will consider a peer group with a greater number of companies, which usually results in a wider range of possible values. Of course the true market valuation for any good is the price at which there is both a buyer and seller for it, and similarly the true value for a company will lie somewhere in between the high and low limits that arise from using the method we have just described.

Appendix 21.1

Capital asset pricing model

The capital asset pricing model is a cornerstone of modern financial theory and originates from analysis of the cost of capital. The cost of capital of a company may be broken down as shown in Figure 21.1.

The three most common approaches used for estimating the cost of equity are the *dividend valuation model*, the CAPM and the *arbitrage pricing theory*. The CAPM is in a class of market models known as *risk premium* models, which rely on the assumption that every individual holding a risk-carrying security will demand a return in excess of the return they would receive from holding a risk-free security. This excess is the investor's compensation for his risk exposure. The risk premium in the CAPM is measured by *beta*, and it is known as *systematic, market* or *non-diversifiable* risk. This risk is caused by macroeconomic factors such as inflation or political events, which affect the returns of all companies. If a company is affected by these macroeconomic factors in the same way as the market (usually measured by a stock index), it will have a beta of 1, and will be expected to have returns equal to the market. Similarly, if a company's systematic risk is greater than the market, then its capital will be priced such that it is expected to have returns greater than the market. Essentially, therefore, beta is a measure of volatility, with a company's relative volatility being measured by comparing its returns to the market's

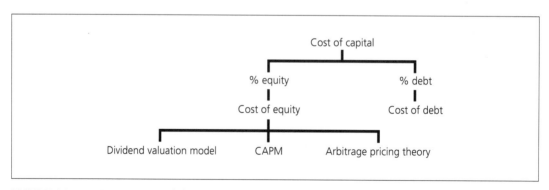

FIGURE 21.1 ■ Components of the cost of capital

returns. For example, if a share has a beta of 2, then on average for every 10% that the market index has returned above the risk-free rate, the share is expected to have returned 20%. Conversely, for every 10% the market has underperformed the risk-free rate, the share is expected to have returned 20% below. Beta is calculated for a share by measuring its variance relative to the variance of a market index such as the FTSE All Share or the S&P 500. The most common method of estimating beta is with standard regression techniques based on historical share price movements over, say, a five-year period.

To obtain the CAPM estimate of the cost of equity for a company, two other pieces of data are required: the risk-free interest rate and the equity risk premium. The risk-free rate represents the most secure return that can be achieved in the market. It is theoretically defined as an investment that has no variance and no covariance with the market; a perfect proxy for the risk-free rate therefore would be a security with a beta equal to zero, and no volatility. Such an instrument does not, to all intents and purposes, exist. Instead the market uses the next best proxy available, which in a developed economy is the government-issued Treasury bill – a short-dated debt instrument guaranteed by the government.

The equity risk premium represents the excess return above the risk-free rate that investors demand for holding risk-carrying securities. The risk premium in the CAPM is the premium above the risk-free rate on a portfolio assumed to have a beta of 1. The premium itself may be estimated in a number of ways. A common approach is to use historical prices, on the basis that past prices are a satisfactory guide to the future, and use these returns over time to calculate an arithmetic or geometric average. Research has shown that the market risk premium for the USA and UK has varied between 5.5% and 11% historically (Mills, 1994), depending on the time period chosen and the method used.

Once the beta has been determined, the cost of equity for a corporate is given by the CAPM as below:

$$k_e = r_f + (\beta \times r_e)$$ (21.5)

where

k_e is the cost of equity
r_f is the risk-free interest rate
r_e is the equity risk premium
β is the share beta.

The primary assumption behind the CAPM is that all the market-related risk of a share can be captured in a single indicator, the beta. This would appear to be refuted by evidence that fund managers sometimes demand a higher return from one portfolio than another when both apparently are equal risk, having betas of 1. The difference in portfolio returns cannot be due to differences in specific risk, because diversification nearly eliminates such risk in large, well-balanced portfolios. If the systematic risk of the two portfolios were truly identical, then they would be priced to yield identical returns. Nevertheless, the CAPM is often used by analysts to calculate cost of equity and hence cost of capital.

If we consider the returns on an individual share and the market as positively sloping lines on a graph plotting return, beta is usually given by:

$$r_s = \alpha_{sI} + \beta_{sI} r_I + \varepsilon_{sI} \tag{21.6}$$

where

r_s is the return on security s

r_I is the return on the market (usually measured for a given index)

α_{sI} is the intercept between s and I, often termed the 'alpha'

β_{sI} is the slope measurement or beta

ε is a random error term.

SELECTED BIBLIOGRAPHY AND REFERENCES

Fama, E., 'The behaviour of stock market prices', *Journal of Business*, January 1965, pp. 34–105.

Fama, E., French, K., 'The cross-section of expected stock returns', *Journal of Finance*, June 1992, pp. 427–65.

Fisher, I., *Theory of Interest*, Macmillan 1930.

Hirshleifer, J., 'On the theory of optimal investment decisions', *Journal of Political Economy*, 1958, pp. 329–72.

Markowitz, H., *Portfolio Selection*, Yale University Press 1959.

Mills, R., *Strategic Value Analysis*, Mars Business Associates 1994.

Mills, R., Robertson, J., *Fundamentals of Managerial Accounting and Finance*, 3rd edition, Mars Business Associates 1993, Chapter 3.

Roll, R., Ross, S.A., 'On the cross-sectional relation between expected returns and betas', *Yale School of Management working paper* 21, 1992.

Ross, S. A., 'The arbitrage theory of capital pricing', *Journal of Economic Theory*, December 1976, pp. 343–62.

Sharpe, W., 'Capital asset prices: a theory of market equilibrium under conditions of risk', *Journal of Finance*, September 1964, pp. 425–42.

Part VI

RATE applications software

In part VI we describe the accompanying RATE software, which was developed specially for this book. It features a yield curve construction calculator, using either money market rates or bond yields, as well as a vanilla interest rate swap and cap calulator.

RATE computer software

This chapter describes RATE application software that is included as part of this book. RATE is designed to demonstrate a selection of interest rate products and market concepts. It has components for modelling the zero curve using either bond yields or a combination of cash money market and derivative interest rate products, which we have called the 'standard' yield curve. RATE also contains interest rate swap and cap valuation tools. The application is reasonably simple to operate and is assembled with a Help file. A reader familiar with Windows-style applications and with interest rate markets will be able to use RATE without any difficulty. However, we recommend that the reader continues with this chapter before using RATE. This chapter not only helps the reader to install and use RATE but also explains the methods and assumptions that are applied by the application.

Comments on the application are welcome and may be sent to the authors care of the publishers. A reduced version of the application may also be downloaded from www.YieldCurve.com, which contains lecture notes and articles on yield curve analytics.

Getting started

RATE is designed for use on Windows operating systems and will function in a Windows 95/98, Windows 2000 and Windows NT environment. On the computer disk provided, run RATESetup.exe to launch the automatic installer. This will guide the reader through the installation options. Select all the default installation options. If the user prefers to customize the installation location of RATE and its data tables, then the data engine path may need to be modified after RATE has been installed. Refer to the last section of this chapter, 'The development environment and code', or RATE's Help file which explains how to modify the data engine path. If the user selects only the default installation options, then no data engine modifications will be required.

Once RATE has been successfully installed and launched, the user will be presented with an opening screen that introduces the application. This is shown in Figure 22.1.

RATE allows the user to construct zero-coupon curves using either a standard yield curve model or a bond yield model. Select a preferred method and click on the 'Bond curve' or 'Yield curve' quick start button. The user will need to capture curve data before a swap or cap can be valued. Ignore the cap and swap options for now!

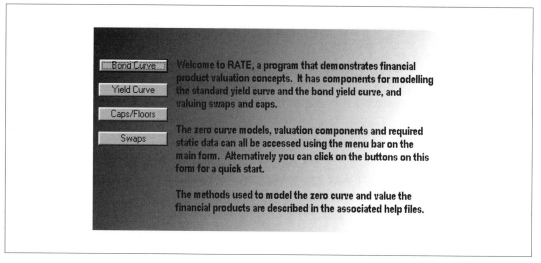

FIGURE 22.1 ■ Opening screen

Using the zero curve models

Defining your curve

RATE's yield curve model constructs a zero-coupon curve using a combination of short-term money market, traded futures and OTC swap instruments. The yield curve screen will initially contain no market data. The basic template is shown in Figure 22.2.

RATE's bond curve model constructs a zero-coupon curve using the effective yield to maturity on coupon-bearing bonds. The empty bond curve screen is given in Figure 22.3.

A RATE zero curve is defined by the value date and currency. These two input parameters are used to filter the underlying input data and therefore determine which market quotes are used to construct a zero curve. It is important to set the value date and currency before attempting to capture any market data.

RATE places no limitation on the number of yield curve or bond curve forms that can be opened. Each form can have its own curve definition. However, where two forms define the same curve (that is, the same currency and value date) but use different calculation parameters, RATE will only display the most recently calculated zero curve.

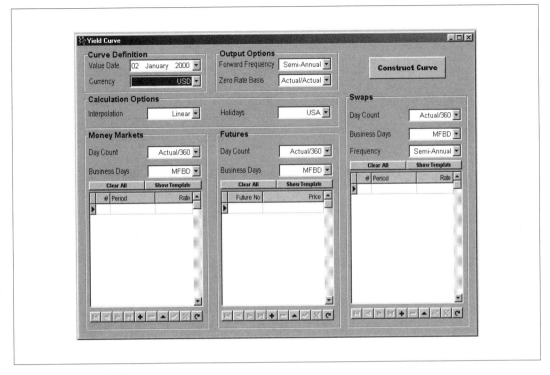

FIGURE 22.2 ■ Yield curve screen

Remember that each new screen utilizes computer memory and will place an extra burden on the operating system. It is therefore advisable to limit the number of forms that are kept open at any one time.

Selecting your calculation parameters

To construct the zero curve, RATE requires calculation parameters. The parameters required are 'holiday country' and 'interpolation method'. Holiday country selects the set of holidays that will be used to identify whether settlement dates are business days or public holidays. A list of holidays can be created, edited or deleted on the holiday form. The holiday form is accessed from the Static Data menu. The interpolation methods are discussed in the section on 'Calculation methods' below.

To calculate the zero curve, RATE needs to know what output options to apply. It is common practice to display the zero curve after applying the actual/actual method to calculate the zero rate. RATE also allows the user to convert discount factors into zero rates using the 360/actual and 365/actual methods. These day-count methods are covered in more detail in 'Calculation methods'.

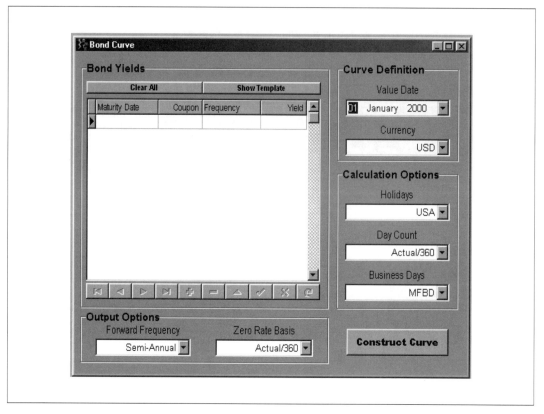

FIGURE 22.3 ▪ Bond curve screen

In addition to calculating the zero curve, RATE calculates and displays the forward rates derived from the zero curve. RATE can align its forward rate periods with the zero curve tenors, but also allows the user you to select the length of the forward rate period. Quarterly, semi-annual and annual options can be applied to the forward rate period. It is common market practice to calculate each forward period using the curve's tenor points.

Capturing your market inputs

When the user is ready to construct a curve for a value date and currency then RATE will need the user to populate the market grid with quoted rates. To simplify this process, an input template can be created using the 'Show Template' button. A template creates a matrix of dates so that only the market rates need to be captured. An example data set where the money markets are populated by the template method is shown in Figure 22.4. The user may of course select his/her own dates without recourse to the template.

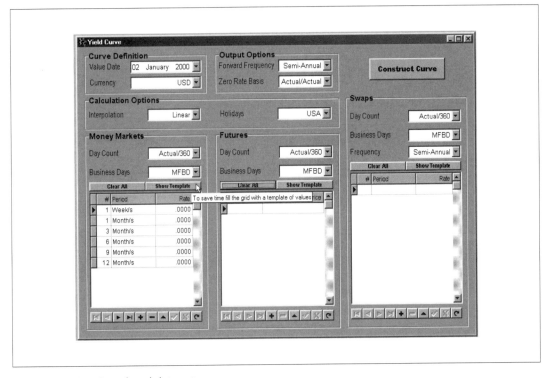

FIGURE 22.4 ■ Populated data set

RATE automatically saves market data in underlying data tables. The data grid on the yield curve and bond curve screens provides a method of capturing and editing this market data. Once data has been captured it is automatically saved to the underlying tables. This auto-save feature works each time the cursor moves from one record to the next. The most recent data item to be input or edited will not be saved until the cursor is moved to the next record, or the 'Post' button on the data editor is pressed. The user should generally change the day count basis, business day basis and, where applicable, the coupon payment frequency to match the market's standards. When using the bond model, a coupon frequency – generally annual or semi-annual – is required for each bond.

To return to previously input data, simply change the currency and value date to the relevant curve definition and the input data will be displayed. Be careful to ensure that the curve value date and currency are correctly defined before market data is captured. Data captured to the incorrect value date or currency can only be corrected by recapturing this information to the properly defined curve.

For any particular value date and currency, market inputs should have only one quoted rate for each maturity date. RATE prevents duplicate maturity dates and will highlight this with a 'key error' when there has been an attempt to create a duplicate entry. A 'key error' is explained in more detail in the application's Help file.

The tab and arrow keys can be used to move through the input grids. If the cursor is positioned in the last cell in the data grid then the tab key will create a new record.

Below each market data grid is a data navigator and editor (*see* Figure 22.5). This data editor provides assistance with capturing and editing market data.

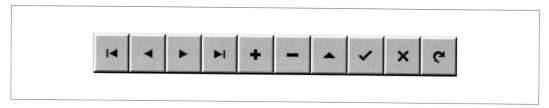

FIGURE 22.5 ■ Data navigator

Each button on the editor performs the following functions:

First	Moves to the first record.
Prior	Moves to the previous record.
Next	Moves to the next record.
Last	Moves to the last record.
Insert	Inserts a new record before the current record.
Delete	Deletes the current record and prompts for confirmation before deleting.
Edit	Puts the record in Edit mode so that it can be modified.
Post	Saves changes to the data.
Cancel	Cancels any edits to the current record.
Refresh	Refreshes the data grid from the underlying data.

The zero curve output display

To calculate and display the zero-coupon and forward curves, press the 'Construct Curve' button (*see* Figure 22.4). On the zero curve output form there is a data grid for reference rates (*see* Figure 22.6). Reference rates are rates that can be manually input or edited and then compared to the calculated zero rates, input rates or forward rates. This enables the zero construction model to be benchmarked against market data such as bond strips or alternative zero curve construction methodologies. You can input any reference rate for any date. To save input time, the reference grid can be populated using the input rates, zero rates or forward rates. Selecting the input rates enables you to compare the calculated spot rates to the bond yields.

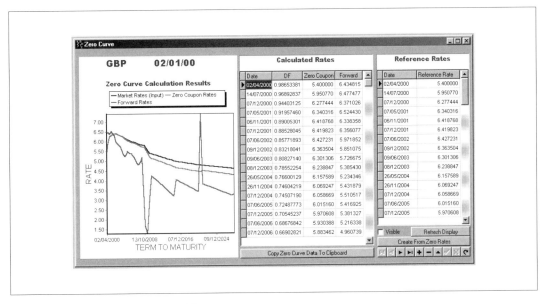

FIGURE 22.6 ■ Zero curve output form

When a new zero curve is constructed, the reference rates remain unchanged. This allows the user to perform currency or date comparisons for different zero curves. If the output data is required in a different application, such as Excel or Word, then use the button 'Copy Zero Curve Data To Clipboard' and simply paste it into Excel or Word. This enables the user to manipulate further the application's output.

Observations on using the application

The zero-coupon yield curve serves a number of purposes in the debt markets. The theoretical spot curve is the key valuation tool used in the analysis of interest rate products such as bond options. The forward curve is used to price FRAs and swaps.

The bond yield curve may be used to demonstrate relative value trading. For example, consider a curve generated from government bond prices. The output curve indicates the theoretical yield applicable for zero-coupon bonds. The price of the coupon bonds may then be compared back to the spot curve to check which are cheap or dear to the curve. The spot yields may also be compared to the yields on actual zero-coupon government bonds (strips) to check fair value. Where the actual bonds are seen to be cheap or dear, the trader may position the book to exploit these pricing differences. This is an effective analysis of the fair value of government strips. A further comparison may be made by using actual zero-coupon bond yields as inputs. Viewing the 'reference curve' in the application enables the user to make an immediate visual check on the yield state of market instruments.

Calculation methods

Standard yield curve construction methodology

RATE uses discount factor methodology to construct the curve. In other words, all market inputs are translated to discount factors before building the curve. The yield curve model does this in three phases. First the money market curve is built, then the futures are spliced with the money market and finally the swaps are bootstrapped. The money market discount factors are calculated using each money market quote from the earliest maturity date to the first maturity date that overlaps the swap inputs. If no swaps are input then all money market quotes are used. To construct a standard curve without money market quotes is not possible and we suggest using the bond curve model.

Where money market inputs mature in less than one year then a discount function that has no compounding is applied. Money market discount factors for periods of more than one year are calculated using a discount function that has annual compounding. These equations are set out below.

When calculating discount factors for a maturity that is greater than one year we use:

$$df = \frac{1}{(1 + r)^B}.$$

(22.1)

When calculating discount factors for a maturity that is less than one year we use:

$$df = \frac{1}{1 + (r \times B)}.$$

(22.2)

where B is the day-count fraction and R is the quoted money market rate.

The day-count fraction is discussed later in this chapter.

Once all money market quotes are translated into discount factors then the futures are spliced with the curve. For the purposes of date generation, RATE assumes that futures are quarterly contracts that have effective dates on the third Wednesday of each quarter. Each contract is assumed to be exactly 90 days in length. The curve can be built without futures' inputs if preferred. Where futures are input, they are spliced from the first futures contract to the date of the earliest swap maturity. Where no swap quotes are available all futures contracts are used.

Based on the assumption that futures contracts are exactly 90 days in length, their discount factors are calculated using a function that has no compounding, that is:

$$df_{90} = \cfrac{1}{1 + \left(\left(\cfrac{100-P_{fut}}{100}\right) \times B_{90}\right)} \qquad (22.3)$$

where df_{90} is the discount factor at the starting date of the futures contract for the 90-day futures contract period, P_{fut} is the future contract quoted price and B_{90} is the day-count fraction for a 90-day period.

Any discount factor calculation requires two dates: the start date and the maturity date. The start date for money market quotes is a date that coincides with the starting point of the curve (the value date). Futures, however, have a future start date. In other words, when we calculate the discount factor for a futures contract, it does not represent a calculation for today but rather a discount factor for a strip of time (90 days) starting on a future date. This means that this discount factor needs to be spliced with one that runs from the value date to the start of the futures contract.

Figure 22.7 displays a futures contract F_1. We can calculate the discount factor for the contract F_1 using formula (22.3) above. However, this is only applicable to its future strip, the 90-day time period F_0 to F_1. F_1's start date falls between two money market contracts M_3 and M_4. In order to get the discount factor applicable at the start of the contract, we must interpolate between M_3 and M_4. The futures contract F_1 can now be spliced with the curve by multiplying the discount factor calculated by interpolation with the discount factor for F_1. This provides F_{DF}'s discount factor, which is a discount factor for the entire period. Each and every subsequent futures contract can then be spliced in the same way by applying this formula.

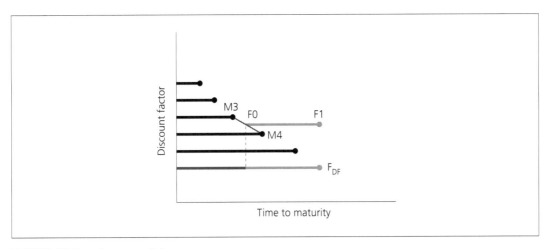

FIGURE 22.7 ■ Futures splicing

$$df_T = \frac{1}{1 + \left(\left(\frac{100 - P_{ful}}{100}\right) \times B_{90}\right)} \times df_m. \tag{22.4}$$

In equation (22.4) df_T is the discount factor for the period from value date to the futures contract maturity date and df_m is the money market discount factor at the futures contract start date, calculated by interpolation.

A zero curve can be constructed without swap inputs, but where swap quotes are available then they must be overlapped by the money market or future quotes. If there is no overlap then the curve will be built without swaps. Swaps are calculated using bootstrapping. Bootstrapping applies to swaps and bonds and therefore follows the discussion on 'Bond yield curve construction methodology' below.

Bond yield curve construction methodology

Bootstrapping cannot be applied to the first bond. A discount function is calculated for each coupon period of the first bond. The formula that RATE applies to the first bond is the no-compounding discount function:

$$df = \frac{1}{1 + (r \times B_t)} \times df_{t-1} \tag{22.5}$$

where df_{t-1} is the discount factor for the previous coupon payment and r is the quoted yield to maturity.

For subsequent bonds the discount factors are obtained using bootstrapping.

Bootstrapping

Unlike cash and futures contracts, bonds and swaps have associated interest settlements or coupons. The quoted rate for a swap contract, or yield to maturity on a bond, represents not only the settlement at maturity date but also the collective rate for each and every interest coupon. The quoted rate represents the cumulative quote of a number of rates that span the term structure of the bond or swap contract. The construction of a zero curve needs to strip out these various coupon payments and identify the appropriate rate applied to each. This is done by 'bootstrapping' the swap or bond. This technique was described in Chapter 4.

In Figure 22.8 a swap contract with settlement dates i_1, i_2, i_3 and i_4 is shown. In addition, money market contracts M_3 and M_4 and futures contract F_{DF}, for which discount factors have been calculated, are available. These discount factors, together with a choice of interpolation, can now be used to calculate an appropriate discount factor for coupon

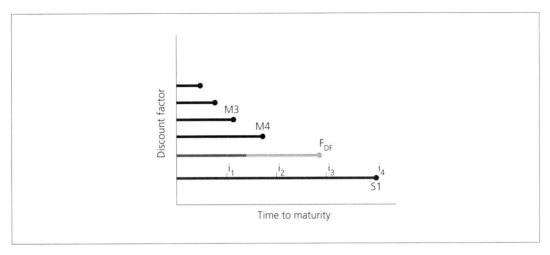

FIGURE 22.8 ■ Bootstrapping

points i_1 and i_2. The difficulty with i_3 is that this swap coupon has a settlement date that lies past the previously calculated discount factors. Interpolation cannot be used to calculate a discount factor for i_3. To solve this problem RATE creates a fictitious swap (*see* Figure 22.9).

This fictitious instrument, S_f, is a sub set of S_1. It is the same as S_1 up to and including coupon i_3 but excludes the last coupon. In other words, the fictitious maturity date is point i_3 and not point i_4.

Our intention is to calculate a discount factor for S_f. However, a discount factor for S_f cannot be calculated because we do not have a swap rate. We cannot simply use the swap rate for swap contract S_1, because S_1 has a different maturity and its rate would be

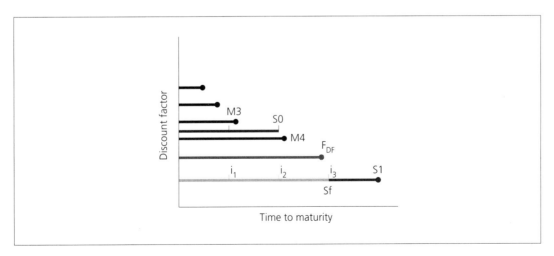

FIGURE 22.9 ■ Overlapping coupon

inappropriate. A rate for S_f needs to be estimated using interpolation. The swap rates for the previous swap, S_0, and the next swap, which is now S_1, are used. By using interpolation a rate for S_f is calculated from the quoted rate of S_0 and S_1. We should point out that the linear interpolation method is in-built (or hard-coded) when swap rates are interpolated for the overlapping swap coupon. This is a hard-coded assumption that can only be changed by altering RATE's source code.

As a result of this estimation technique used by RATE it is an important requirement, in the case of the standard yield curve model, that quotes for the cash and/or futures market overlap the first swap maturity. If they do not, then RATE cannot perform this calculation and will ignore all swap inputs.

RATE will now calculate the zero-coupon discount factor for the period of the swap S_f. The function that is applied by RATE is given by:

$$df = \frac{1 - (1 \times r \times \sum_{i=1}^{t-1} (df_i \times B_i))}{1 + (1 \times r \times B_t)} \tag{22.6}$$

where r is the quoted swap rate, and df_i is the discount factor for each coupon period excluding the last coupon settled at maturity. Similarly, B_i is the day-count fraction for each coupon period from 1 to $t-1$ (i.e. all excluding the last coupon), and B_t is the day-count fraction for the last coupon period.

Each swap discount factor can now be calculated in turn. S_1 once calculated can be fed into the calculation of S_2, and S_2 into S_3, and so on. This is the process that is termed 'bootstrapping', so called because when you lace your bootstraps you must start from the bottom and work your way up to the top.

Bonds can be bootstrapped in much the same way. There are two key differences when applying bond bootstrapping. First, there are no cash or futures markets in the bond model. The first bond is therefore not bootstrapped. Instead the yield to maturity for the first bond is applied to all coupon and principal settlement points on the bond. Second, a bond has a price. This is applied to the bootstrapping function as shown at (22.7):

$$df = \frac{P_{bond} - (1 \times r \times \sum_{i=1}^{t-1} (df_i \times B_i))}{1 + (1 \times r \times B_t)} \tag{22.7}$$

Interpolation

The cash, futures and swaps quotes are quotes for a set of fixed points in time (tenors). When we need a rate or discount factor for a point in time that does not coincide exactly with the quoted tenors, then a method of estimating the rate or discount factor is required. This is achieved using interpolation. There are various methods of interpolation that have become widely accepted and used in the market, for example linear, exponential and cubic spline. RATE currently supports only the linear interpolation. An introduction to cubic splines and B-splines is given in Chapters 8–9.

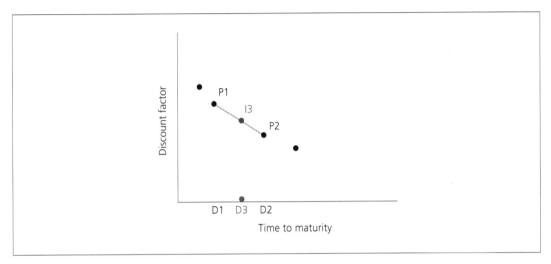

FIGURE 22.10 ■ Interpolation

As illustrated in Figure 22.9, discount factors have been calculated for a number of points on the zero curve. How does one determine the discount factor for a date D_3 that lies between points P_1 and P_2?

Using linear interpolation a straight line is drawn between the two points P_1 and P_2 and where they cross the date D_3 the interpolated rate is determined. This is achieved mathematically using the function given at (22.8):

$$I_3 = P_1 + \left(\left(\frac{P_2 - P_1}{D_2 - D_1} \right) \times \left(D_3 - D_1 \right) \right). \tag{22.8}$$

Business days

Contracts settle on business days. If a contract's maturity date happens to fall on a weekend or public holiday then the nearest business day needs to be determined. Two generally accepted business day standards are implemented by RATE:

■ following business day (FBD)

■ modified following business day (MFBD).

The following business day identifies the first business day that falls after the contract's maturity date and uses that as the settlement date. In the case of the modified rule, the following business day is applied, but if the following business day falls in the next month, then the first business day prior to the contract maturity date is used. Sterling and euro settlements are usually determined using the modified following business day basis.

Day-count basis and the day-count fraction

Calculation of future value (with annual compounding) is given by:

$$FV = PV \times (1 + r)^B.$$ (22.9)

The day-count fraction is a consistent means by which B can be reflected after taking into consideration the day-count basis, for example actual/360 or actual/365. For example, using a day-count basis of actual/365, the day-count fraction would be calculated using (22.10):

$$B = \frac{d}{365}$$ (22.10)

where d is the number of days from value date to maturity or the contract length expressed in days.

Instrument valuation

The swap calculator

The swap calculator returns the value of an interest rate swap. A standard yield curve definition is enforced after the swap parameters have been captured. This means that RATE can be used to value the same swap against any zero curve. The calculation parameters of value date, currency and interpolation do not therefore form part of the swap parameters.

RATE calculates and displays the cash flows for the fixed leg and floating leg separately (see Figure 22.11). The present value of each leg is determined and aggregated to return the net present value of the swap. Where the effective date precedes the value date then the swap is being valued after it has started accruing interest. Accrued interest for the current coupon is therefore displayed.

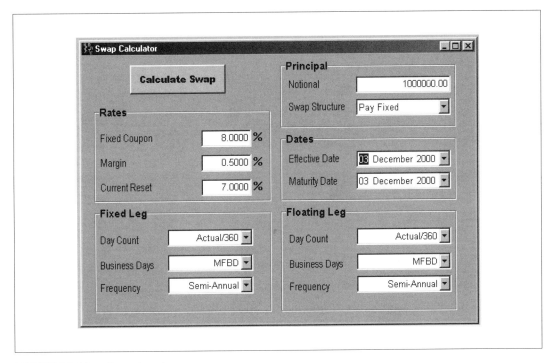

FIGURE 22.11 ■ Swap input

Cap/floor calculator

The cap/floor calculator calculates the value of an interest rate cap/floor based on the selected zero-coupon curve (*see* Figure 22.12). As with the swap calculator, the cap calculator enforces a standard yield curve definition when the option is valued.

Value date, currency and interpolation are determined when the zero curve is constructed. It is therefore not possible to apply different methods of interpolation to the option valuation and zero curve construction. The option value is calculated using the Black 76 model. No other option calculators are currently supported by RATE.

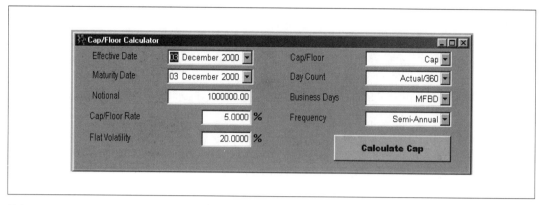

FIGURE 22.12 ■ Cap input

Static data and drop-down lists

Within RATE there are a number of drop-down lists available, for example Currency. In some cases the static data for these menus will need to be maintained. For example, to create or delete a currency code, access to this static data is required. The three types of static data that the user can update within RATE are currencies, countries and holidays. These are all accessed using the Static Data menu on the main form.

The development environment and code

All of the source code (program code) for RATE has been made available on the enclosed application CD-ROM. Readers will need to be familiar with a number of items before delving into the heart of RATE. These are discussed below.

Program code

RATE has been developed using Borland C++ Builder 5 (Professional). The following file types are therefore provided:

■ *Code files – .cpp files*: These are the primary code files. It is possible to view these in a text editor or an alternative C++ development environment.

■ *Header files – .h files*: These are the C++ header files. Once again, these can be viewed with a standard text editor or in an alternative C++ development environment.

■ *Project file – .bpr file*: This is the Borland project file. For more information on Borland C++ Builder visit Borland's website (www.Borland.com).

Programming can at times be more of an art than a science. Application code will therefore express some degree of personal preference. Given that this is a book about financial products and not one about C++, we wanted RATE's code to communicate financial product concepts rather than programming concepts. In addition, we wanted to make the code more readable to C++ beginners. We have therefore tried to avoid C++ syntactics that may not be obvious to beginners. The object-oriented programming features of C++ have been applied by designing abstract financial market types. There are classes for deposits, futures, swaps and bonds that implement market-related operations for these types of quoted instruments.

We have not made use of any custom components or library files. All the components used by RATE are those that are packaged as standard within the Borland C++ Builder 5 development environment. Borland includes the Visual Component Library (VCL) written in Object Pascal. RATE makes use of the components available in this library.

Database structure

To store market and static data, Paradox-type data tables have been used. RATE makes use of these tables through a local data architecture that facilitates scaling up in a two-tiered environment. This is achieved using the Borland Database Engine (BDE). The BDE can be accessed from the Windows control panel using the BDE Administrator.

Within the BDE Administrator resides a database called RPMCFinCalc. This is the RATE source data and should be configured to point to the Paradox tables located in the RATE install directory. If a different install directory was chosen, or if the data tables have been moved, then this directory path may no longer be valid. The BDE Administrator can be used to edit the database path and point RPMCFinCalc to the correct data directory. Similarly, it can be used to point to a directory on a common server or at an ODBC source.

SELECTED BIBLIOGRAPHY AND REFERENCES

Josuttis, N., *The C++ Standard Library*, Addison Wesley Longman Publishing 1999.
Lippman, S., Lajoie, J., *C++ Primer*, 3rd edition, Addison Wesley Longman Publishing 1998.

Index